EARLY GEORGIA MAGAZINES

EARLY GEORGIA MAGAZINES

Literary Periodicals to 1865

by

BERTRAM HOLLAND FLANDERS

1944

THE UNIVERSITY OF GEORGIA PRESS

ATHENS

Paperback edition, 2010
© 1944 by the University of Georgia Press
Athens, Georgia 30602
www.ugapress.org
All rights reserved
Printed digitally in the United States of America

The Library of Congress has cataloged the hardcover edition of this book as follows:
Library of Congress Cataloging-in-Publication Data
LCCN Permalink: http://lccn.loc.gov/44042497

Flanders, Bertram Holland, 1892–
    Early Georgia magazines; literary periodicals to 1865, by Bertram Holland Flanders.
    xiv, 289 p. illus. (map) 22 cm.
  Bibliography: p. [233]–248. Bibliographical references included in "Notes" (p. 251–274)
    1. American periodicals—Georgia. I. Title.
PN4897.G6 F55
051   44-42497

Paperback ISBN-13: 978-0-8203-3536-0
ISBN-10: 0-8203-3536-3

TO

MY WIFE

LILLIAN STUCKEY FLANDERS

Preface

MY PURPOSE in this work is to show the extent to which literary periodicals were published in Georgia before 1865, to point out the types of literature included therein, and to indicate the editors and contributors involved. It is also my purpose to show the centers of literary activity in the state as indicated by the interest in the production of periodical literature. In this way we may be able to learn what was the contribution of Georgia magazines to literary culture in Georgia.

My plan, first of all, is to discuss each literary periodical in detail as far as extant files permit. I have adopted the plan of dividing these publications into chronological periods, which are the result of chance rather than of any particular unity binding the members of a group together. One periodical seems to have been followed by others within the space of a few years, but all sank out of sight after a short existence. Then, after an interval of several years, the process was repeated, always with the same result. Since there appears to be little unity within any given group, no attempt has been made to draw any conclusions relative to the publications appearing in any period. Only general conclusions involving the entire list seem valid in the face of so many and so varied efforts to establish periodical literature in the state. In more than a score of instances, periodicals were published for which no files have been located. Sometimes the prospectus was issued for a magazine which is never referred to thereafter as having appeared. In both instances the periodicals have been included in the introductory section to the group in which each belongs chronologically. In only one important instance does a periodical run beyond the assigned limit: the *Countryman* (Turnwold), in the "Third Period: 1859–65." But since it expired in the early part of 1866, its complete history does no violence to the title of this work. With one exception the history of a Georgia periodical stops, as far as this discussion is concerned, when it is removed from the state, for with the removal passes its significance to Georgia cultural history. The *Orion*, this exception, survived removal only six months; hence its entire history is covered. In each case, however, the subsequent history of the magazine is sketched as far as it can be ascertained.

The non-literary magazines of the state though not treated in this discussion, indicate, too, the interests of Georgians. During the period in question there were begun in the state ten agricultural, fifteen medical, and twenty-four religious magazines, besides others devoted to temperance, education, politics, business and industry, and Masonic interests. The religious periodicals were, in the main, the longest-lived, inasmuch as they had a constituency to support them upon whom the editor could depend, even in financial depressions. Examples of these are the Baptist *Christian Index*, begun in Philadelphia in 1821 and removed to Georgia in 1833, and the Methodist *Wesleyan Christian Advocate*, begun in 1837. Both these periodicals are still in existence. Another long-lived periodical is the current *Southern Cultivator*, an agricultural journal begun in 1843 and appearing variously in Augusta, Athens, and Atlanta. For readers who are interested in knowing what was being published in these other fields in Georgia, I have added an appendix containing a list of such publications.

It has been extremely difficult to locate files of Georgia magazines. In some instances the only ones are in private possession. In some cases they are located in distant or out-of-the-way places, and photostats or microfilms had to be obtained. In finding and gaining access to many files I wish to express my great indebtedness to the late William Kenneth Boyd, of Duke University, who labored untiringly to add to the Duke Library what is possibly the most valuable collection of Georgia periodicals before 1865. In some cases he has obtained the only files known to exist. Without his work, as well as his kind advice, great gaps would occur in this history of periodical literature.

The identity of the countless number of authors who appended pseudonyms to their contributions to Georgia magazines presents a problem of superhuman proportions. I have succeeded in penetrating the disguises of some writers through diligent study, but most of them still remain a mystery. In a discussion of each Georgia periodical I have included a list of pseudonyms and initials (excluding single initials) used by contributors, and in Appendix C have included the same pseudonyms as a possible aid to anyone interested in pursuing the subject further.

In a discussion of Georgia literary periodicals it is necessary, perhaps, to define the term *literary periodical*. To include all types of periodicals in the state up to 1865 would make this volume several times as large as it now is, for more than twenty-five important publications in the fields of agriculture, medicine, education, and religion would have to be included. In my use of the word *periodical* I exclude daily and weekly newspapers, gift books, annuals, official reports, and publications of societies. A *literary periodical* is here understood to mean any journal or magazine whose principal interest lies in literature, or which has a special department devoted to literature, with a special editor in charge. College publications, though referred to, are excluded from this discussion because their productions are academic exercises rather than well-defined attempts to develop periodical literature. In order to avoid the constant repetition of the word *periodical*, I often use the terms *journal, work,* and *publication* as synonyms.

In footnotes referring to Georgia periodicals I depart from the usual method of giving the volume number, page or pages, and date in parentheses. Instead I give both volume number and issue number, followed by the date in parentheses. Page numbers, if necessary, follow the date, always preceded by *p.* or *pp.* For periodicals running only a few months, simply the date of each issue is given. This departure from the usual method of reference is due to the fact that some libraries record files of magazines by the number of both volume and issue, while others record files only by dates. Such a departure facilitates the checking and identification of references. Needless to say, the usual method is followed with out-of-the-state periodicals.

I wish to express my indebtedness to Prof. Clarence Gohdes, of Duke University, who aided in getting this project under way and who has given much sound advice since that time concerning methods of treating the subject; to Mr. J. P. Breedlove, of the Duke Library, for giving me valuable assistance in procuring the loan of rare material from other libraries all over the United States; and to Prof. Ralph Betts Flanders, of New York University, for advice relating to the phase of the subject dealing with Southern history. My deepest appreciation goes to Prof. Jay B. Hubell, of Duke University, who has made many valuable suggestions while the work was in progress, and who has in numerous ways assisted in making this an exhaustive treatment of Georgia literary periodicals.

I wish to express my deep appreciation to the following for aiding me in various ways, both in locating the material involved and in making it available for use at all times: Miss Jane Green, Mr. Carl Pratt, and Miss Allene Ramage, of the Duke Library staff; Miss Sallie Aiken, Washington Memorial Library, Macon, Georgia; Miss Ruth Blair, Atlanta Historical Society Library; Miss Margaret Jemison, Emory University Library; Miss Jane McDaniel, North Georgia College Library, Dahlonega, Georgia; Mr. P. W. Thompson, Waynesboro, Georgia; Miss Dorothy Edwards and Miss Frances Edwards, Durham, North Carolina; Rev. Spencer B. King, Blakely, Georgia; and Prof. H. Prentice Miller, Emory University. In the reading and revision of proofs and in the preparation of the final index I am indebted to Prof. C. C. Chadbourn, Jr., Prof. Kenneth England, Miss Vernelle Ray, and my wife—all of the North Georgia College.

BERTRAM HOLLAND FLANDERS

Dahlonega, Georgia
February 12, 1944

Symbols Used for Library Files[1]

ALABAMA
   A—Department of Archives and History, Montgomery

CALIFORNIA
   CL-S—Stanford University, Los Angeles

CONNECTICUT
   CtY—Yale University, New Haven

DISTRICT OF COLUMBIA
   DE—U.S. Bureau of Education
   DLC—Library of Congress
   DS—Smithsonian Institution
   DSG—U.S. Surgeon General's Office

GEORGIA
   G—Georgia State Library, Atlanta
   GA—Carnegie Library, Atlanta
   GAH—Atlanta Historical Society Library, Atlanta
   GAt Co—E. M. Coulter, Athens
   GAuY—Young Men's Library, Augusta
   GCL-E—Ledger-Enquirer, Columbus
   GE—Emory University, Atlanta
   GM—Mercer University, Macon
   GMM—Washington Memorial Library, Macon
   GMW—Wesleyan College, Macon
   GMiC—Georgia State College for Women, Milledgeville
   GSR—Keith Reade, Savannah
   GU—University of Georgia, Athens
   GU(D)—DeRenne Library, University of Georgia, Athens
   GVG—Georgia State Woman's College, Valdosta
   GWaynT—P. W. Thompson, Waynesboro

ILLINOIS
   ICN—Newberry Library, Chicago
   ICU—University of Chicago
   IEG—Garrett Biblical Institute, Evanston

IOWA
   Ia—Iowa State Library, Des Moines

MASSACHUSETTS
   MB—Boston Public Library
   MBAt—Boston Athenaeum Library
   MH—Harvard University, Cambridge
   MHi—Massachusetts Historical Society, Boston
   MWA—American Antiquarian Society, Worcester

NEW JERSEY
   NjP—Princeton University, Princeton
   NjR—Rutgers University, New Brunswick

---

[1] Symbols used here are taken from, or based upon, those in the *Union List of Serials*.

New York
- *N*—New York State Library, Albany
- *NN*—New York Public Library, New York City
- *NNC*—Columbia University, New York City
- *NNHi*—New York Historical Society, New York City
- *NNN*—New York Academy of Medicine, New York City

North Carolina
- *NcD*—Duke University, Durham
- *NcU*—University of North Carolina, Chapel Hill

Ohio
- *OClWHi*—Western Reserve Historical Society, Cleveland

Pennsylvania
- *PCC*—Crozer Theological Seminary, Chester
- *PPL*—Library Company of Philadelphia
- *PU*—University of Pennsylvania, Philadelphia

Rhode Island
- *RPB*—Brown University, Providence

South Carolina
- *ScChC*—College of Charleston
- *ScChL*—Charleston Library Society
- *ScU*—University of South Carolina, Columbia

Texas
- *TxDM*—Southern Methodist University, Dallas
- *TxU*—University of Texas, Austin

Virginia
- *Va*—Virginia State Library, Richmond
- *VaRCM*—Confederate Museum, Richmond

Wisconsin
- *W*—Wisconsin Historical Library, Madison
- *WHi*—Wisconsin State Historical Society, Madison

ABBREVIATIONS USED IN FILES
- CF—Complete File
- mut.—mutilated
- inc.—incomplete

Contents

	PAGE
PREFACE	vi

CHAPTER
    INTRODUCTION: FIRST EXPERIMENTS IN PERIODICAL LITERATURE   3
    1. Savannah—*Georgia Analytical Repository* (1802–03)   6
    2. Savannah—*Ladies' Magazine* (1819)   13

I   FIRST PERIOD: 1837–46   22
    Introduction
    1. Macon—*Southern Post and Literary Aspirant* (1837–39?)   28
    2. Augusta *Mirror* (1838–41)   30
    3. Macon—*Southern Ladies' Book* (1840–43)   38
    4. Macon—*Family Companion and Ladies' Mirror* (1841–43)   61
    5. Penfield—*Orion* (1842–44?)   68
    6. Madison—*Southern Miscellany* (1842–46?)   88

II   SECOND PERIOD: 1848–54   91
    Introduction
    1. Eatonton—*Turner's Monthly* (1848)   93
    2. Athens—*Southern Literary Gazette* (1848–53)   95
    3. Athens—*Schoolfellow* (1849–57?)   106
    4. Athens—*Mistletoe* (1849)   108
    5. Athens—*Wheler's Magazine* (1849–50)   110
    6. Savannah—*A Friend of the Family* (1849–51?)   118
    7. Athens—*Roath's Monthly Magazine* (1853)   119
    8. Augusta—*Southern Eclectic* (1853–54)   123

Contents

CHAPTER		PAGE
III	THIRD PERIOD: 1859–65	129
	Introduction	
	1. Atlanta—*Medical and Literary Weekly* (1859)	134
	2. Augusta—*Southern Field and Fireside* (1859–64)	136
	3. Atlanta—*Hygienic and Literary Magazine* (1860)	148
	4. Eatonton—*The Plantation* (1860)	150
	5. Newnan—*Southern Literary Companion* (1860?–65?)	157
	6. Atlanta—*Georgia Literary and Temperance Crusader* (1834?–61?)	160
	7. Turnwold—*Countryman* (1862–66)	164
	8. Griffin—*Bugle-Horn of Liberty* (1863–?)	177
IV	SUMMARY AND CONCLUSION	179
	APPENDICES	
	A. Georgia Literary Periodicals to 1865	211
	B. Georgia Non-Literary Periodicals to 1865	216
	C. Contributors to Georgia Literary Periodicals to 1865	221
	BIBLIOGRAPHY	235
	NOTES	251
	INDEX	275

EARLY GEORGIA MAGAZINES

MAP OF GEORGIA

SHOWING IMPORTANT TOWNS

State Capital During Civil War Marked ★
Principal Colleges in Towns Marked ⊙
Literary Periodicals Were Published in Towns Underlined, with
Number of Important Periodicals in Parenthesis

INTRODUCTION

*First Experiments in
Periodical Literature*

THE ATMOSPHERE of pioneer life is scarcely conducive to the production of works of literature. Nor is there much time for reading such works as may be written elsewhere. Men have to concern themselves with exploring the land newly occupied, with building houses, and with battling against unfamiliar foes of all kinds. Such was the situation in Georgia, the last of the thirteen colonies, for some time after its settlement in 1733.

The first English settlers in Georgia were the victims of a debtors' system that had aroused the sympathy of James Edward Oglethorpe and numerous others. When they settled on the site of the present-day city of Savannah, they began the difficult task of rehabilitating themselves in a strange land. This small band of Englishmen was soon augmented by a band of Salzburgers, who settled at Ebenezer, not far from Savannah. In 1735 the town of Augusta was laid out on the western bank of the Savannah River at the head of navigation, and was soon in a thriving condition. The colony was augmented later by Moravians, Scotch Highlanders, and Irish Protestants, besides smaller and less important groups of settlers. As time passed, the population began to push southward and westward, opening up the promising lands in Middle Georgia.

There was undoubtedly plenty of room in Georgia for thousands of settlers, for in 1790 the population of the state was only 82,548, as compared with 249,073 in South Carolina, 395,005 in North Carolina, and 747,610 in Virginia.[1] Middle Georgia, however, was populated, in the main, by direct colonization from Virginia, North Carolina, and South Carolina and not by descendants of the debtors whom Oglethorpe planted on the Georgia coast. Small centers of culture, such as Macon, Athens, Penfield, and Madison, sprang up throughout Middle Georgia as the section became more thickly populated, and it was in these centers that the important literary periodicals of *ante-bellum* Georgia were published. Within this section, too, besides the state capital, Milledgeville, were the University of Georgia (Athens), Emory College (Oxford), Mercer University (Penfield), Oglethorpe College (Midway), and the Georgia Female College (Macon)—all founded in the 1830's.

Magazine activity had begun in the American colonies with the appearance in 1741 of two periodicals, the first having priority by only three days: the *American Magazine, or A Monthly View of the Political State of the British Colonies* (January–March, 1741), by Andrew Bradford; and *The General Magazine and Historical Chronicle, for all the British Plantations in America* (January–June, 1741), by Benjamin Franklin, both printed in Philadelphia.[2] Both magazines devoted most of their space to state affairs, but Franklin's periodical contained more varied reading matter. The first important magazine in the colonies was the *American Magazine and Historical Chronicle* (1743–46), published in Boston and modeled after the *London Magazine*. Later periodicals were the *American Magazine and Monthly Chronicle* (1757–58), Philadelphia; the *Royal American Magazine* (1774–75), Boston; *Pennsylvania Magazine* (1775–76), Philadelphia, of which Tom Paine was a contributing editor most of its life; the *Boston Magazine* (1783–86); the *Gentlemen and Lady's Town and Country Magazine* (1784), Boston, the first periodical in which women were given any special attention; and the *American Magazine* (1787–88), New York, edited by Noah Webster

First Experiments in Periodical Literature 5

and devoted to education. The four most important magazines of the eighteenth century in America were: the *Columbian Magazine* (1786–92) and the *American Museum* (1787–92), both published in Philadelphia; the *Massachusetts Magazine* (1789–96), Boston; and the *New-York Magazine* (1790–97), New York City. The only magazine south of Baltimore in the eighteenth century was the *South Carolina Weekly Museum* (1797–98), edited in Charleston by T. P. Bowen. Practically all the above-mentioned magazines were eclectic in character and more or less imitated the English periodicals of the day, especially Cave's *Gentleman's Magazine*.

The nineteenth century witnessed greater magazine activity than ever before. Most important of the periodicals coming before 1820 were: *Port Folio* (1801–27), Philadelphia, published by Joseph Dennie and pre-eminent for the first part of the century; *American Review and Literary Journal* (1800–02), New York, published by Charles Brockden Brown as a successor to his *Monthly Magazine and American Review* (1799–1800), New York; *Literary Magazine and American Register* (1803–07), Philadelphia, published by Brown; the *Portico* (1816–18), Baltimore; and—most scholarly of all—the *North-American Review* (1815–to date), published in Boston.[3] Numerous other magazines of minor importance appeared during this period, most of them lasting only a few years at the very longest.

The very first attempt to establish a periodical of any kind in Georgia took place in the seacoast town of Savannah, which had a population in 1800 of 5,146,[4] and which was a place of some intellectual activity. Bethesda College, founded as an orphanage by the Rev. George Whitefield in 1739, with "A Seminary of Literature and Academical Learning" added in 1764,[5] was trying to meet the higher educational needs of the community, together with numerous private schools set up in the city in the latter part of the eighteenth century.[6] The circulating library, started by George Lamb in January, 1798,[7] was ministering to the reading appetites of the people. As early as 1783 *The Fair Penitent,* by Nicholas Rowe, was given for the benefit of the poor; [8] and in 1785 a regular theater was opened, where dramas were presented at irregular intervals thereafter.[9]

Savannah residents were not only buying books from the North and from England, but subscribing to at least one reputable literary periodical. When the *Port Folio,* a Philadelphia weekly devoting much space to literature, was begun in 1801 by Joseph Dennie, it numbered among its first subscribers people from Savannah. Subscriptions to this Northern periodical apparently increased to such an extent that the one Georgia agent for the work was given three helpers, all from Savannah, within a few months.[10] In the midst of this intellectual activity the first attempt was made to establish a magazine in the state.

1. SAVANNAH—*GEORGIA ANALYTICAL REPOSITORY*
(1802–03)

TITLE: *Georgia Analytical Repository*
FIRST ISSUE: May & June, 1802   LAST ISSUE: March & April, 1803
PERIODICITY: Bi-monthly
PUBLISHERS: Seymour, Woolhopter & Stebbins, Savannah
EDITOR: Rev. Henry Holcombe
LOCATION OF FILES: *GU(D):* Vol. I, No. 4. *NNH:* (Inc.). *PCC:* CF. *RPB:* CF. *WH:* CF

What seems to have been the first periodical of any kind, exclusive of newspapers, in the state began in Savannah in May, 1802. It was entitled the *Georgia Analytical Repository,* and was of both literary and religious nature, predominantly the latter. It appeared bi-monthly and was edited by the Rev. Henry Holcombe, a prominent Baptist minister of Savannah. The first issue was dated "May & June, 1802," and consisted of 48 octavo pages, without column divisions. The life of the magazine was short, for only the six numbers of Volume I exist, the last being dated "March & April, 1803." Whether any further numbers were issued is not known, though there is no indication in those extant that the editor had any intention of abandoning his project.

First Experiments in Periodical Literature 7

Henry Holcombe (1762-1824), a native of Virginia and a captain of cavalry in the American Revolution, came to South Carolina in early manhood, and there, as a Baptist preacher, served as pastor until 1799, when he moved to Savannah. The religious tolerance of the man is evidenced by the fact that he served as pastor of a Presbyterian congregation for several months before a Baptist church was organized in the city.[11] Holcombe was so interested in humanitarian projects that he originated, says one historian, the "penitentiary system which abolished sentence of death for ordinary crimes." [12] He was the recipient of two degrees: the D.D. from South Carolina College, and the M.A. from Brown University.

For some years prior to the founding of the *Georgia Analytical Repository,* Holcombe seems to have been deeply interested in the moral condition of the country. His concern may be noted in his preface to the first number of the work:

In a land mourning on account of such sins, and pained with the irremediable inefficacy of *human laws,* some have asked if these, and other existing means of order and happiness, might not be aided, at this time, by a *periodical publication.* The *cautious* reply has been, "We are not ripe for any thing of this nature. It must be deferred to a future day. Learning and religion, here, are in their infancy. Let us depend on foreigners, well known to fame, to write for us, and improve our minds by their learned labors. For us to attempt, without better qualifications, to publish a work, in this age of refinement, would be only to expose ourselves."

The anxious *querists,* at first, were chilled, and palsied by these suggestions; but they have since considered that in countries where Arts and Sciences most flourish, they were very imperfect in their origin; that they must forever rise into perfection by slow degrees; that writing, and publishing, whether we are treated with silent contempt, or honored with public notice, are some of the best means of improving us in these Arts; and that dissuasion from introducing a periodical work, till we are qualified to conduct it, with taste and ability, is like an injunction not to go into the water, till we learn to swim, or not to attempt saving our beloved country, nor precious souls, from *ruin,* by using some of the most powerful means we have, till we can more smoothly round our periods!

And feeling the great need for experimentation as a means of literary growth, he further remarks:

> Urged by, what we still conceive to be, the *necessity* of the measure, we again, respectfully enquire, if we may not, though infants in learning and religion, rationally indulge the pleasing hope of contributing, with effect, towards the maturity of both literature and piety, by combining and properly directing our efforts, in the encouragement and support of a *periodical piece,* for that *important,* because *all-comprehending purpose?*
>
> We can, at least, make the *experiment,* and be but where we were, if we *fail* in this *Repository.* To justify almost any liberties of which young hands may wish to avail themselves, was a motive that influenced the choice of a *title* for this piece. Among Georgians especially, to whom it will probably, with a few exceptions, be eventually confined, it promises admission, and security, to *whatever sketches* may be considered interesting in a religious, or moral view, without *engaging* to furnish any purely original, or completely finished productions.

The editor further states that the magazine will contain *"analized* intelligence from every part of the christian world," accounts of religious bodies in Georgia, general church news, *"short* judicious essays on *any* subject of importance," sermon outlines, "interesting deaths, of persons of all descriptions, well authenticated anecdotes, select sentences, poetry," etc. "Ministers of the gospel," he pursues, "in this state especially, by a liberal combination of their abilities, and their prayers, it is confidently expected will largely contribute to the success of this adventurous enterprize."

. Holcombe doubtless felt the difficulties of the task of editing such a periodical, for he makes the following confession at the conclusion of the preface:

> I freely own myself to be very unequal to a business of such delicacy and magnitude. But I am consoled with a hope, that my deficiencies will be in some degree concealed, by friendly assistance, till the arduous concern can be placed in more competent hands.

The magazine was dedicated to Josiah Tattnall, Governor of Georgia, whom Holcombe called an "excellent Theophilus," a "public character, to patronize 'religion and virtue' . . ." As far as can be ascertained, Holcombe used no particular periodical as a model for the *Repository*. He perhaps allowed his publishers to arrange his material in the manner most attractive to them.

The *Georgia Analytical Repository* does not seem to have been a sectarian periodical, for it contains historical sketches of denominations other than the Baptist, together with items of general interest. Nothing whatever may be learned from the extant numbers as to the subscription price, number of subscribers, or reception of the work elsewhere. Frank Luther Mott lists the magazine in his "Chronological List of Magazines," [13] and histories of Georgia and Savannah merely state that such a periodical was published in 1802–03, but little else seems to be known. Even the contemporary newspapers *Columbian Museum & Savannah Advertiser* (Savannah), Augusta *Chronicle*, and Augusta *Herald* make no mention of this magazine in their pages; hence it must have attracted very limited support and interest.

An examination of the first number of the *Repository* reveals the general character of the work. This issue, "May & June, 1802," devotes practically all its space to articles of a religious nature. "Religious Intelligence" contains news items about revivals and events of religious significance. There are historical sketches of the Congregational Church at Medway,[14] and of Christ's Episcopal Church in Savannah; a brief biography of the late Rev. Daniel Marshall; an account of the "Ordination, of Rev. Henry Francis, a man of color, whose freedom was recently purchased of Mrs. Hammond, in consideration of his character, and ministerial gifts, by a number of the gentlemen of Savannah"; and a didactic narrative of "A Most Awful Death," the account of the horrible death of a woman of ill fame. But by far the greatest space is given to "Rice's Biography," a biographical sketch of John Rice, executed in Savannah for theft on May 20, 1802, whose "life and death, however wicked and disgraceful, appears [*sic*] to us improvable to valuable purposes." This sketch concludes with the appeal of the editor to all sinners to forsake their evil ways and repent. The first number of this periodical closes with a half-page of miscellaneous anonymous aphorisms of a decidedly didactic nature.

The succeeding five numbers of the *Repository* are similar to the first, with additional accounts of "Happy Deaths" and "Tragic Deaths," and with extracts from letters to the editor relating revival experiences. Now and then hymns are quoted, usually in long prose articles, but only two poems appear for their own intrinsic worth. One, signed "E," is entitled "Retirement" and consists of two four-line stanzas in ballad meter. The poem is quoted in full as typical of the religious verse of the period as found in newspapers and periodicals:

> Rerired [sic] from all noise my silent thoughts
>   On things celestial muse;
> Reflection calmly looks behind,
>   While faith the future views.
>
> Here all is rest, and sweet repose.
>   Here all my sorrows cease;
> For Jesus meets my spirit here,
>   And kindly whispers peace.[15]

The other poem is entitled "Extract from a young minister's diary. March 4, 1792, on reading rev. *Oliver Hart's* Sermon entitled, '*The Gospel Church Portrayed.*'"[16] It consists of twenty-seven lines of heroic couplets, the last three lines forming a tercet. In the closed-couplet manner of Pope the poem praises the Church. Two lines will suffice to give a flavor of its diction:

> Portrayed by Hart's divinely skilful hand,
> What admiration does the Church command!

By far the most interesting article in the whole volume is the "Address. To the Friends of Religion, on Civil Government," written by the editor. Running through three issues,[17] it defends civil government as a divine institution, further declaring that "even the worst form of government, and that badly administered, is preferable to entire anarchy." [18] The writer doubtless experiences an intellectual reaction to the French Revolution, even though Georgia has heard only an echo of it in the newspapers. The following extract from this address reveals the writer's interest in "natural rights": "Ascertaining our own natural rights, as good citizens will always do, we ascertain those of all other men, with equal precision; and we should honestly, and diligently seek, and boldly avow the truth." [19] In reference to Tom Paine, at that time in Washington, the national capital, Holcombe continues in this vein:

... the fallacious orators of this "Age of Reason," among other essential distinctions, have artfully blended natural and acquired rights, and stimulated the very refuse of society to rise up, under the influence of an imaginary equality, and treat their superiors with the most brutal insolence and barbarity. ... Pretended patriots are strenuously insisting that all men are equally entitled to a voice in the expression of the public will; though it is evident, that where inequalities exist as to acquired rights, they should be respected in all social compacts. Constitutions are radically defective, and to a degree subversive of their existence, which do not provide for the security of every man's legal possessions. Hence in apportioning the number of representatives from the different states, in Congress, respect was had to *wealth,* as well as *population.* Without a just regard to both, in representation, the poor are liable to oppression, or property is insecure. Voters too, as with us, should everywhere, and always, have pecuniary qualifications. ... As to a form of government, God has left men to the exercise of their own reason, regulated by a natural desire of happiness, to enter into such compacts and to form such regulations, as are most agreeable to their tempers and their circumstances: But he has made it our duty to view him as the foundation of all subordinate authority, whether it be conferred in judgment, or in mercy. ... However deeply legislators, and magistrates, are stained with crimes, it should not destroy our respect for the station which they fill, nor for the wholesome laws that they frame and execute.

. . . .

In the constitution of a free people, provision is made for legally rectifying all errors and abuses, whether in law or administration.

This is highly proper; but . . . the generous spirit of christianity will enable us to bear many inconveniences, rather than disturb the public peace. . . . and if governments become grievously oppressive, to effect a reform, or even a *revolution* may be a desirable and important object; but it should always be done, *if possible,* by constitutional, and moderate means. . . . And should the sword of tryanny be unearthed to enforce submission to inequitous [*sic*] measures, the only, and therefore lawful alternative, is, to oppose *force* to *force.*[20]

Holcombe here seems to be voicing the general American opposition to the Deism of Paine. He also seems fearful of the presence in the United States of Paine, who, he thinks, may be able to sow in America the insidious seed that produced the French Revolution. He refers to his opponent as "the infamous apostate from the principles of 'Common Sense,' and author of the detestable 'Age of Reason,' " who "has arrived at the seat of government, and unfurled the banners of infidelity under patronage too respectable to be treated with contemptuous silence."[21] Paine, he further declares, "has not recanted a syllable in the Age of Reason," nor is he "now occupied solely in politics, on the principles of *Common Sense,*" for he "continues to be the avowed enemy of all who bear the Christian name—the avowed enemy of God our Savior."[22] In conclusion, says Holcombe:

We live, and *happily,* under a Government, *a representative republic,* which affords us full as much liberty as we have virtue to improve. It has a tendency, it must be owned, to an aristocracy; but we may easily check this, by the general encouragement of learning and Religion . . .[23]

Deism never attained the influence in the South that it had in the North, except possibly in Virginia under the patronage of Thomas Jefferson. It did, however, attract the attention of John Wesley, who found the movement of such proportions in Georgia in 1737 that he felt obliged to preach special sermons against it.[24] The return of Tom Paine to the United States in 1802 at the invitation of Jefferson resulted in a militant campaign against the deistic philosophy by the Methodists, Baptists, and Presbyterians of the South, and the revival movement that swept America from Maine to Georgia in the first decade of the nineteenth century practically ended the cause of militant Deism.[25] By means of these evangelistic campaigns in behalf of "old-fashioned" religion, Deism had been almost totally erased from the South by 1830,[26] and the religious field was left to the three above-mentioned evangelical denominations, together with the Episcopal Church, which had been little affected by the emotionalism of the revival movement. The fervor of the campaign against Deism is reflected in the writings of the editor of Georgia's first magazine.

The *Georgia Analytical Repository* soon ceased to exist, but such was the case with practically all magazines of that period, North or South. The Savannah magazine might not have been a true representation of the culture of the city. It might not have appealed to Georgians because it was non-sectarian; and the State at the beginning of the nineteenth century was decidedly narrow in its religious viewpoints. The work possibly would have been more nearly a success had its editor made it a Baptist paper and made Baptist doctrines its rallying point. Regardless of what might have been, the periodical was of no great literary value in itself; nevertheless it represented an interest in the cultural welfare of the state, and as such it was a milestone in the development of periodical literature in Georgia.

2. SAVANNAH—*LADIES' MAGAZINE* (1819)

TITLE: *Ladies' Magazine*
FIRST ISSUE: February 13, 1819   LAST ISSUE: August 7, 1819
PERIODICITY: Weekly
EDITORS AND PUBLISHERS: Barton & Edes, Savannah, February 13–May 8, 1819; Russell & Edes, Savannah, May 15–August 7, 1819
LOCATION OF FILES: *MH:* CF *NcD:* CF (photostats). *W:* CF

Between 1803 and 1819, the year of the establishment of Savannah's second periodical, some progress had been made in Savannah in intellectual and educational circles. The Chatham Academy, chartered by the State legislature in 1788,[27] was formally opened on January 5, 1813, with 219 pupils the first day.[28] Both the Academy and Bethesda College, the latter established by the Rev. George Whitefield, were endowed institutions,[29] and were apparently well equipped to give a classical training to the youth of the city. The drama was still popular, for we learn that the season for 1818 was opened with a performance of Andrew Cherry's comedy of *The Soldier's Daughter*.[30]

The second periodical established in Georgia and the first devoted exclusively to female readers was the *Ladies' Magazine*, published weekly in Savannah in 1819 from February 13 to August 7. The first number carried the following address "To Our Patrons":

> In devoting our publication to the amusement and instruction of the LADIES, we pay only a just tribute of respect to the virtues, and talents, of our fair Countrywomen. . . . We must all acknowledge, that much depends upon the impressions imbibed in infancy; and that the character of the man is usually marked by the traits, the passions, and dispositions manifested in boyhood. From whom are these passions, traits, and dispositions, in a great measure derived? From the MOTHER. . . . Hence the importance of Female Education in this point of view, particularly as it bears upon the interests of this form of government. . . . Cornelia, instead of exhibiting to her vain and ostentatious friend, pearls, rubies, and diamonds, produced her sons, the Gracchi, as the most valuable and only inestimable jewels in her possessions. This is the pride which, in a Republic like this, it ought to be our anxious wish to see indelibly impressed upon the deportment and character of an American Female. . .
>
> Under these impressions, we assume the task of contributing by our labours, to the general mass of Female information; and with such original matter as may be furnished, we shall call to our aid the best selected matter from the pages of history and science. —In all things we shall endeavor to discharge with fidelity our engagements to the public; and flatter ourselves with the hope, that the Ladies of Savannah will not be disappointed in any expectation they may have formed of our zeal in enlarging the sphere of their amusement and instruction.

This periodical, printed and edited by Barton & Edes (William C. Barton and Richard W. Edes), was to be published "every

First Experiments in Periodical Literature 15

Saturday evening, on fine paper, with new type in octavo," [31] and was advertised at $5.00 per year, one half in advance for "city subscribers," and one year in advance for "country subscribers." With one exception, which will be noted later, each issue consisted of eight pages of two columns to the page.

A magazine for ladies, though a new venture in the South, had been attempted elsewhere at an earlier period. The first attempts were made in Philadelphia: the *Lady's Magazine* (1792–93); the *Ladies' Museum* (1800); the *Repository and Weekly Register,* later the *Repository and Ladies' Weekly Museum* (1800–06); and the *Ladies' Magazine and Musical Repository* (1801).[32] Only one other such periodical was published, the *Lady's Weekly Miscellany* (New York, 1805–08),[33] before the *Ladies' Magazine* appeared in Savannah. None of the early Southern ventures made more than a ripple on the surface of periodical literature, yet, says Bertha-Monica Stearns in a recent study of "Southern Magazines for Ladies (1819–1860)," all of them "played their little parts in the life of an earlier time, and, absurd as many of them are, they tell a story of struggling enterprise and of determination to give to the lady-reader of the South what editors in other regions were supplying to their country-women." [34] *Godey's Lady's Book,* which ran from 1830 to 1898, was the most successful of all efforts in behalf of female readers of the century, but these earlier ventures deserve notice because they blazed the trail for their more fortunate successors.

The first issue of the Savannah *Ladies' Magazine* contained a letter, in the Addisonian tradition, to the editors from "Your Correspondent, TOM QUEERFISH." [35] This letter, a humorous discussion of the meaning of the word *magazine* as "a place in which arms, ammunition, provisions, &c. are deposited," ends with the declaration that "if other than the purest motives influence your labour, I sincerely hope you may be *blown up;* not with gunpowder, but by the keen invectives of that portion of animated beauty, whose frowns alone can kill, and whose smiles alone can reanimate." The "Ladies' Department" carried miscellaneous tributes to the dignity and worth of woman in the world; while "Miscellany" included as its most important item a short tale entitled "Mary," which "A Subscriber" declared to be "the production of G. Minor, Esq. the Editor of the Village Record." "Gleanings," "Marriages," and "Deaths" completed the contents of the first issue except for "The Recess," which, occupying the last page, consisted of three short poems selected from other periodicals. The *Ladies' Magazine* seemed careful to give credit where such was possible. Certain contributions were headed "For the Ladies' Magazine," while selected matter was attributed to miscellaneous works, both in America and in England. The following periodicals were named in the composite file:

Vermont Intelligencer
Boston *Recorder*
London *Magazine*
Boston *Intelligencer*
Catskill Recorder
N. E. Galaxy
Baltimore *Telegraph*
Philadelphia *Daily Advertiser*
Gloucester (N.J.) *Farmer*
Christian Spectator
Augusta (Ga.) *Chronicle*
New York *National Advocate*
Boston *Palladium*
New York *Ladies' Literary Cabinet*
Darien (Ga.) *Gazette*
Georgia Advertiser
Poulson's Daily Advertiser [36]
Providence *Patriot*
Philadelphia *Gazette*
Saratoga *Sentinel*
Boston *Kaleidoscope*
American Daily Advertiser [36]
New-York *Columbian*

Utica *Patriot*
Charleston *Times*
London *Lady's Magazine*
British Magazine
Boston *Gazette*
Baltimore *Federal Republican*
Independent Balt.
Franklin Gazette
Georgetown *Messenger*
Richmond *Enquirer*
Savannah *Georgian*
American Farmer
Virginia Herald
Columbia (S.C.) *Telescope*
Philadelphia *Union*
Bath (Eng.) *Herald*
Mount-Zion (Ga.) *Missionary*
Ladies' Miscellany
Port Folio
Aberdeen *Journal*
West Jersey Gazette
People's Watch-Tower
American Magazine
 [unidentified]
Troy *Budget*
Augusta (Ga.) *Herald*

Of the periodicals and newspapers from which selected material was drawn, fully three-fourths came from the Northern states, with four from England and eight from Georgia. This seems to indicate an intellectual dependence upon both the North and England, although selected material was often of the miscellaneous type, sometimes acting as an apparent filler for one or more pages. Yet at least the editors were keeping up with what was going on in the rest of the world, and they had sufficient material for an eclectic magazine if they had desired to conduct one of that nature. Doubtless many of the listed periodicals were received entirely by way of exchange and were of secondary importance. To say the least, however, the editors of the *Ladies' Magazine* had a decided variety of material at their command whenever they needed it. Eclectic material occupied most of the space in each issue and was far superior to the original matter included. It is impossible to tell how much of the latter material came from residents of Savannah, but doubtless some of it came from personal friends of the publishers interested in the venture.

The aim of the *Ladies' Magazine* was not only to entertain but to instruct. The didactic note is struck in a selection from "Gleanings" entitled "One Thousand Dollars Reward," in which a "Toper" is depicted as offering a reward for the return of his estate, which has been totally lost "after being put in motion by the magic art of one Intemperance, who lived in the family." Among the most interesting, as well as most important, articles and tales appearing in the work during its short life of six months are the following, specially contributed except as stated otherwise:

"A Fragment," contrasting a household of sin with one of purity [37]
"A Proclamation," by Benjamin Symmetry, who, though seventy years old, wants as a wife some "deserving young woman of 16" [38]
Letter from Polly Proportion, in answer to Benjamin Symmetry's "Proclamation" [39]
Letter from Saffronia, in answer to Benjamin Symmetry's "Proclamation" [40]

Letter from Benjamin Symmetry, in answer to the above two letters [41]
Letter on the Fine Art of Dancing, by "Comus" [42]
"Fatal Curiosity," from the London *Magazine* [43]
"Julia and Palmira," a tale by Miss Eliza Yeames [Source not indicated] [44]
"Sentence of Death Pronounced by Judge Berrien against Jonathan Evers, for the Murder of Mr. Jones" [45]
"An Over-Ruling Providence," from *D'Oyly's Discourses* [46]
"The Serpent Charmed," from Chateaubriand's *Beauties of Christianity* [47]
"A Hint to Parents and Guardians of Children," by "An Observer" [48]
"Duelling," by Coelebs [49]
"The Wife," from the Sketch-Book of Geoffrey Crayon (Washington Irving) [50]

The longest poem to be published was "Maria; or, The Victim of Jealousy," by Junius, quoted from the New York *Ladies' Cabinet*.[51] Other poems, both original and selected, bore such titles as "One Glass More" (on temperance),[52] "Extempore Reflection at Twilight,"[53] "The Patriotic Soldier,"[54] "Female Piety,"[55] "The Negro Boy,"[56] "To Peace,"[57] "On Profane Swearing,"[58] etc. In the issue preceding the last one[59] appeared "The Times," which is "from a friend in Charleston, and presents a good picture of the times." The last of the three stanzas possibly shows the financial situation of the editors, who were soon to suspend publication of the periodical:

> Oh! curse upon the banks;
> No credit's there.
> They issue nought but blanks;
> No cash is there,
> *Hard times,* the men do cry,
> *Hard times,* the women sigh;
> Ruin and mis-e-ry!
> No cash is here!

The difficulties of the editors of the *Ladies' Magazine* seem to have been very great. Barton, with the issue of May 8, disposed of his interest in the publication to Henry P. Russell,

First Experiments in Periodical Literature 19

and the firm became Russell & Edes. Except for the printing notices of the proprietors themselves, no advertisements appeared in the pages of the periodical until the issue of July 3, which was a sixteen-page attempt to gain the favor of an unresponsive reading public. The issue stated that "Advertisements not exceeding a square, or 16 lines, will be published for *fifty cents* for the first insertion, and *twenty-five cents* for each continuance;—longer ones in the same proportion." Advertisements offered to the public "Muslins and Cambric Trimmings," "Millinery," "Rose Water," Card Games, Books, Perfumery, Portrait Painting, "Mineral Waters," and the advantages of J. Humphrey's School, besides the "Wanted" items regarding domestic servants and apprentices. These advertisements appear on the first two and the last two pages of the July 3 issue, so that the "outside leaves will prevent the body of the work from being soiled, and may be taken off at pleasure, without interfering with the Miscellaneous parts of it, when the owner wishes to have the numbers bound up in a volume."[60] The editors make a strong plea for their magazine, citing, by way of example, the New York *Ladies' Literary Cabinet*, which, though one of fourteen competing publications in New York City, has a total subscription list of some 1,400 people.[61] This issue for July 3 carried a humorous tale entitled "Pilgarlick's Magnanimity; or, An Unsuccessful Attack upon a Regiment of Musquetoes," by Ralph Nipshaw, quoted from the *Ladies' Miscellany*. Other interesting items were: "Mrs. Pilkington," a biographical sketch of an actress; "Josephine. A Tale of Truth," from the London *Ladies' Magazine;* a review of Byron's "The Vampyre" [*sic*], from the *Literary Cabinet;* and "Useful Recipes."

The ambitious experiment of July 3 brought no substantial results, for in the next issue,[62] which consisted of only eight pages, we find the editors commenting as follows:

Being satisfied, from the experiment made last week, that the present is an unfavorable time (on account of the numerous removals from the City, for the summer season), to pursue the proposed plan of enlarging the paper, the Editors have concluded to publish it of the same size as heretofore, until the expiration of the current six months. In the mean time, subscriptions will be opened for its enlargement; and if, within that period, sufficient encouragement shall be given, it will then be published in *sixteen* pages, agreeable to the specimen given in the last number.

Advertisements in the last number occupied less than one page. The general quality of the periodical did not decline as the work neared its end, but a lack of financial success brought its career to a close in the very year that saw its birth. The financial panic of 1819 was doubtless a contributing factor in the death of the magazine. The editors, in the concluding number,[63] thus outlined their reasons for suspending publication of the *Ladies' Magazine:*

The present number (26) of this paper terminates one half year since the commencement of its publication, and three months since it fell into the hands of the present proprietors. To those who have promptly complied with the terms of the paper they tender their warmest thanks, but they are sorry to say, there are many who have, as yet, been only *nominal* patrons; and it is owing to the latter circumstance, together with the want of more general support, that the Publishers are reluctantly compelled to announce, their intention of *suspending* at least, if not discontinuing entirely, its publication after the present number. They would take peculiar pride and pleasure in affording instruction and amusement to the female part of this enlightened community; and a *literary* paper is one which, of all others, they would prefer publishing, provided it met with adequate encouragement and support; but as the taste and ardor for reading seem to have abated with the approach of warm weather, and the general decline of business, in consequence of the numerous removals from the city, for the summer season . . . they see no other alternative than to let the paper cease for the present. In the fall, when the citizens shall have generally returned to their homes, they propose issuing a prospectus for its recommencement, upon a different plan from that heretofore pursued; and if sufficient encouragement shall offer, the publication will be resumed.

In 1819, when the *Ladies' Magazine* suspended publication, the State of Georgia was probably still too small in population

First Experiments in Periodical Literature

to make any kind of magazine successful. The growth of the State in population from 1790, when the first official census was taken by the federal government, to 1830 is indicated in the following figures from the U.S. Census:

Year	Whites	Slaves
1790	53,284	29,264
1800	102,697	59,404
1810	147,215	105,218
1820	191,331	149,654
1830	299,292	217,531

Another reason for the failure of Georgia's first two magazines may be the fact that the editors of these two periodicals—like far too many of their successors—founded literary periodicals without really understanding the problems involved, and without reckoning in advance with the problem of getting contributors and subscribers. Running a magazine is no job for an amateur, yet most Georgia editors (in fact, many others, for that matter, all over the country) tackled the job like amateurs, thinking it a good thing if Georgia or a certain Georgia town had a magazine of a certain type. Only men and women of journalistic experience ever succeeded, in *ante-bellum* Georgia, in founding any periodical that ran for more than a few months.

CHAPTER I

First Period: 1837–46

INTRODUCTION

THE POPULATION of Georgia did not, as might have been expected, branch out from Savannah as a center. Some settlers from the coastal region did, it is true, push southward and westward to open up new lands, but they had little to do with the settlement of Middle Georgia. This latter section was, in the main, colonized by people from the Carolinas and from Virginia, and with the coming of these new settlers the center of population in the State shifted from the coast to the regions of Middle Georgia. In consequence there was a shifting of enterprise from Savannah to Macon and to the rich lands in the center of the State. Southwest Georgia remained a sparsely settled country until the middle of the century, and played little part in the production of Georgia literature of any sort except in the establishment of a few newspapers. Middle Georgia, after the 1830's, took the lead in both economic and literary fields, and furnished to the State, with few exceptions, all her distinguished sons during the decades immediately preceding the Civil War.

During the 1830's the chief influence in the development of periodical literature in the South was the rise of the sectional spirit. Ever since the trying years of the late eighteenth century, when the newly-freed American colonies were trying

First Period: 1837–46

to establish a permanent government, there had been a dividing line between the interests of the North and of the South. Slavery played as yet only a small part in this division, which went back even to colonial times. As the Industrial Revolution spread to the New World, the North devoted itself mainly to industry, commerce, and banking, while the South concerned itself almost exclusively with agriculture. The injection of the slavery question, however, into the already-present differences between the two sections merely served to crystallize sentiment so strongly that a long and bloody Civil War finally resulted.

The congressional debates leading up to the Missouri Compromise of 1820 were perhaps the cause of the Southern awakening to a defense of slavery, which, as a sectional issue, had remained practically dormant since the compromise brought about in the Constitutional Convention.[1] In 1831 occurred the Southampton (Virginia) slave insurrection, led by a negro named Nat Turner, in which more than sixty whites, mainly women and children, were killed. The South naturally believed that Northern abolitionists were responsible for this uprising, and centered their attacks upon the *Liberator,* the abolition newspaper established in Boston in January of the same year by William Lloyd Garrison, a Massachusetts reformer. The founding of the American Anti-Slavery Society in Philadelphia in 1833, together with the British emancipation of slaves in the West Indies in that year, emphasized the abolition sentiment so greatly that in a short while hundreds of abolition societies were established in the North. As a natural consequence the South bristled to defend herself from Northern attacks, which were sometimes merciless. It was, therefore, only after 1833 that we find Southern sentiment concentrating upon a defense of the South in any very definite fashion.

The Old South, imbued with this new spirit of sectionalism, under different conditions might have produced a great literature. Composed of a more homogeneous white population than that of the North, and bound together by agricultural interests, the South early became conscious, to a considerable extent at least, of her sectional unity. Yet the very intensity of the slavery controversy handicapped all literary production except that in the political realm. Congressional debates were eagerly read all over the South, for politics was the arena in which most great Southerners endeavored to meet their Northern opponents. Slavery came to be defended as a God-given institution for the uplift of the under-privileged race; and the plantation as the stronghold of slavery was so idealized in the South, perhaps most of all in Virginia and in South Carolina, that eventually much of Southern literature was colored by its glamor.

Sectional feeling and prejudice ran high in Georgia, to be sure, though perhaps not so high as in South Carolina. There was a strong anti-secessionist sentiment in the State that made itself felt in the Secession Convention of 1861; yet, almost to a man, Georgians, like most Southerners, defended slavery even while they disagreed over the methods of meeting Northern attacks. Georgia writers, however, except in political discussions, generally avoided slavery as a literary topic. Their literary themes were usually drawn from those of religion and morality, of early American history, or of love and adventure in European countries. For this reason we find the early magazines of Georgia subordinating sectional prejudice to a desire to entertain and instruct. Part of this subordination was due to the editorial labors of William Tappan Thompson and of William C. Richards, natives, respectively, of Ohio and England. These two men early made Georgia their adopted home, and both expressed sympathy with Southern principles; but their pleas for the establishment of a purely Southern literature were free from the usual bitterness found in the editorial columns of Southern publications. The study of Georgia periodicals after 1833, then, involves a study of the attempts to found a Southern literature independent of Northern influences.

First Period: 1837-46

After the discontinuance of the *Ladies' Magazine* in Savannah in 1819, eighteen years passed before another attempt was made to establish a literary periodical in Georgia. In this interval the Savannah *Times*, calling itself "A Commercial, Miscellaneous, and Literary Journal," devoted some space to literary interests, usually, it seems, the last of its four quarto pages to an issue.[2] Other newspapers of the period included poems and tales of some length, but none can be classified as other than a news journal. An interesting little Georgia (?) magazine, whose first number is dated September, 1831, is the *Youth's Repertory and Child's Magazine*, whose only extant issue is in the Library of the College of Charleston (South Carolina). It is a duodecimo magazine of 36 pages, but with no title page to indicate either place of publication, editor, or printer. It lists the governors of Georgia, gives an outline of the Georgia Constitution, Judiciary, etc., and contains a biographical sketch of George Walton, Georgia signer of the Declaration of Independence. The magazine contains more general information, historical and biographical, than anything else. It is reasonable to suppose that the periodical was published in Georgia, since this State plays an important place in the first issue of the magazine.[3]

After 1833 several periodicals were either planned or begun in Georgia with literary interests in mind. Following is a list of those for which no files have been located:

Scottsboro (Baldwin County)——*Georgia Academician and Southern Journal of Education*. Semi-monthly, 8 pages, published by Robert C. Brown, and to begin November, 1834. Prospectus in Augusta *State Rights' Sentinel*, April 10, 1834.

Athens——*Athenian*,[4] published by the alumni of Franklin College, monthly. To contain 64 royal octavo pages, with the object of fostering literature in the South. Prospectus in Augusta *State Rights' Sentinel*, October 18, 1836.

Augusta——*Southern Pioneer*. Weekly quarto, edited by Charles Wyatt Rice, and published by Browne, Cushey & M'Cafferty. To begin October, 1839. Prospectus in *Southern Post* (Macon), II, 31 (May 25, 1839).

Columbus——*Southern Bee.* Weekly quarto, edited by William J. Ellis and James H. Ticknor, and published by John M. McMurray. Prospectus in *Southern Post* (Macon), II, 37 (July 6, 1839).

Savannah——*Literary Messenger.* Weekly, published by H. S. Bell in 1842.[5]

Columbus——*Youth's Companion.* Monthly quarto, 16 pages, published by the Rev. Thomas M. Slaughter. First number has been received, says *Southern Miscellany* (Madison), II, 1 (April 1, 1843).

Aside from the above-mentioned periodicals, nothing of literary importance to periodical literature appeared in Georgia during this period except those discussed below.

While all this was taking place in Georgia, periodicals in the North were entering upon an era of success. In Philadelphia *Graham's Magazine* (the *Casket* combined with *Burton's Gentleman's Magazine*) was becoming a remarkably successful periodical.[6] Several Southern periodicals contained the types of reading matter found in the average issue of *Graham's*, such as short stories, light essays, biographical sketches, literary articles, and a "considerable amount of poetry—narrative, lyrical and didactic."[7] In 1841 Edgar Allan Poe joined the editorial staff of *Graham's*, and during his fifteen months' connection with it did some of his best writing.[8] *Graham's* possibly influenced most of the *ante-bellum* Georgia periodicals through "its contents [which] were designed to be amusing rather than profound: in its lighter essays we have the beginnings of what came to be magazinish writing in contradistinction from the dull and heavy review style all too prominent at that time."[9] Georgia periodicals, however, seldom published engravings or musical selections in their pages, and absolutely avoided the colored fashion plates that adorned the pages of *Godey's, Graham's,* and certain other Northern magazines. The expense of such "extras" was prohibitive to most Georgia publishers.

The *Knickerbocker* magazine (New York), belonging to the class of lighter periodicals, is possibly the one which most

Georgia monthlies before 1860 resembled, at least in type of reading matter. During its long life from 1833 to 1865,[10] it is often referred to in Georgia periodicals. It may have furnished the model of William C. Richards in his "Editor's Table" in the *Orion* (Penfield) and the *Southern Literary Gazette* (Athens). The *Southern Quarterly Review,* begun in New Orleans in 1842 but removed to Charleston in the same year, appeared until 1857. It was a "heavy" work of a general nature, but its comparatively long life argues some degree of popularity. It seems to have exerted little influence on Georgia periodical literature in spite of the prominence of such of its editors as D. K. Whitaker, J. B. D. DeBow, and William Gilmore Simms. The several periodicals with which Simms was connected doubtless furnished models of various kinds for Southern journalists, and Georgia magazine editors, in general, were pleased to receive contributions from the eminent Charlestonian. The student of Georgia periodicals will see in this period the close connection most of them maintained with Charleston.

The dominant force in Southern periodical literature before 1860 was, of course, the *Southern Literary Messenger* (Richmond), established by Thomas W. White in 1834.[11] The most famous of its editors was Edgar Allan Poe, who was with the magazine from December, 1835, to January, 1837, but since Georgia had no literary periodical running during those months, we have no way of connecting Poe with what was going on in the state except his review of Longstreet's *Georgia Scenes* in the *Messenger* for March, 1836.

In addition to the above-mentioned magazines, numerous other prominent and popular periodicals were in existence outside the South, among which the following are possibly the best: *North American Review* (Boston), 1815–current; *New York Mirror,* 1823–57?; *Casket* (Philadelphia), 1826–40; *Ladies' Magazine* (Boston), 1828–36; *Godey's Lady's Book* (Philadelphia), 1830–98; *Ladies' Companion* (New York), 1834–44; *Ladies' Garland* (Philadelphia), 1837–49; *Brother*

Jonathan (New York), 1839–45?; *Ladies' Pearl* (Lowell, Mass.), 1840–43; *Ladies' Repository* (Cincinnati), 1841–76; *Peterson's Ladies' National Magazine* (Philadelphia), 1842–98; *Ladies' Wreath* (New York), 1846–55? The *Southern Ladies' Book,* established in Macon in 1840, represents Georgia's interest in the nation-wide appeal to feminine readers.

1. MACON—*SOUTHERN POST AND LITERARY ASPIRANT* (1837–39?)

TITLE: *Southern Post and Literary Aspirant,* September 2–November 24, 1837; *Southern Post,* December 1, 1837–October 26, 1839 (?)
FIRST ISSUE: September 2, 1837   LAST ISSUE: October 26, 1839 (?)
PERIODICITY: Weekly
PUBLISHER: Cornelius R. Hanleiter, Macon
EDITORS: Cornelius R. Hanleiter, September 2–November 24, 1837; Philip C. Pendleton, December 1, 1837–October 26, 1839 (?)
LOCATION OF FILES: *GMM:* Sept. 9, 1837–Oct. 26, 1839

The first periodical of any real literary importance in Georgia was the *Southern Post and Literary Aspirant,* founded in Macon by Cornelius R. Hanleiter in September, 1837.[12] It was published weekly, four pages to the issue, in quarto size most of the time, at $2 per year.[13] Publication was not regular, for it sometimes suspended publication for several weeks before being resumed. With the issue of December 1, 1837,[14] the name became simply the *Southern Post,* and Philip C. Pendleton joined the periodical as editor. Through his connection with the work its quality was improved, for Hanleiter was more of a publisher and printer than an editor. William Tappan Thompson, editor of the Augusta *Mirror,* later declared that the *Post,* "though not devoted exclusively to literature, sustains a high literary character, and has done much for the advancement of the cause of southern literature. The Post is ably conducted, and, combining as it does, the useful with the entertaining, should be liberally patronized." [15] Although the *Post* devoted some space to news and advertisements, it became more and more literary as time passed, until it ceased to appear during the latter part of 1839.[16]

First Period: 1837-46

The literary contents of the *Southern Post,* mainly eclectic material, consisted of poems and prose articles, taken variously from the London *Athenaeum, Southern Literary Messenger, Knickerbocker, Metropolitan Magazine, Blackwood's, Bentley's Miscellany,* and the New York *Mirror.* The editor was swamped by poems sent in to him,[17] but published many, often under pseudonyms. Excellent local color is found in the "Third Letter of William Barlow, Esq., to His Cousin Robert. The Female Examination"[18] and in similar letters in later issues. Besides selected matter from Bryant, Holmes, Whittier, and others, contributions came from the following: Mrs. Abdy, Robert M. Charlton, Mrs. Dulany, Mrs. Caroline Lee Hentz, Mrs. C. Ladd (Vineville, Georgia), J. H. Mifflin (Florence, Georgia), Lieut. G. W. Patten, and E. M. Pendleton.

The following initials and obvious pseudonyms were attached to contributions: Ada; Adolphus; Alceus; Anthropos; Billy Barlow (Warren County); Blondel; Carolina (Irwinton, Alabama); Caroline V—; Clio (George F. Pierce); E.C.P.; Frank; G.A.P.; Hedas; Heinfred; Henry (South Carolina); H.E.M.; Ines; Ireneus; Jamie (Florence, Georgia); Janus; J.C.E.; J.H.B. (Sparta, Georgia); J.H.T. (Florence, Georgia); Juliet; Leelin; Mark Anthony Snubs; M.M.N.; Mustapha; Muza; Oscar; P.E.C.; Philologus (Macon); Q. (Vineville, Georgia); Stafford (Mt. Zion, Georgia); Tim Fudge; Valeria (Warrenton, Georgia); Village Bard; W. (Warrenton, Georgia).

The *Southern Post* is important mainly for the fact that it pointed the way for the Augusta *Mirror,* established in 1838, and for the *Southern Ladies' Book,* which Philip C. Pendleton and George F. Pierce started in Macon in 1840. Hanleiter had a hand in several other periodicals, one, the *Southern Miscellany* (Madison), 1842-46, proving even more important because of William Tappan Thompson's connection with it for a brief period.

2. AUGUSTA *MIRROR* (1838–41)

TITLE: Augusta *Mirror*
FIRST ISSUE: May 5, 1838   LAST ISSUE: December 18, 1841
PERIODICITY: Semi-monthly. (No numbers between August 24 and November 30, 1839; between July 25 and September 19, 1840; or between December 26, 1840, and April 24, 1841.)
PUBLISHERS: William Tappan Thompson & James McCafferty, a few months in 1838, Augusta; William Tappan Thompson, 1838–41, Augusta
EDITOR: William Tappan Thompson, assisted by Augustus Baldwin Longstreet during part of 1840
LOCATION OF FILES: *DLC:* III (1840–41). *GAuY:* II, 2–16, 18–22, 24–26 (1839–40). *GMiG:* May 11, 25, June 29, July 13, 27, Aug. 10, 1839. *GWaynT:* CF (also cover pages for II, 4–9; III, 1–8)

The first purely literary paper known to have been published in Georgia was the Augusta *Mirror*, begun on May 5, 1838, by William Tappan Thompson (1812–82), who was both editor and proprietor. The royal quarto periodical, of eight pages to an issue and three columns to a page, bore the subtitle: "A Semi-Monthly Journal. Devoted to Polite Literature and Useful Intelligence. Containing the latest popular pieces of Music, arranged for the Pianoforte or Guitar." Thompson was born in Ravenna, Ohio, of Irish-American stock, but when he was only eleven years of age, the family removed to Philadelphia, where the youth worked in the office of the *Chronicle*. At the age of twenty-five he became secretary to Governor J. D. Westcott, of Florida, and studied law during the term of his secretaryship. In 1835 he was associate editor of the Augusta *State Rights' Sentinel*, but soon gave up this position in order to become a soldier in the war against the Seminole Indians in Florida. At the conclusion of the Florida campaign he returned to Augusta, still interested in journalism. The Augusta *Mirror* was the first of Thompson's several journalistic ventures in the state, which included his connection with the *Family Companion* (Macon), the *Southern Miscellany* (Madison), and the Savannah *Morning News*.[19]

In undertaking the publication of the *Mirror*, Thompson

First Period: 1837–46

was putting into practice a conviction that he thus expressed in the Editorial Department of the first issue of the periodical:

We have been influenced to the present undertaking from a convinction [sic] that a work devoted to literature was demanded by the public interest and taste, and when we have computed the advantages which it must be apparent to all, are likely to result from the establishment of such a journal, particularly to the juvenile [20] portion of the community, we have not been without strong hopes of success. . . . Our aim is chiefly to afford a suitable medium through which the production of southern talent and southern genius, may find their way into the literary world. . . . In the exercise of our editorial duties, we shall always give precedence to matter of home production. . . . In the preparation of the present paper, we have been compelled to rely almost solely upon our own resources, not yet having the advantages of an exchange . . .

To this issue the editor contributed a tale entitled "The General's Horse," but the most entertaining tale is that by Augustus Baldwin Longstreet (under the pseudonym "Baldwin"), "Georgia Scenes, Characters, & Incidents. New Series. Number 1. Little Ben," appearing in print for the first time. Other pieces include the anonymous "MacGirth: or, The Tory's Revenge. A Tragedy"; [21] "A Legend of the Seven Towers," by Miss Pardoe; "To Dyspepsia," a poem by Allan; and "Coronation of the Queen of May," a poetic account of a May Day celebration in Augusta by the pupils of Mrs. H. L. Moise's School, with the speeches written by "A Lady of Augusta." Aside from a few shorter pieces and some fillers, the first number is rounded out by "The Family Circle," a department of miscellany, and by "To Our Patrons," the editorial column.

The Augusta *Mirror* appears to have been received with favor, for the editor's "To Correspondents" of the second issue [22] boasts:

Our subscription list has already increased to a respectable number of names, and every day adds new names to our list; indeed so rapid has been the increase, although, a large number above what we considered the probable demand were printed, we will not be able to supply new subscribers with the first No. in a very short time.

From another source we learn that the *Mirror* began with 200 subscribers, and that at the end of the first year it had 800 in Georgia and as many in the Carolinas.[23] During the second year of the periodical there was a rapid increase in the subscription list. In two weeks' time 150 new subscribers were added, 70 of whom were from Savannah.[24] The excellence of the journal soon attracted the attention of Thomas W. White, editor and publisher of the *Southern Literary Messenger*, who refers to it as "a very neatly printed and well edited periodical."[25] The *Southern Post* (Macon) thus hails the appearance of the *Mirror:* "Its first appearance augurs well for its future usefulness; and located as it is, in one of the first of Southern cities, it will waken up the slumbering genius of the South."[26] The *Independent Monitor* (Tuscaloosa, Alabama) declared that in "appearance and typography it is similar to the New York Mirror; and in excellence and originality much superior to it."[27] Thompson's early success inspired Alexander H. Stephens, in a Fourth of July address at Crawfordville, Georgia, in 1839, to toast the journal as "A lonely but brilliant Star in the long and cheerless night of the Literature of Georgia."[28] The *Mirror* seems to have been popular in Augusta. In 1840 there were over 100 subscribers in that city, which boasted a white population of not more than six or seven thousand. The increase in the subscription list, unfortunately, did not continue, for the list had dwindled to 650 or 700 in 1842.[29] From December 26, 1840,[30] to April 24, 1841,[31] Thompson suspended publication of the *Mirror*, but resumed it for the rest of 1841, with the intention thereafter of making it a weekly publication. Feeling, however, the need of some other form of rejuvenation for his declining periodical, he finally decided to consolidate it with the *Family Companion* (Macon), a union which was consummated with the issue of the latter for March 15, 1842. Thompson became joint-editor

First Period: 1837-46

with Mrs. Sarah Lawrence Griffin of the combined periodicals, which continued to bear the name of the Macon magazine during a short existence thereafter.

Thompson, in spite of his success with the subscription list, was beset by financial difficulties because, he says, "the times are unpropitious . . . and yet we have reason to hope that the friends of the Mirror will not permit it to languish for want of support during the temporary exigency of the time . . ."[32] The financial panic of 1837 was still bearing fruit, and we must remember, too, that it was easy to subscribe to a periodical at that time, for cash was not required in advance; hence many subscribed to the journal and doubtless read it with interest, yet failed to pay for what they had received and enjoyed. With the beginning of Volume II [33] the *Mirror* offered the covers of its pages as an advertising medium, at the same terms as those of the city newspapers. There was a fair response, it seems, for the issue of six weeks later [34] carried a loose outside cover sheet of four extra pages, with one page devoted entirely to advertisements. Such interest, however, did not last long, for soon the *Mirror* carried no advertising matter, as had been the case at the beginning.

When he began to publish the *Mirror,* Thompson, though not a Southerner by either birth or training, was fully aware of the need for greater literary activity in the South. Note his editorial comment during the second year of the existence of his periodical:

Prior to the commencement of the Augusta Mirror, but little interest was felt in our domestic literature. Indeed such a thing did not exist even in name, and it was a rare thing indeed to meet with a literary production from the pen of one of our own citizens . . . and every day furnishes its quota of evidence to prove that the south is as capable of an exalted literature as any other section of country, and that Georgia and Carolina, though long listless upon the subject, are awakening to the importance of its culture. . . . Our southern institutions favor the growth of a purely American literature, in the same degree that they favor practical republicanism and the inculcation of true democratic sentiment.[35]

Other difficulties beset Thompson. Sometimes he had trouble in getting paper for printing the *Mirror*.[36] Sometimes it was difficult to get original matter for the journal.[37] From August 24[38] to November 30, 1839,[39] he had to suspend publication of the paper because of an epidemic of yellow fever in Augusta. Because he himself at this time was afflicted with "chronic affection of the liver, and . . . great irritability of the lungs,"[40] he fled for safety to Warrenton, Georgia, where he remained till all danger had passed. And from December 26, 1840,[41] to April 24, 1841,[42] he was forced, for some unknown reason, probably financial, again to suspend publication of the *Mirror*. During at least a part of 1840 Thompson employed as co-editor Augustus Baldwin Longstreet, author of the famous *Georgia Scenes*.

In order to stimulate the production of Southern literature, Thompson, in the second issue of his periodical, offered the following prizes for original contributions:

> For the best Tale, founded upon incidents connected with the early history of Georgia or South Carolina, is given the latest edition of the complete works of Sir Walter Scott, with a biography.
> For the best Tale, the author to make choice of the incidents, locality, &c, will be given splendid editions of Bulwer's and Marryatt's Novels, complete.
> For the best Poem, not over a half-page in the *Mirror*, a copy of *Byron's Works*.
> For the best Essay on the subject of Political Economy, Hume Smollett and Miller's *History of England*, in 4 vols.
> For the best Biography of a distinguished southern character, the *Lives of the Signers of the Declaration of Independence*, in 4 vols.
> For the best description of Georgia Scenery, a copy of Noble and Rose's *Landscape Illustrations*, 1 vol.

A one year's subscription to the *Mirror* was added to each of the above prizes. Compositions appear to have been submitted in only two contests, for only the following awards were ever announced: for the best tale, to Miss M. E. Moragne of South

Carolina for "The British Partizan, A Tale of the Times of Old"; [43] for the best poem, to Robert M. Charlton of Savannah for "The Moral of Winter." [44] The judges were the Hon. John W. Wilde, the Rev. A. N. Cunningham, Captain E. Starnes, and the Hon. Augustus Baldwin Longstreet.[45]

The Augusta *Mirror* did not lack contributors, at least during the first two years of its existence, although those sending in contributions could expect nothing but thanks for their efforts. Except for prize awards, as indicated previously, contributors to *ante-bellum* Georgia periodicals received little if any compensation whatever for their literary labors. In spite of this fact, however, some of the leading literary figures of the South contributed to Thompson's periodical. Among them were William Gilmore Simms, Richard Henry Wilde, Henry Rootes Jackson, Robert M. Charlton, and Augustus Baldwin Longstreet. Thompson himself, in addition to writing miscellaneous articles for his journal, contributed some of his own humorous tales, among them the following: "The General's Horse," [46] "Judge Lynch Outwitted," [47] "The Alarm," [48] "My First and Last Fire Hunt," [49] "The Duelist and the Devil," [50] "Adventures of a Sabbath Breaker," [51] and "John's Alive! or The Bride of a Ghost." [52] Augustus Baldwin Longstreet contributed several of his "Georgia Scenes" under the pseudonym of "Baldwin": "Little Ben," [53] "Darby Anvil," [54] and "A Family Picture." [55]

Contributions to the *Mirror* came from the following writers: Rev. G. W. Bethune; Robert M. Charlton; Mrs. M. S. B. Dana; S. B. Edwards (Fayetteville, North Carolina); Mrs. E. F. Ellet (South Carolina); Rev. William H. Fonerden (Augusta); Louisa Medina Hamblin; Henry W. Hilliard; Henry Rootes Jackson; Augustus Baldwin Longstreet; Mrs. Margaret Martin; Miss Mary Martin; Alexander Means; Alexander B. Meek (Tuscaloosa, Alabama); J. H. Mifflin; Miss M. E. Moragne (South Carolina); Samuel C. Oliver (Montgomery, Alabama); Mrs. [Frances S.] Osgood; Miss Pardoe; E. M. Pendleton; Hamilton Raiford; Charles Wyatt Rice; T.

Addison Richards; William C. Richards; Mrs. L. H. Sigourney; William Gilmore Simms; W. Wragg Smith; Mrs. Ann S. Stevens; [56] Samuel M. Strong (Macon); M. R. Suarez (Barnwell, South Carolina); Charles West Thomson; W. Waybridge; Richard Henry Wilde; E. L. Wittich (Madison, Georgia); H. V. Wooten.

Many contributors used either initials or pseudonyms, some of which may be readily identified, but most of which are still a mystery: Albanio (Augusta); Algeroy (Sparta); Allan; Alligator (Savannah); Alpha; Archaeus; A.R.P.; Ashman (Edgefield, South Carolina); Baldwin (Augustus Baldwin Longstreet); Barnard (Augusta); Bertha (Augusta); B.F.G.; Botanist; Miss C— (Washington, Georgia); A Carolinian; C.D.O.; C.E.F. (Dahlonega, Georgia); Charles; Mrs. C.M.H.; Chips (T. Addison Richards?); Cora (Sandersville); F.H.; F.H.R. (Clinton, Mississippi); Frank (Columbus); A Gothamite; H. (Penfield); H. (Sandersville); Harietta (Augusta); Hinda; H.M.K.; Holcomb; Homer; H.R.; Jamie (Brooksville, Georgia); J.E.R.; J.P.H.; Juvenis (Athens); J.W.B. (Milledgeville, Georgia); A Lady of Augusta; A Lady from Georgia; Leila; Leon; Marcus; M.G.M. (Augusta); M.J. (Augusta); M.L.C.; P— (Augusta); P.A.C.; Peter Pepper (Warrenton, Georgia); P.H.; The Preacher; Rambler; R.A.R.; R.S.; R.S.S. (Fryer's Pond, Georgia); S.A.M.; S.B.E.; S.B.M.; S.C.O. (Montgomery, Alabama); Senex; Seroc; S.W.C. (Calhoun, South Carolina); S.W.E. (Crawfordville, Georgia); Tirtium [sic] Quid; Valeria (Macon); Venator; Viator (Newton, Georgia); W. (Warrenton, Georgia); W. C. R[ichards].; W.F.; W.F.H. (Pocotaligo, South Carolina); W.L.H. (Augusta); Young.

The exchange list of the Augusta *Mirror,* if we may judge from reprinted matter, included such periodicals as the New York *Ladies' Companion, Knickerbocker, Burton's Magazine,* New York *Mirror, Southern Literary Messenger,* Mobile *Literary Gazette,* the *Southron, Blackwood's, Bentley's,* and the *New Monthly.* By the end of 1841 the Augusta *Mirror* consisted, for the most part, of matter selected from other periodicals. Selected material usually bore a caption to indicate the source, while contributions written especially for the *Mirror* were headed "Original," though doubtless some of the latter were the work of the editor himself. Contributions were often sent in that had previously appeared in print elsewhere. Some of Thompson's humorous writings appeared in several Georgia periodicals.

Thompson seems to have made little effort toward any form of literary criticism at first, unless he is the "Rambler," who contributed to the *Mirror* "The Life and Writings of Sir Richard Steele," [57] "The Yankee Abroad: or, Letters from a Stray Collegian," [58] and "The South the Natural Home of Literature." [59] His first critical effort that we are sure of is a review of "Tortesa the Usurer. A Play in Five Acts by N. P. Willis." [60] Another work of his is "Our Own Writers," in which he attempts to discuss the American writers of his own day.[61] He goes to French literature for the sketch entitled "The Life and Times of Chateaubriand," which appeared serially in seven issues of the *Mirror*.[62]

The Augusta *Mirror* had a great variety of literary types, the poems being the least important, since they were usually extremely short and light in quality. The prose articles and tales are, by far, the most important and most interesting contributions. The following different types will serve as examples of the prose contents week by week: "On the Study of the Classics," by W. Waybridge; [63] "The Seasons," by "A Lady from Georgia"; [64] "Painting," by T. Addison Richards; [65] "Poetry," by Henry Rootes Jackson; [66] "Sir Walter Scott," by S.W.E.; [67] "The County of Habersham," by Bertha; [68] and "The Mississippi. (From the Atala of Chateaubriand)," by "A Lady of Augusta." [69] For the musical members of the family each number of Volumes I and II carried on the last page a musical selection, either a piano number or a song with both words and music, following the practice of its contemporary, the New York *Mirror*. The original tales in the *Mirror* were the usual romantic, sentimental tales that were found in all

American periodicals down to 1860. In the following, all original, the editor was catering to the taste of his reading public:

"Clement Maurice: A Tale of Florida," by Juvenis (Athens) [70]
"Catherine of Lancaster: or, The Tournament of Toledo," anonymous [71]
"The Indian Captive," by E. L. W[ittich] [72]
"Clara: The Blind Parson's Daughter," by Mrs. Ann S. Stevens [73]
"The Orphan Julia," by Mrs. M. S. B. Dana. Prize Tale of 1840 [74]

One of the best of the longer poems contributed to the *Mirror* was "Pekasina, the Beautiful, or 'The Daughter of the Sun,' a Legend in 4 Cantos," by Samuel C. Oliver, which ran serially in 1841.[75] The shorter poems were usually addressed to some young lady, such as: "To My Friend Mary Ann, with a Boquet [sic]," [76] "Stanzas to Elizabeth," [77] and "To a Young Girl," [78] by William C. Richards; "To a Young Lady Weeping," by Henry Rootes Jackson; [79] and "To a Dark-Eyed Georgian," by A. B. Meek.[80]

The main purpose of Thompson's periodical seems to have been to entertain. The literary level of its reading matter was not, of course, very high, nor was it low. But the Augusta *Mirror* marks the real beginning of Georgia literary periodicals, and Thompson may be said to have opened the way for later attempts by such men as Philip C. Pendleton, Cornelius R. Hanleiter, William C. Richards, Charles L. Wheler, and Joseph Addison Turner.

3. MACON—*SOUTHERN LADIES' BOOK* (1840–43)

TITLE: *Southern Ladies' Book,* January–December, 1840; *Magnolia:* or *Southern Monthly,* 1841–June, 1842; *Magnolia:* or *Southern Apalachian,* July 1842–June, 1843
FIRST ISSUE: January, 1840 LAST ISSUE: June, 1842 (in Georgia) June, 1843 (in S.C.)
PERIODICITY: Monthly
PUBLISHERS: Cornelius R. Hanleiter, Macon, January–April, 1840; Benjamin F. Griffin, Macon, May–October, 1840; H. S. Bell, Savannah, November, 1840–December, 1841; Philip C. Pendleton, Savannah, January–June, 1842; Burges & James, Charleston, July, 1842–June, 1843

First Period: 1837–46

EDITORS: George F. Pierce and Philip C. Pendleton, January–October, 1840; Philip C. Pendleton, November, 1840–March, May, 1842; Philip C. Pendleton and William Gilmore Simms, April, June, 1842–June, 1843
LOCATION OF FILES: *A:* Jan.–June, 1842; July, 1842–June, 1843. *CtY:* III. *DLC:* I, 1–3, 4–6; III (inc.)–II (N.S.). *GA:* July–Dec., 1842. *GE:* I. *GMM:* II. *GMW:* Jan.–Aug., 1840; Jan.–Dec., 1841. *GU:* Aug., Oct., 1840; Jan., Apr. (inc.), 1842. *GU(D):* I, 3, 5–6; II, 1–3, 5–6; N.S. II, 1–6; III, 1–12. *Ia:* N.S. I–II. *ICN:* IV–N.S. I–N.S. II (inc.). *MHi:* N.S. I–N.S. II. *NN:* N.S. I. *NNHi:* III–N.S. II. *NcD:* I, 2–3, 5–6; II, 1–6; III, 1–12; IV, 1–6; N.S. I, 2–3, 5–6. N.S. II. *NcU:* N.S. I–N.S. II. *ScU:* III–N.S. II. *TxU:* N.S. I–N.S. II (inc.). *WHi:* III (inc.)–N.S. II

In January, 1840, in Macon, home of the Georgia Female College (now Wesleyan College), the first college in the world to grant degrees to women, a new magazine appeared, the *Southern Ladies' Book: A Magazine of Literature, Science and Arts*. The editors of this periodical were George F. Pierce, newly-elected president of the Georgia Female College, and Philip C. Pendleton, both native Georgians. The venture was the outgrowth of a feeling long prevalent in the South that this section of the country needed the literary stimulation that comes from a periodical literature of a high order. As one Southerner has said:

> The South was beginning [c. 1839] to feel the need of a distinctly Southern literature, and the *Southern Literary Messenger* was in successful operation in Richmond. A young friend and companion of Mr. Pierce's, Philip C. Pendleton, proposed to establish a magazine in Macon, the *Southern Ladies' Book,* and invited Mr. Pierce to edit it for him. I suppose no man ever lived who had less taste for the labors of the editor than George Pierce had in 1840. He, however, was exceedingly anxious for the success of the Georgia Female College, and for the advance of Southern literature, and anxious that his young friend should succeed in his daring venture. The cooler head of his old friend, Judge Longstreet, saw this project of Mr. Pendleton in a different light from the sanguine editor . . .[81]

Augustus Baldwin Longstreet, the "Judge" of the above quotation, was a native Georgian of some journalistic experience in Augusta, where he had edited the *State Rights'*

Sentinel from 1834 to 1836; and he had undoubtedly learned something of the vicissitudes of a magazine editor from William Tappan Thompson, at that time editor of the Augusta *Mirror*. He therefore gave some practical advice to young Pierce in the following extract from a letter to him dated November 4, 1839:

> As to the main subject, not much space is necessary for my views of that. "The Southern Ladies' Book" will do for a name, if book it will be, which I doubt. But I should have preferred something less commonplace. The plan is well conceived, will go into operation, progress twelve or eighteen months, and expire, because subscribers won't pay, though dunned from the first number to the last. It will start pretty fair, grow lame and lamer at every step until it expires; simply because your long list of presidents wont write for it. May be Brother Jesse Mercer may give you a few lines alamode The Cluster, but I doubt it.[82] I question whether you ever get more from him than some *didactics* upon Bapto and Baptizo. Your only hope of escape from these issues is in the minimum which [you] have fixed for your subscription list, before you start. You'll run up to five hundred so fast that you'll almost wish you had made three thousand the minimum—from five to seven hundred you'll begin to think surely the prospectus has not been half circulated—from seven hundred to one thousand you'll begin to fret at the want of public spirit in the South—and between one thousand and fifteen hundred it will gradually ease out of notice. It would have been more likely to succeed as a quarterly than as a monthly publication, because many will write by the quarter who would not per month, if it ever gets under way. I dare not promise to write for it, because I know not that I will be able to do so without neglecting imperative duties; but I hope and *think* I shall.[83]

Macon, situated "in the heart of a thickly settled and fertile country, and on a navigable river," [84] seemed an ideal place from which to radiate a cultural influence through periodical literature; and its three printing offices, two book binderies, and two bookstores, together with two newspapers, indicated an intellectual atmosphere above the average. The population of the city proper in 1840 was 3,927,[85] and it had been estimated in 1837 that the town, with its environs, included about 5,000 people.[86] The Macon Lyceum and Library Society, with Dr. A. Baber as president, had been incorporated on December 26, 1835, and organized on November 16, 1836; and the reading room had been opened on March 1, 1837, with fifty papers and twelve reviews and periodicals.[87] And, too, the Georgia Female College, which had a registration of 168 students in July, 1839,[88] was attracting attention all over the state; hence its group of students and teachers furnished an excellent nucleus with which to begin a literary periodical.

The Prospectus of the *Southern Ladies' Book* throws light on the ambitions of the young editors:

Of the few literary papers published South of the Potomac, there is NOT ONE exclusively dedicated to the LADIES! We have felt this as a want which ought to be supplied. . . . In offering the plan of a SOUTHERN LADIES' BOOK, we do not intend that it shall be precisely similar to a work of like name, at the North. We leave to our Northern cotemporary pictorial representations of fashion and dress, for the embellishment of the person: be it ours to provide a garb of purity, elegance, refinement and grace, for the adornment of the mind. . . . Arrangements for regular aid will be made with several Ladies, whose productions have already gained them high fame in the literary world—and several gentlemen of distinguished attainments have already been secured as contributors, from whom scientific tracts, with notes, and observations on the Arts may be expected. . . . It only remains to obtain the requisite number of subscribers—say two thousand—and if the Ladies will smile upon, and aid our efforts, that number will not long be wanting.[89]

Yet, add the editors, the work is not designed solely for female readers:

We certainly design to labor in behalf of Female character, education, taste, refinement, instruction and entertainment, but we look to the general good—we propose to range over the whole field of Literature, and to cull, combine and furnish such specimens and preparations as, in our judgment, will find acceptance with the reading *public*. The *name* is a guarantee that nothing indelicate, impure, or offensive, shall appear upon our pages.[90]

The use of the name "Ladies' Book" soon attracted the attention of the editors of *Godey's Lady's Book,* who spoke rather caustically of the name:

Another in want of a name. A new work has been started at the west, called "The Western Lady's Book." It is presumed that the contents of the work must be very poor, as the publishers have not invention enough for a name; but must steal one ready made. It will meet the fate we presume of its quondam namesake, the Southern Lady's Book. Ours is *The* Lady's Book, intended for the North, South, East, and West. Nothing can be more indicative of the popularity of our work than the frequent attempts to rob us of our name, and the host of rogues who infest the country, procuring subscribers unauthorized by the publisher. Not a number of the Book is published that we do not have occasion to mention one or two new names.[91]

To this the editors of the *Southern Ladies' Book* replied:

The name we have adopted was not chosen with any reference to the popularity of his [Godey's] work, of which we know little or nothing, (having never been amongst its readers,) save perhaps the bare fact of its publication. The "Southern Ladies' Book" will be continued although every number of Godey's Lady's Book should pronounce its discontinuance.[92]

The Macon periodical rounded off its answer to Godey's charge by declaring that the accurate title for *Godey's* should be "Godey's Lady's *Picture* Book."

The Southern Ladies' Book has been called by Frank Luther Mott a "Methodist miscellany" and a "Methodist parlor magazine," [93] but the periodical itself shows no marks of being a Methodist publication, even though George F. Pierce, one of the editors, was a Methodist minister and later bishop in the Methodist Episcopal Church, South. Contributions to the magazine came from members of many churches.

The *Southern Ladies' Book* was published monthly at $5 per year, in semi-annual volumes, publication being suspended in October, 1840, to be resumed in January, 1841, in Savannah under a new name: *Magnolia: or Southern Monthly,* and edited solely by Pendleton. Feeling, however, a moral responsibility toward those who had subscribed for a full year to the magazine, Pendleton promised to publish during 1841 the November and December numbers for 1840 and send them to the subscribers, who had taken the magazine in good faith.[94] True to his promise, he published the two missing numbers for 1841 some time during the summer of 1841 and thus preserved his integrity as a journalist.[95]

In the first issue of the *Magnolia* in Savannah, that for January, 1841, the editor makes the following confession:

> We are ready to acknowledge to all the world, and hereby do make humble confession to the public, that the execution of our Book, heretofore, has not borne favorable comparison with that of other periodicals, and were it all our own fault, conscience would certainly trouble us, because it has not appeared regularly, and at that precise date which each number bore upon its face. . . . We have . . . endeavored to supply matter—original when our contributors would afford it—and the very best selections, when they would not; but it surpassed our power to manufacture paper, mould type, or make printers. . . . We have been disappointed in our expectations, and we will endeavor to make atonement, by future improvement in external appearance, and punctuality in our issues, for all past faults.[96]

An additional reason for the removal to Savannah is given in the same issue: "We had hoped also, by this removal, to enlist a greater number of literary gentlemen in the enterprize. In which matter we have succeeded beyond our most sanguine expectations." [97] The editor goes to some length in explaining the reason for the change of name for the magazine. The following is an extract from his explanation:

> As to that of the name of the work, there are many reasons which have led us to this course. . . . We wished one entirely original, so as to prevent any confusion of conflicting interests with other publishers of similar works. In using the name "Southern Ladies' Book," the impression went abroad that we should give occasionally engravings of new fashions in dress, notwithstanding our positive disclaimer of such an intention. . . . We thought we were paying a compliment to our fair Southern readers, by presenting them with a work which addressed itself alone to the understand-

ing. . . . Others are under the impression, that a work bearing such a title, should contain no article that was not expressly written for them, having in view their feelings and sentiments as different from the other sex. Such was not the view we had taken of the conduct of such a work, and we find it necessary to use a title under which we shall have greater liberty with the various subjects of which it may be necessary to speak or treat . . .[98]

The *Magnolia* remained in Savannah for eighteen months, during which time it attained an excellence far beyond that of the first year of its existence in Macon. With the issue of July, 1842, the magazine was removed to Charleston,[99] where, with the aid of William Gilmore Simms, it became a different periodical, though not necessarily a better one, as its friends had fondly hoped.

The first issue of the *Southern Ladies' Book*, published in January, 1840, consisted of 64 pages of royal octavo paper, each page printed, for the most part, in two columns of pica type. After an editorial introduction of two pages the first article is an eleven-page discussion entitled "Address on Female Education," by George F. Pierce. Then after two short poems, one by "Clifford" and one by Robert M. Charlton, there is a long discourse on "Georgia Marble," by Dr. Alexander Means, Professor of Physics at Emory College, Oxford, Georgia. The rest of the number is given over to miscellaneous articles, tales, and short poems. The longest of these original tales are: "A Tale Illustrating the Passions," by G. P. R. James, and the anonymous "Glimpses into the History of Frank Thurston, and Other Characters," which ran serially in later issues. A letter from William Gilmore Simms to the editors, quoted in the first number, reveals an interest in the undertaking:

. . . I assure you that I wish all success to your endeavors; and, so far as consistent with my engagements, will strive to co-operate with you.—You are at perfect liberty to say thus much to your readers, and I will feel honored in finding myself ranked among the excellent contributors already referred to in your design.[100]

The succeeding numbers for 1840, through October, pursue the same general policy of including such articles as "Female Education," by Lovick Pierce,[101] "The Georgia Female College," by George F. Pierce,[102] and "Southern Literature," by Samuel M. Strong.[103] The eminent author of the *Georgia Scenes* is honored by the inclusion in the second number of the "Inaugural Address of Hon. A. B. Longstreet, President of Emory College, before the Faculty and Students of that Institution, at its Commencement, Feb. 10th, 1840." Numerous poems, usually short, dot the pages of the *Southern Ladies' Book*. Most of these are signed either with initials or with obvious pseudonyms, though the names of Robert M. Charlton (Savannah), Henry Rootes Jackson (Savannah), and William Gilmore Simms (Charleston) are appended to some. George F. Pierce himself sometimes wrote for the periodical under the pseudonym of "Clio." [104] The eclectic character of the work may be gathered from the occasional selections from Mrs. [L. H.] Sigourney,[105] Henry W. Longfellow,[106] and Washington Irving.[107]

Before going any further, we should be made well aware of the general editorial policy toward material submitted for publication. The editors doubtless knew that many of the articles, and especially the bulk of the poems, submitted to them were inferior in quality, yet they aimed to encourage, as far as possible, the development of literature in the South. This editorial policy is stated in the issue for February, 1840:

> While we are on this subject, we will remark that we earnestly desire to elicit the latent genius of the South, and are not disposed to repress, by ungenerous criticism or cold rejection, the kindling fire of any spirit that seeks redemption from its obscurity. We want to encourage the art of composition—to create a taste for writing —to cultivate the habit among the young and promising of each sex. In the outset, many of these productions must be necessarily crude and faulty, if judged by the standard of a rigid and practised taste, and yet may have thought, sentiment, style, to demand in their behalf, such encouragement as a publication may afford.

Without intending, therefore, to encumber our book by a multiplicity of jejune compositions, we expect to publish, occasionally, an article, the faults of which must be excused because of the youth or the want of exercise on the part of the writer.[108]

The poems written especially for the *Southern Ladies' Book* are usually the sentimental and didactic poems of a popular sort, but some of them are narratives based on Biblical or historical subjects. Besides the more common stanzaic forms, they employ the heroic couplet, the tetrameter couplet, and blank verse, the latter meter predominating.

With the beginning of 1841 the *Magnolia: or Southern Monthly*, retaining the volume number of its predecessor, and under the editorship of Pendleton alone, began a new journalistic policy. Though it retained practically the same format, it followed what the editor called "the English plan" of printing stories of some length "continuing from month to month, even though they should amount to the dignity and length of an ordinary Novel." [109] Issues for 1840 had carried tales of different kinds, such as "An Eligible Match—A Tale of a Country House," by Mrs. Abdy,[110] "The Spirit of Contradiction—A Tale," by Mrs. Abdy,[111] "The Stranger at the Banquet," by Mrs. Caroline Lee Hentz,[112] "Remorse," by G. P. R. James,[113] and "Ellen: A Tale of the Frontier Settlement," by E. L. Wittich,[114] but very little space had been devoted to prose fiction of any nature. To excite the interest, therefore, of his subscribers, Pendleton gave, in January, 1841, the first installment of Dr. William A. Caruthers' "The Knights of the Golden Horse-Shoe," a tale which was continued each month until its conclusion in October, 1841. The editor felt that he had a "scoop" in being able to present to his reading public the first printing of this Virginia story, which would have been published earlier by Harpers except for the accidental destruction of the first manuscript.[115]

There seems to have been no rabid prejudice in the mind of Pendleton as he labored for the development of literature in the South. In a remarkably sane and clear fashion he proceeded, toward the end of 1841, to outline his views on the relation of sectional literature to national literature. A short extract from the "Editor's Table" for the November number follows:

> While, therefore, we desire, so far as this periodical is concerned, to give our readers the *best* products of American literature, we would not forget the offerings of *first fruits,* which, though they may not have the mellow ripeness of perfect maturity, are yet the beginnings of a golden harvest. . . . There are, however, and ever must be, some characteristics of Southern literature, which do not pertain to Northern; the whole arrangement of domestic Society, the productions of the soil, the aspects of nature, hereditary feeling, physical constitutions, and even the powerful influence of climate, are all different from the North, and ever will bear it, for we hope the time will *never* come, when a foreign style of thought and feeling shall be substituted for the genuine growth of our own sunny clime.
>
> These *characteristics* of Southern writers, do not, however, constitute sectional literature . . . but add to the harmony and symmetry of American literature, as the splendid colors of the iris, give perfection to the beautiful bow of the covenant.[116]

This last statement of Pendleton, contending that the production of Southern literature would but contribute to "the harmony and symmetry of American literature," is unusual in that most Southern editors were contending for sectional independence in literature without giving a thought to this broader aspect of the question. Nowhere else is this note sounded in Georgia *ante-bellum* literary periodicals.

Another prominent feature of the *Magnolia* for 1841 was a series of two articles on "Southern Literature," by William Gilmore Simms, in the issues for January and February. Simms was very frank, in the first article, in his opinion of Pendleton's periodical. He says, in part:

> When, something like a year ago, you drew my attention, by letter, to the Literary project which you had in view, and solicited my aid in its behalf, it was with a degree of indifference . . . that I yielded to your wishes, in a promise of compliance, to a certain, but very limited extent. It was not that I was unfriendly to your

purpose. That was noble, and I could admire its aim, however much I might question its policy. But I had no faith in the project then; and, you will pardon me if I confess, I have very little more faith in it now. I have had so much experience, either as an editor or as a contributor, in the making of Southern Magazines, and know so thoroughly their history, and the inevitable event, that my conviction of the almost certain fate which awaits them, inspires me with a feeling, very like disgust, when I am told of any new experiment of this kind in contemplation. . . . I cannot help but doubt;—and when I sit down to write for a Southern periodical—which I do only as a professional duty—I do so under the enfeebling conviction that my labors and those of the editor are taken in vain;—that the work will be little read, seldom paid for, and will finally . . . sink into that gloomy receptacle of the "lost and abused things of earth," which, I suspect, by this time possesses its very sufficient share of Southern periodical literature.[117]

In the course of time Simms became involved in some unpleasant notoriety that came from the publication of his "The Loves of a Driver," which appeared in the issues for May, June, and July, 1841.[118] The tale involves the amours of a young negro and deals very frankly and realistically with his affairs. In the June, 1841, number of the *Magnolia* is a letter to Pendleton, signed "A Puritan," protesting against the publication of the tale. The objector thus speaks of Simms:

He descends from his introduction, to which no serious objection can be made, into the low valley of his story; and be his intents, wicked or charitable, he cannot expect from such a story, be it ever so highly wrought, to wear laurel—it must be ivy—his classic wreaths will no more flourish on his brow, and he must descend with the specific gravity of the conception of such a subject.

Waving [sic] these considerations, the whole texture of society forbids the introduction of such a romance.[119]

W. P. Trent, in his *William Gilmore Simms,* believes that "critics were doubtless right in assailing this story," [120] but Pendleton came quickly to the defense of Simms with an especially sane and clear answer:

The story of Mr. Simms, in our judgment possesses rare merit, graphically illustrating and comparing the characters of the Indian and Negro races, and justly describing both as they are known to us. Although the scenes are low, they are truthful and characteristic; had he made them otherwise, he would have signally failed in faithful portraiture of character, that greatest merit of the dramatist and novelist.

The very disgust which we are made to feel in perusing the story, is the author's condemnation, and instead of its having a debasing influence upon the mind, will have the contrary effect of rendering more odious, that which is already so. . . . If an excellent article, in the main, possessing more than ordinary degree of merit, is to be rejected because of a few blemishes, even which latter is a subject of difference between men of taste, and in such a case who are to be the judges? [121]

Simms's reply, which he calls a justification of Pendleton rather than a defense of himself, appeared in the form of a "Letter to the Editor" in the *Magnolia* for August, 1841. Simms disclaims any intent to write an immoral story, but defends his realistic story in the following words:

There is nothing surely very attractive in Negroes and Indians; but something is conceded to intellectual curiosity; and the desire is a human, and very natural one, to know how our fellow beings fare in other aspects than our own, and under other forms of humanity, however inferior. No race is so very low, or so debased, as to deprive them of the power of exciting this interest in the breasts of men. . . . Their modes of life, passions, pursuits, capacities and interests, are as legitimately the objects of the analyst, as those of the best bred people at the fashionable end of London. . . .[122]

He adds further that there is too much "mock modesty" in our country and that the moral of his tale is very much the same as that of Shakespeare's *Othello*. The controversy apparently ended here, for no further reference is made to it in later issues of the *Magnolia*.

A few words might be said regarding the two belated issues of the *Southern Ladies' Book* for November and December, 1840, which were printed in midsummer of 1841, as previously stated. From his new Savannah establishment Pendleton issued them, bound together under one cover, to the subscribers to his 1840 periodical. These numbers partake of the character of the *Magnolia* rather than of the *Southern Ladies' Book*. The November number contains two interesting tales: "Ellen Clifford," by "A Lady," and "The Misanthrope," by L.D.D., of Savannah. The long article of the December number is "A Lecture on the Art of Living," by Dr. W. A. Caruthers, previously delivered at the First Presbyterian Church at the request of the Savannah Temperance Society. These two issues show marks of haste, but Pendleton was really in a hurry to redeem his promise of earlier days. From that time on, his periodical began to improve, and during the first six months of 1842 he issued what was in many respects the best literary periodical in Georgia in the *ante-bellum* period.

The difficulties of the editors of the *Southern Ladies' Book* were numerous. Pierce knew little or nothing about editing a magazine, and Pendleton was also new at the business. For the first ten issues of the periodical they had to use an inferior grade of paper, and they did not succeed very well in making the content as attractive as it might have been. For the general difficulties, note the editorial explanation in the issue for September, 1840:

> One of the Editors, who is also proprietor, has all the business department on his hands, and of course but little leisure for writing—the other, when he preaches three or four times in the week, and attends to the *thousand* and one calls connected with his office in the College, has not time for composition. We should never have undertaken this project, but for the strong assurances of help from those who have talents to make the work what it ought to be. If the people who find fault with *us*, will just turn their guns upon our *"contributors,"* we will feel better, and will even throw in a shot or two ourselves. . . . The misfortune is, "Our contributors" have too much leisure. They do not like to work for the country, though they *are patriots*—they are the *friends* of literature, but they never bring an offering to her altars—zealous to exhort others to give—but niggard in their own donations—philanthropists on the tongue, but misers in heart. . . . We must have "works," or else we despair of the Literary Republic, if these be her guardians.[128]

First Period: 1837–46 51

This explanation accounts for the fact that numerous articles were written by Lovick Pierce,[124] father of George F. Pierce, by the professors of the Georgia Female College, and by professional men in other walks of life. With the change of name and removal to Savannah, however, contributors became more generous, and the contents of the periodical increased in interest and variety. The editors in 1840 were continually disturbed by the fact that few subscribers had paid for their magazines. But such a situation was not a local one. It existed all over the United States before the Civil War, as well as for years afterward.

Pierce and Pendleton believed that writers should be compensated for their productions, but they also saw that it was not a customary thing in the South. Note their views in October, 1840:

> To secure talents to the support of a periodical publication, they must be paid for, and the truth is, the laborer in this vineyard is as worthy of his hire, as in any other. But this does not seem to be generally understood, or believed to be necessary. The writer will carry his wares to the best market, just as naturally as the merchant, or mechanic, and none will say that the fruits of his labor are less important or useful than either of the above class.
>
> The Southern public are liberal enough at subscribing, to support any laudable undertaking, but a want of promptness in another, and certainly not less important matter, often frustrates and places it out of the power of a publisher to do himself or that public justice, unless he has a small fortune to spend in his patriotic undertaking, and then probably, after two or three years of such service, he will begin to receive something for his labors.[125]

Southern writers had to write only for fame, many of them sending contributions to Northern periodicals, sometimes receiving pay and sometimes not.

It was to be expected that the *Magnolia* would be received with favor by other Southern periodicals. The Lexington (Virginia) *Star* typically declared:

> We received by the last Saturday's mail this most excellent monthly. We have examined its articles with great care, and con-

cur most fully in the complimentary notices which we have seen from the various journals of our own and other States. The contributors are men of decided literary reputation—such as William A. Caruthers, . . . W. Gilmore Simms, . . . Richard Henry Wilde, and G. W. Patten, poets of no inconsiderable celebrity . . .[126]

From New England the Portland (Maine) *Tribune* stated that the *Magnolia* "is one of the best monthlies in our country. . . . Among its contributors are some of the most talented minds in our country. The Southerners should be proud of this work."[127] The Newburgh (New York) *Telegraph* went to greater length in commenting on the *Magnolia:*

It seems indeed to be a work which reflects honor on the literature of the South, and we are disposed to award much credit to its talented editor, Mr. Pendleton. We notice as contributors to its pages, the names of the most distinguished men of the South, and we really have no hesitation in pronouncing it equal to any periodical of the kind published in the United States.[128]

From the *Knickerbocker* (New York), a monthly magazine like the *Magnolia,* came these words:

"The Magnolia, or Southern Monthly," is the present title of "The Southern Lady's [sic] Book," which has assumed a more *manly* character, and is now published at Savannah, in a greatly improved form. It is conducted with editorial tact and talent, and has a corps of good contributors. We wish the Editor could be aware of the hearty sympathy and cordiality with which we invoked for him abundant success, while perusing his spirited appeal, on the last page of the number before us. The "Magnolia," or we greatly mistake, will prove an honor to the periodical literature of the South.[129]

And the same editor, later in the same year, says that "the existence of such works as the 'Southern [Literary] Messenger,' 'Augusta Mirror,' 'Macon [Georgia] Companion,' Savannah 'Magnolia,' Cincinnati 'Repository,' and the like, abundantly proves the correctness of the remark [that 'American talent is not local nor provincial']."[130] The *Magnolia* scarcely expected any support from the North, as we learn from an editorial comment in April, 1842:

> We expect no help, and scarcely any countenance, beyond the Potomac. Southern literature has never found any favor beyond that limit. We doubt if the Southern Review [published in Charleston in 1828-32] had ten subscribers North of Virginia. They are too hostile in that quarter to what is called a "sectional literature" to encourage any that does not grow in their own section.[131]

The support of the South, however, was more gratifying, at least in the number of subscribers obtained. Before the end of 1840 the editors declared that they had enough subscribers to "pay all the expenses of the work" if these would pay for their subscriptions.[132] But advertisements were not forthcoming; hence financial difficulties always beset the periodical.

One interesting bit of comment during 1842 concerned the visit of Charles Dickens to America that year. In March, after reading newspaper accounts of the acclaim with which the British novelist was received in the North, Pendleton wrote a long editorial, of which the following is only a part:

> If Mr. Dickens comes to the South, he will receive a Southern welcome. But he will not receive the public evidences of our esteem which have signalized his northern tour. He will we hope find courtesy tempered with dignity, and our open hearts, guarded by open judgments. . . . We have been led into these remarks not by any ill feelings to Boz, because we have none, but by a desire to lift up our voice feeble as it is against this excessive and nauseating adulation which is offered to our visiters [sic] from the old world. They receive us with cautiousness and distrust; we credulously fold them in our arms and see not our hasty error till we feel the sting of their envenomed darts rankling in our bosoms.[133]

On the same page of this issue of the *Magnolia,* Pendleton pays a tribute to the greatness of Washington Irving and commends his appointment that year as Minister to Spain. He also compares Irving with Dickens, saying that although Irving is the superior, he cannot be expected to be received with such acclaim when he visits Europe as Dickens has received in the

United States. This criticism, of course, was written some months before the publication of Dickens' *American Notes,* which created a great furor upon its appearance in America.

The literary offerings of the Macon and Savannah periodical represent, in the main, the current taste for tales of love, adventure, and humor, and for all types of sentimental poems. The following original tales are the best:

"Glimpses into the History of Frank Thurston, and Other Characters," anonymous [134]
"Our Pastor's Manuscript," by Ludovic Paedagogus (Lovick Pierce?) [135]
"The Spirit of Contradiction," by Mrs. Abdy [136]
"The Stranger at the Banquet," by Mrs. Caroline Lee Hentz [137]
"An Eligible Match—A Tale of a Country House," by Mrs. Abdy [138]
"Ellen: A Tale of the Frontier Settlement," by E. L. Wittich [139]
"Auto-Biography of a Married Man," by Col. Butterball [140]
"The Knights of the Golden Horse-Shoe," by Dr. William A. Caruthers [141]
"The Adventures of the Last of the Abencerage," by Miss L. R. L. [142]
"The Loves of the Driver: A Story of the Wigwam," by William Gilmore Simms [143]
"Tales of the Packolette," by James Edward Henry [144]
"Myra Cunningham, A Tale of 1780," by James Edward Henry [145]
"Castle Dismal; or, The Bachelor's Christmas," by G. B. Singleton (William Gilmore Simms) [146]
"Henry Herbert. A Tale of the Revolution," by Clifton [147]
"Turgesius: A Historical Romance of the Danish Dominion in Ireland," by Charles Kyle [148]

Articles, critical and otherwise, all specially contributed apparently, covered a wide range of subjects:

"Address on Female Education," by George F. Pierce [149]
"Georgia Marble," by Alexander Means [150]
"Vocal Music," by Victor La Taste [151]
"The Georgia Female College," by George F. Pierce [152]
"On Female Education," by Lovick Pierce [153]
"Inaugural Address of Hon. A. B. Longstreet, President of Emory College, before the Faculty and Students of that Institution, at its commencement, Feb. 10th, 1840." [154]

First Period: 1837–46

"Female Education," by Eugenius A. Nisbet [155]
"Education of the Poor," by Lovick Pierce [156]
"The Evils of Fashionable Education," by Dr. [Timothy?] Dwight (from his *Travels?*) [157]
"Expedition into the Interior of Africa," by James E. Alexander [158]
"Music, Poetry and Religion," by W. [159]
"Importance of Home Education," by Vindex Veritatis [160]
"American Botany," anonymous [161]
"Southern Literature," by Samuel M. Strong [162]
"General Superiority of the Ancients to the Moderns," by J.R.D. [163]
"Thoughts on a Journey to the Moon," by C. J. H[adermann]. [164]
"Southern Literature," by William Gilmore Simms [165]
"The Library of Alexander A. Smets," by William Bacon Stevens [166]
"The Antiquitates Americanae," by William Gilmore Simms [167]
"Montgomery's Messiah," by William Gilmore Simms [168]
"Transcendentalism," by J. E. Snodgrass [169]
"Ancient and Modern Culture," by William Gilmore Simms [170]
"Southern Periodicals," by William Gilmore Simms [171]

The *Southern Ladies' Book* and the *Magnolia* carried so many short poems that it is impossible to mention more than a very few, all of which conform to the sentimental and didactic type found in most American periodicals of the time. Many popular poets of the country, mainly Southerners, sent in original contributions, among which a few above the average may be cited:

"Revenge," by Dr. E. M. Pendleton [172]
"The Language of Gems," by Mrs. [Frances S.] Osgood [173]
"The Language of Flowers," by M.M. [174]
"Thoughts Suggested by Passages in the Prophecy of Daniel," by J.R.D. [175]
"The Whip-Poor-Will," by Henry Rootes Jackson [176]
"The Stars," by Amelia B. Welby [177]
"Memories of the Past," by E. M. Pendleton [178]
"To Narcissa," by William C. Richards [179]
"A Poem," by Alexander B. Meek [180]
"Greek Mother's Lullaby," by J. L. L[awrie]. [181]
"Death," by William C. Richards [182]
"Arcana Angelorum: or The Mystery of the Angels," by John Love Lawrie [183]

"Song and Sonnet: or, The Lays of Early Days," by William Gilmore Simms [184]
"The Living Picture," by Mary E. Lee [185]

The poems in this periodical were the usual didactic and sentimental types, like those often found in *Godey's* and in the *Southern Literary Messenger*. Besides using Biblical and religious subjects, the poets wrote to lady loves, such as "To Narcissa," to birds and flowers, and on subjects like "Memories of the Past," "Revenge," and "Greek Mother's Lullaby." These poems were usually short sentimental lyrics, using the more common metrical forms, with ballad meter, blank verse, and heroic couplet predominant.

As usual with writers of the period, many authors used only initials or pseudonyms appended to their contributions. Excluding single initials, the following initials and pseudonyms were used by contributors to the periodical: Annette (Camden, South Carolina); Arion; Aristeus; Aros (Darlington, South Carolina); Col. Butterball; Clara (New County, Georgia); Clifford; Clifton; C.S.K. (Spartanburg, South Carolina); D.C.C.; Delta; E.A.W. (Augusta); Eliza N. (Savannah); Eliza; Elwin; Ephemerus; Etowah Bard; E.W.H.; Filicaja (Pike County, Georgia); Freeman; Fusbos Secundus; Geraldine; Giovanni (Forsyth, Georgia); G.L.H.; A Grandfather; G.R.D.; Harold (Savannah); Henri (Macon); H.R.; Inez (New York); Imlac; Inisfael (Macon); Irene; Janett (Cokesbury, South Carolina); J.H.B. (Columbia); J.H.M.; J.M.P.; J.R.D. (Oxford, Georgia); J.T.D.; J.L.H. (Irwinton, Alabama); B. A. Keem (A. B. Meek); A Lady of Milledgeville; L.D.D. (Savannah); Lothaire (South Carolina); Miss L.R.L.; Ludovic Paedagogus (Lovick Pierce?); Melodia (Mrs. Madeline V. Bryan); M.L.G. (Vernon, Alabama); Medicus; M.M. (Columbia); N.L.L. (Greenville, Georgia); Philander (Milledgeville, Georgia); R.R.D.; G. B. Singleton (William Gilmore Simms); S.R.; Stafford (Mt. Zion, Georgia); S—— S.; Studens (Mercer University); T.C.; Telescope; Vere-Dicus; Viator; Vindex Veritatis; Viola; W.B.S.; Y.G. (Oxford, Georgia); A Young Lady of

First Period: 1837–46

Columbus (Georgia); A Young Lady of Hamilton, Harris County, Georgia; Xylon (Washington, Georgia); The Stranger.

The known contributors to the *Southern Ladies' Book* and *Magnolia*, many of whom were prominent professional men and writers in the South, were as follows: Mrs. Abdy; James E. Alexander; Hon. G. Anders (Washington, Georgia); Col. Jorn Billups (Lexington, Georgia); Hon. Edward J. Black (Jacksonboro, Georgia); Dr. J. W. Boatwright (Columbia); E. W. Butt; Major Calder Campbell; C. K. Campbell; Dr. William A. Caruthers; S. T. Chapman (Columbus, Georgia); A. H. Chappell (Macon); Robert M. Charlton; D. A. Chittenden; Alonzo Church (Franklin College, Athens); Mrs. Clifton; Rev. J. H. Clinch; W. T. Colquitt (Columbus, Georgia); Rev. Daniel Curry; Mrs. Mary S. B. Dana; Thomas Dick; Dr. John Dickson; Dr. [Timothy?] Dwight; Abraham Elder; William Ellison (Georgia Female College); Rev. I. A. Few (Ex-President Emory College); Professor William H. Fonerden (Forsyth, Georgia); Leonidas Franklin (Macon); Mrs. Ellen B. F. Freeman; Mrs. M. E. Gifford; Mrs. Caroline Gilman; Professor C. J. Hadermann; General James H. Hammond (South Carolina); John M. B. Harden; James Edward Henry (South Carolina); Mrs. Caroline Lee Hentz; J. L. Hunter; Ludwig Inkle (Marianna); Henry Rootes Jackson; G. P. R. James; Charles Kyle; Maria Gertrude Kyle (Savannah and Covington, Georgia); Victor La Taste; Judge (William) Law; John Love Lawrie (Savannah); Mary E. Lee (South Carolina); Augustus Baldwin Longstreet; Col. J. L. Lumpkin (Lexington, Georgia); Miss H. B. Macdonald; Mrs. Margaret Martin (Columbia); Adolphus Maussenet (Georgia Female College); Dr. Alexander Means (Emory College); Alexander B. Meek (also under pseudonym of "B. A. Keem"); Rev. Jesse Mercer (Washington, Georgia); A. K. Merrill; J. H. Mifflin; N. C. Munroe (Macon); Eugenius A. Nisbet (Macon); Mrs. (Frances S.) Osgood; Miss Phebe Paine; Lieut. G. W. Patten, U.S.A.; Dr. E. M. Pendleton (Sparta, Georgia); Rev. George F. Pierce; Rev. Lovick Pierce (also probably under pseudonym of "Ludovic Paedagogus"); D. Postell; Dr. Reed; William C. Richards; Rev. G. H. Round (Covington, Georgia); Mrs. (L. H.) Sigourney; William Gilmore Simms; G. G. Smith, Jr.; Mrs. Seba Smith; Dr. J. E. Snodgrass (Baltimore); Alexander H. Stephens; William Bacon Stevens; Rev. W. H. Stokes (Washington, Georgia); Samuel M. Strong (Macon); Rev. J. R. Thomas (Talbotton, Georgia); J. Tomlin (Jackson, Tennessee); Professor J. P. Waddel (Franklin College); J. A. Wade; Amelia B. Welby; Richard Henry Wilde; E. L. Wittich (Madison, Georgia); Dr. H. V. Wooten (Lowndesboro, Alabama).

As stated before, the *Magnolia* improved greatly in appearance and in content with the beginning of 1842, while it was still in Savannah. And all this seems to have come about through the efforts of Pendleton alone, with little outside assistance. At the end of 1841 he had promised his readers that if they would "use their exertions to extend the circulation of the Magnolia *one thousand,* more than it now has," he would "engage the services of W. Gilmore Simms, Esq. and another distinguished literary gentleman as Co-editors of the work." [186] Then, with the first number for 1842, Pendleton further stated: "We begin the year with hopes [,] new publishers, new contributors, new subscribers, new designs." [187] It was not, however, till March, 1842, that he announced that Simms would become associate editor at an early date.[188] The work of Simms on the periodical began with the number for April, 1842, was interrupted the following month by the death of his youngest daughter,[189] and was resumed in June, 1842. Simms is probably the author of an interesting discussion of "The Conduct of a Magazine," which outlines the duties of an editor. Following is an extract:

It is necessary . . . . that he should study with care; elaborate with patience, and pronounce impartial judgments. He must keep pace with the progress of letters and science around him; he must conciliate the awards and favors, of the wise, the virtuous and the tasteful. . . . His object must be to elevate the standards of criticism to a proper level, and to strengthen the cause of letters against the indiscriminate and dishonest trade in eulogy, forcibly styled 'puffery,' which is one of the besetting evils attending our national criticism. . . . Every reader of the day, must have been led, in numberless instances, to note the miserable inconsistencies of judgment which mark the opinions of our literary journalists. The same journal speaks a different language from itself, in the brief space of a single month—speaking through anonymous mouthpieces, with a total want of responsibility, which naturally produces an equally total disregard to shame.[190]

The removal of the *Magnolia* to Charleston with the issue for July, 1842, ends its literary importance in connection with Georgia, for the name, with a change in subtitle, became the *Magnolia: or Southern Apalachian,* and the volume number was changed to "New Series." Hence it may be considered, in some respects, a new periodical, although both Simms and Pendleton continued their connection with the work.

The reasons for removing the *Magnolia* to Charleston are the same that animated editors for years to come as they contemplated the possibilities of the city that eventually came to be called "the graveyard of periodicals." The *Magnolia* thus explains its action:

The literary facilities of Charleston are, in some respects, superior to those of Savannah. It lies more conveniently in the line of the great thoroughfares, East and West; and its population, being so much larger, it necessarily combines the prospects of a greater literary and pecuniary patronage in behalf of the work. The very considerable increase of its subscribers within the last two months, particularly in South Carolina, naturally prompts its proprietors to a greater outlay of effort in promoting—along with the wishes of its friends—the extension of its own facilities and means of influence. This change of the place of publication, however, will imply no preference in favor of Charleston over our former publishing city. The work will be delivered to subscribers on the same day in both cities. The new arrangement will also effect that desideratum in the business department of all periodicals, the punctual delivery of the journal to the subscribers when due; an object which has hitherto eluded all our efforts, and has been so frequently productive of mortification to ourselves and dessatisfaction [sic] among our friends and readers. It is proposed to publish the Magazine, simultaneously, in the four cities, of Savannah, Charleston, Columbia and Augusta, in each of which agents of character will be established, who will always be prepared with the adequate supply for subscribers, in sufficient season for delivery, on or before the first day in every month. . . . Its subscribers are increasing daily. . . . The Editorial duties will chiefly devolve upon Mr. W. Gilmore Simms, whose services we have secured to a greater degree than before.[191]

The general plan of work of the new *Magnolia* is to resemble that of the *Southern Literary Messenger,* states the Prospectus, and Pendleton is to travel the remainder of the year in the South in the interest of the periodical. In looking over the accomplishments of the past months, the editor sounds a concluding note of optimism:

We rejoice to believe that the day of Southern lukewarmness to the necessity of culture, in our land, has gone by forever.—There is a glorious awakening. We have daily signs that a Southern literature is demanded. . . . We feel the sentiment of Southern intellectual independence, every where, beginning to breath [sic] and burn around us. It will be no fault of ours if we do not maintain its fires. . . . The creation of a national literature is, next to the actual defence of a country by arms, against the invader, one of the first duties of patriotism.[192]

How good a periodical, we may ask, was the *Magnolia* in comparison with other magazines of the day? It had only two Georgia rivals of the same general quality: the *Orion,* published in Penfield from 1842 to 1844, and the *Family Companion and Ladies' Mirror,* published in Macon from 1841 to 1843. The reading matter of these three is of the same literary type and degree of excellence, but the *Magnolia,* at least during the first six months of 1842, surpassed its two rivals. It is far superior to the *Southern Rose,* edited by Mrs. Caroline Gilman in Charleston from 1832 to 1839. Resembling the *Southern Literary Messenger* (Richmond) somewhat in format, it contains reading matter that is lighter, and, consequently, sometimes more popular. In comparison with Northern magazines, the *Magnolia* is not so good as *Graham's* and *Knickerbocker*, but is as good as the New York *Ladies' Companion* except that it lacks the musical selections and the engravings of the latter. And it is fully as good as the *Ladies' Repository*, which began in Cincinnati in 1841. It also compares favorably with the *Ladies' Pearl, and Literary Gleaner*, conducted in Lowell, Massachusetts, by Daniel Wise. In short, the *Magnolia*, at its best period, was a magazine of no small importance—one which Georgians could feel justly proud of. Its removal to Charleston in July, 1842, made it a more scholarly and perhaps less popular periodical than it had been in the hands of Pendleton in Savannah. After a short existence in its Charleston home the *Magnolia* succumbed.[193]

4. MACON—*FAMILY COMPANION AND LADIES' MIRROR*
(1841–43)

TITLE: *Family Companion and Ladies' Mirror*, October 15, 1841–March 15, 1842; *Family Companion*, April, 1842–February, 1843
FIRST ISSUE: October 15, 1841   LAST ISSUE: February, 1843
PERIODICITY: Monthly. (After March 15, 1842, name of month without date is used. No issues for October and November, 1842.)
PUBLISHER: Benjamin F. Griffin, Macon
EDITORS: Mrs. Sarah Lawrence Griffin, October 15, 1841–February 15, 1842; Mrs. Sarah Lawrence Griffin and William Tappan Thompson, March 15–June, 1842; Mrs. Sarah Lawrence Griffin, July, 1842–February, 1843
LOCATION OF FILES: *GMM:* I. *GMW:* I, 1 (mut.)–6; II, 1–6 (mut.). *NNL:* I–II; III, 1, 3. *NcD:* II, 3

Macon, with its Georgia Female College, was a center of culture in the 1840's. The college in its midst seems to have been the incentive for the establishment of two of the most important *ante-bellum* periodicals designed for the female readers of the South. The *Southern Ladies' Book*, established in January, 1840, was the first of these, but its removal to Savannah in the autumn of the same year prepared the way for a second experiment, the *Family Companion and Ladies' Mirror*. This new periodical, to which contemporary publications referred as the *Family Companion*, was begun on October 15,

1841, by Benjamin F. Griffin, and was edited by his wife, Mrs. Sarah Lawrence Griffin. She had edited numerous *Readers* for Southern and Western children, among them: *The Southern Primary Reader, The Southern Second Class Book, The Southern Third Class Book,* and *Familiar Tales for Children.*[194] The *Family Companion* was an octavo monthly, priced at $5 per year, with sixty or more pages to each issue.

The purpose of the editor, in her own words, was to make the magazine—

fit for that holiest place in the world, the Family Circle—a Mirror from whose reflections images may be formed, which will be models worthy of being copied into the life, actions and sentiments of the Ladies who may peruse its pages. . . . In the multiplicity of periodicals . . . the Family Circle has been almost entirely neglected. It will be our endeavor to supply this neglect. Science, stripped of its mystery, tales, education, the house and the garden will each receive its share of attention in our pages. . . . While by our tales and essays we would enliven the fancy, cultivate the taste, and establish correct moral principles, we would cultivate the higher intellectual powers by essays of a more labored character, for the subjects of which the vast fields of Science afford ample materials.[195]

In a later issue we find a desire to encourage more of the "Ladies of Georgia" to produce literature:

We . . . hope that our COMPANION may be the means of giving impetus to the talent of the ladies of Georgia, and become the organ of conveying some spark of the fire from Heaven, which shall burn forever in increasing brightness—which shall obliterate narrow prejudice, and viewing the broad field of truth by the light of revelation, walk through its fair paths without stumbling or falling by the way.[196]

The outward appearance of the *Family Companion* is enhanced by its etchings, a full-page one in each issue, sometimes in colors. Georgia scenes are featured, as well as men famous in Georgia history. Pendleton had not been able to put illustration in his *Southern Ladies' Book,* but Mrs. Griffin, perhaps copying *Godey's Lady's Book,* felt that her magazine would have a wider appeal with feminine readers if it was more like its popular Northern rival. The reading matter of the periodical is not inferior to the etchings, which compare favorably with those in *Godey's*. The *Southern Miscellany*, in speaking of the *Companion*, comments thus: "Its appearance is equal to that of any periodical in the United States: its matter is good and varied." [197] A month later the *Miscellany* says that the *Companion* is "one of the first literary periodicals of the country, either North or South. . . . Some of the ablest pens in the Union are engaged to contribute to its pages." [198] *Brother Jonathan*, a popular magazine published in New York, also commends the Macon periodical in these words: "It appears to be gaining favor on all hands, East, West, North and South, and better still, to *deserve* it. It is beautifully printed—contains a very large amount of reading matter, is wholly original, and among its regular contributors, are some of the best living writers." [199]

The first number of the *Family Companion* begins with an eight-page article, "The Poetry of the Bible," by Thomas Curtis, D.D., pastor of the Macon Baptist Church, the first of a series of lectures delivered before Macon audiences the preceding year in the Methodist Church of the same city, which lectures the *Companion* undertook to publish serially.[200] To this same issue Mary E. Lee, the versatile writer from South Carolina, contributed "The Leper of Capernaum." At the end of the number were departments especially for feminine readers: "The Flower Garden" and "The Kitchen [Vegetable] Garden." The issue for Nov. 15, 1841, added the "Educational Department," by Prof. J. Darby, of the Georgia Female College, and "Literary Notices," which reviewed *The Gift for 1842*, edited by Miss Leslie, *The Lady's Book of Flowers and Poetry*, *The Amaranth*, the *Southern Literary Messenger* (commended as really Southern), and *Georgia Illustrated*, published by William C. Richards from drawings by his brother, T. Addison Richards. The *Family Companion* did not use the customary "Written for the Companion" or "Original" at the head of contributions. Its policy was this: "No article appears in our pages that is not original, save an occasional extract to fill a corner, which is invariably credited as such upon the cover." [201]

The *Companion* had not been long in existence before its proprietor realized the need of help, both for himself in the printing department and for his wife in the editorial management. Noting the financial straits of the Augusta *Mirror*, published by William Tappan Thompson, Griffin negotiated for the merging of the Augusta with the Macon periodical. Thompson, wishing for less strenuous duties because of ill health, soon came to terms with Griffin, and with the March 15, 1842, issue of the *Family Companion and Ladies' Mirror* the union was consummated under the name of the Macon periodical. According to the agreement between Thompson and Griffin, the former was to become joint-editor with Mrs. Griffin for the sum of $1,000 a year, and was to receive $400 in payment for the subscription list of the *Mirror*. In his first editorial contribution to the *Companion*, Thompson thus referred to Dickens, the English novelist, who toured America in 1842:

> While his ludicrous scenes are perhaps a shade too broad, and his detail and description rather too minute and full for the all-pervading interest which he never fails to excite in the reader, his touches of pathos are natural, and steal upon us and melt our hearts before we are aware of it.[202]

To this same number Thompson also contributed one of his own humorous tales, "Great Attraction! or, The Doctor 'Most Oudaciously Tuck In,'" which took up more than six pages of the issue.

The new editor had not been working long at his duties before friction developed between him and his office associates. First of all, Thompson, in ill health at the time, was irked by his arduous duties. Griffin wanted him to perform the labors of a journeyman in the printing establishment. Thompson was editor, contributor, and general superintendent of the office. He read proof sheets, made up the pages of the magazine, and directed and assisted in the job work. He had no control over what went into the *Companion* or what was left out of it. For this latter reason he soon came into conflict with his fellow-editor. In the issue of January 15, 1842, had appeared the first of a series of anonymous sketches called "Cousin Betsey's Letters on Matters and Things." This first sketch was decidedly tiresome and inane, and when Thompson came to look over the material intended for his first number with the periodical, he found the second of these "Letters." He protested in vain against its publication, not knowing, of course, the identity of the author. He soon learned, however, that Mrs. Griffin had written the "Letters." Both Mrs. Griffin and her husband turned against Thompson, and the latter's position became unbearable. After only a few months' connection with the *Companion,* Thompson severed his relations with it, and in August of the same year became editor of the *Southern Miscellany,* published in Madison, Georgia, by Cornelius R. Hanleiter. Both Griffin and Thompson aired their views of the controversy in the papers of the day, and strong words were used on both sides. Griffin charged Thompson with failure to perform his assigned duties in the printing establishment, and Thompson accused his opponent of failure to live up to the terms of the original agreement. The *Southern Miscellany* published several of Thompson's "Letters to the Public," in one of which Mrs. Griffin was called "a vain vulgar woman."[203] The *Family Companion* did not long survive the controversy. Mrs. Griffin ceased her duties as editor with the issue for February, 1843, and the work was apparently discontinued.[204] Nothing is known about the circulation of the *Family Companion,* but it attracted attention beyond the borders of Georgia, as we learn from the issue of June, 1842,[205] which speaks of having agents in South Carolina, Alabama, Maryland, Virginia, Massachusetts, and Maine.

The reading matter of the *Companion* consisted mainly of the romantic tales of love and adventure popular throughout the whole country during that period. There were, it is true, articles intended to instruct, such as "The Poetry of the Bible," mentioned previously, and various discussions of the excellence of Ancient Literature; but the people of the South seemed to want tales of love and adventure, of humor and mystery. Among the most interesting of the original tales are the following:

"The Ins and Outs, or The Last of the Bamboozled," by A Disappointed Man (Mrs. Sarah Austin) [206]
"Oakatibbe," by William Gilmore Simms [207]
"The Countess of Beltokay," by John Neal [208]
"Diana," by Mrs. Charlotte M. Wood [209]
"The Fair Rosamond," by Mary E. Lee [210]
"The Deed of Gift," by Samuel Woodworth [211]
"Jacques Callot. A Tale of Art, from the German," by Mrs. E. F. Ellet [212]
"Mary Bishop, or The Transformation," by John Neal [213]
"Great Attraction! or The Doctor 'Most Oudaciously Tuck In,'" by William Tappan Thompson [214]
"The Blind Organist," by Mary E. Lee [215]
"Cecelia," by Miss M. E. Walley [216]
"The Lottery Ticket," by Clifton [217]
"The Fisherman's Daughter," by William Tappan Thompson [218]
"Boss Ankles, the Man What Got Blowed Up with a Sky-Rocket," by William Tappan Thompson [219]
"Florita. A Spanish Tale," by Mrs. Charlotte M. Wood [220]
"Letter from Joseph Jones," by William Tappan Thompson [221]
"Homespun Yarns, No. 1. Polly Peablossom's Wedding," by John B. Lamar [222]
"A Thanksgiving Tale," by Psyche [223]
"Timothy Teasewell, the Everlasting Story Teller," by B. [224]
"Party-Spirit. A Tale of the South," by A Lady of South Carolina. $200 Prize Tale [225]

Book reviews played only a small part in the *Family Companion*, but several original articles appeared that deserve mention:

"Education," by Prof. J. Darby [226]
"Outlines of an Essay, On the Causes Which Contributed to Produce the Peculiar Excellence of Ancient Literature," by G.H.H. [227]

First Period: 1837-46

"Intellectual and Moral Culture," by Dr. H. V. Wooten [228]
"Eighteen Months in Russia. By a Professor of Arms," translated from the French by Miss M. E. Walley [229]
Review of Dickens' *American Notes* (very unfavorable) [230]
"Modern Refinement," by O. L. Smith [231]

The original poems appearing in the *Companion* are usually very short, but as good as the average in American periodicals. The following are possibly the best illustrations:

"Heart Fancies," a series of sonnets by William Gilmore Simms [232]
"Lines Written for Viscountess ——'s Album," by Richard Henry Wilde [233]
"Exodus, or The Passage of the Red Sea," by William C. Richards [234]
"The Poetry of Flowers," by Clifton [235]
"Sabbath at Home," by Mary E. Lee [236]
"The Missionary's Hymn," by Mirabeau B. Lamar [237]
"Prayer," by Henry Rootes Jackson [238]

Pseudonyms and initials did not often appear appended to contributions to the *Companion,* but there were a few:

Barnard (Augusta); Clifton; Eugine; A Georgia Woman; G. F. H(olmes?); G.H.H.; Hamilton; A Lady of South Carolina; M. G. M(ilward?).; Psyche; Rinaldo; Somers.

Signed contributions came from the following writers, Northern and Southern, two-thirds of them out-of-state and possibly a dozen from the North:

T. S. Arthur; Mrs. Sarah Austin; Mrs. E. Carter; Dr. (William A.) Caruthers; S. W. Catlin; Robert M. Charlton; D. A. Chittenden; Dr. Thomas Curtis; Mrs. Mary S. B. Dana; Prof. J. Darby; J. C. Edwards; Mrs. E. F. Ellet; William B. Ellison (Macon); Mrs. Emma C. Embury; Mrs. Sarah Lawrence Griffin; J. E. Henry; Mrs. Caroline Lee Hentz; George Frederick Holmes; Rev. William Houser; Prof. William G. Howard; Henry Rootes Jackson; John B. Lamar; Mirabeau B. Lamar; E. Lawrence; Mary E. Lee; J. H. Mifflin; Mrs. Maria G. Milward; John Neal; Dr. S. C. Oliver; Miss Caroline F. Orne; Mrs. Caroline Orne; Mrs. Frances S. Osgood; Lieut. G. W. Patten; Rev. George F. Pierce; William C. Richards; William S. Rockwell; Mrs. L. H. Sigourney; William Gilmore Simms; O. L. Smith (Oxford, Georgia); Mrs. Susan A. Smith;

J. Evans Snodgrass; Mrs. Ann S. Stevens; William Tappan Thompson; Miss Mary E. Walley; General James Watkins; Richard Henry Wilde; Mrs. Charlotte M. Wood; Samuel Woodworth; Dr. H. V. Wooten.

The *Family Companion* stands at the very top of Georgia *ante-bellum* monthlies, sharing honors with the *Magnolia* (Savannah) and the *Orion* (Penfield). Mrs. Sarah Lawrence Griffin, though not the best judge in the world of reading matter, in some way managed to get contributions that were among the best to be found in Southern periodicals. William Tappan Thompson's stay with the magazine was too short to have any permanent effect on its policies, but if he had remained longer, there is no doubt that the *Companion* would have been better than it was.

5. PENFIELD—*ORION* (1842–44?)

TITLE: *Orion*
FIRST ISSUE: March, 1842   LAST ISSUE: August, 1844 (?)
PERIODICITY: Monthly. (No numbers for April, October, 1842; May–August, 1843; double number for March & April, 1843.)
PUBLISHER: William C. Richards, Penfield, March, 1842–February, 1844 (actually printed in New York, according to contemporaries); Charleston, March–August, 1844 (?)
EDITOR: William C. Richards
LOCATION OF FILES: DLC: I–III. G: I–III. GA: I. GE: I–III. GM: I–II. GMM: I–II. GMW: I. GU: I–III. GU(D): I; II, 1, 3, 4, 5–6 (inc.); III, 1–5, 6 (inc.). Ia: I, III. MBAt: I (inc.). NNHi: I–III, IV (inc.). NcD: I, 1, 2 (inc.), 3–6; II, IV. NjP: I–II. PPL: I–II. PU: I. ScChL: CF. TxU: I–III. WHi: I, II, III (inc.), IV

The *Orion* made its initial appearance in March, 1842, in the little town of Penfield, seven miles north of Greensboro, in Greene County. Penfield had been laid out as the site of Mercer University, established by the Georgia Baptists in 1838, but it never contained more than a few hundred inhabitants. As the fountain head, however, for that denomination in the state, it was chosen as the site for the establishment of a magazine by William Carey Richards, himself a young Baptist minister, who appears to have been named for William Carey, the great Baptist missionary from England to India in the nineteenth century. The *Orion,* however, was not a denominational periodical, nor even a religious publication. Its aim was to foster and develop literature in the South, and Richards, the twenty-four-year-old editor, was well qualified for the work.

Richards was born in London, England, in 1818, the son of a Baptist minister who emigrated to America in 1831 to become pastor of a church in Hudson, New York. The son graduated from Madison University (Hamilton, New York) in 1840, and the following year married Cornelia Holroyd Bradley, in the meantime having set up his residence in Georgia. During the ten years he labored in that state, he had a hand in three of the most important literary periodicals in Georgia: the *Orion* (Penfield), the *Southern Literary Gazette* (Athens), and the *Schoolfellow* (Athens), a magazine for children. From Georgia he removed to Charleston, South Carolina, but after a few years of residence there settled in the North, where he spent the rest of his life, dying in Chicago in 1892.[239] Two other members of the Richards family achieved prominence. Thomas Addison Richards, a younger brother, became a well-known artist and engraver, and also wrote numerous tales and sketches that appeared in various Southern periodicals. Kate Richards, a younger sister, who married Charles W. DuBose of Sparta, Georgia, contributed many poems and tales to her brother's periodicals, often under the pseudonym of "Leila Cameron." The wife of William C. Richards was also a writer, sometimes under the pseudonym of "Mrs. Manners," and sometimes as merely "C.H.B.R." [240]

William C. Richards was a prolific writer. In his early journalistic career he found time to write many poems and tales of different types. His tales of humor are entertaining, most of them appearing in the *Orion.* Some of them are: "The First Lecture at Smithville," [241] "The Smithville Gas Frolic," [242] "The Smithville Debating Society," [243] and "Major Theophilus Bandbox Bubble, or The Nice Young Man." [244] His poems, usually short lyrics, are at times very sentimental, but sometimes they are above the average of the day. His writings appeared not only in the periodicals he himself edited, but also in the *Southern Quarterly Review* (Charleston), the *Christian Review* (Boston), *Knickerbocker* (New York), *Southern Ladies' Book* (Macon), Augusta *Mirror*, and *Family Companion* (Macon). After his removal to the North in the 1850's Richards devoted himself mainly to religious work and wrote articles of a religious nature.

The first number of the *Orion*, dated March, 1842, bears a very close resemblance, in typography and general appearance, to the *Knickerbocker*, published in New York during that period. Both magazines, octavo in size, have the same type of material and the same general arrangement of it. Richards, however, denied any intentional imitation of his New York contemporary and declared that his periodical was no more like the *Knickerbocker* than it was like any other American magazine.[245] The *Orion* was, nevertheless, a work above the average, as may be seen by glancing at the Table of Contents. The first issue, consisting of 64 pages, made a decidedly popular appeal, with the following high lights:

"Tallulah," a tale by Miss M. E. Moragne
"Lights and Shadows of the Heart," the first installment of a tale by C.H.B.R. (Mrs. William C. Richards)
"The Trysting Rock: A Tale of Tallulah," first installment, by T. Addison Richards
"Dante Alighieri," poem by Richard Henry Wilde
"Autumn Reveries," essay by Henry Rootes Jackson
"The Lost Child," poem by Orionis (William C. Richards)
"Regrets," essay by Charles Lanman
"Let the Banner Men Advance," poem by Robert M. Charlton
"My Native River," poem by J. H. Mifflin
"Thoughts. From the French of Paschal [sic]," twenty aphorisms in prose
"Literary Review," with reviews of *Memoir and Poems of Lucretia M. Davidson*, "The World of London," from *Blackwood's Magazine*, and *Biographical Memorials of James Oglethorpe*, by Thaddeus Mason Harris
"Editor's Department," with an informal essay on "The Tooth-

Ache," a formal essay on "International Copy-Right Law," and reviews of *Ballads and Other Poems,* by Henry W. Longfellow, and *The Parted Family, and Other Poems,* by Mrs. M. H. [sic] B. Dana
"Monthly Chat with Readers and Correspondents"

The talent of Richards is best seen in his informal essays, which appear in almost every subsequent issue of the *Orion,* and in his "Monthly Chat," in which he addresses himself to correspondents, one by one, giving reasons for rejecting certain contributions, and commending others which are soon to appear in the *Orion.*

Richards' periodical, as the editor explains in the first number, was named for "the most magnificent constellation in the southern hemisphere," the name being proposed by William Tappan Thompson, editor of the Augusta *Mirror,* who was to "stand godfather to the newly born." [246] The original sketches and drawings appearing in the magazine were the work of the editor's brother, T. Addison Richards, and the engravings were done by James Smillie, "without question the best landscape engraver in the United States." [247] "Our plate—" continues the editor, "every plate we publish —for sketching, drawing and engraving alone, costs us THREE HUNDRED DOLLARS!" [248] The duty of T. Addison Richards was to travel all over the South, make drawings of notable scenery, and write descriptive articles about the places visited. The editor promises "one splendid southern landscape [in] every number" as soon as the subscription list warrants the expense incurred thereby. All this, however, could not at that time be furnished adequately by any Southern printing establishment; hence Richards was forced to have his periodical printed in New York City, though it was actually distributed from Penfield.[249] The *Southern Miscellany,* published in Madison, Georgia, attacked the *Orion* for being printed in the North in imitation of Northern magazines,[250] but Richards' practice was not unknown among Southern editors, who could always get their periodicals printed on better paper and at cheaper prices in the North than could be had anywhere in the South. Joseph Addison Turner, also of Georgia, even as late as 1860 had his quarterly, the *Plantation*, printed in New York City.

The breadth of Richards' views on Southern literature may be judged from his address to "Our Southern Contemporaries":

> Entering as we do upon the same broad field of literary effort with our contemporaries in Georgia, we may be allowed to express our sympathy with them in their struggles to secure and maintain an independent existence. We *know* how hard it is to establish a popular and permanent magazine; we have regarded with deep interest the experiment of the Mirror, the Magnolia, and more recently of the Family Companion, and we have urged upon our friends the duty of supporting them, and aiding their proprietors in the accomplishment of their common noble aim—the advancement of literature in the South—we will not say southern literature, for we have a decided distaste for such local expressions, as if literature were of different characters in the South and in the North. It is the same every where except in degree and tone, and its advancement, its elevation in the South, is the proper object of our desires and efforts.
>
> Called as we are by circumstances, and especially by the public voice—the voice of *our readers* we mean—into the same arena with the works already mentioned, we would assure their conductors of our continued sympathy, and our very warmest wishes for their complete success. . . . To them, one and all, we most cordially extend the right hand of fellowship, and beg to be esteemed a true, if humble, co-laborer.[251]

In July, 1842, Richards emphasized these views:

> We have said, in a previous number, that we disliked the term "southern literature; as if literature were of different characters in the North and South." To our mind there is but one literature, whether it exists in the North or the South, in the East or the West. Its existence in different stages of development, or in different degrees of elevation—is another thing. In name it is unique, in character various. Have we of the South different standards from the people of the North, for determining the merit of literary production? Have we even different matériel for producing literature?

Do our authors write with other aims than northern writers? Do our poets construct their verse by different rules? . . . If we localize literature, we render it unworthy of the name. . . .

We are the warm advocates of literature in the South. For its advancement we will toil and hope to see the fruit of our toil. For this we have displayed our constellation in the southern literary firmament, and invited our authors to become its stars. . . . We labor for the advancement and refinement of intellectual taste and habit in the South; and most happy are we to have the cooperation of our literary brethren beyond our great sectional landmark. If we are asked—"Why then not suffer the North to supply the material for this end, and save the toil, the money, the *sacrifices,* necessary to establish the means at home?" We answer, 1. Because we deem it a disgrace to our people, that they should be servilely dependant [sic] on the North for all their intellectual supplies—when God has given them mind in abundant measure; and 2. Because through our own organs alone can we vindicate ourselves from aspersions and misrepresentations, when they are hurled at us from abroad, and because they alone can be the true exponents of our interests.[252]

Richards was not able to do all that he wished in the *Orion,* for it is only with Volume II that he was able to include as many engravings as he wished. In that volume appeared one in colors, "The Table Rock, S.C.," the others being the usual black-and-white cuts, one at the front of each number. From the first, however, Richards followed the plan of including serial stories at frequent intervals, some of the longest and best of which were written by T. Addison Richards. Mrs. Anna L. Snelling (New York), Mary E. Lee (Charleston), and William Gilmore Simms (Charleston) were also authors of serials, which will be named later. In the first number of Volume II [253] Richards declared that he had procured vigilant and able correspondents in the cities of New York, Philadelphia, Boston, and London, who would send advance copies of all new English and American publications, of which notices would appear in the *Orion.* Acquainted as he was with people both in the North and in England, Richards made use of such contacts to further the interests of his work. He was more cosmopolitan than William Gilmore Simms, perhaps the leading literary editor in the South, and much more ambitious to establish a popular periodical of the highest type in the South. The *Orion* was superior in every respect to the *Southern Rose,* edited by Mrs. Caroline Gilman in Charleston until its discontinuance in 1839, and also superior to the *Ladies' Pearl, and Literary Gleaner,* edited in Lowell, Massachusetts, by Daniel Wise from 1840 to 1843. Though not containing quite so much material as the *Magnolia* (Savannah), published by Philip C. Pendleton during the first half of 1842, the *Orion* compared favorably with that magazine, and had the virtue of making a better general impression upon the reader than did the earliest issues of the *Magnolia.* Richards never says anything in the *Orion* about the size of his subscription list or about any financial difficulties. He never burdens the reader with long discussions of the trials of an editor except as he treats them in a humorous manner. Sometimes the most interesting features of an issue are the "Editor's Department" and the "Monthly Chat," which reflect a critical judgment above the average of *antebellum* Southern editors. He strikes a humorous note in one issue, in which he shows his reason for rejecting a poem entitled a "Parody on Lord Byron's Maid of Athens." He quotes only the first stanza as an example:

> Cherubina! female wizard,
> Give, oh! give me back my gizzard;
> But since that has left my craw,
> Keep it now and be my squaw.[254]

In the second number of the *Orion,* mindful of the host of amateur poets who were sending their contributions to editors, Richards grows sarcastic in his advice to them:

We have before us a . . . task . . . to administer a word of advice . . . to the thousand half-fledged bardlings, who in this *aetas scribendi* bring ridicule and contempt upon the name of poetry by their vile attempts to manufacture rhymes and stanzas, and who . . . must, in the exceeding generosity of their souls, inflict these rhymes upon some unfortunate editor, obliging him to pay the postage of the MS., break its seal—a Byron's head perhaps or an Apollo's lyre!—then to read the enclosed verses, distinguished only by long and short lines placed alternately, and each beginning with a capital letter; when, as if to cap the climax of generosity—he is "at liberty to print in his valuable Magazine, the first efforts of a young Poet," or "the report of my first ride on Pegasus!"—"my first blossom culled on Parnassus"—"my first pebble picked from the spring at Castaly," or something equally poetical! Shade of Homer! Spirit of Milton! What a privilege! [255]

In the same column Richards quotes the first stanza of "To the Beautiful Black Eyes of My Cousin Sally," a poem sent in to him by a youthful bard:

> My beauteous cousin Sally's eyes,
>   Like diamonds bright do sparkle;
> Or like the sparks which upwards rise
>   When burning thorns do crackle! [256]

The only comment the editor makes in conclusion is, "We hope he will never make a second effort!"

Richards was a literary critic of no mean ability. He had standards that were based upon a wide range of reading from authors of all types. And he did not hesitate to give his candid opinion wherever he thought it advisable. His frank remarks about some early poems of William Gilmore Simms cannot be truthfully attributed to any jealousy of the *Magnolia*, which had begun printing, in November, 1841, the "Early Lays" of Simms.[257] Richards, feeling that Simms was scarcely as good a poet as he was a novelist, thus expressed his views:

We should not have chosen the "Early Lays" of the author of Atlantis [sic] as affording choice pleasure, or evidencing the existence of the true poetic spirit among us. Mr. Simms is hardly adding to his reputation in publishing, at this late day, such endless series of these "Early Lays." [258]

Richards joined other Southern editors in attacking Griswold's *The Poets and Poetry of America*, an anthology of supposedly representative poetry that devoted very little space to Southern poets. The *Orion* thus came to the defense of the South:

Our contemporaries in Charleston have justly found fault with Mr. Griswold's "American Poets," alleging that he has performed his task only in part, and what is worse, with evident partiality. While he has given considerable space to the productions of second-rate bards in New-England and other northern regions, he has not even named several in the south who have certainly written much that is superior to many of the specimens of the *favored* ones. . . . We regret this, inasmuch as a work professing to embody our *national* anthology should have done justice to *all* sections of the country. Among those names which should have appeared in "The Poets of America" we will allude to that only of . . . Henry Jackson, Esq.[259]

An interesting attitude toward novel-reading, though not a very liberal one for the 1840's, appeared in an early number of the *Orion*. The reading of prose fiction was condemned by the more puritanical people of the United States in *antebellum* days and afterwards, but Richards, though a Baptist minister, had broad views on the subject, as can be seen in the following statement:

We are not of the class called novel-readers in the extended sense of the term, nor can we approve of a general and indiscriminate reading of the works of fiction which issue from the press in the present day. Apart from the decidedly injurious tendency of many—perhaps a majority of them—their very numbers . . . require that they be read only in selection. The mawkish taste, ridiculous philosophy, and threadbare sentiment, not to speak of the positive and openly vicious character, of the mass of novels, render them very unfit companions for the young and pureminded reader. These however are not the characteristics of Mr. [G. P. R.] James' novels, and the one we have announced [*Morley Ernstein, or The Tenants of the Heart*] we are disposed to rank, after a fair perusal, as one of the best productions of this gifted novelist.[260]

Like all other Southern editors, Richards did not mince matters in reviewing Dickens' *American Notes for General Circulation,* published in the autumn of 1842, in which Dickens made some unfavorable criticism of the American people after his visit to the New World in the early part of the same year. Yet Richards had a good word for the English novelist, as may be judged from his review:

> We . . . were gratified to find that Mr. Dickens had uttered no libels, none wilfully at least, upon our country, our people, our manners, or our institutions, except that of slavery; in treating of which he displays his utter ignorance of the subject, and his natural and to-be-expected bitterness against the system and its upholders. We could wish that Mr. Dickens had visited the South, and judged for himself, before he penned his stale and often-refuted calumnies upon our citizens, and his gross misrepresentations of a system which, at the worst, is infinitely superior, even by the confession of Mr. Lester, an abolitionist, to the system of white slavery so fearfully prevalent in some parts of the author's land. We are sorry that the "amiable Boz," as he has been often called, laid aside in this instance his amiability, and suffered his prejudices to control his heart and his pen. In other respects we find little to condemn in the "American Notes;" little cause for the tempest of "critic wrath" which some reviewers have raised. There are many instances of exaggeration in the book; many caricatures. . . . But we observe that these caricatures are not generally of national character, or of important matters, but rather of ludicrous incidents, or, it may be, of much-prevailing habits which deserve ridicule—and worse! . . .
>
> There are many beautiful passages in the "Notes;" passages in which the author of the "Old Curiosity Shop" appears to the reader in all his exquisite genius and power. . . . His book, taken as a whole, is not a happy literary performance. We apprehend it never was designed to be . . . and if it *adds* nothing to the author's reputation, which is likely, we hardly believe it will seriously diminish it, even with its disaffected readers.[261]

Dickens did not come any farther South than Virginia, but he saw enough of slavery to condemn it without reserve. It is no wonder, then, that Southern editors bristled in defense of their cherished institution.

Possibly the most extended bit of literary criticism that Richards indulged in related to Thomas Holley Chivers, the prolific Georgia poet, whose relations with Edgar Allan Poe led to a controversy (over who influenced whom) that is not yet absolutely settled. Chivers had submitted his poem "To Allegra Florence in Heaven" to Richards for inclusion in the

Orion, but the latter mercilessly picked the poem (which antedates Poe's "Raven" by two years) to pieces in his "Monthly Chat" in the double number for March and April, 1843. This piece of criticism is too caustic to be omitted; hence it is quoted with only minor omissions:

"To Allegra Florence in Heaven" is a most unequal performance. It contains some stanzas of *poetry,* and occasionally verses of much beauty, but as a whole we are compelled to decline it. We shall take the liberty, however, of presenting a few extracts from the poem by way of dealing poetical justice to the author. The following is the opening stanza, and one of the best:

> "When thy soft round form was lying,
> On the bed where thou wert sighing,
> I could not believe thee dying,
>   Till thy angel-soul had fled;
> For no sickness gave me warning,
> Rosy health thy cheeks adorning,
> Till the Hope—destroying morning—
>   When my precious child lay dead."

This is natural and poetical—but as an offset to it we give the fourth:

> "Like some snow-white cloud *just under Heaven,* some breeze has torn asunder,
> Which discloses to our wonder
>   Far beyond, the tranquil skies;
> Lay thy pale cold lids half closing,
> While on Death's cold arms reposing,
> Thy dear seraph-form seemed dozing
>   On thy violet-colored eyes!"

Here is a sad jumble of snow-white clouds "just under Heaven" (we should like to know whose topography the author follows!) tranquil skies, dozing seraphs, and violet-colored eyes.

The meaning is very obscure with the author's punctuation, but by making a parenthesis of the sixth and seventh lines we are enabled to discover it. . . . The author should study perspicuity of style.

> "Bathed in sunny dews, adorning
> One white lily bed, while scorning
>   All the rest, however bright!"

There is some obscurity even in this stanza. "All the rest" what? All the rest of the lily beds—scorning? Is that it? The following comparison in the opening of the eighth stanza is decidedly bad —decidedly. It is.

> "For as birds of *the* same feather
> On the earth will flock together
> *So around thy* HEAVENLY FATHER,
> They [angels] now gather there with thee!"

Here the author has come the "wicy warcy" on Napoleon's "step from the sublime to the ridiculous"—and has stepped from the ridiculous in imagery—to the sublime in reality. Don't do that again, Doctor! There is poetry and genuine feeling in the next stanza.

> "With my bowed head thus reclining
> On my hand, my heart repining,
> Shall my salt tears, ever shining
>   On my pale cheeks flow for thee:
> Bitter soul drops ever stealing
> From the fount of holy feeling,
> Deepest anguish now revealing—
>   For thy loss, dear child, to me!"

But what shall we say of the ensuing one?

> "As an egg which broken, never
> Can be mended, but must ever
> Be the same crushed egg forever,
>   So shall this dark heart of mine"—etc.

Shade of Blair, what a figure of speech! An egg and a heart in the same category. With what intensity does the poet declare the important fact that a broken egg cannot be repaired! We learned the same truth theoretically, when we were five years old in the following *parallel* lines—we mean parallel to our author's—which were propounded as a riddle—

> "Humpty-dumpty sit [sic] upon a wall,
> Humpty-dumpty had a great fall;
> All the king's horses and all the king's men
> Couldn't put humpty-dumpty together again!"

Humpty-dumpty, reader, is the Dutch or something else for an egg! We have handled our author's egg rather severely we confess, but we have done it "more in sorrow than in anger" that he should have *laid* it—on our table for judgment! If as we are disposed to think these oddities are an affectation of the writer—a studied quaintness—in other words *a way of his,* we must candidly inform him that *his way* is a most ridiculous and miserable one, and ought to be amended at once.[262]

A survey of the contents of the *Orion* indicates varied, colorful, and entertaining reading matter. In June, 1842, Simms had stated, in the *Magnolia,* then edited by him, that in the *Orion* he had seen "nothing . . . indicative of very great intellectual superiority," [263] yet nobody had ever claimed any "great intellectual superiority" for the *Orion,* not even its editor. It was what it claimed to be: a periodical that aimed, in a popular way, to encourage the production of literature in the South. Its reading matter, therefore, is its excuse for existence. The following serial stories were contributed to the *Orion:*

"The Trysting Rock: A Tale of Tallulah," by T. Addison Richards [264]
"Lights and Shadows of the Heart," by C.H.B.R. (Mrs. William C. Richards) [265]
"The Wanderer. Translated from the MSS. of an Italian Monk," by D. A. Chittenden [266]
"The Miser's Curse," by Maria Gertrude Kyle [267]
"Alice Seyton," anonymous [268]
"The Village Postmaster," by T. Addison Richards [269]
"Clarence Grahame; or, The Capture of Burgoyne," by Mrs. Anna L. Snelling [270]
"The Fulton Folly, or, The First Steamboat," by T. Addison Richards [271]
"A Spanish Chronicle," by Mary E. Lee [272]
"Il Campanetto; A Romance of a Summer," by T. Addison Richards [273]
"The Hickory Nut," by James Hungerford [274]
"The Hermytte of Drowsiehedde," by William Gilmore Simms [275]

Tales other than serials written especially for the *Orion,* appeared in each issue, of which the following are the best:

"The First Lecture at Smithville," by William C. Richards [276]
"Margaret Donaldson: or The Fortune Huntress," by T. Addison Richards [277]

First Period: 1837–46

"Records of the Past," by C.H.B.R. (Mrs. William C. Richards) [278]
"The Smithville Gas Frolic," by William C. Richards [279]
"Agnes. A Story of the Revolution," by Mrs. Anna L. Snelling [280]
"The Two Ediths," by C.H.B.R. (Mrs. William C. Richards) [281]
"The Smithville Debating Society," by William C. Richards [282]
"Mauvaise Honte: or, 'Don't Be Bashful,' " by T. Addison Richards [283]
"Major Theophilus Bandbox Bubble, or The Nice Young Man," by William C. Richards [284]
"Mary Linton's Wedding," by William C. Richards [285]
"Mateo Falcone, An Incident Illustrative of Corsican Life," from the French of Prosper Merrimee, by the author of the "Corsican Revenge," etc.[286]

The fact that members of the Richards family wrote so many of the above-mentioned tales does not mean that they wrote most of the contents of each number; but it does mean that their stories were better than those by most other contributors.

Numberless original poems appeared in the *Orion* from month to month, among which the following are the best and most representative:

"Harold," anonymous satire in the style of Byron's *Don Juan* (almost certainly the work of Henry Rootes Jackson) [287]
"The Lost Child," by Orionis (William C. Richards) [288]
"Let the Banner Men Advance," by Robert M. Charlton [289]
"My Native River," by J. H. Mifflin [290]
"To a Flying Swan," by Louis L. Noble [291]
"To a Mocking Bird," by Orionis (William C. Richards) [292]
"Row Merrily, Fisherman, o'er the Sea," by John Love Lawrie [293]
"To Thee, after Marriage," by William C. Richards [294]
"Hast Thou Forgot Me?" by Mary E. Lee [295]
"The Poet's Destiny," by Maria Gertrude Kyle [296]
"The Rainy Day," by Mary E. Lee [297]
"My Father," by Henry Rootes Jackson [298]
"Genesis," by William C. Richards [299]
"On Leaving Florence," by Richard Henry Wilde [300]
"To Kate," by Orionis (William C. Richards) [301]
"Eginhard and Emma; or Love's Stratagem," by Mary E. Lee [302]
"Skiddaway Narrows by Night," by John Love Lawrie [303]
"To the Keowee," by William C. Richards [304]
"Ysobel; or The Ivy Vine," by James Hungerford [305]

These poems are in many different meters. "To Kate" and "Skiddaway Narrows by Night" are in Spenserian stanza, while the rest are in blank verse or in stanzaic form of some variety. "Harold" is an excellent imitation of the Byronic manner of rambling narrative, with humorous exaggerations continually creeping in. The best portion of the poem is the song "To the Whip-Poor-Will." The first stanza of this unfinished poem, for only two cantos are given, is typical of the spirit of the whole work:

> The grass was green on Bay-street, for the dog-days
>   With glowing Sol, and skies of brazen sheen,
> When sale of julaps [sic] mix'd of ice and grog, pays
>   More than the best bank dividends, I ween—
> Had but commenced: on Bay-street, in Savannah,
> Young Harold sauntered *à la Byron* manner.[306]

One stanza of "To the Whip-Poor-Will" is sufficient to show its lyricism:

> Bird of the night, sad Whip-poor-will,
>   Alight upon yon waving tree,
> And with thy sweetest warblings fill
>   The star-lit grove for me!—
> And I will listen to the strain,
> While eve is on her peaceful wave,
>   And echo on her hill,
> And Nature drops her dewy tear,
> And holds her softest breath to hear
>   Thy ditty—Whip-poor-will! [307]

One of the best lyrics ever to appear in an *ante-bellum* Georgia periodical is the "Row Merrily, Fisherman, o'er the Sea," by John Love Lawrie, an unidentified poet from Savannah. A quotation of the entire poem will not be amiss:

ROW MERRILY, FISHERMAN, O'ER THE SEA

by

John Love Lawrie

Oh prescator dell' onda,
  Fi da lin;

> Oh prescator dell' onda,
>   Fi da lin,
> Vien prescar in qua,
> Colla bella tua barca
> Colla bella se ne va,
>   Fi da lin, lin la.   Venetian Boat Song.

Row, merrily, fisherman, o'er the sea,
Where the waters murmur melodiously;
Go forth on the golden waves that leap,
In glittering myriads along the deep,
And watch by the light of each waning star,
How speedeth thy lonely course afar;
    Row merrily, merrily.

Still the last steps of the rosy day,
On the dusky portals of the night delay,
And through the breathless expanse of air,
The twilight glideth with starry hair;
While the chant of the ocean swells and dies,
Or mingles its voice with the sea bird's cries;
    Row merrily, merrily.

Fisherman, heard ye the castanet,
That broke o'er the wave when the daylight set:
Heard ye the laughter and measured beat
From the shore, where our dark-eyed maidens meet,
Blending its tones with the water's [sic] hoarse,
To cheer thee along on thy trackless course?
    Row merrily, merrily.

Fisherman, would I could go with thee,
So merrily over that silver sea;
We would row afar on our shining way,
And sing to the moonbeam that smiled so gay,
And we'd gaze at the water's deep bed of blue,
While we counted each star that was shining through;
    Row merrily, merrily.

Row merrily, fisherman, o'er the sea,
Where the waters murmur melodiously;
Go forth on the golden waves that leap,
In glittering myriads along the deep,
And watch by the light of each waning star,
How speedeth thy lonely course afar;
    Row merrily, merrily.[308]

General articles in the *Orion* include the following original work:

"The Origin of Slave Labor in Georgia," by William Bacon Stevens [309]
"Autumn Reveries," by Henry Rootes Jackson [310]
"The Bardolphian Nose," by Dr. (William A.) Caruthers [311]
"The Harpsichord of Marie Antoinette," translated from the French by C.H.B.R. (Mrs. William C. Richards) [312]
"A Chapter on the Supernatural," by William Gilmore Simms [313]
"Glimpses of Switzerland," by Rev. W. C. Dana [314]
"The Poetry of Our Periodical Literature," by C.B.N. [315]
"Luis de Camoens," by William Bacon Stevens [316]
"Luther and the Reformation," by H. M. Spofford [317]
"The Lusiad of Camoens," by William Bacon Stevens [318]
"Edmund Burke," by J. R. K(endrick) [319]
"Felicia Hemans," by C.H.B.R. (Mrs. William C. Richards) [320]
"Revolutionary Poetry," by Hon. Judge (John Belton) O'Neall [321]
"The Moral Character of Hamlet," by William Gilmore Simms [322]
"The Old English Writers," by Rev. J. R. Kendrick [323]

Richards devoted some attention to reviews of current books, usually book notices rather than reviews in the strictest sense of the word. A list of the more important of these reviews shows the varied interests of the *Orion*:

Ballads and Other Poems, by Henry W. Longfellow [324]
Biographical Memorials of James Oglethorpe, by Thaddeus Mason Harris [325]
Conjectures and Researches concerning the Love, Madness and Imprisonment of Torquato Tasso, by Richard Henry Wilde [326]
The Poets and Poetry of America, by Rufus W. Griswold [327]
Poems, by Alfred Tennyson [328]
American Notes for General Circulation, by Charles Dickens [329]
Martin Chuzzlewit, by Charles Dickens (advance notice) [330]
Poems, by Robert M. Charlton and Thomas J. Charlton [331]
Forest Days: A Romance of Old Times, by G. P. R. James [332]
The Last of the Barons, by Sir E. L. Bulwer [333]
Sweethearts and Wives; or Before and After Marriage, by T. S. Arthur [334]
A Christmas Carol, by Charles Dickens [335]
Arabella Stuart, by G. P. R. James [336]

First Period: 1837–46

Tales of Every Day Life in Sweden, etc., by Frederika (*sic*) Bremer [337]
Poems, by Frances Anne Butler [338]
Coningsby, or the New Generation, by B. D'Israeli [339]
The Spanish Exile, play by William Gilmore Simms [340]
Excursions through the Slave States, etc., by G. W. Featherstonhaugh [341]
Rose D'Albret: or Troublous Times, by G. P. R. James [342]

The *Orion* was variously received in the South by contemporary periodicals. The *Southern Miscellany* (Madison) in June, 1842, declared: "The Orion is the *star* magazine of the South in point of typography: in fact, in that particular, it is equal to any in the country." [343] But in October of the same year it was calling the *Orion* a "precious humbug" for being printed in the North.[344] William Gilmore Simms, writing in the *Magnolia* for June, 1842, felt himself forced to admit that Richards "writes with ease and good humor." [345] The *Southern Literary Messenger* thus notices the *Orion* for September, 1843:

The September number contains a lithographic representation of the Falls of Slicking, highly picturesque.—Some of the prose articles are vigorous and spirited, and there is one exquisite poetic gem, "He came too late," contributed by Mrs. Welby of Kentucky. The Editor enforces with sound argument and commendable zeal, "the claims of Southern periodicals upon the South"—in all of which we fully concur. We heartily wish the Orion success.[346]

The following year the *Messenger* was of the opinion that "the work will now improve as it has got into a good Literary atmosphere" by removing to Charleston; [347] but in this instance the Richmond periodical was wrong, for the *Orion* withstood the shock of removal only six months.

The *Knickerbocker* (New York), which Richards had been accused of imitating in his periodical, declared in May, 1842:

The deserved success of the Richmond (Va.) *"Messenger"* . . . has given rise to other Southern publications, some of which (from out the number of those that must needs ere long expire) bid fair to emulate its merit, and to earn a like popularity. Chief among these, it is easy to perceive, will be "THE ORION," a very neatly printed, well supplied, and admirably embellished monthly Magazine, under the care of Mr. RICHARDS, late editor of "Georgia Illustrated." . . .[348]

The *Georgia Illustrated* referred to was not a periodical but a collection of engravings illustrating the scenery of Georgia as viewed through the drawings of T. Addison Richards.

Richards had literary and business connections with Robert Sears of New York, editor and publisher of *Sears' New Monthly Family Magazine,* "a rival in appearance and interest," declares Richards, "of the great London Penny Magazine in its palmiest days."[349] Speaking of the new monthly of Sears, Richards says: "Anticipating its immense value and popularity, the publisher of our Magazine [Richards himself], desirous of securing for it a vast Southern circulation, entered into an arrangement with Mr. Sears, by which he has become an associate editor and publisher of the work."[350] The *New Monthly,* therefore, was printed in New York and issued there and in Penfield. Nothing further is said about the venture anywhere in the later issues of the *Orion;* hence its success is problematical.

Contributors to the *Orion* often availed themselves of pseudonyms, among which are the following, including initials also:

Beta; A Carolina Contributor; C.H.B.R. (Mrs. William C. Richards); Claude; Clifton (Columbus, Georgia); H. V. W(ooten). (Lowndesboro, Alabama); J.R.H. (Georgia); L. (St. Mary's College); A Lady of South Carolina (Pendleton, South Carolina); La Georgienne; Orionis (William C. Richards); Rigel; A Student at Law; Wallace (William Wallace Webster, New York); X.Y.Z.; Yona (Clarksville, Georgia).

The contributors who signed their own names were not numerous, but they included some of the leading writers of the South, as well as a few from the North:

Park Benjamin (New York); Rev. J. Newton Brown (New-Hampton, New Hampshire); Miss Mary Bates; Dr. (William A.) Caruthers; Robert M. Charlton (Savannah); D. A. Chittenden (Augusta); Thomas Holley Chivers (Washington, Georgia); F. W. Cole (Albany, New York); Rev. W. C. Dana (Charleston); Mrs. E. F. Ellet; Hannah F. Gould (Massachusetts); General Andrew J. Hansell; W. W. Hazard; James Hungerford; Henry Rootes Jackson (Savannah); Prof. A. C. Kendrick (Hamilton, New York); Rev. J. R. Kendrick; Maria Gertrude Kyle (Covington, Georgia); Charles Lanman; John Love Lawrie (Savannah); Mary E. Lee (Charleston); A. B. Meek (Tuscaloosa, Alabama); Grenville Mellen (Maine); J. H. Mifflin (Savannah); Miss M. E. Moragne; Abiel L. Nettleton; Louis L. Noble; Hon. Judge (John Belton) O'Neall; T. Addison Richards; William C. Richards (also under pseudonym of "Orionis"); Lydia H. Sigourney (Connecticut); William Gilmore Simms (Charleston); Mrs. Anna L. Snelling (New York); H. M. Spofford (Massachusetts); E. G. Squier (Albany, New York); William Bacon Stevens (Savannah); Richard Henry Wilde (Savannah); Miss Leonora Wilson.

Little more remains to be said relative to the career of the *Orion*. Since it lasted only six months after its removal to Charleston, its existence there has been included in an account of its history. Richards transferred the magazine to the South Carolina city, as he himself tells us, "because we consider that city as the most important point in the South, and such a work as ours should, by all means, emanate from the headquarters of the region in which it is designed especially to circulate." [351] For various unknown reasons the change of location did no good. With the issue of August, 1844, the *Orion* joined the great number of publications sleeping in the "graveyard of periodicals"—Charleston. The work of Richards in the field of literature deserves more attention than it has heretofore received. His literary productions are not, of course, great pieces of literature, but they indicate a poetic talent above the average of Southern editors. In conclusion let us quote one of his sonnets, which appeared in the Editor's Department of the *Orion*:

JUNE SONNET

    Hail first and fairest of bright Summer's train,
        That comést with thy leafy honors crowned!
        From myriad voicéd Nature all around—
    Are poured sweet songs to welcome thee again.
    Beneath thy smile the fields of yellow grain
        Sway gently to the motion of the air;
        And countless graceful shapes, as frail as fair,
    Bloom from the dawn, to Daylight's crimson wane.
        Thou comest laden with the treasure free—
        Which bounteous Nature "hangs on every tree,"
    The luscious fig—the downy peach are seen,
    In ripened beauty through the curtaining green—
        Though but a foretaste of the lavish sweets,
        With which our taste the bright Midsummer greets.[352]

6. MADISON—*SOUTHERN MISCELLANY* (1842–46?)

TITLE: *Southern Miscellany*
FIRST ISSUE: April 5, 1842   **LAST ISSUE:** 1846 (?)
PERIODICITY: Weekly
PUBLISHER: Cornelius R. Hanleiter, Madison, 1842–46; Atlanta, 1846–?
EDITORS: Cornelius R. Hanleiter, April 5–August 13, 1842; William Tappan Thompson, August 20, 1842–February 9, 1844; Cornelius R. Hanleiter, February 16, 1844–46 (?)
LOCATION OF FILES: *DLC:* Dec. 8, 1843. *GMM:* I–II. (Missing—Oct. 15, 1842; Mar. 4, 1843)

On April 5, 1842, appeared the first number of the *Southern Miscellany*, a weekly periodical "Devoted to Literature, The Arts, Science, Agriculture, Mechanics, Education, Foreign and Domestic Intelligence, Humor, etc." It was published in Madison, a thriving town in Middle Georgia, at the western end of the Georgia Railroad. The editor describes the place as "one of the most eligible villages, in the very heart of our State, at the head of rail-road communication, and surrounded by rich and well settled counties—with all of which we enjoy unusual mail facilities—there is no reason why a well conducted journal . . . should not receive a competent support."[353] The publisher of this journal was Cornelius R. Hanleiter, who, from 1837 to 1839, had published in Macon the *Southern Post and Literary Aspirant*.[354] The *Southern*

Miscellany was a quarto periodical printed on imperial sheet, six columns to a page, and contained four pages to each issue. The subscription price was $2.50 per year. It was truly a family periodical, with about one-fourth of its space devoted to news. At first each issue contained at least one good story and one or more poems, besides miscellaneous comments, news, and selections from both Northern and Southern periodicals. Advertisements occupied two or three columns, and were priced at one dollar per square of 14 lines for the first insertion, and fifty cents for the second.

A very favorable criticism of the periodical comes from the *Family Companion* (Macon), which thus describes the *Southern Miscellany:*

> It is among the handsomest and most readable family newspapers that reach us from any quarter, and if anything may be argued from its matter and manner, is destined to become a popular journal. Madison county alone, has the taste and liberality to sustain such a paper; but we should be surprised, indeed, if it did not in time obtain a wide circulation, wherever true merit is appreciated.[355]

Hanleiter attempted to conduct the paper with no outside editorial help, but he soon found that he needed some able assistance. He therefore secured the aid of William Tappan Thompson, who had recently severed his connection with the *Family Companion.* The new editor, who was paid a regular salary, and who had already had a varied experience in the journalistic field, greatly improved the contents of the Madison journal, and during his connection with the paper from August 20, 1842, to February 9, 1844, he succeeded in making it one of the best literary weeklies of the period, and second only to William C. Richards' *Southern Literary Gazette* (Athens). The financial difficulties of the periodical were like those of all such periodicals at that time, and Hanleiter relinquished the services of Thompson only because he felt himself unable to employ a salaried editor.[356]

Thompson contributed much to the contents of the *South-*

ern Miscellany. Many of his "Major Jones' Letters" appeared in its pages,[357] as well as the following tales: "Boss Ankles," [358] "John's Alive! or, The Bride of a Ghost," [359] "The Doomed Maiden," [360] "The Patriot Brothers. A Tale of the Revolutionary History of Georgia," [361] and "The Mystery Revealed," a Pineville Sketch.[362] E. M. Pendleton, Henry Rootes Jackson, D. A. Chittenden, and W. H. Campbell were among the most important contributors to the work. An interesting feature of 1842 was the serial appearance in the *Southern Miscellany* of "A Night in the Cars," by Augustus Baldwin Longstreet,[363] which is missing from collected tales of the author.

Hanleiter's periodical undoubtedly had merit, and it was commended by the *Mechanic and Farmer* (Pictou, Nova Scotia) as "in point of mechanical execution . . . one of the handsomest weeklies we have ever seen. The contents, both original and selected, are acceptable to every reader, and must, we think, secure quite an extensive circulation." [364] With the departure of Thompson the journal devoted less space to literature and more to news and advertisements. It had been liberally patronized during the first two years of its existence,[365] but in later years its patronage fell off to a great extent. Finally it "was moved from Madison to Atlanta in 1846, and survived for a brief period." [366] Nothing is known about its life in Atlanta, but doubtless the new location was still too small to support such a work. With its discontinuance ended the first period of attempts to establish a literary periodical in Georgia.

CHAPTER II

Second Period: 1848–54

INTRODUCTION

GREATER LITERARY activity was manifested in the period 1848–54 than during the preceding period. Magazines were started at such educational institutions as the University of Georgia (Franklin College), LaGrange College, and College Temple (Newnan). Periodicals devoted to humor and satire began to appear, like the *Horn of Mirth* (Athens) and the *Tomahawk* (Macon). Another periodical was planned, and the Prospectus issued, but no number ever appeared. This was the *Microcosm*,[1] to be published in Athens and edited by Thomas A. Burke and James A. Sledge. The editors, in abandoning the project, made arrangements for their advance subscribers to be supplied with *Wheler's Monthly Journal,* which appeared in Athens for a few months in 1848.[2]

The State of Georgia had been steadily growing during the 1840's. The white population, according to the U.S. Census, increased from 407,695 in 1840 to 521,572 in 1850, and the bulk of the increase had been in Middle Georgia. Educational institutions, such as Emory College, Mercer University, Oglethorpe College, and the Georgia Female College, all of which had sprung up in the 1830's, were attracting more students than heretofore, and bookstore advertisements in newspapers increased in number. An illustration of the widespread interest in history is the fact that in a short length of time 100 copies (in a cheap edition, it is true) of Macaulay's *History of England* were sold in Athens as "The Great Book of the Day." [3]

The following periodicals, arranged in chronological order, include all those actually begun in Georgia from 1848 to 1854 of any literary value except those discussed later in detail:

LaGrange—*Rose-Bud.* Monthly quarto, edited by young ladies. First number actually appeared, says *Southern Literary Gazette* (Athens), I, 17 (September 2, 1848), p. 135. No files located.

Athens—*Horn of Mirth.* Humorous monthly, running from July 4, 1849, to August 10, 1850, and edited by Thomas A. Burke.[4] U.S. Census for 1850 records 1,200 subscribers. No files located.

Atlanta—*Monthly Miscellany.* Religious and literary monthly, published by Joseph S. Baker, simultaneously at Richmond, Atlanta, and New Orleans.[5] Baptist periodical of minor literary interest. Files: *NcD:* I, 1–7 (January–July, 1849).

Augusta—*Youth's Friend.* Monthly quarto, 8 pages, edited by Miss W. C. Tyson. First number appeared February 8, 1850, says Augusta *Chronicle* (February 9, 1850). No files located.

Oxford—*Southern Literary Journal.* Edited by Mrs. Rebecca Haynes Riley. Periodical actually appeared, says *A Friend of the Family* (Savannah), II, 13 (June 1, 1850). No files located.

Milledgeville—*Gem.* Monthly, published by J. C. Reagan. Prospectus in *A Friend of the Family* (Savannah), II, 17 (June 29, 1850). U.S. Census for 1850 records 2,000 subscribers. No files located.

Macon—*Youth's Gem and Southern Cadet.* Semi-monthly in common newspaper form, edited by J. C. Reagan, probably the same man who edited the Milledgeville *Gem.* First number actually appeared, says *Southern Ladies' Companion* (Nashville), IV, 2 (January, 1851). Probably a continuation of the Milledgeville *Gem,* removed to Macon. No files located.

Milledgeville—*Day Star of Truth.* Monthly, edited by the Rev. Mr. Reagan. U.S. Census for 1850 records 2,000 subscribers. Reviewed in *A Friend of the Family* (Savannah), II, 14 (June 8, 1850). No files located.

Athens—*Georgia Home Gazette.* Edited and published by Messrs. Smythe and Whyte, beginning in January, 1852. Reviewed in

Second Period: 1848–54   93

Roath's Monthly Magazine (Athens), I, 2 (February, 1853), p. 82.[6] No files located.

Augusta—*Georgia Home Gazette*. Family journal, edited and published by Messrs. Smythe and Whyte. Quoted from in *Southern Eclectic* (Augusta), II, 12 (September, 1853). Possibly the same as the Athens *Georgia Home Gazette*, with error in name of city somewhere.[7] Files: *MWA:* Dec. 22, 1851; June 16, 1852.

Athens—*Georgia University Magazine*. Published for the Senior Class of Franklin College, by Christy & Kelsea, at Franklin Job Office. Established March, 1851. Files: *GU:* I, 1–5; II, 1–2, 4; III, 1–2, 5; IV, 3–4; V, 1–3, 5; VI, 1–5; XII, 1.

Buena Vista—*Literary Vade Mecum*. Published by James W. Gaulding. Contributors: T. P. Ashmore, Thaddeus Oliver, and M. A. Smith.[8] No files located.

Macon—*Tomahawk*. Published by B. F. Griffin, and edited by Peter Pickle (pseudonym of Joseph Addison Turner).[9] Each number a volume in itself. Aim was to dissect "the various follies and absurdities of the present day."[10] Only one number ever issued.[11] No files located.

Macon and Madison—*Southern School Journal*. Monthly. Begun probably in January, 1853. Published in Macon, and edited by the Rev. E. H. Myers. Then removed to Madison and edited by John G. Clarke, with issue of September, 1854. Files: *CL–S:* II (inc.). *DE:* II (inc.)–III. *DS:* III, 2. *NcD:* II, 4–12; III, 1–3.

Newnan—*Fly Leaf*. Quarterly, published by Senior Class of College Temple. U.S. Census for 1860 records 1,000 subscribers. Photograph of title page to VII, 1 (May, 1861), in *Coweta County Chronicles*, edited and compiled by Mary G. Jones and Lily Reynolds (Atlanta, 1928), p. 229. Begun presumably in 1854. No files located.

1. EATONTON—*TURNER'S MONTHLY* (1848)

TITLE: *Turner's Monthly*
FIRST ISSUE: January, 1848   LAST ISSUE: March, 1848
PERIODICITY: Monthly
PUBLISHER: C. L. Wheler, Madison; distributed from Eatonton
EDITOR: Joseph Addison Turner
LOCATION OF FILES: *GAH:* I, 2

The first attempt at a literary periodical during the period 1848–54 was *Turner's Monthly,* begun in Eatonton presumably in January, 1848, by Joseph Addison Turner, then only twenty-two years of age.[12] It was called by its editor "A Miscellaneous Journal and Review," and was printed by C. L. Wheler at Madison, Georgia. It consisted of 24 octavo pages, two columns to a page, and was advertised at $1.50 per year. The only copy known to exist is Volume I, Number 2 (February, 1848), from which can be gathered an idea as to the general character and policy of the periodical. In his "Editorana," Turner plunges at once into a defense of his work:

> We hear one say, "Why should I subscribe for your Magazine, when I can get a better one somewhere else?" We admit you can get some superior magazine. But is it to be found in Georgia? Have you no *State pride* which will prompt you to support a home literature in its incipiency, and nourish the tender plant until it becomes a sturdy tree? . . . We have the talent in our State. All that is wanted is, that this talent should be excited to action, and properly developed. . . .
>
> We know . . . that there are many Northern papers which you had better pay one dollar to keep out of your family than allow them to enter for nothing. What kind of principles do they teach? Are you sure that they are not filled with abolitionism, and other kindred *isms,* which are at war with our nearest and dearest interest? . . . Are you sure that your daughters will not have their tastes vitiated by the miserable stuff in its foolish *"tales"* and *"sentimental love-stories?"* From the great fountain-head of corruption, Paris, there flows a poisonous stream of literature which is flooding many of our literary productions. Even where our news-papers and magazines do not give verbatim Parisian literature, its colorings and corruption are so nearly imitated, that a very good substitute is furnished us. No where is this more the case than in our large cities? [*sic*]

Contributions are solicited, Turner says, but "lengthy articles are not expected or desired."

The issue that has been preserved contains some excellent pieces of light literature. Besides several anonymous poems such as "Chanticleer and Partlet. A Fable" and "Beauty, Wit and Gold," we have the poem "The Poor Flower Girl," by Miss C. W. Barber; the tale "Il Zingaro," by Mrs. Emma C. Embury; and the tale "Bingo," by "X," from "A Georgia

Lawyer's Portfolio." Since the editor was himself a lawyer and had begun to write as early as 1846, he may be the author of the last-named tale. He had also published, in 1847, a volume of juvenilia entitled *Kemble's Poems*.[13] Another interesting contribution to *Turner's Monthly* is called "Essays." "No. 1—Introductory Essay" begins with a quotation from Horace, while "No. 2—Love" begins with one from Virgil. The author, who calls himself "Jonathan Falstaff," is probably Turner, for the "Essays" show the Turner characteristics found in his "My Uncle Simon's Plantation, or Sketches of Southern Life, &c," which, under the pseudonym of "Abraham Goosequill," appeared serially in the *Southern Literary Gazette* (Athens) later in the same year. No authors' names appear as contributors other than those already mentioned.

Nothing is known as to how *Turner's Monthly*, obviously an immature piece of work, was received by its contemporaries. We find no reference to it in other periodicals and newspapers of the time. Since we find Turner, later on in 1848, contributing to the *Southern Literary Gazette* and the *Southern Literary Messenger*, we suspect that *Turner's Monthly* did not long survive its second number;[14] for with no advertisements in its pages, it surely needed more support than its short list of twenty-one subscribers could possibly contribute.[15]

2. ATHENS—*SOUTHERN LITERARY GAZETTE* (1848–53)

TITLE: *Southern Literary Gazette*, May 13, 1848–April 28, 1849; *Richards' Weekly Gazette*, May 5, 1849–April 27, 1850; *Southern Literary Gazette*, May 4, 1850–53
FIRST ISSUE: May 13, 1848   LAST ISSUE: December 22, 1849 (in Georgia)
PERIODICITY: Weekly (fifty numbers to a volume)
PUBLISHERS: C. L. Wheler, Athens, May 13, 1848–December 22, 1849; Richards & Walker, Charleston, January 7, 1850–53
EDITORS: William C. Richards, assisted in 1850 by D. H. Jacques
LOCATION OF FILES: *GMM:* II. *GU:* I, 1–6, 9, 11, 13–14, 16, 21. *GU(D):* I. *NcD:* I

The second adventure of William C. Richards into periodical literature, the *Southern Literary Gazette*,[16] published in Athens, was undoubtedly his greatest success. In the first place, there was a considerable reading public in Athens, influenced to a great extent by the presence in its midst of the University of Georgia (Franklin College), with its library of between 8,000 and 9,000 volumes, as well as with the libraries of the two literary societies, each with between 2,000 and 3,000 volumes.[17] Several bookstores carried a stock of the best books of both the United States and England, and Richards himself was agent for a number of the leading periodicals of the country.[18] Then, too, Athens was situated in Clarke County, with an estimated population of 10,343 in 1845,[19] of which more than half were whites. "Its natural advantages, its freedom from malaria, its facilities for educating children all made it an attractive home." [20] The Georgia Railroad had been completed to Athens in 1841, and because of "the increased facilities for getting to Athens, citizens of other towns moved there, attracted by the cultured society of the place, the climate and the advantages of education." [21] It was an excellent center for a successful literary periodical, and Richards soon proved that it was not impossible to make a success, temporary at least, of such a venture. One historian thus speaks of the influence of Richards and his artist brother:

> Two brothers, T. Addison Richards and William C. Richards, were great additions to the growing town in the forties. Addison Richards was an artist of no mean skill, his brother a poet and musician, and both men of more than ordinary literary culture. Mrs. William C. Richards was Principal of a flourishing girls' school called the Athens High School.[22]

Returning from South Carolina, where he had witnessed the demise of the *Orion,* his first attempt at periodical literature, William C. Richards had an undimmed zeal to establish a periodical that would foster and develop the literature of the South. Though not a native Southerner, he saw the need for an intellectual activity in the South in the direction of literary interests, and he devoted himself tirelessly to the task. As to his object in beginning the new periodical note his own words:

Second Period: 1848-54

Up to this time, no Magazine or Journal of Belles-Lettres has been attempted in our midst. . . . And will not all who feel an interest in the intellectual advancement of the South, join the standard we have set up, and help us to unfurl the bright banner of Intellect over the beautiful land we love? . . .

The grand object of the paper we edit, is to develope and foster the intellectual capital of the South; to open a channel for literary communication between the scholars of our wide-spreading territory, to incite to diligence latent talent, and to awaken from its trance, slumbering genius in our midst, that "the wilderness may blossom like the rose." . . .

We seek, then, to establish a paper that shall be avowedly sectional in its purpose; but while we thus speak openly, let us not be misunderstood. We love the South—for here all our interests for life are centered. We mourn that the South, preeminent in physical beauty and resources, is, beyond cavil, behind the North in intellectual development and cultivated taste. . . . We labor to promote Southern literature—because it has been mournfully neglected amongst us. We have engrafted the title, "Southern" upon our very name . . . to suggest, if no more, to our people, that Literature is as congenial and indigenous to the South, as to any other region. . . . Strictly neutral in partisanship, we shall present our readers with a bare synopsis of political intelligence, possessing general interest. Literature is the staple of our Journal.[23]

And he further assures his subscribers of his financial backing:

By private effort a large and generous list [of subscribers] has been obtained, and upwards of ONE THOUSAND SUBSCRIBERS have pledged their support to the paper. Until this was accomplished, the editor was unwilling to publish his Journal, but it is now given to the public with the unequivocal assurance that it shall be permanent.[24]

The first issue of the *Southern Literary Gazette: An Illustrated Weekly Journal of Belles-Lettres, Science and the Arts* appeared on Saturday, May 13, 1848. It was an eight-page quarto sheet, with four columns to the page, and was advertised at "Two Dollars per annum, *in advance*." The reading matter consisted "of matter both original and selected; and . . . Tales, Essays, Sketches of Travel, Poetry, Criticism, and a General Miscellany of information in all departments of Literature, Art and Science." [25] The first issue contained much original matter headed "For the Southern Literary Gazette," as well as "The Southern Eclectic" section, quoting William Gilmore Simms's "Chevalier Bayard" and Mary E. Lee's "The Poets." The prose high lights are: "All About: With Pen and Pencil," by T. Addison Richards; "Influences of Spring," by C. Vavasour Holroyd; "London Letters—No. 1," by S.F.G.; and "New-York Letters—No. 1," by Flit. The last-named article is an illuminating sketch of the religious, dramatic, operatic, and commercial activities of the Northern metropolis. "London Letters—No. 1" is devoted to a discussion of political conditions and activities in the great city of England. It promises, however, "literary intelligence . . . in subsequent communications." Only one column is given over purely to news. Short poems appear by Mrs. Joseph C. Neal (sister of Richards' wife), Leila Cameron (pseudonym of Mrs. C. W. DuBose, Richards' sister), and William N. White. The editor includes "Our Gossip Column," where, he says, "we shall serve up, in such quantity as we may, those literary *tit-bits* that are always palatable, and in most cases, so eagerly sought for by the general reader.[26] "Our Book Table" reviews *The Life of Chevalier Bayard,* by Simms, *Dombey and Son,* by Charles Dickens, and several other works of less importance. "The American Weekly Press" reviews the humorous periodical *John Donkey* and *Neal's Saturday Gazette.* Humor plays a part in this first number, in "A Column Erected to Fun," as well as in Thomas Hood's "Black, White and Brown," quoted in "The Eclectic of Wit." Advertisements are confined to the last page and take up little more than one column, exclusive of those inserted by Richards himself concerning his own interests, which include a bookstore.

The *Gazette* was received with enthusiasm by the *Southern Literary Messenger,* edited by John R. Thompson, in these words:

Second Period: *1848–54* 99

There prevails, among certain periodicals of our country, a ridiculous practice, based upon affected superiority, of passing over *sub silentio* contemporary magazines, and quite disdaining to notice the first efforts of a literary enterprise. With them, the attractive and neatly printed journal, whose caption we have written above, would perhaps be considered altogether beneath the dignity of the monthlies. For ourselves, we are proud to hail it as a promising coadjutor in the field of letters. . . . We regret that we did not receive the first issue of the Gazette, as we could have wished to read the salutatory address of its editor. We hazard nothing, however, in declaring, from the evidences before us, in the well-filled columns of Nos. 2 and 3, that he is a man of taste and judgment, and will walk worthily of the vocation wherewith he is called.[27]

Thompson was mistaken in this instance, for the Athens periodical was favorably reviewed by several Northern and Western publications. *Neal's Saturday Gazette* says: "We take pleasure in noticing the advent of an able weekly paper, devoted to Southern interests and Southern literature. . . . The number before us is filled with original contributions. . . ."[28] The Boston *Yankee Blade* states that "the paper is brimful of choice matter, original and selected, and the typography is worthy of the contents."[29] The Buffalo *Western Literary Messenger* notes that it "is edited by W. C. Richards, Esq., a young gentleman of fine literary taste, with whose writings we have been conversant for the last eight or ten years. The Gazette looks well."[30] The Cincinnati *Great West* thinks that the periodical "bids fair to maintain an elevated position among the weekly literary papers of the Union."[31] And the *Knickerbocker* (New York) sees it as "quite in the form and style of the old 'New-York Mirror'[32] . . . The 'Gazette' bids fair to do much towards extending the literature of the South. We hope often to hear through its columns from Mr. [J. M.] Legaré and Mr. [Henry Rootes] Jackson. Both these gentlemen are true poets."[33] Other favorable comment came later from the New York *Mirror of the Times* and the Boston *American Union*,[34] as well as from the Boston *Excelsior and Ram-*

bler, the New York *Literary American,* and the *National Intelligencer.*[35]

Some of the most prominent Southern writers who contributed to Richards' periodical were William Gilmore Simms, Mary E. Lee, Robert M. Charlton, Henry Rootes Jackson, J. M. Legaré, Thomas Holley Chivers, Mrs. Caroline Lee Hentz, and Joseph Addison Turner (sometimes under the pseudonym of "Abraham Goosequill"). Tales, sketches, and essays of excellence are numerous throughout the periodical as long as it was published in Athens. Among the serials specially contributed were:

"All About: With Pen and Pencil," by T. Addison Richards—sketches of travel over the country, with descriptions of places visited [36]
"La Roulette," anonymous, translated from the French [37]
"Libussa's Lamp. A Story from the German," by Mary E. Lee [38]
"The Listener, etc., Not by Caroline Fry," anonymous essays [39]
"My Uncle Simon's Plantation, or Sketches of Southern Life, &c," by Abraham Goosequill (Joseph Addison Turner) [40]
"Evelyn Hamilton: Or, The Sisters," by Miss Eliza G. Nichols [41]

Interesting tales also appeared in shorter form:

"The Country Cousin," by Miss C. W. Barber [42]
"Pauline de Meulan," by J. A. Turner [43]
"The May-Party: or, Love's Masquerade," by Florio [44]
"The Victor Monarch's Bride," by Mrs. Caroline Lee Hentz [45]
"Marian Gray, or The Wife's Devotion," by Stephenia (Savannah) [46]
"The Lady Pilgrim," by Miss C. W. Barber [47]
"The Indian Mound: A Tale of Southern Country Life," by Caroline Howard [48]
"Percy: or, The Banished Son," by Mrs. Caroline Lee Hentz [49]

Two humorous tales are of especial interest:

"The Hen-Pecked: or, How He Cured Her," by T. Addison Richards [50]
"Maj. Theophilus Bandbox Bubble, or, The Nice Young Man," by William C. Richards [51]

Long original poems sometimes appeared, such as:

"Eginhard and Imma: or Love's Stratagem," by Mary E. Lee [52]
"Sketches among the Alleghanies," by Henry Rootes Jackson [53]
"The Stars," by William Gilmore Simms [54]
"Wachullah," by Mrs. C. W. DuBose—Prize Poem [55]
"Tallulah Falls: A Legend of Georgia," by D. W. Belisle [56]

Richards very ably reviewed a number of books for his periodical. Having been educated in the North, he had doubtless come in contact with the best literary productions of that section, and seemed to possess a discriminating taste. Among the important books reviewed were the following:

Dombey and Son, by Charles Dickens [57]
Life of Chevalier Bayard, by William Gilmore Simms [58]
Lectures on Shakespeare, by H. N. Hudson [59]
Lays of the Palmetto, by William Gilmore Simms [60]
Orta-Undis, and Other Poems, by J. M. Legaré [61]
The Oak Openings, by James Fenimore Cooper [62]
A Search after Truth, by Thomas Holley Chivers [63]
Poems by Currer, Ellis and Acton Bell (by Charlotte, Emily, and Anne Bronte) [64]
A Fable for Critics, by James Russell Lowell [65]
Works of Washington Irving, 2 volumes [66]
Life and Voyages of Christopher Columbus, by Washington Irving [67]
Literary Sketches and Letters. Final Memorials of Charles Lamb [68]
Life, Letters, and Literary Remains of John Keats, edited by R. M. Milnes [69]
History of England, by Macaulay [70]

An interesting item appearing in the *Southern Literary Gazette* for March 3, 1849, is the tale "Death in a School-Room," by Walter Whitman, reprinted from the *Democratic Review* (New York) for August, 1841.[71] There is little literary merit in this story by Walt Whitman (who, in his early life, had been called "Walter"), but Richards apparently liked it for its emotional appeal, and judged that readers of his periodical would be pleased with it. This reprinted tale hardly represents any direct connection between Whitman and Richards, nor does it indicate any special interest on the part of Richards in the poet who was soon to attract widespread attention. The Southern editor was looking for a sentimental type of reading matter for his constituency, and he found it in the *Democratic Review*.

The vicissitudes of an editor are many and varied, as we learn from Richards himself.[72] The greatest task, he finds, is that of supplying readers "with instruction and pleasure," for the editor must write much that appears in his periodical. Then, too:

> It is not alone the actual amount which the Editor himself contributes to his paper: this, indeed, is a very small part of the toil. It is the care of providing for the various departments—of determining the fitness of this or that contribution—a delicate operation, by the way, and one involving many nice issues; of writing soothing letters to "the authors of rejected addresses,"—of ransacking old books for choice material to adorn the Eclectic columns—and, we had forgotten almost to say, of revising accepted manuscripts, and particularly Poetry; supplying here a deficient foot; remedying there a disallowed rhyme—now furnishing a word to complete the author's meaning, and anon hunting up an idea to suit the author's rhyme. All of these are weekly—nay, daily duties—from which there is no honorable escape.[73]

An illustration of the material that often comes to an editor's hands is seen in the following, taken from "Notices to Correspondents":

> "Charles." We must respectfully decline your verses addressed "To a young lady whom I saw washing her lily-white hands on the back piazza at sunrise in the morning." The inscription reminds us forcibly of some stanzas once published in the Augusta Mirror, (if we mistake not,) addressed "To a child reposing in its nurse's arms under a rose-bush in Jasper county." [74]

The editor of the *Southern Literary Gazette* was untiring in his efforts to stimulate literary thought in the South. His "Editor's Department" usually began with a discussion of some contemporary problem, among which are the following: "International Copy Right," [75] "The State Temperance Convention," [76] "The Insurrection in Paris," [77] "Scientific Progress," [78] "Puns and Punsters," [79] "Light Literature," [80] "Lit-

Second Period: 1848–54

erary Associations," [81] "The Value of Books," [82] "A Medley on Music," [83] "Singing in Our Churches," [84] "On the Cultivation of Taste," [85] "Winter Evenings," [86] "Public Lectures," [87] "Literary Composition," [88] "Demoralizing Literature," [89] "Fugitive Poetry," [90] and "Influence of the Press." [91] There is nothing pedantic about the style of Richards. He was a master-editor in making the contents of his periodical interesting, yet of a high quality.

Besides the departments already mentioned, others were added in the course of Volume I, such as "The Working Man," "Newspaper Analects," "Our Bowl of Punch," "Philosophy for the People," "Opinions of the Press," "The American Periodical Press," "The Essayist," and "The Family Circle." Advertisements increased in number until they took up the whole of the last page. The success of the *Southern Literary Gazette* may be judged by the words of the editor himself, as he outlines to his subscribers his plans for Volume II, which was to be entitled *Richards' Weekly Gazette*:

> Contrary to the expectations of, perhaps, a majority of its subscribers, and . . . contrary to the predictions of croaking friends and jealous foes, the Gazette has lived and *flourished,* so that it will begin its second year under brighter auspices, and with multiplied claims upon the public favor. . . . Our dependence for success is not upon Southern pride, or Southern liberality, for these have been appealed to a hundred times in vain; but it is upon our indefatigable exertions, our fixed and irrefragible [sic] purpose, to succeed in the task we have begun. . . . Let our friends, then, understand that we depend upon ourself, while we earnestly invoke their coöperation, for the establishment of a permanent weekly Journal of Letters in the South.[92]

The *Gazette,* under its new name, was to be "Less exclusively devoted, than heretofore, to Literature, the Arts, and the Sciences," and the editor hoped to make it a "Choice Family Newspaper." [93] The issue of October 14, 1848,[94] had announced "Valuable Prizes" to be given for the purpose of developing and encouraging literary talent in the South, to be divided as follows:

Fifty Dollars for the best Tale of the South
Twenty Dollars for the second best Tale of the South
Twenty Dollars for the best Poem
Ten Dollars or a copy of *Harper's Pictorial Shakespeare* for the second best Poem

After some delays the prizes were finally awarded as follows:

First Prize Tale—"Percy, or, The Banished Son," by Mrs. Caroline Lee Hentz (Columbus, Georgia) [95]
Second Prize Tale—"The New Aria," by A.E.F. (Augusta, Georgia)
First Prize Poem—"Wachullah," by Mrs. C. W. DuBose (Sparta, Georgia)
Second Prize Poem—"The Sword and the Pallette," by J. M. Legaré (South Carolina)

The first-prize Tale and Poem appeared in the first issue of *Richards' Weekly Gazette* (May 5, 1849). The judges were Philip Clayton, Dr. Henry Hull, and James W. Harris, Esq.[96]

Numerous writers contributed to Richards' periodical during its nearly two years' existence in Athens. As was customary with writers of the day, many used initials or pseudonyms, some of the most common being: Alphonso (Lowell, Massachusetts), Aleck (Athens), Alton (A. L. Taveau, South Carolina), Alpha, Aglaus (Henry Timrod),[97] Bayard (Roswell, Georgia), Bachelor, Bard of Saratoga, Conjux, E. H. (Charleston), Florio, A Lady of Georgia, P. H. H(ayne?). (Charleston), and Tim Whetstone. The following writers contributed at various times:

David R. Arnell; Miss C. W. Barber; General William O. Butler; Mrs. M. F. Baber; Rev. J. D. Baldwin; Miss Mary Bates; D. W. Belisle; Robert M. Charlton; Leila Cameron (Mrs. C. W. DuBose, Sparta, Georgia); L. Maria Child; Rev. J. H. Clinch; Thomas Holley Chivers; H. H. Clements; Mrs. C. W. DuBose; Mrs. Mary S. B. Dana; William E. Davis; L. T. Doyal; Mrs. E. Jessup Eames; John P. Ellis; Mrs. E. F. Ellet; Richard Fairfax (Virginia); Walter H. Griswold; Abraham Goosequill (Joseph Addison Turner); Mrs. Caroline Gilman; Gertrude Gaultier; S. Gilman; C. Vavasour Holroyd; Mrs. S. C. Hall; Mrs. Caroline Lee Hentz; Rev. C. H. Hall; Mary Howitt; Caroline Howard (Mrs. Caroline Gilman Jervey); J. W. Hanson; Edwin Heriot; Henry Rootes Jackson; Jacques

Journot (D. H. Jacques, Athens); Thomas W. Lane; Charles Lanman; L. La Taste; Mary E. Lee; J. M. Legaré; Charles Lufton; O. A. Lochrane; Cotton Mather Mills; Clara Moreton; Eliza G. Nichols; Mrs. Joseph C. Neal; B. F. Porter; George D. Prentice; Edward J. Porter; Dr. Eugene Percy; C. F. Quintard; T. Addison Richards; William C. Richards; John G. Saxe; William Gilmore Simms; Rev. William Bacon Stevens; Charles Southman; Mrs. Ann S. Stephens; Mrs. (L. H.) Sigourney; Parish Saxon (South Carolina); A. L. Taveau; Camilla Toulmin; Joseph Addison Turner; William N. White; C. L. Wheler; William Cumming Wilde; Robert A. White (South Carolina); Edward Youl.

In addition to the most common pseudonyms quoted above, the following, together with initials, also appeared now and then:

An Amateur; Ann E.; Alfred Crowquill; Benedict Bayard (or simply "Bayard"); C.H.H.; Delta (Athens); E.F.G.; E.G.N.; Epsilon; Eremus (Athens); Erwin; Flit; Gertrude; Hetty; H.M.J. (Montgomery, Alabama); J.A.S.; J.C.W.; J.F.H. (Athens); J.H.N. (Midway, Georgia); J.L.; Josiah Allspice, Esq. (Augusta); Juvenis (Charleston); A Learner; P.P. (Franklin College); Rab; Samivel (Savannah); W.C.W.; Wilfred; Willhelmine (Augusta); Xury (Marietta, Georgia).

Volume II, under the title *Richards' Weekly Gazette,* as stated previously, was less devoted to literary interests and more intent upon producing "A Choice Family Newspaper." For this reason its importance in our connection is less than that of Volume I. From its files we learn that by the end of 1849 Richards had sold one-half interest in the periodical to Joseph Walker, of Charleston, and that the journal was removed to the latter city in time for the first issue of 1850. On May 4, 1850, the title again became the *Southern Literary Gazette,* which name was unchanged until December, 1852, when Richards severed his connection with the work and moved to New York City, to which city he also transferred the publication of the *Schoolfellow,* "a juvenile periodical that . . . [had] risen to great favor under his auspices." [98] Early in 1853 the *Gazette* was merged with the *Weekly News,* edited by Paul Hamilton Hayne, but its usefulness in Georgia literary history had long since passed away.[99]

3. ATHENS—*SCHOOLFELLOW* (1849–57?)

TITLE: *Schoolfellow*
FIRST ISSUE: January, 1849   LAST ISSUE: 1857 (?)
PERIODICITY: Monthly
PUBLISHERS: William C. Richards, Athens, 1849; Richards & Walker, Charleston, 1850–52; New York, 1852–57 (?)
EDITOR: William C. Richards
LOCATION OF FILES: *DLC:* I–VI, VIII–IX. *MWA:* IV, 6. *NN:* VI, VIII. *NNHi:* II. *NcD:* I. *ScChL:* I

In the midst of his labors with the *Southern Literary Gazette* in 1848, William C. Richards conceived the idea of a monthly magazine exclusively for boys and girls. Although he had not long been a resident of Georgia, he realized that—

> The absence of those tastes for Literature and the Fine Arts, which is so often deplored by our writers and our orators, will continue to be felt until a generation of *educated* youth comes upon the stage of society; and to educate the young, in the true sense of the term, their tastes, their minds and their hearts, must all undergo careful culture.[100]

The first number of the *Schoolfellow,* Richards' contribution to the proper education of the young, and "the very first enterprize of its kind in this region," [101] appeared in January, 1849, in a 32-page duodecimo form, with excellent woodcuts throughout. In the opening "Address" the editor states his aim:

> As the kind *schoolfellow* is not less ready to help his associates to learn a hard lesson than he is to join them in any proper amusement, so he will be, at once, your teacher and your playmate—not less ready to inform you of curious facts in History, Philosophy, and other Sciences, than to share with you in those innocent pastimes which constitute the charm of boyhood and of girlhood.

The magazine, advertised at $1 per year, ran for one year in Athens and attained great popularity. Richards himself states that before the end of 1849 it had reached a circulation of 10,000 copies.[102] In December, 1849, the editor removed his publishing office to Charleston, transferring both the *Schoolfellow* and *Richards' Weekly Gazette* to that city. In 1852 the former periodical was removed to New York City, where, still in Richards' hands, it continued until 1857.[103]

The *Schoolfellow* received favorable criticism from the Tallahassee *Floridian*,[104] as well as from the New York *Literary American*, which declared that the "South has reason to be proud of these exponents [*Richards' Weekly Gazette* and the *Schoolfellow*] of its genius." [105] Even *Godey's Lady's Book* praised the periodical, in the later years of the *Schoolfellow*, in these words:

> This is a very neat and valuable little work. . . . It presents a great amount of information, conveyed in a familiar, but fascinating style, and embraces among the number of its contributors several of the most popular practical writers of the country.[106]

True to his word, Richards filled the pages of the magazine with stories, poems, biographies, historical sketches, besides articles on "Table Etiquette" [107] and "Table Manners," [108] and descriptions of various specimens of animal life. The main spirit of the periodical is, of course, didactic, though many stories appear solely for the amusement of youthful readers. The following titles of original tales illustrate the general contents of the *Schoolfellow*:

"Harry's Vacation: or, a Month at Beechwood," by William C. Richards [109]
"Harry Horton and His Sister," by Aria [110]
"The Prize at School; or, The True and the False Friend," by Caroline Howard [111]
"Laduli and His Golden Dreams," by Charles L. Wheler [112]
"The Broken Necklace: or, The Falsehood," by Caroline Howard [113]
"Keeping a Journal. Or, Miss Percival's New Rule," by Mrs. Joseph C. Neal [114]

Three members of the Richards family wrote for the *Schoolfellow*. The editor's sister, Mrs. C. W. DuBose, sometimes wrote under her own name, but more frequently under the pseudonym of "Leila Cameron." She was probably, too, "Cousin Leila," whose contributions often appeared. Richards' wife also contributed stories and articles under the name of "Mrs. Manners," and she was probably the "Mrs. C. H. Richards," whose name often appears in the periodical.[115] Richards wrote many pieces of various types for the *Schoolfellow*. In addition to selected matter from Mrs. Mary Howitt, Thomas Hood, Caroline Gilman, Miss C. M. Sedgwick, and others, contributions came from the following: Miss C. W. Barber; Mrs. Caroline Lee Hentz; Caroline Howard (Mrs. Caroline Gilman Jervey); Jacques Journot (D. H. Jacques, Athens); Annie F. Law; Clara Moreton; Mrs. Joseph C. Neal; and Charles L. Wheler.

Richards left Georgia probably because he thought Charleston a better place for publishing a periodical. With his removal from the state went one of the most powerful factors in the development of periodical literature. Coming to Georgia with no previous journalistic experience, he was instrumental, in his efforts with the *Orion*, the *Southern Literary Gazette* (with its continuation, *Richards' Weekly Gazette*), and the *Schoolfellow*, in stimulating to literary activity such men as Charles L. Wheler and David L. Roath, and possibly both J. W. and T. A. Burke. Such adopted Georgians as William C. Richards and William Tappan Thompson, who, without reservation, accepted the heritage of the State as their heritage, aided greatly in setting the State on a literary eminence not below that of any other Southern state. The literary activity that Richards exemplified and stimulated in Athens has never been approached at any period in that city since the Civil War. The time was ripe, and another Athens saw, at least in part, her "Golden Age."

4. ATHENS—*MISTLETOE* (1849)

TITLE: *Mistletoe: A Magazine of the Sons of Temperance*
FIRST ISSUE: January, 1849   LAST ISSUE: March, 1849
PERIODICITY: Monthly
PUBLISHERS AND EDITORS: J. W. and T. A. Burke, Athens, January–February, 1849; Cassville, March, 1849
LOCATION OF FILES: *NN*: Jan. (pp. 1–6 missing)–March. *NcD*: Jan. (pp. 1–6 missing)–March (microfilm)

The *Mistletoe: A Magazine of the Sons of Temperance* was a monthly magazine edited and published in Athens and Cassville by John W. and Thomas A. Burke, native Georgians and sons of an Irish immigrant who had married a Georgia woman. John W. Burke was an interesting figure. After editing and publishing the Cassville (Georgia) *Standard* from 1848 to 1854, he joined the Georgia Methodist Conference, and after a few years was put in charge of the book and publishing department of the Methodist Episcopal Church, South, Publishing House in Macon. His one important literary work was his *Life of Robert Emmett, the Celebrated Irish Patriot and Martyr*.[116] Thomas A. Burke possessed a vein of humor that cropped out on numerous occasions. In 1849 and 1850 he edited and published the *Horn of Mirth*, a humorous monthly printed in Athens, which seems to have attracted much attention and actually reached a circulation of 1,200 in 1850,[117] but which appears to have entirely disappeared from view. Thomas A. Burke also edited, in 1851, a collection of humorous tales called *Polly Peablossom's Wedding; and Other Tales*,[118] which he dedicated to Johnson J. Hooper, the Alabama humorist. This collection of tales includes two by the editor: "A Losing Game of Poker, or, The Gambler Outwitted," and " 'Doing' a Sheriff. A Georgia Sketch."

The *Mistletoe*, advertised at $1 per year, appeared in only three numbers, January to March, 1849, each number consisting of from 16 to 24 pages. Its aim was to foster the Arts and Sciences in the South, as well as to promote the cause of Temperance, one of the few "isms" that flourished in the South. Each number of the periodical contained articles and poems of fair literary merit, among which are the following specially contributed:

"The Angel Hope," poem by C. L. Wheler [119]
"The Intemperate: A Thrilling Story of the West," by Mrs. L. H. Sigourney [120]
"The Child's Dream in Summer," Prize Poem by Miss Catherine W. Barber [121]

"The Sciences, Arts and Mechanics of the Ancients," by Charles L. Wheler [122]
" 'Tis the Voice of Frail Woman," poem by Edwin Heriot [123]
"Sunshine in the Cottage," poem by Miss C. W. Barber [124]
"The Bridal Eve: A Legend of the American Revolution," tale by George Lippard [125]

The *Mistletoe* also included selected articles from both British and American writers. Original contributions came from Miss Catherine W. Barber, Thomas A. Burke, J. H. Fleming, Edwin Heriot (Charleston), J. O. Rockwell, Mrs. L. H. Sigourney, and Charles Southman (Athens).

The editors and publishers ran into difficulties after two numbers had appeared, and the third was issued from Cassville, Georgia, where John W. Burke was conducting the *Standard*. This third number apologized for its delay and promised to be more regular thereafter, but no other numbers were forthcoming. The Burkes eventually turned their subscription list over to C. L. Wheler in Athens, who fulfilled the obligations the same year by sending to the *Mistletoe* subscribers his own monthly periodical, *Wheler's Magazine*, which began in July, 1849.

5. ATHENS—*WHELER'S MAGAZINE* (1849-50)

TITLE: *Wheler's Magazine*
FIRST ISSUE: July, 1849   LAST ISSUE: January, 1850(?)
PERIODICITY: Monthly
PUBLISHERS: C. L. Wheler & Bro., Athens
EDITOR: C. L. Wheler
LOCATION OF FILES: *NN:* I; II, 1. *NcD:* I; II, 1. *NjR:* II, 1

Wheler's Magazine, which began with the issue of July, 1849, was the first important literary adventure of its editor, Charles L. Wheler. It had, however, two predecessors which, after checkered careers, turned their subscription lists over to *Wheler's Magazine* for fulfilment of obligations. The first of these was *Wheler's Monthly Journal*, begun in October, 1848, by "C. L. Wheler & Bro.," Athens.[126] It has been described as "a neat little pamphlet of 16 pages—handsomely printed and freely embellished with wood cuts. . . . Its object is to afford instructive reading at a cheap rate and no one will question that it answers its end." [127] It was issued at "Fifty Cents a year," but seems to have lasted only three numbers.[128] The second predecessor of *Wheler's Magazine* was the *Mistletoe*, edited by J. W. and T. A. Burke in Athens and Cassville. When its publication was suspended after three months, the subscription list was turned over to Wheler, who completed its obligations with his own periodical. In an editorial address to the former subscribers to the *Mistletoe*, Wheler makes the following plea:

We NEED the money, and we ask every Son of Temperance (of whom we are one) to do us JUSTICE, in the name of "Love, Purity and Fidelity!" . . . Magazine Publishers live on bread and butter, just like other people. The idea that they live on air, chameleon-like, is not founded in fact. Hence we want "l'argent," that we may NOT want bread and butter.[129]

The connection of *Wheler's Magazine* with the *Monthly Journal* is indicated by the fact that the new publication begins with "New Series."

Very little is known about Charles L. Wheler beyond the fact that he had formerly been connected with the Madison (Georgia) *Family Visitor*, "which under his administration gained a good name," [130] and the fact that he had conducted the *Monthly Journal*. We do know that he contributed poems, tales, and prose articles, not only to his own periodicals, but also to the *Southern Literary Gazette, Richards' Weekly Gazette, Schoolfellow*, and *A Friend of the Family*. He was also printer for William C. Richards' *Southern Literary Gazette* from May 13 through August 12, 1848,[131] but severed his connection with that periodical to start his own *Monthly Journal*, whose Prospectus first appeared in Richards' *Gazette* for August 26, 1848.[132] Wheler, convinced that the subscription price for Southern magazines was too high, voiced his belief in the first issue of his *Magazine:*

The great fault of Magazines heretofore published at the South has been the comparative highness of their subscription price. The Southern people have repeatedly been called upon to support five-dollar Magazines which contained no more reading matter than the Northern three-dollar Magazines, for the reason that they were SOUTHERN MAGAZINES. . . .

A Dollar Magazine, of sterling merit, has been long considered a desideratum at the South. To meet this, we now offer an illustrated Magazine equal to any Northern cotemporary of the same class. We think the Dollar Magazine best suited to the wants of the Southern people. And we are not alone in this opinion. In Holden's Magazine, for May, 1849, the Editor says, (in a note touching Southern Literature,) "In starting a Magazine at the South, I would not select Graham's as the beau ideal of all excellence * * * I should greatly prefer a Dollar Magazine." [133]

The title of Wheler's periodical varies, even in the pages of the work itself. The first number bears the title *Wheler's Magazine* on its inside pages, but sometimes on the cover page it is called *Wheler's Southern Monthly Magazine*. The last extant issue [134] bears the caption *Wheler's Monthly Magazine* throughout its pages.

The first number of *Wheler's Magazine* makes a pleasing appearance, with its 24 octavo pages of two-column reading matter. It opens with two etchings: the first, of Macaulay; the second, of the "Boston Custom House." A gesture of good will is contained in the first article, a long letter from William Gilmore Simms to the editor on "Periodical Literature," which must be quoted in part:

Dear Sir—You are pleased to ask at my hands a leader for the first number of your contemplated periodical. I am scarcely in a condition to serve your purpose. . . . But I have every disposition to promote your objects; and, if the brief and hurried considerations which are here set down will contribute in any degree to your design, they are cheerfully at your service. . . . The great body of the Southern people are better informed in political affairs—on the great questions which affect the interests of the Nation—in the absolute terms of the Constitution, and in many of the subtleties which belong to the various constructions put

upon certain of its provisions—than any other people in the Union.
. . . The monthly and weekly Journals not only afford much useful and interesting material, but are usually so various in their contents, and in the many writers whom they employ, that it is scarcely possible but that every mind in a family, however they might severally differ, must discover something in their pages which shall compel thought into activity, and gratify those tastes which are most necessary and grateful to the intellectual man.
. . . The periodical, which is devoted to *all* the departments of art, letters and science, however superficial in each, is perhaps the most *suggestive* medium which Literature could employ for the benefit of the young beginner. . . .

One objection which our people entertain to subscribing to the Southern periodical, arises from the so frequent failure of the enterprize. But this failure is scarcely more frequent here than in other regions, in proportion to the number of experiments. At the North, magazines are constantly rising to the surface, only to sink out of sight in the course of a single season. Hundreds, to my knowledge, have perished within the last twenty years, which scarcely survived the first. . . . I suppose that Godey's and Graham's Magazines are the most firmly established of any, and the most profitable. Of periodicals of higher pretensions, there are very few that afford any profit to their proprietors—as few pay their contributors for articles, and most of them provide their contents by the contributions of amateurs, who, in their anxiety for print, disdain all vulgar consideration of the *money* value of what they write.

Simms closes his letter with a description of the ideal editor:

An Editor should be a gentleman, as a matter of course—governed by a high sense of propriety—calm, firm, steady, unobtrusive, and studiously just and careful in his judgments. His principles must be fixed and certain—his taste refined and always vigilant, and his manners—the manners of a periodical are, by the way, quite as essential as its morals—such as would grace the best bred courtier in the best society.

The contents of this first number appear to be entirely from Southern writers. The editor contributed an Indian tale, "The Lost Isle: A Legend of Lake Sunapee"; Jacques Journot (D. H. Jacques), "A Chapter on Guide-Posts"; Mary Lamar

(Macon), "The Lovers. A Beautiful Sketch from the German"; Olinthus Orthopolitan (Georgia), an article on the "Condition of the Mechanic Arts at the South"; and Prof. James P. Waddel (University of Georgia), a botanical article on "The Rose." Poems were contributed by Jacques Journot (D. H. Jacques), Mrs. Mary S. Whitaker (wife of D. K. Whitaker—South Carolina), Dr. Osborne A. Lochrane, and the editor. The caption "For Wheler's Magazine" appears above most of the contributions. "Editorial Bureau" occupies the last three pages of this issue—miscellaneous bits of information and anecdotes, the best of the latter being "Who'll Pay the Bill? A Humorous Sketch," by Aleck. The editor not only invites the contributions of amateur authors, but joins in the complaint "that justice has not been rendered the South by Mr. Griswold, in his 'Poets and Poetry of America.' " He promises, therefore, "to put a volume to press, containing specimens of Southern poetry, with short critico-biographical notices of our Poets." Wheler follows the custom of the day in including a short section addressed "To Correspondents," in which the editor addresses miscellaneous remarks to contributors, who are called by name, pseudonym, or initials. The first number of *Wheler's* makes interesting reading, and though its general excellence does not equal that of its contemporary, *Richards' Weekly Gazette* (continuation of the *Southern Literary Gazette*), it now and then surpassed the latter in some of its contributions.

The popular appeal of *Wheler's Magazine* is shown in the variety of its contents. The embellishments [135] consisted of portraits of Macaulay, Washington at Prayer, Cowley, Goldsmith, and Longfellow (with a very youthful face), besides such scenes as "Castles in Europe and Asia," "Moses Commanding Water out of the Rock," "Boston Custom House," "The Gallery of the American Art-Union," "The Canary," "Passing Moments," "Vignette," "Vignette to the 'Stormy Night,' " "Childhood Personified," and "Model Cottage." Among the important prose contributions are:

Second Period: 1848–54   115

"The Sunday Christian," by T. S. Arthur [136]
"The Poetry of the Rainbow," by Charles Southman [137]
"Three Scenes," by Miss C. W. Barber [138]
"The Enchanted Field," by J.C.W.—(Charleston) [139]
"The Morality of Cheating," by Olinthus Orthopolitan [140]
"The Inside of a Pie," by J. M. Legaré [141]
"Ben Houraud and the Angel. A Sketch of Persia," by Charles L. Wheler [142]
"A Story of Venice," by E.F.E. [143]
"Henry Wadsworth Longfellow," by Jacques Journot (D. H. Jacques) [144]
"The Cannon of the Palais-Royal," by Calla, "A Lady of A—" [145]
"Fate, Fortune and Co.," by O. A. Lochrane [146]
"The First Mesmeriser: or, Why 'Squire Jones Lost His Seat in the Church, A Georgia Scene," anonymous [147]
"Inez Guevara: or, The Unknown Minstrel," by "A Lady of South-Carolina" [148]
"Poetry and Poets," by Charles L. Wheler [149]
"Aaron Burr," by John Neal [150]
"Catochus; or, Burying a Man Alive," by W. W. Story [151]
"The Timely Pardon," by Thomas A. Burke [152]
"The 'Frinnolygist' at Fault," by J. J. Hooper [153]

The following poems are among the best in *Wheler's:*

"Solitude," by Osborne A. Lochrane [154]
"Song of the Georgia Farmer," by C. L. Wheler [155]
"The Three Songs," by Mrs. E. F. Ellet [156]
"Oconee," by Henry Rootes Jackson [157]
" 'Neath the Shadow of the Vine," by Robert M. Charlton [158]
"Time, Faith and Energy," by C. L. Wheler [159]
"The Prisoner," by Mrs. Mary S. Whitaker (South Carolina) [160]
"Stanzas," by William Gilmore Simms [161]
"Espanola: or, The Flower of the Everglades. . . . An Indian Legend," by Edwin Heriot [162]
"A Lay of Courage," from the Danish of Ove Malling, by Henry UU. [sic] Longfellow [163]
"The Two King's-Children," by J. M. Legaré [164]
"Where Grows the Green Palmetto Tree," by Hon. Benj. F. Porter [165]
"Love Not the World," by Miss M. J. E. Knox [166]

Possibly the most interesting contribution to *Wheler's Magazine* is the Longfellow poem, "A Lay of Courage," a translation from the Danish of Ove Malling (1746–1829). Unknown seemingly for many years because of its appearance in a little-known Georgia periodical, it was brought to light recently and reprinted in *American Literature*.[167]

The following writers contributed articles, tales, and poems to the magazine:

T. S. Arthur; Miss C. W. Barber; Thomas A. Burke; Robert M. Charlton; John D. Collins; Matilda F. Dana (Boston); Mrs. E. F. Ellet; Theodore A. Gould (New Orleans); Edwin Heriot; J. J. Hooper; Henry Rootes Jackson; Jacques Journot (D. H. Jacques, Athens); Miss M. J. E. Knox; Mary Lamar (Macon); J. M. Legaré (South Carolina); Dr. Osborne A. Lochrane; Henry W. Longfellow; John Neal (Maine); Hon. Benj. F. Porter; Edward J. Porter (Kingstree, South Carolina); Charles P. Shiras; William Gilmore Simms; Charles Southman (Athens); James P. Waddel (Athens); C. L. Wheler; Mrs. Mary S. Whitaker (South Carolina); William N. White (Athens).

Only a few contributors used pseudonyms and initials, such as: Calla, A Lady of A—; Delta (Franklin College); Glenmore; A Lady of South-Carolina; Olinthus Orthopolitan; O. A. L(ochrane).; S.P.W. (Munroe, Georgia).

It was to be expected that other Georgia periodicals would favorably review *Wheler's*, and such was the case with *A Friend of the Family* (Savannah),[168] as well as with *Richards' Weekly Gazette* (Athens).[169] *The Southern Literary Messenger* (Richmond) also gave a cordial greeting to the Athens periodical in these words:

Through inadvertence we failed to greet the first number of this pleasing little monthly, which made its appearance in July last. We have now to make our acknowledgements to the Editor for two subsequent numbers, and to welcome him cordially to the Literary Press of the South. He is supported in his undertaking by a corps of able contributors, and we shall look to him for substantial assistance in the good work of fostering a taste for letters in the Southern States.[170]

Except for a one-page notice of the publication of *Haynes' Baptist Cyclopaedia*,[171] *Wheler's Magazine* contained no advertisements, unless they appeared on the outside covers of the periodical, which are usually torn off and discarded when the separate numbers are bound. Beginning with the issue for September, 1849,[172] the editor includes in each number a section entitled "Literary Items" or "Literary Mems," miscellaneous comments on writers, books, literary events, etc. One interesting item reads thus: "Edgar A. Poe, the poet, has joined the Sons of Temperance." [173]

Literary criticism in *Wheler's Magazine* consisted of little more than a bare comment on some work just published. The practice of the writers of the day is best illustrated by the article "Henry Wadsworth Longfellow," by Jacques Journot (D. H. Jacques), in which the critic speaks thus:

> We have not spoken of Longfellow's defects as a poet; nor of the faults of his style, not because such defects and faults do not exist, but because we choose the pleasanter task of seeking for merits and beauties—
> "Seeing only what is fair.
> Sipping only what is sweet." [174]
> [Emerson, "The Humble Bee"]

The editor himself gives some frank criticism in his "Poetry and Poets," from which the following sentences are culled:

> Poetry is the offspring of a "goodly mixing" of mind and matter —an emanation from the Creator himself. . . .
> Poets are as necessary to humanity as are flowers to the field. . . .
> [Man] should contemplate Nature, and descend into his own deep soul, and silently commune there. Not like Byron should he disparage man to ennoble nature. . . .
> . . . Burns' is the Language of Nature,—a language which her offspring will understand in all coming time. But Byron's is the language of lecherous Art and affected Supernaturalism. . . . [Byron] was a wayward child—a rebellious spirit. Spoiled in infancy—soured in youth by a variety of trifling adversities—in manhood carried away by a fake philosophy, his life was indeed an "awful chaos." His friend Shelley, imbued with the same philosophy, was theoretically bad, yet practically good; but Byron was almost the opposite in character. . . .
> Byron threw himself upon the rack, and called the world to

witness his wounds; but whenever his disciples attempt the same thing, it were as they should say, "Come, look at these sores!" [175]

One interesting item in *Wheler's* is the statement that the editor offers to pay "a fair compensation for *Original Tales,* whether by professional or amateur writers." [176] He also offers his magazine for one year in return for acceptable short prose articles, and any three-dollar magazine for "any article, over two and less than five" printed pages.[177] This is the first instance where a Georgia editor is recorded as paying for contributions.

No reason can be advanced for the discontinuance of *Wheler's Magazine* except that it very probably did not have the financial support necessary to keep it going. Its Athens competitor, *Richards' Weekly Gazette,* was already in the field when *Wheler's* began, and since the former had already attained a degree of success, there was scarcely room for even a monthly periodical in that section of the state. Thus ended Wheler's efforts in behalf of Southern periodical literature.

6. SAVANNAH—*A FRIEND OF THE FAMILY* (1849–51?)

TITLE: *A Friend of the Family*
FIRST ISSUE: March 1, 1849   LAST ISSUE: March 1, 1851(?)
PERIODICITY: Weekly
EDITOR AND PUBLISHER: E. J. Purse, Savannah
LOCATION OF FILES: *GMM:* I–II (March 1, 1849–March 1, 1851)

On March 1, 1849, appeared the first number of *A Friend of the Family,* devoted to "Literature, Science, and Art, the Sons of Temperance, Odd Fellowship, Masonry, and General Intelligence." It was a weekly quarto of four pages, published in Savannah by E. J. Purse at $2 per year. In 1850 the subscription list had reached 1,000,[178] but this seems to have been the height of its popularity, for nothing is heard of it after the issue of March 1, 1851.

Susan A. Stuart, of Savannah, one of the principal contributors to this periodical, wrote numerous tales which appeared serially in its pages. C. L. Wheler, L. T. Voigt, A. B. Meek, and Annie Lee also wrote for the publication. The most popular contributions, however, appear to have been those of William Tappan Thompson. Exploits of "Major Jones" appeared in its pages, among them the following: "The Augur-Hole in the Chimney-Piece," [179] "The Baby's Ghost," [180] and "What Made the Baby Cry." [181] The longest of Thompson's contributions was "Major Jones' Courtship, or Adventures of a Christmas Eve: A Domestic Comedy in Two Acts," a dramatization of the famous Christmas-Eve adventure of Major Jones, in which he offers himself to his lady-love by placing himself in a large sack hanging on her back porch. This drama ran serially from March 23 to April 20, 1850.[182] It is not a drama in the true sense of the word, but is rather an arrangement in dramatic form of the dialogue of the original tale, which had appeared in 1840 in his *Major Jones' Courtship*.

Another interesting local-color story, the anonymous "First Mesmeriser: or, Why Squire Jones Lost His Seat in the Church," appeared in the number for November 15, 1849,[183] being reprinted from *Wheler's Magazine* (Athens).[184] *A Friend of the Family*, like many of its predecessors and contemporaries, aimed at being a family paper, and as such it, too, in all likelihood proved to be "an interesting and instructive fireside companion" [185] to a few people as long as it was published.

7. ATHENS—*ROATH'S MONTHLY MAGAZINE* (1853)

TITLE: *Roath's Monthly Magazine*
FIRST ISSUE: January, 1853   LAST ISSUE: February, 1853(?)
PERIODICITY: Monthly
PUBLISHERS: Christy & Kelsea, Athens
EDITOR: David L. Roath
LOCATION OF FILES: *NcD:* I, 1–2

Standing almost alone in the 1850's is *Roath's Monthly Magazine*, begun in Athens in January, 1853, and published by Christy & Kelsea. Though the editor's name is nowhere mentioned in the periodical, we learn elsewhere that he was David L. Roath, of Athens, whose name had been "long and favorably known in the literary circles of our country." [186] He is the Roath who, in 1851, published *Zara: A Romance*,[187] a satire in the manner of Byron's *Don Juan*, with the scene laid in Georgia on the banks of the Savannah River, and who, the following year, published *The Five Love Adventures of Solomon Slug, and Other Sketches*.[188] Though the magazine was published in Athens, the editorial office was in Augusta. Six numbers were to constitute a volume, and the price was $1 per volume. Roath's policy was that "No name will be entered without the cash." [189] Mindful of the fate of previous Georgia periodicals, the editor makes the following promise in the first number:

> One volume of this Magazine will be published, whether we receive adequate support or not. . . . We consider the proprietors of every periodical under an implied contract with their subscribers, to furnish them with the publication or to refund the money.—This contract will be most faithfully adhered to on our part.[190]

Whether this promise was fulfilled or not is not certain, for only the first two issues of the periodical survive. Both numbers, consisting each of 48 octavo pages, two columns to a page, are printed in blue ink. The workmanship is very neat and artistic, the reading matter being far superior to that of most earlier Georgia periodicals.

Roath seems to have had the highest ideals for his magazine, as we see from his first "Editor's Table":

> Foremost among the necessaries of civilized life, at this day, are magazines and newspapers. They are the only source of information accessible to thousands of our countrymen. In view of this fact, then, should we not consider it an absolute duty to establish and sustain a home literature? . . . We have, within our control, all the material for acquiring and establishing literary reputation. . . . Georgia, the Empire State of the South . . . has scarcely a single Journal devoted to general literature, and designed for the lighter amusement . . . of her citizens. . . . We shall not make any extraordinary efforts to get our Magazine before all or any portion of the public. . . . If our intention was to

get the greatest amount of money possible, in the shortest time, our course would be extremely different.[191]

No author's name is anywhere attached to any poem, article, or tale. Roath thus explains: "We have, after deliberation, adopted the plan of publishing each article without the name of the author. For this course we shall, probably, at some future day, give our reasons."[192] No reasons are forthcoming from the two extant numbers, but from a close examination of the contents one suspects that the editor himself wrote most of the contributions. Yet there is decided merit in everything of any length. There is a spirit of satire running all through the periodical. The best examples of this spirit are "Trials of an Author,"[193] "Model Letters,"[194] "First Grand Exhibition of the Squashville Academy of Science,"[195] and "Mr. and Mrs. Skinflint; or, One Week of Married Life."[196] The last-named piece is one of the best to be found in any *ante-bellum* Georgia periodical, yet it is free from the coarseness that often characterizes early Georgia humor. Roath caters to sentimental readers in "Parson Paul: A Tale of the Revolution"[197] and "The Triumph of Love."[198] The political element is found in a eulogy of "Henry Clay."[199] The poetry consists of the humorous "Recollections"[200] and "The Amazed";[201] the narrative "Snow-Storm,"[202] in the manner of Wordsworth's "Lucy Gray," but with a happy ending; and "The Continentals";[203] the sentimental "'Smile of Aidenn,"[204] "The Shadow,"[205] and "To a Friend";[206] and the stirring "Song of the Revolution,"[207] strongly suggestive of Longfellow's rhythm. Passing over the little "fillers" scattered throughout, we turn to Roath's literary criticism.

Roath discusses only three works in his "Literary Notices." The first is the *Lays of the Scottish Cavaliers, and Other Poems*, by William Edmondstoune Aytoun,[208] editor of *Blackwood's Magazine*,[209] which he calls "a great book." "We have not enough of such publications," pursues Roath. "Our authors and publishers are too busily engaged in pandering to a morbid appetite of the public—they find too good an account in ministering to the excitable natures of a class unable to comprehend any other style but the one appropriately denominated the 'blood and thunder' style." One of the *Lays*, "The Execution of Montrose," which Roath considers the "gem of the whole collection," is quoted at some length as an example of beauty. The second book reviewed is *A Faggot of French Sticks, or, Paris in 1851*, by Sir Francis Head, author of "Bubbles from the Brunnen of Nassau," [210] which is commended as "a most *piquant* volume—combining with an entertaining facility of description a large fund of valuable information." The third work is *The Book of Ballads*, edited by Bon Gualtier, New York, 1852,[211] which Roath describes as "a work like the Dutchman's razors, 'made to sell!' " He quotes one ballad, "Parr's Life Pills," but refrains from quoting more, for "a few more extracts might tend to injure the sale of the book!" In an article entitled "Cheap Literature" [212] the editor defends the cheap editions of works of literature as ministering to the needs of "a territory fast filling with a population whose natural gifts are unsurpassed, and whose desires for knowledge and amusement will increase in exact proportion to the speed with which those desires can be gratified." He does, however, condemn the "flimsy romances," which "are the delight of the young of both sexes, and which with their feeble flights of a diseased fancy are as welcome to them as is food to the starving."

Roath's Monthly Magazine seems to have been favorably received, at least by the Press.[213] "The blue ink takes very generally," declares the editor, "and we think justly, for we regard it as far more beautiful than black ink. Out of the large number of notices we have seen, but two have voted 'no' to the *blue*. The authors of these are perhaps, like old mill-horses, who have been accustomed for so many long years to hobble a beaten round, that it is utterly impossible for them to appreciate anything like novelty." [214] There is nothing pedantic about Roath's periodical. It was an attempt to instill an element of freshness and originality into Georgia periodical literature, and with the demise of the magazine, probably some time in 1853, disappeared the promise of some worth-while humorous satire and criticism. And with it passed the last attempt to make Athens a center for periodical literature in *ante-bellum* Georgia.

8. AUGUSTA—*SOUTHERN ECLECTIC* (1853-54)

TITLE: *Southern Eclectic*
FIRST ISSUE: March, 1853   LAST ISSUE: June, 1854(?)
PERIODICITY: Monthly
PUBLISHER: J. H. Fitten, Augusta
EDITORS: J. H. Fitten, March–April, 1853; J. H. Fitten and James M. Smythe, May–June, 1853; J. H. Fitten, July–August, 1853; J. H. Fitten and Daniel K. Whitaker, September, 1853–February, 1854; Daniel K. Whitaker, March–June, 1854(?)
LOCATION OF FILES: *A:* II, 12. *DLC:* I–III (inc.). *GAuY:* II. *GU:* I, 1–6; II, 7–8, 10; III, 13, 15, 16. *NcD:* I, 1–3, 5–6; II, 7–12; III, 13–16. *NcU:* I–II

The only purely eclectic magazine in *ante-bellum* Georgia was the *Southern Eclectic,* established in Augusta in March, 1853, by J. H. Fitten, editor and proprietor, about whom nothing is known beyond the fact that he was a native Georgian.[215] The first number consisted of 80 pages, "Composed chiefly," says the outside cover, "of Selections from the Best Journals of Europe." Very little space is devoted to American works. In fact, out of thirteen articles in this number only three are on American topics; and out of eight book reviews only three are of American works. The percentage of American articles and reviews for the six numbers of Volume I is actually smaller than that for the first issue: out of sixty-seven articles only nine are on American topics, and out of forty-seven book reviews only four are of American works. The first issue of this new Augusta monthly is typical of all subsequent issues, at least for the first volume, and includes, besides minor articles, such selected writings as:

Review of *The Works of Daniel Webster,* 6 vols., from the *Westminster Review*
Review of Thackeray's *Henry Esmond,* from the *Eclectic Review*

Review of *Memoir, Journal, and Correspondence of Thomas Moore,* from *Fraser's Magazine*
"Concerning British Free Negros [sic]," letter to editor of *Fraser's Magazine*
"The Golden Guillotine," tale by Shafto D'Abzac, from the *Dublin University Magazine*
"Captain Fitzroy Smith's Adventures in Connaught," from the *United Service Journal*
"England and the United States," from the London *Times*
"On the Literature of the Island of Cuba," translated from the German of the *Weser Zeitung*, for the *Southern Eclectic*

For the issue of May, 1853, Fitten was joined in the editorship by James M. Smythe, who, after remaining with the periodical only two issues, resigned to accept the postmastership of Augusta. Smythe, also a native Georgian,[216] a few years later published a novel entitled *Ethel Somers*.[217] In September, 1853, the *Southern Eclectic* was combined with *Whitaker's Southern Magazine* (Columbia) under the former title, and continued to be published in Augusta. Daniel K. Whitaker, the new associate editor with Fitten, was born in Massachusetts in 1801, but soon after graduation from Harvard had settled in South Carolina. He had edited the *Southern Literary Journal* (Charleston), 1835-37, and the *Southern Quarterly Review* (New Orleans and Charleston), 1842-47, before establishing *Whitaker's Magazine* (the first title used) in July, 1850.[218] Whitaker began to include a few original contributions after he joined the periodical, many of which were by his wife, Mary Scrimzeour, who was already a well-known poet when he married her in 1849. In March, 1854, Whitaker became sole editor of the *Eclectic,* which he conducted till it was combined with the Augusta *Home Gazette,* some time in the fall of 1854, after which time its literary importance ceased.

The aim of the *Southern Eclectic* may be summed up in the words of Fitten and Smythe in the third number of the periodical:

There is no other work similar to that of the Southern Eclectic south of Mason and Dixon's line. This is, therefore, emphatically *The Southern Eclectic*. If there be a patriotism in Literature, as there is in politics, we would appeal to it on this occasion. Certainly the South should rely more upon herself than she now does, for her intellectual gratifications. The Editors of the Southern Eclectic are Georgians by birth, and are ready to contribute everything in their power to the common stock of Southern mental enjoyment, as they are to Southern prosperity and security. . . . It will be seen that the ECLECTIC will contain *nine hundred and sixty pages* of reading matter for the year, in a form suitable for binding and preservation.[219]

An additional comment on the character of the reading matter of the magazine is found in the editors' outline of policy:

Whatever is remarkable in the forms or changes of Government or Society, illustrious in Character, striking or novel in Art or Science, with whatever is richest in the range of the world's Literature, will be strikingly illustrated. We intend that it shall meet the wants even of an *arbiter elegantiarum*, as well as of those who would be so versed in the grand features of human progress as to feel, at least, composed, among those who claim to be upon the summit level of the great empire of Mind.[220]

The *Southern Eclectic,* in its attractive octavo form, elicited favorable criticism in many places. Besides praises from Georgia papers, compliments came from all over the South.[221] The *Southern Quarterly Review* (Charleston) describes the reading matter of the *Eclectic* as "selected with judgment, and with reference to the special wants of American readers." [222] The *Southern Literary Messenger* (Richmond) thus comments on the *Eclectic:* "It is composed of selections from the best journals of Europe on the plan of Littell's Living Age [London], and from the number before us we have no hesitation in declaring that these selections evince the best taste and discrimination of the editor." [223]

Fitten and Whitaker, in "An Appeal to the Citizens of the South in Behalf of the Southern Eclectic," plead the cause of

Southern periodicals as opposed to the support of those coming in from the North:

> The North has never been willing to give the South a hearing on this subject [slavery and social conditions]. . . . While Southern periodicals are wholly precluded from northern circulation simply because they emanate from the South where slavery prevails, there is no good reason why any extraordinary eagerness should be manifested at the South to sustain the interests of northern periodicals . . . provided, we can have periodicals of our own of equal ability, and which are unexceptionable in this particular.[224]

The predominance of European interests over American interests in the *Eclectic* is explained chiefly by the absence of any international copyright agreement; hence Southern periodicals could use British periodical literature at no expense to themselves. The fact that the circulation of the *Eclectic* reached about 2,100 in 1854 [225] indicates, too, that Southerners were interested in the literature and affairs of the world in general.

Following is a list of foreign periodicals from which selections were taken for the *Southern Eclectic:*

Westminster Review (London)
Fraser's Magazine (London)
Dickens' Household Words (London)
Dublin University Magazine
London *Times*
Diogenes (London)
Hogg's Instructor (London)
Tait's Magazine (Edinburgh)
Weser Zeitung (Bremen)
London *Quarterly Review*
Ainsworth's Magazine (London)
Colburn's New Monthly Magazine (London)
Eliza Cook's Journal (London)
Gentleman's Magazine (London)
London *Athenaeum*
Chambers's Edinburgh Journal
London *Examiner*
Revue des Deux Mondes (Paris)
Constitutionnel (Paris?)
Retrospective Review (London)

Eclectic Review (London)
Bentley's Miscellany (London)
Punch (London)
London *Spectator*
London *Critic*
North British Review (Edinburgh)
London *Literary Gazette*
Sharpe's London Magazine
Edinburgh Review
London *Literary Journal*

Selected matter from American periodicals came only from the Charleston *Courier*, the New Orleans *Delta*, and the *United Service Journal* (New York).

The best of the selected articles and reviews are the following:

"The Golden Guillotine," tale by Shafto D'Abzac, from the *Dublin University Magazine* [226]
"Christopher Marlowe," by Rev. Alexander Dyce, from *Fraser's Magazine* [227]
"Julius Caesar and Napoleon Buonaparte," by J.W.C., from *Dublin University Magazine* [228]
"Ancient English Ballad Poetry," from *Retrospective Review* [229]
"The Religious Poets of the Eighteenth and Nineteenth Centuries. James Thompson [sic]," by George Gilfillan, from *Hogg's Instructor* [230]
"The Critics of the Age. Hazlitt and Hallam," by Apollodorus, from London *Literary Journal* [231]
"Literary Movements in Germany," translated from the *Revue des Deux Mondes* [232]
"Wanderings through London," from *Fraser's Magazine* [233]
"What Constitutes a Poet," from *Hogg's Instructor* [234]
"Thackeray's Works," from *Westminster Review* [235]
"American Authorship," by Sir Nathaniel, from *Colburn's New Monthly*, dealing with Irving, Dana, Hawthorne, Melville, George William Curtis, Holmes, Longfellow, Bryant, N. P. Willis, and Donald G. Mitchell [236]
"John Knox," from *Westminster Review* [237]
"Poe and Poetry," from *Dublin University Magazine* [238]
"The Crown and the Dagger. A Tale of the Third Crusade," from *Dublin University Magazine* [239]
"Modern British Authors," by George Gilfillan, from *Hogg's In-

structor, dealing with Edmund Burke and Richard Brinsley Sheridan [240]
"Memoranda by a Marine Officer," from *Hogg's Instructor* [241]
"Electro-Biology and Mesmerism," from London *Quarterly Review* [242]
"The Life and Times of Madame de Staël," from *North British Review* [243]

With the coming of Whitaker to the editorship of the *Southern Eclectic*, original compositions were added to the reading matter. Such contributions came from Alpha, Alteram Partem, C. (New Orleans), Thomas Bibb Bradley (Huntsville, Alabama), Julien, D. K. Whitaker, Mrs. D. K. Whitaker, J. W. D(avidson?)., T.W. (Marietta, Georgia), and W. W. Poems were scarce, but tales and prose articles appeared to be popular. The following are possibly the best of those "Written for the Southern Eclectic":

"Southern Literature," by J. W. D[avidson?] [244]
"The War of the Fanatics," by Alpha—on slavery [245]
"Florence Mortimer; or, The Force of Love," by Mrs. (D. K.) Whitaker [246]
"Freedom in England and Slavery in America," anonymous [247]
"Legislative Interference with the Education of the People," by T.W. [248]
"The Two Books of Revelation," by Julien [249]
"American Colleges," by W.W. [250]
"The Rights, Duties and Responsibilities of the Conductors of the Press," by W[hitaker] [251]

The *Southern Eclectic* had no rival of any importance in Georgia, and should have had a support sufficient to keep it going. Why it did not succeed we cannot tell, unless it was the usual indifference of Southerners to works published in their midst. As an eclectic magazine it was as good as the average in the country, but it needed something more than excellence to guarantee a continued existence, and that something was not forthcoming.

CHAPTER III

Third Period: 1859–65

INTRODUCTION

THE PERIOD 1859–65 in Georgia represents one of renewed intellectual activity on many lines. The population of the State had made a substantial increase between 1850 and 1860, according to the U.S. Census. Whereas in 1850 the population was 521,572 whites and 381,682 slaves, in 1860 it was 591,588 whites and 462,198 slaves. Not only was the oratorical and political interest at its height, but interest in literature seemed to be increasing. The drama was popular in certain towns, as we learn from the newspapers of the day. Even in 1863, when the Civil War was in full swing, dramatic performances in Augusta included such original productions as *The Viviandiere, The Scouts, The Prisoner of Monterey,* and *King Linkum the First,* the latter a "comical burletta on the Cabinet at Washington." Prof. J. H. Hewitt, the "Father of American Ballad Poetry," was the author of several of these.[1] Mr. Waldron, of the "Thespians," the Augusta theatrical troupe, was at that time offering $300 for the best melodrama in three acts, and $200 for the second-best, "founded on events of the present war."[2] On March 14, 1863, the Thespians, after a successful season of some seventy nights, closed their stay in Augusta with *Still Waters Run Deep,* by Tom Taylor, and *The Veteran,* an adaptation from the French, by J. H. Hewitt.

From Augusta the troupe went to Savannah for performances.[3] In addition to drama given in Atlanta,[4] during the war presentations were given in Macon of Shakespeare's *Merchant of Venice*, as well as of *Pocahontas: or, The Gentle Savage*, the famed extravaganza by John Brougham, of London. *Camille* [5] also had more than one performance in that city.[6]

The first effect of the Civil War was to stimulate a movement for a purely Southern literature, since the South had definitely declared herself an independent nation. This movement was partly responsible for the many attempts to establish periodicals and to set up adequate printing and publishing houses in the South. West & Johnston started a large publishing house in Richmond to rival the firm of Harpers, and magazines sprang up almost overnight all over the South. War and the blockade of Southern ports cut off the section from Northern and English books and periodicals, and the South had to depend upon her own resources for new reading matter. By 1863, of course, conditions became increasingly unfavorable, and with a shortage of paper, ink, and labor, Southern papers and magazines began to die off in increasing numbers. During the war, however, it seemed a patriotic duty to write for the Southern cause, and some writers who had never before written anything began to contribute to periodicals. All these conditions were doubtless responsible for the degree of success attained by two Georgia magazines: the *Countryman* and the *Southern Field and Fireside*, both of which apparently had large circulations during the war.

Southern opinion concerning literary vassalage to the North at this time may be seen crystallized in the words of Atticus G. Haygood, then a young man, but later a bishop in the Methodist Episcopal Church, South. In the *Educational Repository and Family Monthly* (Atlanta) for February, 1861, he thus propounds his views:

The South must know the absolute necessity of having an *indigenous literature;* she must second the efforts that are and shall be made, with a generosity worthy of her name; and her gifted sons and daughters must rally to the defense of all true Southern interests, and unite in rearing a pyramid of learning, that may stand when our enemies live only in history. . . . And there is a peculiar *balance* about the Southern mind, that will effectually shield us from the wasting influences of the various "Isms," that like monstrous *fungi*, have grown out from Northern character. . . . The peculiar forms of infidelity that have torn down so many sacred altars in the North, will not flourish so luxuriantly under the influence of a Southern philosophy.[7]

Perhaps the most potent contention of Haygood in this article is one borne out by history itself in its more general aspects:

Great moral, or political, revolutions nearly always inaugurate new eras in literature. Witness that period in English authorship called the Elizabethan. . . . In America, the conclusion of the Revolution was the beginning of a new and a greater era in our literature. . . . We are now in the midst of a great revolution—we are to be "a peculiar people," and our literature ought to bear the impress of our distinctive characteristics. It must, then, *be created; and never was there a more glorious prospect than is now inviting Southern talent.*[8]

The "glorious prospect" referred to by Haygood was soon crushed by the oppression of War, and the Civil War drained the South in so many ways that a New South had to emerge before a greater era in Southern literature could be born.

Literary activity was going on all over the South just before the Civil War. One of the best monthlies of the Old South was running during the early part of the period 1859–65. *Russell's Magazine* (Charleston) had been established in 1857 by John Russell under the editorship of Paul Hamilton Hayne and W. B. Carlisle as a medium for the expression of Southern thought and feeling.[9] The magazine, however, did not last long; it was discontinued in 1860 ostensibly because the editors were forced to devote their energies to other demands. The cordial relations among most Southern periodicals at this time is reflected in the notices they published about each other. Both *Russell's* and the *Southern Literary Messenger* (Richmond) made favorable comments on the Georgia periodicals of this period.

In the North were several excellent literary periodicals at this time. The *North American Review* (Boston), in existence since 1815, was perhaps the leading quarterly in the country, with a circulation which, though small, "was distributed throughout the country." [10] The *Atlantic Monthly* (Boston), established in 1857 under the editorship of James Russell Lowell, stood at the top in literary excellence, with contributions from Emerson, Whittier, Lowell, Longfellow, Holmes, and other prominent New Englanders.[11] *Harper's Monthly Magazine* (New York), established in 1850, was another flourishing periodical, with tales and articles from both British and American authors.[12] Perhaps the most popular Northern magazines at this time were *Godey's Lady's Book* (Philadelphia), *Knickerbocker* (New York), and *Graham's Magazine* (Philadelphia), all of which are constantly mentioned in their Georgia contemporaries.

Besides the important literary periodicals of this period in Georgia there were a number of lesser ones that apppeared. For the benefit of the soldiers of the Confederacy two periodicals were published in the State during the war:

Atlanta—*Soldiers' Friend.* Devoted to the Intellectual, Moral and Religious Interests of the Soldier. Edited by J. J. Richards, and published every Saturday by A. S. Worrell. First number, January 10, 1863. Files: *GAH:* 1864, Feb. 25 (mut.); Mar. 3 (mut.); Apr. 14 (mut.); May 12; May 26 (mut.); June 2 (mut.); June 9 (mut.); June 16, 30.

Macon—*Army and Navy Herald.* "Published weekly for gratuitous circulation amongst the soldiers of the army and navy, supported by voluntary contributions of their friends at home." Edited by Robert J. Harp, with the Rev. J. W. Burke as Treasurer of the Soldiers' Tract Association, Macon. Begun in 1864. Files: *DLC:* 1865, Jan. 5, Mar. 16, 23, 30. *MWA:* 1864, Nov. 1; 1865, Mar. 30. *NNHi:* 1863, Nov. 1; 1865, Mar. 16–Apr. 13. *NcD:* 1865, Feb. 9; Mar. 16, 23, 30; Apr. 6. *OClWHi:* 1865, Feb. 23.

Five educational periodicals appeared, published either in the general interest of education or by students of some educational institution:

Forsyth—*Educational Journal.* Weekly, 1857-61. U.S. Census for 1860 gives 800 subscribers. No files located.[13]

Covington—*College Miscellany and Orphan's Advocate.* Monthly, published by the Masonic Female College, 1858-59? No files located.[14]

Marietta—*Kennesaw Gem.* Quarterly, "Devoted to Improvement in Composition, the Promotion of Female Education, and the Elevation of Woman." Published in 1859 by the "Young Ladies of Marietta Female College." Notice that a copy has been received is found in *Southern Field and Fireside* (Augusta), I, 25 (Nov. 12, 1859), p. 196. No files located.

Atlanta—*Educational Repository and Family Monthly,* 1860-61. Organ of the Educational Institute of the Methodist Episcopal Church, South. Edited successively by the Rev. J. Knowles, Prof. W. H. C. Price, and Greene B. Haygood. Files: *DE:* I (inc.). *DLC:* CF. *GE:* I. *GMW:* I *IEG:* I (inc.). *N:* I (inc.). *NcD:* I, 1-10; II.

Lumpkin—*Educational Monthly.* Published and edited during the Civil War by Mrs. Mary A. McCrimmon, who lived at Lumpkin. Statement of *Living Female Writers of the South* (Philadelphia, 1872), p. 212. No files located.

Other periodicals of literary interest during the period were:

Fayetteville—*Literary Casket.* Weekly, 1859-? U.S. Census for 1860 gives 1,200 subscribers. No files located.[15]

Waynesboro—*Gopher.* Semi-weekly humorous periodical. U.S. Census for 1860 gives 50 subscribers. No files located.

Greenville(?)—*Georgia Weekly.* Quarto established by William Henry Peck in 1860. "After a brief struggle for existence, it went down," says James Wood Davidson, *Living Writers of the South* (New York, 1869), pp. 408-409. No files located.

Macon—*Child's Index.* Monthly, published and edited by Samuel Boykin. Probably a Baptist Sunday School paper. Begun September, 1862. Circulation of 4,000, says issue of February, 1863. Joel Chandler Harris, at age of fifteen, contributed "Charlie Howard; or, Who Is the Good Boy?"—a very sentimental and didactic short story—to the issue for July, 1863 (I, 7). Files: *GE:* June, 1863. *NcD:* I (1862-63); II (1864), 1-7, 9-12; III (1865), 2-4. *VaRCM:* Jan., 1865.

Macon—*Children's Guide.* Monthly, 1864-? Files: *VaRCM:* Oct., 1864.

Atlanta—*Scott's Monthly Magazine.* Edited by J. J. Toon. Begun in 1865. Files: *NcD:* I, 1–2, 5–6; II, 1, 3, 5–6; III, 1, 5. [For further files see *Union List of Serials.*]

1. ATLANTA—*MEDICAL AND LITERARY WEEKLY* (1859)

TITLE: *Medical and Literary Weekly*
FIRST ISSUE: May 7, 1859   LAST ISSUE: October 22, 1859
PERIODICITY: Weekly
PUBLISHERS AND EDITORS: Dr. V. H. Taliaferro and Dr. A. G. Thomas, Atlanta, May 7–October 15, 1859; Dr. V. H. Taliaferro, Atlanta, October 22, 1859
LOCATION OF FILES: *NNN:* 1859, May 14 (mut.), 28; Aug. 6, 20, 27; Sept. 10, 17, 24, 31 [sic]; Oct. 8, 15, 22. *NcD:* Photostats of above file

The strangest hybrid in the periodical literature of *antebellum* Georgia was the *Medical and Literary Weekly,* established in Atlanta on May 7, 1859, by Dr. V. H. Taliaferro and Dr. A. G. Thomas as editors and proprietors. The aim of these two men seems to have been to appeal to the general public in a "double-barrel" fashion, for there was no connection between the medical and the literary departments except that both were printed together as one issue. Since the medical department contains nothing of literary interest, our attention will be confined to that part devoted especially to literature. Each number consisted of eight quarto pages, the first three of which were usually devoted to medical interests, the next three to literature, one to news, and one to advertisements. Although no special editor is assigned to it, the Literary Department contains, week by week, contributions that are still entertaining. Atlanta, incorporated in 1847, was a fast-growing little city, with an estimated population in 1859 of 11,500;[16] and since it was rapidly becoming a central point for the distribution of periodical literature, it seemed an admirable location for reaching a responsive constituency.

The first number of the *Medical and Literary Weekly,* dated May 7, 1859, is not extant, but the second is typical of the twelve numbers still preserved. Each of the twelve contains one or two tales, sometimes in serial form, and one or more short poems. Selected matter appears now and then, such as "The Maid of Treppi,"[17] an anonymous tale from the *Westminster*

Third Period: 1859–65

Review (London), and "Shadow.—A Parable," by Edgar A. Poe.[18] The original contributions are, with a very few exceptions, decidedly mediocre, yet several prominent writers, mainly women, wrote for the periodical. In the second number the public is informed that the editors have fitted up a reading room where "Especial attention will be given to the literary department . . . for the benefit of the Ladies."[19] In the fourth number [20] the editors offer a prize of $200 "For the best original Romance," and a silver cup "For the Best Poem," besides other prizes for articles on hygiene, etc. The awards for these two literary prizes were announced in the issue for October 15, 1859,[21] as follows: "Jessie Randolph," [22] for the best romance,[23] and Dr. A(lexander). Means, for the best poem.[24] The prize-winning contributions appeared the following year in the *Hygienic and Literary Magazine* (Atlanta), the successor to the *Medical and Literary Weekly*. The judges were announced as Prof. W. H. Brown,[25] Mr. W. T. C. Campbell,[26] and Mr. J(ames). S. Slaughter.[27] The last number of the periodical, that of October 22, 1859,[28] informed the public that owing to the removal of one of the editors, Dr. Thomas, from Atlanta, the paper would be changed to a monthly, beginning in December of the same year. Not only did delays intervene, but the entire printing establishment was destroyed by fire in November of the same year; [29] consequently the new monthly did not appear till January, 1860. Dr. Taliaferro, in the last issue of the *Weekly*, speaks of the "well established success" of the periodical; hence we presume that he was not disappointed in the popular support of his undertaking.

The most important articles and tales appearing in the *Weekly* were:

"Alice Harcourt. A Story of Excitement," by James Summerfield [30]
"A Sketch from Real Life," by Kitty Clyde [31]
"England and Napoleon Bonaparte," by K.[32]
"Pencil Sketches of the Mammoth Cave," by Tallulah [33]
"The Flower Basket," by M. Louise Rogers [34]
"Letters from Tallulah Falls," by Tallulah [35]

"Where Tallulah's Thunder-Waters Fall," by M. L. R[ogers] [36]
"Heart Changes," by La Josse [37]

Several poems of some degree of merit appeared:

"No Land So Free as Ours," by Finley Johnson [38]
"A Summer Day," by M. Louise Rogers [39]
"The Holy Stars Are Out, Mother," by Jennie Woodbine (Annie R. Blount) [40]
"How to Win Her," by Jennie Woodbine (Annie R. Blount) [41]
"Woman's Love," by Jennie Woodbine (Annie R. Blount) [42]
"Love's Maladies," by Mary E. Bryan [43]
"Day Dreams," by Leola (Mrs. Loula Kendall Rogers) [44]

Contributors to the *Medical and Literary Weekly* made frequent use of initials and pseudonyms. The following appear in the pages of the periodical: Dogwood; F.W.C. (Atlanta); Jennie Woodbine (Annie R. Blount); K.; La Josse; Le Ferve (Mrs. Dr. Riley); Leola (Mrs. Loula Kendall Rogers); Marinda (Oak Grove, Georgia); [45] M.L.F.; M.L.R.; Tallulah. The following names are attached to contributions: Mary E. Bryan; Kitty Clyde; Finley Johnson (Baltimore); and Miss M. Louise Rogers (Atlanta). A few names are listed as belonging to contributors, but their works do not appear in the extant numbers: Mr. A. D. Burns (Texas); Mr. W. T. C. Campbell (Atlanta); Mr. Theodore Hunter (Abbeville, South Carolina); Prof. B. L. Jones (Savannah); Nette Jones; Jessie Randolph (Atlanta); Mr. George P. Screven (Savannah); Mr. James S. Slaughter (Atlanta); Mrs. T. I. Slaughter (Atlanta); Miss O. L. Thomas (Alabama); Mrs. W. F. Westmoreland (Atlanta); and Mr. J. P. C. Whitehead (Augusta).

2. AUGUSTA—*SOUTHERN FIELD AND FIRESIDE* (1859–64)

TITLE: *Southern Field and Fireside*
FIRST ISSUE: May 28, 1859   LAST ISSUE: October 29, 1864 (in Georgia)
PERIODICITY: Weekly. (No numbers between November 15, 1862, and first Saturday in January, 1863.)
PUBLISHERS: James Gardner, Augusta, 1859–63; Stockton & Company, Augusta, January–October, 1864. (Afterwards moved to Raleigh, North Carolina.)
EDITORS OF LITERARY DEPARTMENT: W. W. Mann, May 28, 1859–May,

1860; John R. Thompson, May, 1860–?; James Nathan Ells, 1860-62; S. A. Atkinson, 1862-63; no editor indicated, 1863-64.
LOCATION OF FILES: *A:* I. 1–52. *DLC:* I (inc.)–III. N.S. I–II (inc.). *GE:* I. *GMM:* 1859-60. *GU:* I, 8, 12, 15, 18, 42–45; II, 4–9, 11–28, 32. *MBAt:* Jan. 2, Aug. 30, 1864. *NcD:* I, 1–17, 19–26, 28, 51; II, 8, 11–12, 38, 42; III, 7, 11, 13, 18, 20; IV, 14, 26; N.S. I, 2, 4–8, 11–17, 20–22, 29–30, 37–38; N.S. II, 1, 3–4, 6–9, 11–17, 19–28, 32–34, 36, 38–39, 41–43, 45 (last number published in Raleigh). *TxU:* 1859. *Va:* I, 1–52. *VaRCM:* May 3, 1862; Sept. 12–26, 1863.

The *Southern Field and Fireside,* a weekly folio of eight pages to an issue, made its initial appearance in Augusta on May 28, 1859, with James Gardner as proprietor. It was composed of three parts: the literary, the agricultural, and the horticultural, and was priced at $2 per year. The first issue, with its attractive reading matter and with nearly an entire page devoted to advertisements, was enough to promise success to its proprietor. The publisher's Prospectus runs true to Southern form in stating the aims of the periodical:

Too long the Southern people have been content to look to Northern periodicals for instruction in agricultural matters, and to Northern literary papers for mental recreation. There is, however, a growing spirit of independence and of self-reliance at the South. Our people are awaking to the conviction that we have the elements of success in the experience, knowledge, and scientific investigation, of the dwellers in our own Southern homes. The truth is gleaming upon us, that we have literary resources of our own worthy to be fostered—that among Southern writers should be divided some portion of that vast stream of Southern money that flows perpetually northward to sustain Northern literature.

My aim [as publisher] is to establish a paper that will be a vehicle of information to Southern Planters and Farmers, and a repository of Southern thought, imagination and taste, in the realms of Literature and Art; and to obtain for it such an extent of patronage and success, as will justify the most liberal compensation to all its contributors. Able and experienced editors are engaged, and steps are in progress to secure contributions from the most pleasing Southern writers, of both sexes. Much latent talent will be brought to light, and furnish some agreeable surprises to Southern people.

"Full many a gem, of purest ray serene,"

will flash before their admiring eyes, and cause a generous glow of pride in Southern genius.

The Agricultural Editor is Dr. Daniel Lee, the distinguished Professor of Agriculture in the University of Georgia—editor for many years of the Southern Cultivator [Augusta], and a leading contributor to many Northern agricultural journals of the highest reputation.

The Literary Editor is Mr. W. W. Mann, of this city, an accomplished writer, of fine taste, and scholarly attainments, who, having retired from the active duties of the legal profession, spent many years in Europe, and was for several years the Paris Correspondent of the *National Intelligencer* and *Southern Literary Messenger*.[46]

The first number of the work added a horticultural department under the editorship of William N. White, formerly a printer in Athens, and author of *Gardening for the South*.[47] The Prospectus further states:

THE SOUTHERN FIELD AND FIRESIDE will combine the useful and the agreeable. It will furnish the Southern Farmer information useful in every field he cultivates, and the Southern Family choice literature, the offspring of Southern intellect, worthy of welcome at every fireside. It will be, in all respects, a first class paper—on a scale of expenditure more liberal than has yet been attempted in the South, and designed to rival, in its merits, the most distinguished of the North.[48]

The first number of the *Southern Field and Fireside,* as well as each of those succeeding, devoted a little more than half of its pages to literary interests, and our attention will be centered only on the literary department, since that is the only section that concerns us. The entire first page and a part of the second in this first issue were given over to Augustus Baldwin Longstreet's "Master William Mitten; or, A Youth of Brilliant Talents, Who Was Ruined by Bad Luck," a long tale that ran serially for twenty-six consecutive numbers.[49] This tale, says the editor in the issue for November 12, 1859, "has contributed very largely, we do not doubt, to the success and popularity of *The Southern Field and Fireside.*" The second important tale of the first number was an installment of

"Jack Hopeton and His Friends; or, The Autobiography of a Georgian," by William Wilberforce Turner,[50] bachelor brother of the talented Joseph Addison Turner. Installments appeared also of "Toil and Victory," by Miss Annie R. Blount, and of "Grace Atherton," by Maud Moreton. Miscellaneous matter, including a few short poems, comprised the remainder of the Literary Department. The following Prize Contest was also announced in this issue:

> For the best Novelette, or Tale of Fiction $100
> For the best Literary Essay 50
> For the best Agricultural Essay 50
> For the best Poem not less than sixty lines 25
> For the best Poem less than sixty lines 25

"Our Book Table," which did not begin to appear till the third issue,[51] consisted merely of book notices. Except in the case of a few books, which will be noted later, this "Book Table" never attained any distinction in the way of literary criticism. A few columns were given over to news miscellany, including "Marriages" and "Deaths," and the writings of a "Paris Correspondent" were added on July 9, 1859.[52]

James Gardner, proprietor of the periodical, continued to publish the work till the first part of 1864, when he sold his interests to Stockton & Company, who sold out in October of the same year to William B. Smith & Company, Raleigh, North Carolina, to which city the periodical was removed and consolidated with the *Illustrated Mercury* under the name of the Georgia journal. The name was eventually changed to the *Field and Fireside,* but it became a different work under the new management; hence its importance in a history of Georgia periodicals ceased with the removal. In May, 1860, John R. Thompson, former editor of the *Southern Literary Messenger* (Richmond), became literary editor, to be succeeded after a few months by James Nathan Ells.[53] The latter, in turn, was succeeded by S. A. Atkinson in 1862, who remained with the periodical till some time in 1863, when there seems to have been a change of policy wherein no person is named as literary editor. In January, 1863, the paper changed to quarto size, remaining thus as long as it was published in Georgia.

The editors of the *Southern Field and Fireside* were interested in developing the latent literary talent of the South, as instanced by their continually offering prizes for poems, tales, and essays. Literary winners in the first Prize Contest were as follows:

Best Tale—"Aliene, or The Recovered Treasure," by Maud Moreton [54]

Best Literary Essay—"Prefaces: What They Are, and Are Not: What They Ought and Ought Not to Be," by "A Man Who Never Wrote One in His Life" [55]

Best Poems not less than sixty lines—"Under the Lamp-Light," by Miss Annie R. Blount [56]

Best Poem less than sixty lines—"A Dream of Locust Dell," by Mrs. Julia L. Keyes, daughter of Mrs. Caroline Lee Hentz [57]

Contestants had to submit their entries under pseudonyms, and the judges were James L. Rossignol and George T. Barnes,[58] presumably residents of Augusta. In 1861 a prize of $100 for the best tale was divided between Mrs. Emma Miot, Ellisville, Florida, for "Our Little Annie," and Miss Clara V. Dargan, Columbia, South Carolina, for "Helen Howard." The committee of judges was not named. In 1863, prizes for tales went to "India Morgan; or The Lost Will," by Miss Kate C. Wakelee, and to "The Randolphs of Randolph Hall," by Mrs. S. A. Miner, Covington, Georgia; prizes for essays went to "The Uses of Poetry," by the Rev. Richard Furman, and to the anonymous "Characters of Poetry"; prizes for poems went to the anonymous "Marching to Death," and to "The Rainbow Dream," by Alexander Means. Judges in this contest were Henry J. Osborne and D. G. Cotting. In 1864 the Prize Tale was the anonymous "By-Gone Life," and the Prize Poem was "Judith," by Mrs. Mary C. Bigby. Judges were Lewis D. Ford, David L. Roath, and Henry Cleveland.

An interesting commentary on the journalistic practice of

making only laudatory criticism of contemporary works of literature is illustrated in an article in the *Southern Field and Fireside* for June 4, 1859, by that strongly partisan Southerner, Joseph Addison Turner, of Turnwold, Georgia. The following extract is typical of the whole:

> Soon after the commencement of the Know-Nothing excitement, I received from a New York publisher an account of a book he was about to publish, containing marvelous accounts of the wicked doings of the Roman priests, accompanied by an editorial puff, which he had the audacity to ask me to publish as my own—and that, too, in advance of the publication of this book.[59]

Turner then cites the attempt in 1856 to establish in New York a journal of independent criticism in *The Criterion*, which, he says, soon died because "our authors and publishers would not tolerate independent criticism." [60]

The question "Who is Ned Brace in *Master William Mitten?*" was answered in the *Southern Field and Fireside* for October 8, 1859,[61] by the editor, who, speaking authoritatively, he declares, says that in the original *Georgia Scenes*, Ned Brace at first was a picture of Mr. Dred Pace, but that later in the same tales he was modeled after Edmund Bacon, of South Carolina. In *Master William Mitten*, however, Brace is "a student of Dr. Waddel's school at Willington" about 1806, and is merely a fanciful figure, although many events in the tale actually took place in Dr. Waddel's school.[62] The popularity of Longstreet's *Master William Mitten* is evidenced by the fact that it occupied the front page of the periodical for twenty-six weeks and was editorially referred to several times during that period.

It had not been customary for Southern periodicals to pay for contributions to their works, but we find the *Southern Field and Fireside* in 1863 stating:

> We pay according to the merit of the Composition. For tales, sketches, essays, and poetical effusions of ability, the highest prices are paid. No expense will be spared to sustain the high reputation which this paper has acquired as a literary journal.[63]

And in 1864, just after the periodical had been removed to Raleigh, the proprietors declared: "Our Contributorial Corps consists of over ONE HUNDRED paid writers—a greater number than were ever before engaged upon any one journal in America. . . ." [64] With the exception of *Wheler's Magazine* (Athens) the *Southern Field and Fireside* seems to be the only Georgia literary periodical before 1865 to mention paying contributors except with free subscriptions to the periodical in question.

The *Southern Field and Fireside* was highly acclaimed by its contemporaries. The *Southern Literary Messenger* (Richmond) predicted success for it even before its first issue, forecasting that it would "speedily become an authority in literary matters which even the Northern cliques and journals will not be able to disregard." [65] And after the Augusta periodical had appeared, it was again commended by the Richmond magazine.[66] *Russell's Magazine* (Charleston) thus received its Augusta contemporary:

This hebdomadal has now been established for months, and every additional number seems to be an improvement on its predecessor. Its contributions, consisting of tales, essays, poems, and articles on farming and agriculture, are generally of a high order of merit. Its Editorials are spirited and able; and above all, its proprietors are, we understand, *men of capital*. With *such* advantages, this journal must succeed.[67]

Many Southern newspaper praises of the *Southern Field and Fireside* are quoted in the Atlanta *Southern Confederacy* for May 2, 1861. The New Orleans *Delta* called its writers "the most distinguished in the South." The Louisville *Journal* said it was the "Best Literary journal in the country." The Raleigh *Standard* believed it "Equal, if not superior, in literary merits, to any journal published," while the Charleston *Courier* capped the climax by the statement that it was "The best family paper published."

The *Southern Field and Fireside* was not able to retain its standard of excellence during the course of the Civil War.

Paper, for one thing, was difficult to get, and communications were so often interrupted that contributions were many times delayed weeks in arriving. For some issues there were only four pages. Yet it seems to have been well supported, for the editor says, in May, 1860, that the periodical has had "handsome support" and has "achieved a brilliant success." [68] About a year later the editor speaks of an "unprecedented number of accessions" to the subscription list for the previous months. This success reached such a point that the periodical had at least 13,000 subscribers in 1864.[69] The subscription price, $2 at first, was soon raised to $4, and in 1864, to $8 for six months, in Confederate money, of course. Yet its popularity continued unabated, in spite of the unsettled conditions during the war period. War news, as a natural consequence, took up a large space in the periodical as time passed. The issue for May 30, 1863,[70] gives a full-page map of the "Seat of War in Mississippi," drawn by Alfred Maurice, of New Orleans. During the same year Maurice contributed other engraved illustrations of various kinds.

Serial stories were important features of the *Southern Field and Fireside* in its early years of existence. The following are the best, by far, of those especially written for the periodical:

"Master William Mitten; or, A Youth of Brilliant Talents, Who Was Ruined by Bad Luck," by Augustus Baldwin Longstreet [71]
"Jack Hopeton and His Friends; or, The Autobiography of a Georgian," by William Wilberforce Turner [72]
"Toil and Victory," by Miss Annie R. Blount [73]
"Grace Atherton; or, The Child of the Wreck," by Maud Moreton [74]
"Aliene, or The Recovered Treasure," by Maud Moreton [75]
"Saturday Night," by Mrs. Caroline Lee Hentz [76]
"Three Years of Heart-History," by Katy-Did [77]
"The Pride of Falling Water; A Tale of the Old French War of 1755," by John Esten Cooke [78]
"The Household at Haywood Lodge. A Story of the South," by Mary E. Bryan [79]
"Bellemont," by Mrs. Sue E. Hunt [80]

"Five Chapters of a History: A Georgian Court, Forty Years Ago,"
   by Philemon Perch (Richard Malcolm Johnston) [81]
"The Randolphs of Randolph Hall," by Mrs. S. A. Miner [82]
"India Morgan; or, The Lost Will," by Miss Kate C. Wakelee [83]
"Gerald Gray's Wife," by Mrs. Sue Pettigru [sic] King [84]
"Bannockburn," by Carrie (Mary Caroline Griswold) [85]
"By-Gone Life," anonymous [86]

Original poems in the *Southern Field and Fireside* were not nearly so good as the tales and articles, but the following are typical of them:

"Ballad at Sea," by William Gilmore Simms [87]
"The Old Cob Pipe behind the Clock," by J. A. Turner [88]
"The Beautiful Princess of Cofachiqui," by L. Virginia French [89]
"Mary: the Mother of Washington," by Miss Annie R. Blount [90]
"Ascalon. A Legend of the Crusades," by Herbert [91]
"A Vision of the Millenium," by Rev. Alexander Means [92]
"Extracts from 'Poesy'—A Poem," by A. R. Watson [93]
" 'Twas Night upon the Battle-Field," by Carrie Bell Sinclair [94]
"Wachulla," by Mrs. Kate A. DuBose (Mrs. C. W. DuBose) [95]
"Judith," anonymous (Newnan, Georgia) [96]
"Claude," by Herbert [97]
"A Spring Morning," by William Wragg Smith [98]
"Manassas," anonymous [99]
"Palestine," by J.R.B. [100]

Contributed articles of a critical nature dot the pages of the *Southern Field and Fireside*, of which these are possibly the best:

"American Literature: Considered Especially with Reference to Its Lack of Independent Journalism and Independent Criticism," by J. A. Turner [101]
"The Early Settlers of Georgia—A Contrast," by M. [102]
"Stray Leaves from the Diary of a Country Lady," by M.M. (Walnut Grove) [103]
"Literary Women," by A Lady [104]
"The Uses of Poetry," by Rev. Richard Furman—Prize Essay [105]
"Byron as a Man and a Poet," by A. W. Dillard [106]
"The Importance of Style," by A. W. Dillard [107]

As stated previously, book reviews played only a minor part in the *Southern Field and Fireside*. One anonymous article,

"Tennyson's Last," reviews the British poet's latest collected poems.[108] An unnamed editor reviews, at some length, Augusta J. Evans' latest novel, *Macaria*.[109] But the best three reviews are by John R. Thompson, a professional journalist and one of the literary editors, in which he discusses *Castle Richmond* and *The Three Clerks*, by Anthony Trollope; [110] the *Memorials of Thomas Hood*, edited by his daughter; [111] and the *Autobiographical Recollections*, by Charles Robert Leslie.[112] The last-named is by far the longest and best, especially since it reviews a little-known book of some historical importance. The editor thus speaks of the book:

> The charm of the autobiography itself lies in the delightful sketches and anecdotes it gives us of Leslie's friends and companions, among whom were men eminent in every walk of life. His intercourse with Irving was of long duration and of a most intimate character, and many hitherto unpublished letters of our great American humorist are given in the appendix. He painted Sir Walter Scott, and was honoured with his friendship, and his association was frequent and unreserved with Rogers, Washington Allston and other celebrities in art and literature of his time.[113]

Thompson also quotes recollections of Coleridge and Sydney Smith, with both of whom Leslie was also closely associated. Thompson seems to have been the only man of real literary ability connected with the editorial staff of the Augusta periodical, and, unfortunately, he did not remain long in that place.[114] Later editors of the work apologized for the non-appearance of book reviews in this manner: "We seldom write or publish 'Reviews,' believing that few of our patrons would relish that class of literature, and that we should often become involved in controversy, which, to us, is almost as distasteful as any other kind of quarrel." [115]

The *Southern Field and Fireside*, like all other Southern periodicals, had a checkered career during the Civil War. Sometimes the journal was delayed because paper did not arrive on time. Sometimes the issue appeared with only four pages, and the literary quality greatly degenerated. Not until the removal of the work to Raleigh with the issue of November 5, 1864, did it regain its former excellence, but its consolidation with the *Illustrated Mercury* changed it in so many respects that it became an entirely different paper.

An almost innumerable group of contributors to the *Southern Field and Fireside* used either initials or pseudonyms instead of their real names. Sometimes initials can be guessed at with fair accuracy, but pseudonyms are more difficult to penetrate. Following are those used while the periodical remained in Augusta:

A.B.W.; Achilles Hoplegg, Esq.; Adele; A.F. (Truss, Alabama); Alabama Dallas; Alguno; An American in Paris; A.M.W.; Anon (Augusta); Mrs. A. R. C.; Arena; A.Z. (Augusta); B.B.; Bessie B. (Pine Cottage, Florida); Bernardo; Mrs. B.M.Z. (Augusta); Buena Vista (Columbia); A Carolina Girl; Carrie (Mary Caroline Griswold); C.E.G.; Claudia; Cyrille Merle; Comer; Cousin Dick; Cousin Jessie (Charleston); Cygriet; Daisy (Savannah); De'esting; Edith (Woodlawn, Mississippi); Elton; E.M.M.; Emma Carra (Mrs. Agnes Jean Stibbes); Emmie Emerald; E. M. P[endleton].; E. Louise W. (Old Homestead); E.N.; Enid; Eola; Epsilon; Ethel Deen (Mrs. Augusta DeMilly); Mrs. E. S. W. (Griffin, Georgia); Eufaula; Etta Eton; Evelyn; E.W.R. (Savannah); E. Y[oung?]; Fabian; Fidelis; Florida Forrest; Floy Forrest (Griffin, Georgia); Frank (Augusta); Georgian; G.P.T. (Kanawha, Virginia); Gulnare (Valley Farm); H. (Bellevigne, South Carolina); H. (Ravenswood, South Carolina); Hal; Harmonia; Henri; Henry (Savannah); Herbert (Charleston); H.M.; H.P. (Retreat); Indamird (Savannah); J.C.P.; Jennie Woodbine (Annie R. Blount); J.F.S.; J.G. (Montgomery, Alabama); J.H.C.; J.H.H.; J.L.L.; J.R.B.; J.W.R.; Justitia; K.B.T.; Kate C. W[akelee].; Katy-Did; Kaluptonoma (Augusta); A Lady; Laurence; L.E.; Lilly-Bell; Lily Lightheart; L'Inconnue (Janie Ollivar); L.M.C.; Lois; Lou Bell; M.A.B. (Atlanta); Mabel; M.A.J.; M.A.L.; Marah; Mary; Marion; Marengo; May (Charleston); May Myrtle; Mattie; Melodia (Hollywood); M.C.B. (Newnan, Georgia); M.E.; Mernet; Memet; Minnie May; Mignionette; Magnolia (Locust Hill, South Carolina); A Minister's Wife (White Springs, Hamilton County, Florida); M.J.M.; M.M. (Walnut Grove); M.W.W. (Augusta); Nadamia; N.A.P.; Nettie Nobody; Nina (Oakland Retreat); Nina Addisine (Macon); Nom de Plume (Griffin, Georgia); Novissimus; Oswald; Ouvrier

Third Period: 1859–65

(Perote, Alabama); Panola (Augusta); Parker; P.E.; Philemon Perch (Richard Malcolm Johnston); Pires; Quintus (Columbia); Rambler; R.D.R.; Sallie; Saluda; Mrs. S.B.C.; S.C.S.; Sigma; Mrs. S.J.E.; The Son; "South Carolina" (Charleston); Stella; Stanford; Terence; Theolian; Ursula; Verena; Viator; Viola; A Virginian; W. G. McC.; W.H.B.; Willie, of Camp Bird (Savannah); Wildbrier; Wilson (Mobile, Alabama); W.N.V. (Atlanta); Woodville; W.S.B. (Savannah); Xemia; Xenia; Z. (Augusta); Zena; Ziola.

Contributions came signed with the following names:

Mrs. E. C. Benton; S. Newton Berryhill (Bellefontaine, Mississippi); Mrs. Mary C. Bigby (Americus, Georgia); Miss Annie R. Blount; Mrs. Caroline Hentz Branch; Mary E. Bryan; Margarita J. Canedo; Henry A. Carr; Henry Cleveland; John Esten Cooke; James Wood Davidson; De Louis Dalton; A. W. Dillard (Livingston, Alabama); Charles S. Dod, Jr.; Mrs. Kate A. DuBose (Mrs. C. W. DuBose); L. Virginia French; Robert Fleming; John B. Gorman, Jr. (Talbotton, Georgia); Ossian D. Gorman (Talbotton, Georgia); Helen Grey; Katie Hall (Lynchburg, Virginia); Charles Hallock; Alphonso O. Hamett (Charleston); Mrs. Leila A. Hamilton; E. M. Harrell (Wood Lawn, Florida); Mary E. Hawkins; Col. William S. Hawkins (Tennessee); Paul Hamilton Hayne; J. H. Hewitt; Mrs. Sue E. Hunt; R. C. Kendall (Reistertown, Maryland); Crammond Kennedy (Macon); Mrs. Julia L. Keyes; Eva Lind; Augustus Baldwin Longstreet; Laura Lincoln; S. D. Lucas; Louise Manhiem; Archd. Arne McBride; Mrs. M. A. McCrimmon; Alexander Means; Mrs. Serena A. Miner (Covington, Georgia); Emma Miot (Ellisville, Florida); Maud Moreton; Emma F. Pradt (Montgomery, Alabama); James R. Randall; Jessie Randolph; A. J. Requier; Anna Cora Ritchie; Laura Bibb Rogers; George H. Sass (Charleston); J. Henry Dmochowski Saunders; William E. Screven; William Gilmore Simms; Carrie Bell Sinclair (Savannah); William Wragg Smith; H. P. Spain; Judge Starnes (Augusta); Mrs. C. L. Statham; James M. Thompson (Calhoun, Georgia); John R. Thompson; Joseph Addison Turner; William Wilberforce Turner; Miss Kate C. Wakelee; Augusta Washington; A. R. Watson (Macon); William Cumming Wilde (New Orleans); Charlie Wildwood; M. G. Willison; Robert Windsor (Atlanta); E[dward]. Young.

The *Southern Field and Fireside*, as indicated previously, was one of the best of *ante-bellum* Georgia periodicals, and in its best issues far surpassed the other literary weeklies of the period. Under different circumstances it probably would have been more successful, but the vicissitudes of war altered the plans and hopes of the well-intentioned Southerners who labored in its behalf.

3. ATLANTA—*HYGIENIC AND LITERARY MAGAZINE* (1860)
TITLE: *Hygienic and Literary Magazine*
FIRST ISSUE: January, 1860   LAST ISSUE: March & April, 1860(?)
PERIODICITY: Monthly
PUBLISHERS: Daily Intelligencer Power-Press Print, Atlanta
EDITOR OF LITERARY DEPARTMENT: Mrs. Dr. Riley (Le Ferve)
LOCATION OF FILES: *DSG:* I, 1-3 & 4. *MiU:* I (inc.) *NcD:* I, 2. Also 1-3 & 4 (microfilm)

The *Hygienic and Literary Magazine,* a monthly octavo periodical, began in Atlanta in January, 1860. It followed the policy of the *Medical and Literary Weekly,* which had appeared for twenty-five issues in 1859 in the same city, but which had been discontinued in October. Its general editor and proprietor was M. A. Malsby, who thus outlined his plan:

The Magazine will be about the size of "Godey's Lady's Book," and will embrace three prominent departments; viz, HYGIENIC, LITERARY and EDUCATIONAL. The Hygienic Department, or that pertaining to the Laws of Health, will be under the immediate supervision of Dr. V. H. Taliaferro, and will form a prominent as well as important feature in the reading matter of the magazine. . . .

THE LITERARY DEPARTMENT will be under the management of Mrs. Dr. Riley, henceforth to be known in literature as LE FERVE, and will embrace the productions of the best and most talented writers of the South.

THE EDUCATIONAL DEPARTMENT will contain the opinions and views of the leading educators of the day, and will be devoted to the elevation and improvement of the masses.[116]

The first and second numbers consisted of 64 pages each, while the third, a double number for March and April, 1860, contained 72 pages. The first issue devoted about one-third of its pages to the Hygienic Department, and the rest, including six pages of advertisements, to the other two depart-

Third Period: 1859–65

ments. The proportion of space for hygienic interests remained about the same for the other issues, but the Educational Department was omitted after the first issue, and literary interests took up the remaining pages except for three or four pages of advertisements in each number. Since we are interested only in the literary phase of the periodical, we shall discuss only the section devoted to it. Delays arose to such an extent that a double number for March & April was necessary in order to issue each succeeding number on the first of the month. And with the third issue the magazine probably ceased publication, since that is the last number located.

"Mrs. Dr. Riley" (Le Ferve) has not yet been fully identified, but her Literary Department was about the average in quality for Georgia literary periodicals. Among the best original tales and articles are:

"Zella," a $200 Prize Story, by Jessie Randolph [117]
"Arria. A Tale of the Roman Empire," by Le Ferve [118]
Review of Augusta J. Evans' *Beulah,* by Rymmon (Atlanta) [119]
"Love is Blind," by Bessie B—— [120]
"The Orphan of the Chattahoochee," by Miriam [121]
"The Bible as a Text-Book," anonymous [122]
"Night and Morning.—A Recollection," by Dean Slow [123]

A few good poems were contributed especially to the periodical:

"The Miser," by Le Ferve [124]
"All Goodness Is Not Lost," by Finley Johnson [125]
"A Vision of the Millenium," Prize Poem, by Alexander Means [126]
"The Rose and the Laurel," by Jennie Woodbine (Annie R. Blount) [127]
"Song of the Flowers," by M. Louise Rogers [128]

The contributors to the *Hygienic and Literary Magazine,* including pseudonyms, were as follows: Bessie B——; Carlos; Finley Johnson; Rymmon Jones; Leole; Alexander Means; Miriam; Jessie Randolph; Mrs. Dr. Riley (Le Ferve); M. Louise Rogers; Rymmon (Atlanta); Silver Age; Dean Slow; James Summerfield Slaughter; J. A. Stewart; and Jennie Woodbine (Annie R. Blount).

The "Editor's Table" contains nothing of value, and there are no book reviews of any importance. What the magazine might have amounted to in time is hard to judge, but its three extant numbers are only of minor quality. It was forced to discontinue, almost certainly, because of unsettled conditions immediately preceding the Civil War, when Southern energy was devoted to the struggle over state rights.

4. EATONTON—*THE PLANTATION* (1860)

TITLE: *The Plantation*
FIRST ISSUE: March, 1860. LAST ISSUE: December, 1860
PERIODICITY: Quarterly
PUBLISHERS: Pudney & Russell, New York. Distributed from Eatonton.
EDITOR: Joseph Addison Turner
LOCATION OF FILES: *G:* I, 1; II, 2. *GE:* I, 1. *DLC:* I–II (inc.). *GU:* I, 1–2. *ICU:* II (inc.). *MB:* I–II (inc.). *MH:* I (inc.). *NcD:* I, 1; II, 2. *NjP:* CF. *PU:* CF

Joseph Addison Turner (1826–68), editor of the *Plantation,* is one of the most interesting and colorful figures in the annals of Georgia periodical literature. Born in a county in Middle Georgia into a family of Turners who had but lately emigrated from Dinwiddie County, Virginia, he soon achieved prominence by trying his hand at almost every conceivable type of literature. After spending one term in school at Emory College, Oxford, Georgia, in 1845, he taught school for a year at Phoenix Academy, at that time an institution of some prominence in Middle Georgia. He gave this up for the practice of law, being admitted to the bar in 1847. He had, however, begun to write for the public in his nineteenth year. He soon became a regular contributor to the *Southern Literary Messenger* (Richmond) and the *Southern Literary Gazette* (Athens). He also wrote miscellaneous poems, tales, and articles for *DeBow's Review, Southern Field and Fireside, Godey's Lady's Book, Peterson's Magazine,* and *Scott's Monthly Magazine.* Under the pseudonym of "Abraham Goosequill" he published a series of Southern sketches called "My Uncle Simon's Plantation," which first appeared in the *Southern Literary Gazette,* and then reappeared, with only minor changes, in the *Plantation* in 1860, and in the *Countryman*, another journalistic venture of Turner's, in 1864. In 1847 Turner published a volume of poems called *Kemble's Poems*,[129] juvenilia written in his teens under the pseudonym of "Frank Kemble," and in 1858 published another volume of poems entitled *The Discovery of Sir John Franklin, and Other Poems*.[130] Possibly his best poem, which appeared in the *Countryman* (Turnwold) in 1862, is entitled "The Old Plantation." It is some 1,400 lines in length and is written in heroic couplets, confessedly in imitation of Goldsmith's "The Deserted Village." A further discussion of Turner's work and an evaluation of his literary efforts will appear in the discussion of the *Countryman*.[131]

The aim of Turner in trying his hand at so many types of literature may be learned from his own words:

My aim, from the beginning, has been to contribute my mite to the creation of a separate and distinct Southern literature. From my youth up, I have hated yankees, and yankee literature.[132]

His literary models went back to the eighteenth century, ranging from Addison and Steele to Wordsworth.[133] His aims were not confined to literature. He was also interested in agriculture in the South and wrote numerous articles on that topic for various Southern periodicals. In 1857 he published *The Cotton Planter's Manual*,[134] an agricultural compilation that "makes no pretension whatever to originality." [135] Turner had had but meager experience in the journalistic field before 1860. In 1848 he had edited *Turner's Monthly* (Eatonton) for three months, but had abandoned the project for some unknown reason. In 1854 he had begun the Eatonton *Independent Press*, a newspaper devoted to the Democratic Party, but in the following year had sold it to Philip C. Pendleton, "who converted it into the Central Georgian, in Sandersville." [136] He must have had considerable means of his own, for he never complained of any inability to meet his financial obligations in the course of his several publications.

The first number of the *Plantation* appeared in March,

1860, and during the same year three other numbers were published. Volume I includes the March and June numbers; Volume II, the September and December numbers. This was the first quarterly of literary importance ever attempted in Georgia, and might have achieved greater success if the Civil War had not forced Turner to abandon his publication. It was not, of course, comparable to the leading quarterly of the country, *The North American Review* (Boston), which had been in existence since 1815, nor to any of the other leading Northern periodicals, nor to the *Southern Quarterly Review* (New Orleans and Charleston). It was rather a bold experiment, since the day of quarterlies had passed, even in the South. The *Plantation*, advertised at $5 per year, was distributed from Eatonton, but was printed by Pudney & Russell in New York. In the second issue of the quarterly Turner gives his reasons for such a procedure:

> In the first place, it takes the labor of publication off of our hands, and leaves us more time to devote to the editorial department of this journal. . . . In the next place, *The Plantation* is published by a house which has all the appliances, and all the machinery, for pushing out this journal into a circulation in a section where it is most needed to combat abolition, and to correct misapprehensions even among the friends of the South. . . . Everybody knows that we have no regular publishing house in Georgia; that labor and material are cheaper in New-York; and, above all, that publishers in that city have the machinery in operation to force out a book or journal into a circulation that exists nowhere in the South.[137]

The *Southern Literary Messenger* thus commends the first number of the *Plantation:*

> Here is a Southern Quarterly worthy of the name. It contains 221 pages of prose and poetry, of Southern sense and Southern humor, and presents in every way, both in text and typography, a most attractive appearance. The purpose of the "Plantation," as we gather from the prospectus, is "to defend the institution of slavery from the attacks made upon it, come from quarter soever they may," and the defence is to be "totally unqualified, unreserved, in a moral, social and political point of view." Good! We

commend the "Plantation" to the support of the entire Union, for the North not less than the South is interested in maintaining, defending and extending slavery, without which there is no solvency for the manufacturing States and no safety, no permanence for Republican government. We shall take great pleasure in exchanging with the first-class journal.[138]

Criticism from a Northern paper possibly gives a judgment most free from a charge of partisanship. The New York *Evening Post* (Republican) thus criticizes Turner's quarterly:

THE PLANTATION is a pro-slavery organ, and most of the articles have a direct bearing upon this theme. Among the more general articles the "Goose-Quill Essays" are the best. THE PLANTATION is neatly printed on smooth, elegant paper, and Southerners have now another opportunity of showing whether they can support a Magazine, which, however much we may differ from its politics, we must confess, possesses considerable literary merit.[139]

The "Salutatory" of the first issue makes the following defense of the work:

The South needs a journal of the kind which we propose to publish, for the defence of her rights. Old and New England number their anti-slavery journals by the hundred—not to say by the thousand. Where is the journal in our midst which blends the literary and the political in such a way as to make itself readable like *The Atlantic* on this side of the ocean, and *Blackwood* on the other? We do not propose for ourself a standard lower than that of either of those journals.[140]

The *Atlantic Monthly* (Boston), established in 1857, was a medium of slavery reform. It was pleased "to be considered as the organ of the anti-slavery party," says Algernon Tassin, and thus "sought to enlist not only ready pens but reluctant pennies." [141] The *Atlantic Monthly*, however, which sought to steer clear of mere propaganda and political partisanship, the contrary of the course Turner pursued in the *Plantation*, is still in existence.

A glance at the "Contents" of the first number of the *Plantation* indicates the type of reading matter contained therein:

I.	Salutatory	1
II.	Lines for Lizzie's Album	4
III.	Thoughts Suggested by John Brown's Raid	5
IV.	I Dream	26
V.	Millard Fillmore, Pandora's Box, and Daniel S. Dickinson	26
VI.	Annie Drew	62
VII.	Herschel V. Johnson	62
VIII.	The Old Cob Pipe Behind the Clock	70
IX.	William C. Dawson	71
X.	The Little Birds and the Little Nest	100
XI.	Douglas and Lincoln—Slavery and Territories	101
XII.	Jenny and Johnny	130
XIII.	Cotton on the Plantation	131
XIV.	Link Not Thy Life and Fate to His	149
XV.	The Old Farm House of My Uncle Simon: or, the Goose-Quill Essays	
	1. Introduction—Cotton	149
	2. My Uncle Simon	154
	3. Spring at the South	160
	4. Snipe Shooting	169
	5. The Poultry Yard	174
	6. The Widow	180
	7. Emily	184
	8. The Schoolmaster	189
	9. A Stroll in the Woods	193
	10. Cousin Dorothy in Trouble	198
	11. Brook Fishing	202
	12. Wheat Harvest	206
XVI.	Cable Canticles	
	1. Queen Victoria to James Buchanan	211
	2. Buchanan to Victoria	212
	3. Victoria and Buchanan	213
Editor's Table		219

Advertisements occupied only a small space in the *Plantation*. Never taking up more than eight pages of any issue, they came usually from business concerns in Pennsylvania, New York, and Massachusetts. The main items advertised were books and various types of farm machinery. All periodicals before the Civil War seem to have depended for their profits upon money obtained from subscriptions rather than from advertisements. It was necessary, therefore, for a periodical to have a large paying list of subscribers in order to survive more than a few years.

The "Goose-Quill Essays" have the greatest literary merit of all literature that appeared in the *Plantation* at any time. These compositions of Turner, under the pseudonym of "Abraham Goosequill," are Addisonian in style, and suggest the "Sir Roger de Coverley Papers." Turner employs a country squire, Uncle Simon, and a widow, Mrs. Applegate, and creates a rural atmosphere throughout the "Essays," which appear in the first three issues of the *Plantation*. The lover of Mrs. Applegate, however, is not the rustic old Uncle Simon, but Cousin Aristides, a bachelor. Turner has the soul of a humorist. His "Cable Canticles," a series of three poems that carry on an imaginary cable conversation between Queen Victoria and James Buchanan,[142] is an excellent illustration. But the best example of this humor in the quarterly is his farce-comedy "Julius Sneezer," a satire on abolitionists that takes up more than 91 pages of the issue for September, 1860.[143] In this comedy Turner boldly uses numerous Shakespearean lines to emphasize his points. Most of the material in the *Plantation* seems to have been written by the editor himself, although many of the articles are unsigned. Turner's brother, William Wilberforce Turner, was the author of "The Ball at B———," a tale appearing in the issue for June, 1860. The third and fourth numbers contain the following selections reprinted from other periodicals: "Cornfield Peas,"[144] from the Richmond *Whig;* "The Differences of Race between the Northern and Southern People,"[145] from the *Southern Literary Messenger;* "Recollections of Leslie,"[146] from the London *Quarterly;* "Clay and Calhoun,"[147] from the *Virginia Sentinel;* and "Garibaldi—His Life and Times,"[148] from *Colburn's New Monthly* (London). Each number usually contained articles on slavery and on agriculture, besides miscellaneous short poems and tales.

In literary criticism Turner reflected the usual Southern

attitude toward the North in 1860. In his first "Editor's Table" he thus reviews the novel *Beulah,* by Augusta J. Evans: "No one is in the fashion who has not read 'Beulah,' and, perhaps, criticised it. We feel proud of our distinguished countrywoman, Miss Evans." In reputation he places her as "second only to that of Bulwer, Scott and Dickens," and considers *Beulah* equal to *Jane Eyre,* by Charlotte Brontë. He declares that Miss Evans' novel contains "nothing coarse, nothing masculine, nothing of that woman's-right-ism, which render even Mrs. Stowe's very interesting *Uncle Tom's Cabin* so offensive to refined sensibilities." In conclusion, Turner says that Miss Evans "illustrates the type of the true Southern woman, while about Mrs. Stowe there is a vulgar snobism which all her talents cannot atone for." [149] The issue for December, 1860, the last to appear, contains sketches of the history of the Edinburgh *Review,* the London *Quarterly, Blackwood's Magazine,* and the *Westminster Review,*[150] all of which Turner seems to have read carefully. He comments on the *Southern Literary Messenger* as follows: "We note a very decided improvement in this veteran Southern monthly. It is becoming a live magazine." [151] He voices an adverse criticism of Seba Smith's *Major Jack Downing Letters,* some of which, he says, are "mere trash and rubbish." [152] At the end of the "Editor's Table" for this last issue Turner points out his plans for the following year:

We know not whether we shall be in the Union the coming year or out of it; but whether in or out, the purposes of this Journal will be the same, and we shall work with renewed energy for their accomplishment.[153]

It is to be regretted that the outbreak of the Civil War stopped the publication of the *Plantation,* one of the most ambitious journalistic undertakings made by any man in the Old South. Turner was a cultured Southerner, well qualified to make a success of such a literary undertaking if he could have had time and the proper backing of those in his section. He was to make one more venture in the field of journalism before his

Third Period: 1859–65 157

short life came to a close, and that, too, was fated to end disastrously because of events beyond his control.

5. NEWNAN—*SOUTHERN LITERARY COMPANION* (1860?–65?)

TITLE: *Southern Literary Companion*
FIRST ISSUE: January (?), 1860(?)   LAST ISSUE: May 17, 1865(?)
PERIODICITY: Weekly
PUBLISHERS: Stephens & Company, Newnan
EDITORS: J. V. D. Stephens, 1864; J. S. Bigby, 1865; Miss C. W. Barber, Editress of Ladies' Department
LOCATION OF FILES: *MBAt:* June 15, 1864. *NcD:* June 1, 15, 1864 (photostats); Apr. 19, May 17, 1865. *TxU:* June 1, 1864

The *Southern Literary Companion* began in Newnan, presumably in January, 1860, though very little can be learned about the periodical because only a few issues are extant.[154] It was a weekly folio journal "Devoted to Literature, Arts and Sciences, Agriculture, &c.," and must have been a success from the start, for the U.S. Census for 1860 lists it as having 1,200 subscribers. It was published by Stephens & Company, Proprietors, under the general editorship of J. V. D. Stephens in 1864 and of J. S. Bigby in 1865, with Miss C. W. Barber as "Editress of the Ladies' Department." Miss Barber was a woman of some journalistic experience. Born in Massachusetts, she had come South after her father's death and had received her education at Lafayette Female Seminary at Chambers Court House, Alabama. From 1850 to 1853 she edited the Madison (Georgia) *Visitor,* thence going to Newnan, where she was connected with the *Southern Literary Companion.* After leaving the latter periodical, she edited another Newnan publication called *Miss Barber's Weekly.* She was the author of tales and poems which appeared in many Georgia periodicals, and published two volumes of stories and sketches: *Tales for the Freemason's Fireside* [155] and *The Three Golden Links.*[156] She was married twice, the first time to John C. Towles, of Lafayette, Alabama, in 1867, and the second time to Jett T. McCoy. Her last days were spent in Columbus, Georgia.[157]

Early issues of the *Companion* seem to have been lost, but in 1864 and 1865 the work consisted of a single folio sheet printed on both sides, seven columns to a page, with more than half the space devoted to literary interests. It had doubtless been larger in former years, but scarcity of paper and the generally unsettled conditions during the Civil War forced all newspapers and magazines to reduce their size and sometimes to delay publication for months. The fluctuation in the currency in Georgia in 1865 may be noted in the fact that whereas the issue for April 19 quoted subscriptions at $10 for six months, that for May 17, printed not long after the assassination of Lincoln, quoted the paper at $1 for six months. News in the paper, which sometimes included local items, was confined almost exclusively, of course, to military events, which, however, never occupied a large space in any issue.

The *Southern Field and Fireside* (Augusta) appears to have been the only periodical of any importance to notice the *Companion*. It speaks of the Newnan paper as "the cheapest paper of its size published in the Confederate States," and of the "Editress" as one "who deservedly ranks among the best lady writers of the South." [158]

The issue for June 1, 1864, the earliest extant, is typical of the work. The "Ladies' Department," which occupies the first page, begins with a poem by M.C.B., "The Little Darling," followed by a story by Miss Barber, "Ella Spencer." An anonymous poem "Ellen Radcliff," "Mrs. Gaskill's [sic] Life of Charlotte Bronte," presumably by Miss Barber, and Ellen Ashton's story, "The Diamond Ear-Rings," together with miscellaneous minor items, fill out the rest of this first page. The second page, devoted for the most part to general information and eclectic material, has a "Local Column" and a "News Summary," besides a little more than one column of advertisements. It also contains one interesting poem by "Gamma of Natchez" called "The Heroes of Sumter." The first page, however, is of greater literary interest, especially for its one bit of literary criticism.

"Mrs. Gaskill's Life of Charlotte Bronte," though unsigned,

is doubtless by Miss C. W. Barber, who used the English biography as a basis for arguing that "a better day is dawning upon the world, and a truer womanhood beginning to be recognized" and that "soon all demonstrations upon this false and degrading estimate of woman will be met with the contempt they are entitled to win." In approximately 1,600 words Miss Barber eulogizes Charlotte Brontë, devoting little more than 200 words to a criticism of the biographer. Perhaps the most interesting sentences of the latter section are these:

> Her [Charlotte Brontë's] biographer is . . . not so clear seeing [as Miss Brontë], and not so profoundly emotional; but she brings to her task a clear head and an appreciative, loving heart. She could not fathom the depths of her friend, but she could see all the nobleness of design. She could look on with admiration at what she comprehended—but there was a vast field of observation, inspiration and prophecy totally incomprehensible to her mind; and hence her evident desire to bring Charlotte Brontë within the scope of ordinary vision, her anxiety to show how dainty-nice were her habits, how simple yet careful her choice of dress, her 'three offers of marriage,' and some every-day talk about potatoes and cooking. All this is but natural, and to be expected from one who walks in the sunshine as does Mrs. Gaskill, who covets life in its simplicity and ease, not in the starry hights [sic] or savage grandeur.

Only three other issues of the *Companion* survive. That for June 15, 1864, contains, as of literary interest, the following: "Sonnet," by Grace Herbert; "At the Turnpike Gate," a poem by V.F.T.; "Only Comfortable," a story by C. W. B(arber).; and another story, "Right Round the Corner," by Miss L. A. Bkocksbank (*sic*). The issue for April 19, 1865,[159] contains an installment of Miss Barber's prose tale, "Rose Grey, or Prison Life," and "Reveries No. 3," by Harry Holt (Clara Le Clerc),[160] besides some news and military orders on the single page devoted to news. The number for May 17, 1865,[161] contains a short story, "Nannie Hays," by Miss Barber; "Reveries No. VII," by Harry Holt; "The Haunted River," a poem by Mary E. Bryan; and "At Renwick," an anonymous journal of a schoolgirl's first days in Macon (?) at the college in 1857. No later issues have been located, but it is probable that the paper soon ceased publication, for in this last issue the editor announced that the work would be published only as long as it had patronage sufficient to defray current expenses.

Aside from the contributors already mentioned we have only one bit of evidence for additional names, that is, a list found at the beginning of each extant issue. The following, then, may be said to constitute the contributors to the *Southern Literary Companion*, at least during its last months:

Ellen Ashton, Miss C. W. Barber, Mary E. Bryan, Miss L. A. Bkocksbank (*sic*), Mrs. H. L. Berry, Miss Annie R. Blount, Miss M. A. Campbell, Mrs. A. T. D. Chapman, Harry Holt (Clara Le Clerc), Gamma of Natchez, Grace Herbert, Miss V. A. Jennings, M.C.B., Mrs. Mary A. McCrimmon, Miss Sallie A. Reedy, Currer Lyle (Mrs. M. Louise Crossley),[162] Mrs. Kate Trippe, V.F.T., Mrs. Dr. Riley.

What the *Companion* was like during the first two years of its existence we have no way of learning. Newnan, with its College Temple, a "Female College" that was already issuing its own literary periodical, the *Fly Leaf*, had a cultural atmosphere conducive to the development of literature, but war conditions, as everywhere in the South, ruined all such prospects for years to come.

6. ATLANTA—*GEORGIA LITERARY AND TEMPERANCE CRUSADER* (1834?–61?)

TITLE: *Temperance Banner,* Washington, 1834–?; *Literary and Temperance Crusader,* Penfield, ?; *Georgia Literary and Temperance Crusader,* Atlanta, 1859(?)–September 12, 1861; *Georgia Crusader,* Atlanta, September 19(?)–November 28, 1861(?)

FIRST ISSUE: (1834?) LAST ISSUE: November 28, 1861(?)

PERIODICITY: Weekly

PUBLISHERS: W. H. Stokes and W. A. Mercer, Washington, 1834–?; Benjamin Brantley, Washington, ?; John H. Seals, Penfield, ?; John H. Seals, Atlanta, ?–November 28, 1861(?)

EDITORS: W. H. Stokes, Washington, ?; John H. Seals, Penfield, ?; John H. Seals, Atlanta, ?; Mrs. Mary E. Bryan, Atlanta, 1860(?); Mrs. L. Virginia French, Atlanta, ?–November 28, 1861 (?)

LOCATION OF FILES: *NcD:* Sept. 12, Nov. 28, 1861

It is rather difficult to reconstruct the history of a periodical from only two numbers, especially if those numbers both belong to Volume XXVI. From other sources, however, a few facts can be gleaned that, properly fitted together, aid somewhat in finding out what had happened in previous years. From the volume number of the *Crusader* as it appeared in Atlanta, the periodical was founded probably in 1834, and from the names of editors, as well as from a study of the evolution of the title, the forerunner of the work was probably the *Temperance Banner,* established in 1834 in Washington, Georgia, by W. H. Stokes and W. A. Mercer.[163] The latter was a weekly journal, the organ of the Sons of Temperance and of the State Convention of Georgia. It was removed to Penfield some time before 1852, for in that year we find it in the latter village, published by Benjamin Brantley, of Washington. Though it reached a circulation of 5,000 in 1850,[164] only two issues have been located.[165] In the late 1850's it was published by John H. Seals in Penfield, and is sometimes referred to as the *Literary Crusader* and sometimes as the *Temperance Crusader.*[166] About 1859 or 1860 the periodical was removed to Atlanta, where Mrs. Mary E. Bryan (nee Edwards), then only eighteen years old and already married, became editor for a year. Because of the expense of the removal to Atlanta—

the proprietor did not *consider that his finances justified his paying for contributions;* still he wished to make his paper interesting and to have it contain a variety of original reading-matter. Mrs. Bryan was equal to this emergency. She determined to the best of her ability to supply the place of contributors. She called in play for the first time her remarkable versatility, her power of changing her style "from grave to gay, from lively to severe," and she filled a page of the "Crusader" every week with the required variety of original reading-matter from her own pen.[167]

Mary E. Bryan was less given to sentimentality than many women writers of the day. In 1860, in an article entitled "How Should Women Write?"[168] first published in the *Southern Field and Fireside,* she was arguing against the periodical literature of the day because much of it was mere "dallying with surface bubbles." She called upon women to write honestly and without fear "what they feel and think, even if there be errors in the thought and feeling." She felt it woman's duty to write, always with a distinct and moral purpose, not heeding the criticism of men, who would confine the sphere of her writing to nature and religion.

Only with the removal of the *Crusader* to Atlanta did its literary life begin. Only when Mrs. Bryan took charge of the magazine did it get beyond being solely the organ of the Temperance movement in Georgia. It is for this reason that it is discussed in this period, even though its early years were devoted to the cause of morality.

In 1861 we find Mrs. L. Virgina French, of McMinnville, Tennessee, as literary editor, with John H. Seals as general editor and proprietor. The name at that time was the *Georgia Literary and Temperance Crusader,* which was changed to the *Georgia Crusader* in the fall of 1861. Mrs. French, the new editor, had had some journalistic experience in New Orleans, where she had been associate editor of the *Southern Ladies' Book* [169] in 1852. She had contributed to various Southern periodicals, usually under the pseudonym of "L'Inconnue." During her connection with the *Crusader* she seems to have remained in her Tennessee home, for we find the general editor, John H. Seals, requesting contributors to write to her at that address. How long she remained with the work, or how long it continued to exist is unknown. Only two issues, both for 1861, are preserved, and these tell us little as to what the periodical had been in its earlier years. Our judgment, therefore, must be based upon those issues, as well as upon the judgments passed upon it by people of that day.

In the issue for September 12, 1861,[170] we find the following contributions of literary interest:

"Cushla Machree," poem by L. Virginia French
"The Dead Love," poem by Clara (Mrs. Clara Cole)
"Alone! or The Pastor's Daughter," anonymous tale
"The Nun of Saint Agnes: or The Castled Crag of Drachenfels,"
    anonymous tale

In the issue for November 28, 1861,[171] are the following contributions:

"A Reveille," poem by L. Virginia French
"To-Morrow," poem by Millie Mayfield (Mrs. Mary Sophie Shaw Homes)
"The Debutante; or Dangers of City Life," anonymous tale
"Editorial Correspondence, No. 2," from L. Virginia French, describing Nashville and military activities there

It will be seen that the literary interest in these two issues is small. From another source we learn that Clara Le Clerc, a prolific young Southern writer, contributed to the *Crusader* when she was only fifteen years of age, and that she also wrote a series of "Reveries," under the pseudonym of "Harry Holt," as well as the replies, "Old Maid Reveries," under the pseudonym of "Polly Holt," for the same periodical.[172]

Some of the most prominent men of Georgia praised the *Crusader*, in its earlier years, no doubt. Alexander H. Stephens, Vice-President of the Confederacy, said: "Of all the publications I take, I prize none more highly than the *Crusader* . . . and not one contains more original and readable matter, in prose and poetry. It is the best literary journal south of the Potomac, and I think one of the best of its kind in the whole country." [173] Richard Malcolm Johnston, professor in the University of Georgia,[174] declared: "The *Crusader* has, in my opinion created a greater interest for reading among our people than any other paper ever published at the South." [175] The periodical was also commended by other eminent Georgians, such as Robert Toombs, Judge Joseph H. Lumpkin, President James R. Thomas (Emory College), President N. M. Crawford (Mercer University), and Rev. Alexander Means (Atlanta Medical College).[176]

From the Prospectus [177] and from miscellaneous other sources we obtain the following list of contributors:

Mrs. M. Armstrong (Tennessee); George Baber (Tennessee); Hon. J. R. Barrick (Kentucky); Miss Annie R. Blount (Georgia); Mrs. Mary E. Bryan (Georgia); Miss Martha Haynes Butt; Emily C. S.

Chilton (Nashville); Clara (Mrs. Clara Cole); Miss Mary W. Crean (Louisiana); Col. A. H. H. Dawson (Mobile); B. M. DeWitt (Virginia); Estelle (Mrs. Martha W. Brown, Tennessee); Miss Jessie Ferguson (Tennessee); Mrs. L. Virginia French (Tennessee); Mrs. Minnie W. Hackleton (Mississippi); John E. Hatcher (Tennessee); Miss E. H. Hill (Missouri); Mrs. Martha J. Hill (Kentucky); Mrs. Rosa Vertner Johnson (Kentucky); Richard Malcolm Johnston (Georgia); Mrs. Annie C. Ketchum (Tennessee); Mrs. Julia L. Keyes (Alabama); Clara Le Clerc (Georgia); Madame Le Vert (Alabama); Mrs. Mary A. McCrimmon (Georgia); Millie Mayfield (Mrs. Mary Sophie Shaw Homes, New Orleans); S. C. Mercer (Kentucky); Mrs. Lide Merriwether (Tennessee); John W. Overall; Miss Sallie Ada Reedy (Mississippi); Mrs. S. A. Vaughan; L. L. Veazey (Georgia); Mrs. C. A. Warfield (Kentucky).

7. TURNWOLD—*COUNTRYMAN* (1862-66)

TITLE: *Countryman*
FIRST ISSUE: March 4, 1862   LAST ISSUE: May 8, 1866
PERIODICITY: Weekly. (No issues between June 27, 1865, and January 30, 1866.) Volumes VIII–XVIII, one number to a volume (October 13–December 22, 1863). Four volumes to a year until October 13, 1863. One volume to a year, beginning with 1864
PUBLISHER AND EDITOR: Joseph Addison Turner, Turnwold (Putnam County)
LOCATION OF FILES: *DLC:* 1862, Sept. 29–Dec. 15. *G:* 1862, Sept. 29, Oct. 6–13, Nov. 3–24, Dec. 1–15; 1863, July 7; 1864, May 3–10, June 7, Aug. 16–23, Sept. 13; 1865, Jan. 3–10, 31, Feb. 7–14, 28, Mar. 7. *GAtCo:* 1862, Sept. 29–Oct. 13, Nov.–Dec. 15. *GE:* 1862–63: I, 1–15; II, 1–15; III, 1–12; IV, 1–14; V, 1–13; VI, 1–13; VII–XVIII (each number a volume). 1864: XIX, 1–5, 9, 13–14 (mut.), 17 (mut.)–18, 20, 22–23, 27–52. 1865: XX, 2–3, 5, 7, 13 (mut.), 18–19. 1866: XXI, 8, 11. *GMW:* 1862: III, 1–3, 6–12. *GVG:* 1862: Sept. 29–Oct. 13, Nov.–Dec. 15. *MBAt:* 1863: Apr. 18(?). *NNC:* 1862–66, Apr. 10 (incomplete file)—photostats. *NcD:* 1862–63: III, 1–12; IV, 1–10, 12–14; V, 1–12; VI, 2, 6, 10; VIII–IX; 1864: XIX, 21–24, 33–34, 44. 1865: XX, 2, 7, 14. *OClWHi:* 1864, Jan. 12–1865, Mar. 21

The fortunes of the *Countryman* are inextricably bound up with those of its editor, Joseph Addison Turner, and with those of the Old South. It is the only paper known to have been conducted on a plantation in the South, and as such it attracted attention from the entire section. In some respects it represented the spirit of the Southern struggle for states' rights, especially since its editor belonged to the Southern group that worked, as long as it seemed feasible, for a peaceable settlement of the differences between the North and the South. Turner's quarterly, the *Plantation,* which had ceased after four issues in 1860, was his first attempt at periodical literature since 1848, and was a most ambitious undertaking, but the Civil War stifled its existence. Now that the actual break had come, Turner conceived the idea of publishing a paper that would be, at the same time, both a work of literary art and a spokesman for Southern sentiments. Lameness from childhood had prevented his entering the Confederate army, but he possessed a pen that exerted a potent influence, both in humor and in satire, while those more physically able were wielding the sword.

The plantation of Turner, called Turnwold, was nine miles northeast of Eatonton, in Putnam County. It was a prosperous community, with its more than 100 slaves, a printing office, a hat factory, and a private distillery. The "Big House" was an unpretentious one, but contained a library of nearly 2,000 books.[178] It stood close to the paternal dwelling of William Turner, then occupied by William Wilberforce Turner, the bachelor brother of the editor of the *Countryman.* This latter house also contained a large private library, which at one time had comprised about 4,000 volumes.[179] It was this little community that was responsible for almost all, save the genius itself, of the greatness of Joel Chandler Harris, who, during the formative period of his life, spent four years under the influence of Joseph Addison Turner.

The first number of the *Countryman,* printed on Turner's own press, "a Washington, No. 2" that "had seen considerable service,"[180] appeared on March 4, 1862, and consisted of four quarto pages, four columns to a page. The first pages were devoted to agricultural articles telling Southerners how to win the war by raising large crops. There were also miscellaneous notes on "War Tax," "Drafted Men," and "Our Soldier Boys." The Prospectus, included in the same issue, declared:

The Countryman is published every Tuesday morning upon the plantation of the editor, away off in the country, 9 miles from any town or village. It is emphatically a country paper, and will represent the interests of the country. Our post-office is Eatonton, with which we have daily communication . . .

Three short poems appear, signed "F.K.," probably the composition of the editor himself, who had used the pseudonym of "Frank Kemble" in publishing his juvenilia, *Kemble's Poems*, in 1847. Perhaps the most important item from a literary standpoint is the advertisement that read: "Wanted. An active, intelligent white boy, 14 or 15 years of age, is wanted at this office, to learn the printing trade." It was this item that a few days later brought Joel Chandler Harris to Turnwold "to learn the printing trade."

The aim of Turner may be stated in his own words, appearing in the number for May 6, 1862: [181]

Our aim is to model our journal after Addison's Little Paper, The Spectator, Steele's Little Paper, The Tatler, Johnson's Little Papers, The Rambler and The Adventurer, and Goldsmith's Little Paper, The Bee: neither of which, we believe, was as large as The Countryman. It is our aim to fill our Little Paper with Essays, Poems, Sketches, Agricultural Articles, and choice miscellany. . . . We wish to make a neatly-printed, select Little Paper—a pleasant companion for the leisure hour, and to relieve the minds of our people somewhat from the engrossing topic of war news.

Later in the same year we find this statement:

The Countryman will contain the cream of the world's literature. . . . I shall be more careful and more studious than ever, to make the very best selections for my Little Paper, and only those which will be of permanent interest and value. . . . I have a great storehouse of these things [choice miscellany of wit, humor, anecdotes, poems, etc.] in my library, and will give them to my readers much cheaper, and in more convenient form than they can be obtained anywhere else.[182]

To offset any idea that his paper might be dubbed a newspaper, Turner earlier had declared:

It is not a newspaper, but we seek to make it a miscellaneous journal of choice things, a friend of the right, and an enemy of the wrong. . . . It is folly to talk of making a weekly journal published in the country, a *news*paper. Such a thing cannot be. The Countryman is simply an Essayist: that is all.[183]

The pride of Turner, which seems to have surpassed that of preceding Georgia journalists like William Tappan Thompson, William C. Richards, C. R. Hanleiter, and Philip C. Pendleton, led him to confess to the following:

It is entirely foreign to the nature of a Southern gentleman to advertise himself, or to drum for subscribers. This is one reason that so few Southern literary, or miscellaneous journals succeed. . . . I have got my consent to advertise—but to drum, never! I could not, under any circumstances, ask a man to subscribe for my paper. It is not genteel to do so.[184]

His only experience in "drumming," he says in the same connection, was while he was conducting his quarterly, the *Plantation,* in 1860; but after asking a few friends to subscribe to his magazine, he had become too disgusted to continue.

The *Countryman* devoted most of its space to miscellany. In the third issue we find an article on Chaucer and a review of Dickens' *Hard Times*,[185] and later a discussion of John Gower,[186] James I,[187] and like topics. Turner never lacked copy for his foreman and apprentice. Harris tells us that "instead of clipping from his exchanges, the editor sent to the office three books, from which extracts could be collected. These books were *Lacon*, Percy's *Anecdotes*, and Rochefoucauld's *Maxims*.[188] Turner himself was probably the author of numerous short discussions of the political questions of the day, especially as they related to the controversy between Jefferson Davis, President of the Confederacy, and Joseph E. Brown, Governor of Georgia, in which the latter accused the former of attempting to violate states' rights in his conduct of the military affairs of the Confederacy. The most important contribution to this controversy will be discussed later in another connection.

If Turner had done nothing else besides befriending Joel Chandler Harris, his life would have been well spent, for it was on the Turner plantation that Harris came in contact with the African folklore that produced his "Uncle Remus," the delight of innumerable readers.[189] When Harris was little more than thirteen years old, he became a member of the Turner establishment, where, in addition to his work in the printing office at Turnwold, he had leisure for association with the negro slaves, who were as kindly treated as any ever were in the Old South. In the large Turner library he was able to satisfy his craving for literature, and in his associations with his employer he was treated as kindly and as tenderly as a son. When Harris began to write essays and poems for the *Countryman,* he received the kind of advice a young writer should receive at the hands of an elder. R. L. Wiggins, in his *Life of Joel Chandler Harris,* has revealed the intimacy between Turner and Harris. Among the latter's papers he has found a note that illustrates Turner's kind helpfulness:

> For the first time since you sent in this article I have found time to examine it; and though it has merit, I regret that I have to reject it, because it is not up to the standard of *The Countryman.*
> In the first place, you have made a bad selection in the article you have chosen for a subject. That article is contemptible and beneath criticism. Captain [Henry Lynden] Flash [editor of the Macon *Daily Confederate*] did his paper injustice in publishing it.
> In the next place, there is want of unity and condensation in your article. It is headed "Irishmen: Tom Moore," and then goes off on a great variety of subjects, and is too diffuse on everything it touches.
> In writing, hereafter, first select a good, worthy subject; second, stick to that subject; and, third, say what you have to say in as few words as possible. Study the "nervous condensation" which you so much admire in Captain Flash.
> All this is for your good.
> August 21, 1864.   J. A. TURNER [190]

Harris had not worked long on the *Countryman* before items written by him began to appear in its pages. At first the item was merely a recipe for making ink,[191] an article on "Grumblers," [192] or a conundrum signed "Countryman's Devil." [193] Wiggins, in his biography of Harris, lists more than thirty items by Harris appearing in the *Countryman*,[194] but he fails to mention the youth's first attempt at literary criticism: "Henry Lynden Flash," a review of the collected poems of a young man who was then editor of the Macon (Georgia) *Daily Confederate*.[195] Besides miscellaneous poems, Harris' contributions include several short stories, as well as a long review of *Macaria*, by Augusta J. Evans,[196] and a criticism of Griswold's memoir of Edgar Allan Poe.[197] Harris, as a critic, usually quotes the opinions of other men, yet now and then he utters a personal opinion that is sometimes impressionistic rather than truly critical. As a youth, however, he was laying the foundation for a critical judgment that later proved to be both sound and reasonable.

Turner's views on the negro question were not so narrow as those of many other Southerners. He saw no objection to educating the negro if he proved capable of being taught. In the midst of the Civil War he declared:

> There is a law on our statute book forbidding the teaching of negroes to read. . . . I don't think the statute is of any importance, any way. I think that without it, there would be no more negroes taught to read than are with it. . . .
> Why not take a practical view of this subject?—Is there any sin in the Georgia statute against educating negroes. None whatever. . . .
> The negro is either capable of education, or he is not. (I speak of him as a race.) If he is capable of education, it is a sin to withhold it from him. If he is incapable of it and so created by his Maker, it may be folly to say, by law, he shall not have an education, but it is neither wickedness, nor sin.[198]

The relation of Turner to his own slaves was a patriarchal one. He treated them so well that many of them stayed on the plantation at the end of the war which liberated them. He realized, too, that the negro was an integral part of the Southern social system before the war; hence his statement:

With regard to literature, I do emphatically wish us to have a Southern literature. And prominent in our books I wish the negro to be placed. The literature of any country should be a true reflex, in letters, of the manners, customs, institutions, and local scenery of that country.[199]

The motto of the *Countryman* at first was "Brevity is the soul of wit," but on September 22, 1863, this was changed to "Independent in Everything, Neutral in Nothing," perhaps the most suitable of all for the fiery and outspoken man, who had attracted attention both as a lawyer pleading cases in court and as a member of the State legislature who did not hesitate to express his opinion. On June 6, 1865, after the Southern cause had gone down to a glorious defeat, the motto of the paper was "Independent in Nothing, Neutral in Everything," a pathetic reminder of the fact that Turner himself had suffered the indignity of arrest by the "Yankee" authorities for some strong statements appearing in the *Countryman*. Finally, after a gap of several months—during which the periodical suspended operations—on January 30, 1866, the motto became "Devoted to the Editor's Opinions," remaining thus for the few months left of the life of the work.

The *Countryman* appeared weekly, three months comprising a volume, until the issue for October 6, 1863, when, for twelve consecutive numbers, each volume consisted of only one issue. This procedure put into effect an idea of Turner's which he thus expresses near the beginning of Volume XIX:

It is my desire, if I live to see the close of this unholy war, to go back, and beginning with the year 1846 [when he had first begun to write for the public], to publish a volume of *The Countryman* for every year from that date down to the last of my life, including the year 1846, to embrace all that I have written. By making the volumes of the The Countryman small, I have run them up to a number (19) which represents the number of years I have been writing for the press. Henceforth The Countryman will be published in annual volumes, beginning with this year.[200]

Before the end of 1862 the size of the *Countryman* was reduced,[201] but the number of pages was increased to eight. The latter number, however, was decreased in the course of the war because paper became scarce and because unsettled conditions caused difficulties. In June, 1865, Turner was placed "under military arrest by General Wilson in Macon, Georgia," upon the charge of "publishing disloyal articles" in the *Countryman*.[202] Certain restrictions were placed upon the periodical, so that no issue was published between that of June 27, 1865, and that of January 30, 1866. With the latter date, however, the persecuted editor resumed publication, but not for long. The last number of the *Countryman* was that of May 8, 1866, as we learn from a penciled note by Joel Chandler Harris on a copy preserved among his papers. The note is as follows:

This is the *very last* number of *The Countryman* ever issued. I mean this is the last paper printed; and it was printed by my hand May 9, 1866. It was established March 4, 1862, having lived four years, two months, and four days.[203]

The success of Turner's periodical appears to have been remarkable. In September, 1862, Turner states:

The success of The Countryman has been remarkable. . . . One universal acclaim of approbation has gone up from the Southern press in favor of this journal. . . . Nor has this been the only success of The Countryman. Most remarkable of all, has been its pecuniary success, at a time when it would seem ruin to begin the publication of a newspaper at only $1 per annum. A circulation in Virginia, N. Carolina, S. Carolina, Georgia, Florida, Alabama, Mississippi, Louisiana, Texas, and Tennessee, and which would also have reached Kentucky and Missouri, but for the war, has enabled The Countryman already to more than pay expenses, and opens a bright future for it, when the clouds of war shall be dispelled, and peace once more smile upon our land.[204]

In spite of Turner's dislike for "drumming" for subscribers, he seems in some way to have struck a popular note. In December, 1862, he further declares:

The Countryman is self-supporting. It pays for itself. . . . It is a source of gratification and pride for me to know that upon my whole list, there is not one single non-paying subscriber. As soon as a subscription expires, the name of the subscriber is invariably stricken from the list. . . . Every mail that comes adds a few subscribers to my list, and my circulation is gradually and certainly increasing.[205]

Turner's difficulties are reflected in his statement in April, 1863, that his paper "has almost too many subscribers for the present unfavorable times, and its list is steadily increasing. . . . Now it is read in every state in the Confederacy, and that, too, by ladies and gentlemen of refined tastes, good education, and liberal principles." [206] The circulation reached nearly 2,000 subscribers at one time,[207] a remarkable number for such unsettled times in the South.

Contributions to the *Countryman*, of necessity because of war conditions, came from only a few writers. Besides those by Turner and Harris, contributions came from William Wilberforce Turner, W. H. Sparks, James R. Watts, and from writers who used such pseudonyms as "Sally Poke" (J. A. Turner?), "Herbert" (Charleston), "The Hermit," and "Larry." "Sally Poke" contributed "Letters from Mrs. Poke," [208] which describe, with illiterate spellings and broad humor, conditions at Milledgeville, the State capital, during the session of the legislature. W. W. Turner contributed a column for a number of weeks entitled "My Grand-Father's Chair," [209] which consisted of biographical sketches and informal essays on a variety of topics. The writings of the editor of the *Countryman*, however, were by far the most interesting and most important of all those appearing in the periodical. His "Life of an American Citizen: Being the Biography of William Turner" [210] sketched the life of Turner's father, one of the pioneer settlers in Putnam County in the early nineteenth century. "The Old Farm-House of Uncle Simon" [211] was a series of sketches like those of Sir Roger de Coverley in Addison and Steele's *Spectator* in the early eighteenth century in England. This series had formerly appeared in 1848, at least in part, in the *Southern*

Literary Gazette (Athens), edited by William C. Richards, and in Turner's own *Plantation* (Eatonton) in 1860. These essays picture the social conditions in the Old South in a romantic fashion in the manner of the *Sir Roger de Coverley Papers*. But the best of Turner's writings to appear in his journal will be treated later more in detail.

Turner did not hesitate to state the truth, even about himself. In 1865 he reprinted some scathing criticisms of his *The Discovery of Sir John Franklin, and Other Poems*, which he had published in 1858.[212] The poems in this collection were, as all critics agreed, mediocre, and the poet made no effort to defend himself against these attacks. He seemed to derive rather a degree of satisfaction from the fact that he had been criticized so mercilessly. Others of his contributions were as follows:

"My Impressions of Tom [Thomas R. R.] Cobb"[213]
"Eulogy on Hon. Isaiah T. Irving"[214]
"Autobiography"[215]

Turner also tried his hand at drama in blank verse. "West Point: A Tragedy"[216] is based upon the relations between Benedict Arnold and George Washington during the Revolutionary War, and presents a very sympathetic portrayal of Washington's magnanimity toward his military rival. It is a full-length drama, with some good lines, and, of course, many poor ones. But blank verse in the hands of Turner is not crudely handled. His fault lies in the fact that it often lacks dignity, even though it has a musical sound. He needed polish more than anything else.

The best of his dramas is "Joseph: A Farce—In One Act."[217] Though signed "Addison," it is undoubtedly the work of Turner. It is a blank-verse sketch of a scene in Milledgeville, where Governor Joseph E. Brown is preparing to leave the State capital upon the approach of Sherman's army on its famous "March to the Sea." Joseph, of course, is Joseph E. Brown, and Davus is Jefferson Davis, President of the Confederacy. The drama is a humorous satire on the controversy between Brown and Davis over states' rights and on Brown's nervousness at the approach of Sherman. Some of the closing lines give the reader an insight into the character of Turner himself, who seldom lost an opportunity to give a humorous turn to any event that attracted his attention:

Scout.—(To Joseph)
    Hail, Joseph! I am sent to let thee know
    That Sherman's coming with a mighty host.
    He's passed through Eatonton, burned Denham's shop,
    And Dennis' mill, and 's crossing at Sheffield's.
    If you would save your bacon, now, cut out—
    Lose not a moment, if you would escape.
Joseph.—What, save my bacon, did the fellow say?
    What's bacon worth without a dish of greens?
    Where are my brave militia that I thought
    Would storm the gates of hell, to save old Joe?
Scout.— Why, sir, they're gone, as hard as they can tear.
Joseph.—Well, that's enough to make a preacher swear.

   .   .   .   .

Joseph.—(Solus)
    All gone but me, as I'm a living sinner—
    Yet I have greens and bacon left for dinner,
    When I get home, 'way down in Sumter county,
    Where Davus ne'er shall share this fellow's bounty.
    'Tis very bad! My state has gone at last,
    And soon will I be going pretty fast.
    My country's fallen, and my state enslaved.
    But all my collards, and my conscience, saved.
                    (Exit running)

Some time in 1858 Turner had begun a long narrative poem in heroic couplets entitled "The Old Plantation," which he had completed about a year later. This poem throws a romantic glow over conditions surrounding an old Southern home as viewed by a "Wanderer," returned to gaze upon a deserted plantation. The poet does not deny that his work, in plan at least, is modeled upon Goldsmith's "The Deserted Village," and that "even the phraseology . . . may sometimes . . . nearly approximate that of the sweet singer of home affections," but he does make the following claim: "The local scenery, manners and customs here described, I claim to be true to nature: and I have only mingled with my description, sentiments common to us all, and which more favored writers have used, with better effect, before me. . ."[218] "The Old Plantation" ran serially in eight numbers of the *Countryman*[219] and is about 1,400 lines in length. Because it portrays certain phases of plantation life, as well as certain figures of importance in Georgia history, five selections are quoted from the poem.

The poem opens with the Wanderer soliloquizing on the old plantation, which he views after years of absence:

> Dear sacred spot, secluded vale of shade,
> How oft hath fancy, lingering here, delayed
> To trace the scenes of merry childhood o'er,
> By memory's magic roused to life once more.
> Here, weary wanderer, worn and wasted turned,
> I greet the hour for which my heart hath yearned,
> Where'er my steps by fortune have been cast,
> Blest scenes, my first affection and my last.[220]

The second selection indicates the view of slavery held in the Old South by many people of that section:

> In lengthened line, stretched out by yonder wood,
> The negro servants' humble hovels stood;
> Yet Heaven more bliss dispensed within their huts
> Than splendid gold in many a palace shuts.
> Slaves were they called: but aye the vacant mind
> Was free from chains which freemen often bind.
>
> . . . .
>
> No nobler deeds celestial records hold,
> Than those which feed the hungry, warm the cold;
> No nobler sons to Heaven's reward shall pass,
> Than those which foster Afric's toiling class.[221]

The poem contains a picture of William H. Seward, Senator from New York and later President Lincoln's Secretary of State, who, in his youth, had taught school for a few months near the Turner home in Putnam County. We have Turner's own words as to the identity of this young schoolmaster, as well as to that of the other two characters described later.[222] The following lines portray the young Seward:

> The stranger youth, received with open arms,
> Here, in this vale, enjoyed its rustic charms;
> Here taught the youth committed to his charge,
> 'Mid favors many, and a bounty large . . .
>
> . . . .
>
> But time rolled on, the youth a man became,
> And won his way to fortune and to fame,
> With hatred every act of kindness paid,
> And rabid hosts against our homes arrayed;
> Did all he could to wound the friendly hand,
> And hurl the robber on our Southern land.[223]

The pastor of the little country church is a portrayal of the Rev. William Arnold, who had faithfully served a church near Turnwold:

> As well he strove with heavenly art to please,
> His snowy locks uplifted in the breeze,
> All eyes were turned to view the man of God,
> Cheer 'neath his smile, or bend to take the rod.
>
> . . . .
>
> With manly tears, he spoke of heavenly love,
> And every thought and feeling raised above,
> As melting strains made every listener weep,
> And silence even blasphemers forced to keep.[224]

The final picture is that of Bishop William Capers, of the Methodist Episcopal Church, South, while he was still a young preacher at camp meeting:

> His gleaming eye upon his hearers fell,
> And searched the heart of every listener well;
> His words directed with unerring aim,
> The coldest heart would kindle to the flame.
> Now all the woes the man of God pronounced,
> And now the flesh and all of sin denounced,
> Convicting power descending from on high,
> Like molten metal from a flaming sky.[225]

This poem, with all its faults and eighteenth-century artificiality, possesses some real merit. Except in the pages of the

Countryman and in pamphlet form a few months later, it has appeared nowhere in print. It represents the meditative Turner, whereas most of his other long poems are satirical. After the discontinuance of the *Countryman* he wrote little except a few prose sketches of historical and autobiographical nature, which appeared in *Scott's Monthly Magazine* (Atlanta) in 1867 as "Crumbs from the Countryman's Table." [226] Turner died in 1868, at the age of forty-two, a disappointed and broken-hearted devotee of the Old South.

8. GRIFFIN—*BUGLE-HORN OF LIBERTY* (1863–?)

TITLE: *Bugle-Horn of Liberty*
FIRST ISSUE: July (?), 1863   LAST ISSUE: Oct. (?), 1863
PERIODICITY: Monthly
EDITORS AND PUBLISHERS: Hill & Swayze, Griffin
LOCATION OF FILES: *NcD:* I, 3 (Oct., 1863)

Georgia's only purely humorous magazine in the Old South of which an issue is extant is the *Bugle-Horn of Liberty,* bearing the subtitle of "A Humorous Monthly, Devoted to Fun, Fact and Fancy." Only one issue, Volume I, No. 3 (October, 1863), survives, but the periodical apparently began in July of that year, inasmuch as the *Countryman* (Turnwold) for July 21, 1863, speaks of receiving the first number. It was a quarto magazine, sixteen pages to the issue, with three columns to the page: a format very similar to that of the *Countryman,* which it was probably imitating. Bill Arp (Charles Henry Smith) was a contributor to the work, but the October, 1863, number apologizes for the absence of Arp's usual contribution, saying that his letter has failed to arrive and that he "has gone soldiering with a big gun, and is now guarding a gap in the mountains of Hepsidam, about sixteen miles from Rome." The editor promises that Arp, now a Lieutenant of Artillery, will be on hand in the next number.

The *Bugle-Horn of Liberty* is a mediocre periodical, filled with jokes and amusing anecdotes. The extant issue has six illustrations accompanying jokes mainly about the "impressment" of private homes by the Confederacy for military purposes. The best contribution to this number is an anonymous two-page humorous, illustrated history of "Gen. John Morgan," a satire on military officials. Only two pieces are marked as original: the prose "Outside of a Horse," by John Happy; and a humorous poem, "Paddy O'Conner, or Love and Bad Luck," by Ed. Porter Thompson, dated "Catoosa Springs, Ga., Sept. 1st, 1863." Selected material consisted of "Letter from Currycomb," from the Mobile *Tribune;* "Judy's Letter of Bad News," by Judy O'Halligan; [227] and "An Explanation of the Conscription Act," by Artemus Ward (Charles Farrar Browne), taken from the Boston *Post*. One and one-half columns are devoted to "The Drama," giving items of dramatic interest from all over the United States, none of which is of any importance. The rest of the contents of the *Bugle-Horn* consists of fillers, mainly jokes. The magazine is scarcely more than a hodge-podge of humorous material, and far below the average of Georgia periodicals. It could hardly have survived long during the unsettled conditions of the State in 1863 and 1864.

CHAPTER IV

Summary and Conclusion

THE LITERARY periodicals of *ante-bellum* Georgia are not without significance in the history of Georgia culture, even though attempts to establish them were often sporadic and ill-timed. Certain influences were at work during the period in question, some of them to be found in both North and South, yet some of them more or less peculiar to the South, and possibly to Georgia in particular. Certain definite conclusions can be drawn, when one views the periodicals as a whole, to indicate the extent to which Georgia had the same literary problems found elsewhere, and the extent to which Georgians were interested in the production of a distinctively Southern literature. A survey of the field of Georgia periodicals reveals the factors involved in the success or failure of the editors to meet the cultural needs of a fast-growing state.

1. EDITORS AND PUBLISHERS

With a few notable exceptions the editors of these publications were native Georgians. Of those who established periodicals, none was what might be called, in the true sense of the word, a man of letters. Five of them were licensed preachers: J. W. Burke, Henry Holcombe, George F. Pierce, William C. Richards, and D. K. Whitaker. Only one of these, Richards, was in any marked degree successful in his journalistic undertakings. Only two were lawyers: William Tappan Thompson and Joseph Addison Turner, both of them excellent editors.

The other editors were, in the main, printers or professional journalists. Of the men filling editorial positions in Georgia for any length of time, only three came from outside the State: William C. Richards (England), William Tappan Thompson (Ohio), and D. K. Whitaker (Massachusetts). Although these three adopted the Southern view of slavery as their own, they did not surrender their independence of judgment, but kept in touch and sympathy with literature in the North and abroad. Their aim apparently was to make Southern literature regional rather than sectional. Almost nothing is known concerning the minor editors and publishers of the State. Biographical dictionaries ignore them, and our only source of information is the magazines themselves. Four editors of Georgia periodicals, all belonging in the later periods, are important enough for short biographical sketches.

The best magazine editor of the four was William Carey Richards (1818–92), who was born in London but emigrated to America in 1831. After his education at Madison University in New York he removed to the South, living fifteen years in Georgia and South Carolina. Though a licensed Baptist preacher, he devoted his most productive years in Georgia to authorship and journalism, with his *Orion* (Penfield), *Schoolfellow* (Athens), and *Southern Literary Gazette* (Athens). During the period between 1848 and 1850 he dominated the literary horizon of Athens, where his *Southern Literary Gazette* seems to have been the inspiration for the journalistic ventures of T. A. Burke and Charles L. Wheler, each of whom launched a magazine that was ambitious, if not very successful. And the publication of *Roath's Monthly Magazine* (Athens) was probably also due to the influence of Richards. He contributed at different times to the *Christian Review* (New York), the *Southern Quarterly Review* (Charleston), and the New York *Knickerbocker*. After leaving Georgia, Richards spent a few years in Charleston, whither he had removed his *Schoolfellow* and *Southern Literary Gazette*. Soon thereafter he moved to Rhode Island to enter the regular ministry of his church. Rich-

Summary and Conclusion 181

ards was a writer as well as editor and publisher. He wrote numerous poems and tales for his own, as well as for other, magazines, and contributed many humorous stories, his best work, to his *Orion*. In these stories, such as "The First Lecture at Smithville," "The Smithville Gas Frolic," "The Smithville Debating Society," and "Major Theophilus Bandbox Bubble, or The Nice Young Man," he attempted to picture the primitive social conditions in Middle Georgia of the 1840's, perhaps influenced by the popularity of the tales of Longstreet and Thompson. His poems are usually short lyrics showing a sentimental appreciation of nature and romantic love. As an editor Richards desired to establish a popular magazine of a high type in the South, and in that respect he attained a measure of success. He did not fail to make the contents of his publications both interesting and entertaining. His unbiased efforts in behalf of a Southern literature aided in keeping Georgia periodicals free from the expected attacks upon the North and upon Abolitionism. He, above all other Georgia editors, attempted to stimulate intellectual activity in the South by means of a discussion of miscellaneous contemporary problems in the "Editor's Department" of the *Southern Literary Gazette*. And if we can believe the words of Richards himself, his journalistic ventures were, at least for a time, practically self-supporting.

William Tappan Thompson (1812–82), editor at different times of the Augusta *Mirror*, the *Family Companion* (Macon), and the *Southern Miscellany* (Madison), was a native of Ohio, who after a few years of journalistic experience in Philadelphia had settled in Georgia. At the age of twenty-three he became secretary to Gov. J. D. Westcott, of Florida, under whom he also studied law. He returned to Georgia and in 1835 became associate editor of the Augusta *State Rights' Sentinel*, whose general editor was Augustus Baldwin Longstreet. After military service in Florida against the Seminole Indians he founded the Augusta *Mirror* in 1838, the first literary journal in Georgia. In 1842 this periodical was merged with the *Family Companion* (Macon), but Thompson remained with the new venture only a few months. He then joined the editorial staff of the *Southern Miscellany* (Madison), in which he published many of his famous "Maj. Jones' Letters." From 1845 to 1850 Thompson was in Baltimore as associate editor with Park Benjamin, and later editor and sole proprietor, of the *Western Continent.* In 1850 he removed to Savannah to establish the Savannah *Morning News,* with which he was connected until his death in 1882. On his editorial staff was Joel Chandler Harris during 1870–76. Thompson published, in addition to his tales in various periodicals, three collections of humorous stories: *Major Jones' Courtship* (1840), *Major Jones' Chronicle of Pineville* (1843), and *Major Jones' Sketches of Travel* (1848). The two latter books were still in print, respectively, in 1880 and in 1893. As far as his literary periodicals were concerned, Thompson was more successful as a writer than as an editor. He furnished his readers with plenty of interesting and amusing tales, many of which he himself wrote. It was his desire to develop a regional literature in the South, and his efforts, like those of William C. Richards, helped to keep Georgia periodical literature free from rabid sectionalism. Thompson was primarily a newspaper man who found his life work in the Savannah *Morning News.*

Joseph Addison Turner (1826–68), editor and publisher of *Turner's Monthly* (Eatonton), the *Plantation* (Eatonton), and the *Countryman* (Turnwold), was perhaps the greatest dilettante of all Georgia editors. He tried his hand, at one time or another, at almost every type of literature, and almost always managed to produce a work of a fair degree of excellence, at least in his later years. After studying one term at Emory College (Oxford), Turner taught school for a year before turning to law as a profession. His published works include *Kemble's Poems* (1847), *The Cotton Planter's Manual* (1857), and *The Discovery of Sir John Franklin and Other Poems* (1858), none of them of any literary merit. At different times he contributed to *De Bow's Review,* the *Southern Literary Messenger, Godey's Lady's Book,* and *Peterson's Magazine,* as well as to such

Summary and Conclusion

Georgia periodicals as the *Southern Literary Gazette* (Athens), *Southern Field and Fireside* (Augusta), *Turner's Monthly* (Eatonton), the *Plantation* (Eatonton), the *Countryman* (Turnwold), and *Scott's Monthly Magazine* (Atlanta). In his writings Turner devoted himself to eighteenth-century models, particularly in his "My Uncle Simon's Plantation," a series of essays in Addisonian style that appeared in the *Southern Literary Gazette* under the pseudonym of "Abraham Goosequill," and in his long poem in heroic couplets, "The Old Plantation," which appeared serially in the *Countryman*. During the Civil War, Turner was actively engaged in politics, and since he had been rejected for military service because of lameness, he used his voice and pen in defense of the Confederacy. During this time he used his talents as a satirist in attacking not only the North, but even Governor Joseph E. Brown, of Georgia, who was at odds with Jefferson Davis on the conduct of the war. Turner was the only editor of a Georgia literary periodical to own a plantation with a large number of slaves, and the only one to feel too proud, as he himself stated, to advertise himself or to dun subscribers for money. He was not dependent upon literature for a livelihood, but was interested in the production of a Southern literature, based, he finally declared, on slavery and Southern themes. During the Civil War, when the South was cut off from contact with publishing houses of the North, Turner's *Countryman*, the only journal published on a Southern plantation, had a wide circulation, large enough, the editor declared, to pay all expenses. In fact, Turner stated on several occasions that he had little trouble in making his journalistic ventures pay as they went. Turner's *Plantation*, a quarterly which he published during 1860, might have developed into a magazine of some worth had not the Civil War cut its life short. Founded as a pro-slavery organ, it contained popular reading matter along with political articles and discussions. All in all, Turner, the greatest of the native Georgia editors, was the only one who in any marked degree exemplified the traditional "Southern gentleman." During the closing years of his life Turner was arrested by the military authorities who ruled Georgia in the Reconstruction Period following the war, and because of alleged disloyal articles appearing in his *Countryman,* this journal was suppressed. In 1868 he died a disappointed and heart-broken man.

Daniel K. Whitaker (1801–81), a native of Massachusetts and a graduate of Harvard, settled in the South because of ill health and became a typical "Yankee gone Southerner." With his scholarly interests and love for literature he accepted the sectional tenets of his adopted home and devoted most of his life to the establishment of periodical literature there. His first journalistic experiment in the South was the *Southern Literary Journal* (Charleston), founded to encourage Southern authorship and to develop Southern culture. This magazine was followed by his *Southern Quarterly Review* (New Orleans and Charleston), which in some issues compares favorably with Northern quarterlies. In 1850 Whitaker founded *Whitaker's Magazine* (Charleston and Columbia), which merged in 1853 with the *Southern Eclectic* in the latter's home, Augusta, Georgia, with Whitaker as associate editor. The new editor opened the pages of the magazine to original contributions, many of them by his wife, Mary Scrimzeour Whitaker. Whitaker's journalistic career in Georgia is of little importance, for his new magazine was combined with the Augusta *Home Gazette* in 1854, and ceased to be exclusively literary. Whitaker, however, was an editor of ability, for he was especially successful with the *Southern Quarterly Review,* one of the best quarterlies in the Old South. He was partly the victim of circumstances, as were most Southern *ante-bellum* editors.

In considering the Georgia editors, one is struck by the fact that the magazines of the State were established and run by amateurs at a time when capital and experience were greatly needed. If we except a few men who worked only a short while in Georgia, there were no professional magazinists, no professional writers from whom to draw contributions as in New York and Philadelphia. Editors could pay little or nothing and were forced to rely on amateur writers. Men in the North like N. P. Willis, Godey, and Graham were making money in the forties and fifties with their magazines; and even when a man like William C. Richards did establish a periodical as good as some in the North, Southerners would not adequately support it. Lack of distribution facilities and inability to collect were at the bottom of the failure of many Georgia editors. Exchange lists were expensive or difficult to secure, and the value of advertising was scarcely understood. Even when an editor tied up his literary magazine with other interests, such as in the *Medical and Literary Weekly,* the *Hygienic and Literary Magazine,* and the *Southern Field and Fireside,* he was hardly more successful, except that the last-named journal did circulate more widely than would have been normally expected because it was impossible to get Northern magazines during the war.

Several women edited literary periodicals in the state. Miss C. W. Barber (1823–?), a native of Massachusetts, removed to Georgia, where she first edited the Madison *Visitor.* During the war she edited the *Southern Literary Companion* (Newnan), and afterward, *Miss Barber's Weekly* (Newnan). Mrs. Mary E. Bryan (1842–1913), native of Florida but long a Georgia resident, edited the *Georgia Literary and Temperance Crusader* (Atlanta); Mrs. Rebecca Haynes Riley, the nonextant *Southern Literary Journal* (Oxford); Mrs. L. Virginia French (1830–81), the *Georgia Literary and Temperance Crusader* (Atlanta); and Mrs. Mary A. McCrimmon, the *Educational Monthly* (Lumpkin) during the war. All these women labored earnestly to give Georgians "correct and proper" literature, and as contributing editors, too, they often practically filled the pages of the departments committed to their care. They were not feminists, though Mrs. Bryan was nearest of the group to becoming one, but appeared concerned primarily with questions of morality and good taste.

The best editorial work in Georgia literary periodicals was done by two adopted citizens: Richards and Thompson. The latter was an ardent advocate of a Southern literature, but the former retained a more catholic view. He editorially declared his lack of sympathy with a purely Southern literature, but he had a strong desire for an American literature that would recognize regional elements. His influence doubtless had much to do with keeping the periodical literature of Georgia comparatively free from the sectionalism often found in *antebellum* magazines, especially in those published in Charleston.

As far as publishers are concerned, little can be said, for there were no large publishing houses in the State and few in the South—no large firms like Ticknor & Fields, Harper & Brothers, and G. P. Putnam & Company, which in the 1850's were publishing, respectively, the *Atlantic Monthly, Harper's Magazine,* and *Putnam's Magazine.* In 1859 possibly the two largest and best appointed Southern publishing houses were the Methodist Publishing House at Nashville, and the Franklin Printing House and Book Bindery established in Atlanta by Cornelius R. Hanleiter. It was, then, sometimes less expensive to have a book or periodical printed in the North. Paper and printing presses were sometimes hard to get in the South, and during the Civil War, when Southern publishers had to develop their own paper mills and ink factories, and when conscription near the end of the war made labor hard to find, it required almost superhuman efforts to get anything printed at all. In 1842 Richards was having his *Orion* printed in New York, and as late as 1860 the "Yankee-hating" Turner had his *Plantation* printed there also. It was scarcely profitable, at any period in the Old South, to print magazines in Georgia.

2. MAGAZINES

Between 1802 and 1865, Georgia editors and publishers began more than fifty literary magazines. Of the twenty-four discussed in this work, the *Georgia Analytical Repository* was

Summary and Conclusion 187

a bi-monthly; the Augusta *Mirror* was a semi-monthly; the *Plantation* was a quarterly; eleven periodicals were monthlies; and ten were weeklies. These magazines, with the exception of the *Countryman,* which apparently circulated widely during the Civil War, attracted little attention from out-of-the-state readers, though there is evidence that they were read to some extent in Charleston.

Several interesting publications appeared among Georgia periodicals. At least four college magazines were launched: the *Georgia University Magazine* (Athens), 1851–57?; *College Miscellany and Orphan's Advocate* (Covington), published by the Covington Female College, 1858–59?; the *Kennesaw Gem* (Marietta), by the young ladies of Marietta Female College, 1859–?; and the *Fly Leaf* (Newnan), by College Temple, 1859–?. Humorous magazines were: the *Horn of Mirth* (Athens), 1849–50?; the *Gopher* (Waynesboro), 1860; and the *Bugle-Horn of Liberty* (Griffin), 1863. Juvenile periodicals were: the *Youth's Repertory and Child's Magazine,* at an unknown place, 1831; *Youth's Companion* (Columbus), 1843; the *Schoolfellow* (Athens), 1849; the *Youth's Friend* (Augusta), 1850–?; the *Youth's Gem and Southern Cadet* (Macon), 1851; the *Child's Index* (Macon), 1862–65?; and the *Children's Guide* (Macon), 1864. Of the literary periodicals three titles indicate their devotion to the "Ladies": *Ladies' Magazine* (Savannah), 1819; *Southern Ladies' Book* (Macon), 1840; and *Family Companion and Ladies' Mirror* (Macon), 1841–43. Numerous others, however, had a "Ladies' Department" or section especially for women.

Georgia literary magazines were variously influenced by those from other states, though none were modeled on British periodicals. In types of reading matter *Graham's Magazine* (Philadelphia), the *Knickerbocker* (New York), and the *Southern Literary Messenger* (Richmond) furnished the chief models. All three magazines are constantly mentioned or commended in Georgia publications. The *Southern Ladies' Book* (later the *Magnolia*) and the *Family Companion* especially show the influence of the *Southern Literary Messenger;* the *Orion* and the *Southern Literary Gazette,* that of the *Knickerbocker.* Charleston magazines, even the *Southern Literary Journal* (1835–38), the *Southern Quarterly Review* (1842–57), and *Russell's Magazine* (1857–60), seem to have had little or no direct influence on Georgia periodicals. The advice of William Gilmore Simms, however, was often sought by Georgia editors, who valued his opinions, even though they did not always follow his advice. Joseph Addison Turner was the only editor to veer toward classical standards, especially in his *Countryman* (1862–66), which he claimed to be patterned after the *Spectator* and similar eighteenth-century journals. Both Turner and Richards show polish and urbanity in their essays, the former in his "Abraham Goosequill Essays" in the *Southern Literary Gazette* and the *Plantation,* and the latter in his editorials in the *Southern Literary Gazette,* which strongly suggest the *Spectator.*

Subscription prices for Georgia magazines were about the same as those in the North during the period 1825–50. Although the New York *Knickerbocker* and the Richmond *Southern Literary Messenger* had a subscription rate of $5.00 per year, the standard in the North was usually $3.00—that of *Graham's* and *Godey's* in Philadelphia. Georgia weeklies during this period almost invariably had a rate of $2.00—the *Southern Post,* the *Southern Miscellany,* the *Southern Literary Gazette,* and the *Friend of the Family.* Of the monthlies *Wheler's Magazine* had a rate of $1.00, *Turner's Monthly* $1.50, and the *Southern Eclectic* $3.00. The more successful monthlies had the rate of $5.00—*Southern Ladies' Book, Orion,* and *Family Companion.* The semi-monthly *Augusta Mirror,* which ran for over two years, quoted a subscription price of $3.00; and the quarterly *Plantation* in 1860 had a rate of $5.00. During the Civil War, with the fluctuation of Confederate money, subscription rates ran to an enormous figure; but so did the price of everything else at the same time.

Georgia magazines devoted little space to advertising, like

all early American periodicals. Illustrations were expensive and seldom appeared; and musical selections and fashions were almost never featured. It is strange that Georgia magazines attained even the measure of popularity they did possess, though several claimed fairly large circulations. Turner claimed that his publications made money for him; Richards declared that his periodicals would easily pay for themselves if the subscriptions were all paid for; and the *Southern Field and Fireside* (Augusta) claimed 13,000 subscribers in 1864. Georgia editors generally avoided book reviews (so they said) because they were not interesting to most readers and because quarrels often resulted from them. Heavy and stilted articles on important subjects and sentimental lightness in others indicate a lack of proper discrimination. Yet these magazines often contained interesting reading matter. The editors, in general, did not know how to put the contents of the magazines in attractive form; hence Southern readers usually preferred Northern periodicals, with illustrations, fashions, music, and many other attractive features.

Indicative of the support given Georgia magazines by their readers are the following statistics for Georgia in the U.S. Census figures for 1850:

Georgia in the U.S. Census for 1850

Periodicals	Number	Circulation	Copies Printed Annually
Literary and Miscellaneous	18	29,638	1,411,976
Neutral and Independent	6	3,046	747,340
Political	20	20,900	1,491,350
Religious	3	4,600	239,200
Scientific	4	9,300	181,000

Although Georgians gave little support to most of their local magazines, there are signs that they were sometimes interested in out-of-the-state publications. Issues for 1835–36 of the *Southern Rose,* a bi-monthly published in Charleston, show not only literary contributions from Georgia writers, but also remittances from Georgia subscribers, in addition to agents for the periodical in Augusta, Savannah, and Milledgeville (the State capital). Richard Henry Wilde, in the early days of the *Southern Literary Messenger* (Richmond), obtained 100 subscribers for that magazine in Augusta alone, "and continued for many years to collect and remit their subscriptions."[1] In 1849 we find the editors of *Godey's Lady's Book* (Philadelphia) promising "something pretty" to a lady in Macon, Georgia, who has been a continuous subscriber to the work since its beginning in 1830.[2] *Whitaker's Magazine* (Charleston) in 1850 listed 170 subscribers from Georgia, mainly from Savannah, Augusta, Macon, Milledgeville, and Columbus.[3] Our most important information, however, concerns the circulation of the *Southern Literary Messenger* in Georgia. A careful count of the paid subscription list of the *Messenger* for the period 1834-49, the only figures known to exist,[4] reveals that between 1836 and 1846 Georgia stood next to Virginia, the home state of the magazine, and in 1847 and 1849 stood third. Georgia's largest number of paid subscriptions was 224 in 1842. During the fifteen-year period in question South Carolina, supposed patron of literature, stood in sixth place, surpassed, in order, by Mississippi, Alabama, North Carolina, Georgia, and Virginia. Corroboration of the above figures is found in the fact that in 1842 Georgia had 11 agents for the *Messenger*, second only to Virginia.[5]

3. CONTENTS OF MAGAZINES

Georgia magazines contained practically the same kind of reading matter to be found in periodicals all over the United States: historical tales based upon the American Revolution, pioneer life, and Indian adventures; sentimental and didactic lyrics, often addressed to beautiful ladies, and poems illustrating a love of natural scenery; and essays on varied topics. In Georgia periodicals are found stories by Augusta Evans Wilson, William Wilberforce Turner, Joseph Addison

Turner, Augustus Baldwin Longstreet, William Tappan Thompson, and the Rev. F. R. Goulding; poems by Robert M. Charlton, Thomas Holley Chivers, Henry Rootes Jackson, Maria J. McIntosh, Alexander Means, Dr. E. M. Pendleton, Carrie Bell Sinclair, William C. Richards, and Richard Henry Wilde; essays and sketches by prominent lawyers, doctors, preachers, and college professors. Very little of any lasting literary importance appeared in the newspapers during the existence of these magazines except Longstreet's *Georgia Scenes,* which first appeared, tale by tale, with few exceptions, at different times in the Milledgeville *Southern Recorder* and the Augusta *State Rights' Sentinel.* Travel letters and sketches of foreign countries were seldom published except by William C. Richards in his *Southern Literary Gazette,* nor did any editor ever devote much space to music, painting, sculpture, and the other fine arts. Only the Augusta *Mirror* printed musical selections, and only the *Orion* and the *Family Companion* were ambitious enough to attempt expensive etchings like those of *Godey's* in the North. Scientific articles are uncommon and usually discuss scientific facts from the popular viewpoint. There was little French and German influence in the reading matter of Georgia periodicals. Only now and then were there tales translated from one of these languages or short sketches of some well-known foreign writer.

Selected material came from many sources, sometimes from books and short works by Northern authors like Franklin, Longfellow, Whitman, or Irving, usually reprinted from some other magazine. The most frequently quoted periodicals were: the New York *Knickerbocker,* New York *Mirror,* New York *Ladies' Companion, Burton's Magazine* (Philadelphia), the *Southern Literary Messenger* (Richmond), London *Athenaeum,* London *Quarterly, Blackwood's,* and *Bentley's Miscellany.* Only one eclectic magazine was begun in *ante-bellum* Georgia, the *Southern Eclectic* (Augusta), and this ran only a few months, taking most of its material from British periodicals.

Book reviews were little more than indiscriminate praise of an author or work, and the American or Southern bias was often present when national or sectional differences were involved. In truth, these so-called reviews were really book notices indicating that a certain book, telling of certain conditions, was on the book market. Comments on social customs appeared only in Richards' *Southern Literary Gazette,* in which the author displayed an interest, like that of Addison, in what was going on around him. Richards, alone of Georgia editors, seemed thoroughly conscious of world literature in its broadest sense.

The popularity of the humorous tale in *ante-bellum* Georgia literature cannot be too strongly emphasized. Few of these tales appeared first in book form. In fact, only two of any importance come in this category: *A Hasty Plate of Soup,* edited by Peter Pickle (pseudonym of Joseph Addison Turner);[6] and the *Kups of Kauphy: A Georgia Book, in Warp and Woof,*[7] an anonymous collection of tales and incidents, told sometimes in rather coarse language. Some humorous stories appeared first in newspapers, such as Longstreet's *Georgia Scenes,*[8] which were first published variously, except for a few stories, in the Milledgeville *Southern Recorder* and the Augusta *State Rights' Sentinel.* By far the bulk of Georgia humor appeared first in the state periodicals, and became apparently the most popular type of reading matter and most distinctively Southern. Beginning with the *Ladies' Magazine* (1819) and continuing down through the *Countryman* (1862–66), these tales were often the *pièce de résistance* of individual issues. A list of the most important of these works will indicate their prevalence:

Ladies' Magazine (1819)—Letters of "Tom Queerfish," "Benjamin Symmetry," and "Polly Proportion"
Southern Post (1837–39)—Letters of "William Barlow, Esq."
Augusta *Mirror* (1838–41)—Longstreet's "Georgia Scenes," tales by William Tappan Thompson
Family Companion (1841–43)—W. T. Thompson's "Maj. Jones' Letters," tales by John B. Lamar

Orion (1842–44)—W. C. Richards' "Smithville" tales
Southern Miscellany (1842–46?)—W. T. Thompson's "Maj. Jones' Letters"
Southern Literary Gazette (1848–49)—Tales by W. C. Richards and T. A. Richards
Wheler's Magazine (1849–50)—Tale by J. J. Hooper, and anonymous tales
Friend of the Family (1849–51)—W. T. Thompson's "Maj. Jones' Letters"
Roath's Monthly Magazine (1853–?)—Tales by David L. Roath, editor
Southern Field and Fireside (1859–64)—Longstreet's "Master William Mitten," and tales by Philemon Perch (Richard Malcolm Johnston)
Plantation (1860)—J. A. Turner's "Cable Canticles," "Julius Sneezer," etc.
Countryman (1862–66)—Letters of "Sally Poke," and J. A. Turner's miscellaneous articles and tales
Bugle-Horn of Liberty (1863)—writings of Bill Arp (Charles Henry Smith)

Of Georgia editors, William Tappan Thompson, William C. Richards, David L. Roath, and Joseph Addison Turner were particularly fond of featuring such tales of humor and local color, and the reading public apparently enjoyed most those magazines that included them. This situation in Georgia apparently bears out the statement of Frank Luther Mott in his *A History of American Magazines, 1741–1850* that the period 1825–50 showed humor as "far more prominent in American periodical literature . . . than it had even been before. . . ."[9] Almost without exception the most important and most successful periodicals of *ante-bellum* Georgia were those that featured humorous writings. Perhaps the most popular humorous writer of this period was Augustus Baldwin Longstreet, whose *Georgia Scenes,* picturing a primitive Middle Georgia community with excellent local color, makes entertaining reading even today. William Tappan Thompson's "Major Jones" sketches, another series of popular tales, contain some coarseness of language and incident, but they do not violently distort the picture of a special type of settler in Middle Georgia.

Humor in early Georgia magazines consisted principally of exaggeration and incongruities, seldom racy or vulgar, sometimes in the form of "Letters." Tales by Longstreet, Hooper, and Thompson attempted to picture frontier conditions in the South, the latter two writers employing dialect to lend color. Longstreet and Thompson may, in truth, be considered the high water mark of Georgia humor before the Civil War. Close to them in fame would come Richard Malcolm Johnston and Bill Arp (Charles Henry Smith), who did most of their writing after the war. The humor of Richards may be characterized as urban—light and graceful, even in his "Smithville" tales dealing with small-town life. His writings provoke a smile rather than outright laughter. It remained for Joseph Addison Turner to satirize and caricature his contemporaries. His "Julius Sneezer" and miscellaneous writings in the *Plantation* and the *Countryman* caricature both Jefferson Davis and Governor Joseph E. Brown, of Georgia, and satirize the abolitionists of the North. All in all, the humorists of the State played by far the largest part in entertaining those who went to Georgia literary periodicals for reading matter.

Georgia literary magazines were apparently uninfluenced by such Northern movements as Transcendentalism and general reform. Several Temperance periodicals were founded in the State, but general magazines paid little attention to them. Northern agitation for the abolition of slavery, naturally enough, put the South on the defensive, and the sectional spirit began to color much that was written in that section. Yet the South continued all along to buy magazines from the North. Sectional feeling and prejudice ran high in Georgia, to be sure, yet Georgians, in spite of that feeling, seemed slow to support their own periodicals. Naturally many native authors defended slavery in their writings, but one can scarcely condemn the use of slavery as a background for literary production. Georgia writers and editors had little to say about slavery except when discussing politics, and Georgia periodicals are remarkably free from the expected sectional spirit in its narrow sense. The only quarterly in the State, Turner's *Plantation* (1860), was the only magazine to devote itself entirely to a defense of Southern principles, but that was at the very outbreak of the war. The idea of the "Southern gentleman" was nowhere stressed by Georgia editors. Only Turner ever said anything about Southern pride and chivalric ideals, and that was in connection with conducting a magazine. His "The Old Plantation," published serially in the *Countryman* during the Civil War, is a long romanticized description of the South as it existed in the mind of one who believed that slavery was an unadulterated blessing to the slaves.

The types of reading matter in Georgia periodicals, except for the lack of translations from German poems, are more or less those popular throughout the country at the same time. The chief taboos for contributors to Southern magazines were antislavery sentiment and religious heterodoxy. From the beginning sentimental literature predominated. In the 1830's and 1840's tales of the American Revolution, of frontier life, and of the Indians were popular. With the 1840's came interest in education for women and in popular science, with resultant essays covering these subjects. Of the sentimental and satirical, religious and historical poems appearing in Georgia magazines, the Romantic lyric was perhaps the predominant type, usually on romantic love, the American past, and religion. Some poets adhered to the heroic couplet, but others tried their hands at narratives in blank verse and in other meters. The influence of no particular Northern or British author colored the poetry of Georgia. During the period from 1850 to 1860 the domestic sentimentalists dominated prose with their tearful fiction. In this decade the country was reading such sentimental works as: *Linda* (1850) and *The Planter's Northern Bride* (1853), by Mrs. Caroline Lee Hentz; *The Curse of Clifton* (1853), by Mrs. E. D. E. N. Southworth; *Tempest and Sunshine* (1854) and *Lena Rivers* (1856), by

Mary J. Holmes; *The Wide Wide World* (1850), by Susan Warner; *The Lamplighter* (1854), by Maria S. Cummins; *Ten Nights in a Bar Room* (1855), by T. S. Arthur; and *Beulah* (1859), by Augusta J. Evans (Wilson). Harriet Beecher Stowe's *Uncle Tom's Cabin* (1852), with all its propaganda against slavery, was sentimental to the extreme.[10]

An analysis of the reading matter in Georgia magazines indicates that the reading taste of the State was by no means as old-fashioned as commonly supposed. Georgians kept in touch with books from the North and from England, and enjoyed the novels of Dickens, Bulwer, Marryat, G. P. R. James, Cooper, and those of the "Feminine Fifties." They also read the works of Macaulay, Bayard Taylor, Charles Lamb, Irving, and Simms, besides shorter essays and poems from elsewhere. They liked literature characterized by didacticism, Romanticism, and sentimentality; they wanted it to be "correct and proper." J. S. Buckingham, an English visitor to Georgia in the 1840's, declared: "The literary taste of the South, whether evinced in its newspapers, magazines, or larger works, may be called of the florid composite order, with a singular admixture of the most opposite principles; especially of the most unbridled democracy and an earnest defence of . . . slavery."[11] Georgians, like most Southerners, were less conservative in their reading than in their politics, and though susceptible to new ideas, were slow in adopting them. Their attitude toward slavery made them suspicious of new ideas and movements fostered by abolitionists.

4. CONTRIBUTORS TO MAGAZINES

Contributions to Georgia magazines came from numerous writers, who cannot be classified by states or sections because of the many pseudonyms used. Authorship was scarcely a profession in the South, and talented Georgians, pursuing law and politics for a livelihood, ordinarily had only their leisure time for literary pursuits. Robert M. Charlton, Henry Rootes

Jackson, and Richard Henry Wilde, of Savannah, were such men. College professors and women of leisure, too, by way of avocation, contributed to magazines. Slave-holding was common in the State, but Joseph Addison Turner was the only large planter in Georgia to edit literary periodicals or to contribute to them.

The lesser and younger Northern writers often contributed to Georgia magazines, especially to those edited by Richards:

T. S. Arthur (New York); Park Benjamin (Boston and New York); Mrs. E. Jessup Eames (New York); Mrs. E. F. Ellet (New York and South Carolina); Mrs. Emma C. Embury (New York); Hannah F. Gould (Massachusetts and Vermont); Grenville Mellen (Maine); John Neal (Maine and New York); Mrs. Frances S. Osgood (New York); Mrs. Anna L. Snelling (New York); E. G. Squier (New York); Mrs. L. H. Sigourney (Connecticut); Mrs. Seba Smith (Maine); Mrs. Joseph C. Neal (New York); Mrs. Ann S. Stevens (Connecticut, New York, and Maine); Samuel Woodworth (Massachusetts and New York).

To these might be added the name of Longfellow, who contributed one poem to a Georgia magazine: "A Lay of Courage" to *Wheler's Magazine*. Tales of love and adventure came even from G. P. R. James, the popular British novelist, who had visited Simms in South Carolina in the 1850's, and must have, on that visit, met various literary and journalistic figures in the South.

South Carolina writers made frequent contributions to Georgia periodicals. Mary E. Lee constantly contributed poems, tales, and essays, often sending the same poem to several different magazines at various times. And the prolific William Gilmore Simms frequently contributed works of his, always, of course, at the solicitation of some Georgia editor. Other South Carolina contributors were: Edwin Heriot, J. M. Legaré, Mrs. Mary S. Whitaker, Mrs. Caroline Gilman (formerly of Massachusetts), Mrs. Caroline Gilman Jervey, and Henry Timrod.

A list of Georgia contributors to periodicals of the State would be too long for inclusion here,[12] but it would include most of the prominent writers in the fields of poetry, fiction, and the essay. A great number of these were women, some of them semi-professional writers, who stayed at home and wrote while their husbands or fathers were engaged in business for a livelihood. They began to write in the 1840's and increased in numbers during the 1850's. Among the women contributors to Georgia magazines the names of the following are most frequently encountered:

Miss C. W. Barber (Newnan); Mrs. Mary C. Bigby (Americus); Miss Annie R. Blount ("Jennie Woodbine," Augusta); Mrs. Mary E. Bryan (Atlanta); Mrs. M. Louise Crossley ("Currer Lyle"); Mrs. C. W. (Kate A.) DuBose ("Leila Cameron," Sparta); Maria Gertrude Kyle (Mrs. Buchanan); Clara Le Clerc ("Harry Holt" and "Polly Holt"); Mrs. Mary A. McCrimmon (Lumpkin); Maria J. McIntosh ("Aunt Kitty"); Mrs. W. C. Richards ("Mrs. Manners" and "C.H.B.R."); Mrs. Dr. Riley ("Le Ferve"); Carrie Bell Sinclair ("Clara," Augusta); Miss Susan A. Stuart (Savannah).

The principal aim of these women, it would seem, was to encourage authorship among their sex. The period from 1840 to 1870 witnessed a great increase in the number of women writing for magazines. Writing was almost the only avenue open to them for self-development, since even school teaching was hardly "genteel"; and it afforded an outlet for the pent-up emotions of the wives and daughters of lawyers, teachers, preachers, and other professional men. It was mainly the latter class of women who wrote for *ante-bellum* periodicals in the South—urban women rather than members of the families of planters. These women usually wrote romantic tales such as "The Randolphs of Randolph Hall," "The Household at Haywood Lodge. A Story of the South," and "The Flower Basket"; sentimental lyrics on "Love's Maladies," "The Dead Love," " 'Twas Night upon the Battle-field," and "Sunshine in the Cottage"; or poems descriptive of a beautiful scene in nature. Few women wrote essays dealing with anything except "The Language of Flowers," household hints, or the fine arts. Pseudonyms sometimes hid a woman's identity from her disapproving family; and, too, they afforded a mask for the woman forced to write for pecuniary gain. Some Georgia women, however, disdained the use of pseudonyms, preferring to sail under their own colors rather than to appear affected. Mrs. Mary E. Bryan and Miss C. W. Barber are examples of the latter group.

Georgia writers of both sexes were contributors to periodicals outside the State and sometimes to Northern publications. Except in the case of prizes for literary productions, authors could not expect any remuneration for their work, yet contributions continually poured in, stimulated in part by the desire to create a Southern literature. *Wheler's Magazine* (1849–50) was the first Georgia periodical to state that it paid for regular contributions in anything except free subscriptions; but the *Southern Field and Fireside* (1859–64) seems to have had a long list of regularly paid contributors, even during the Civil War, when it had a subscription list of around 13,000. Yet the vast majority of Southern writers received nothing but thanks for their contributions to any periodical. Such a situation is reflected in Augusta J. Evans' *Beulah,* one of the most popular of Southern ante-bellum novels.[13] The heroine, after submitting a contribution to the editor of a Southern magazine, is told that it is not customary to pay for such work, since most authors write mainly for fame. To this declaration Beulah replies:

> I happen to know that northern magazines are not composed of gratuitous contributions; and it is no mystery why southern authors are driven to northern publishers. Southern periodicals are mediums only for those of elegant leisure, who can afford to write without remuneration. With the same subscription price, you cannot pay for your articles. It is no marvel that, under such circumstances, we have no southern literature.[14]

The editor, after reading her article, agrees to pay her for it, but asks her to say nothing about the contract to anyone.

Anti-slavery agitation undoubtedly had a detrimental influence on Georgia writers. Being constantly on the defensive as regards slavery, they were unable to give a complete or unbiased picture of life on a Southern plantation. Joseph Addison Turner is an extreme example of this bias, for he seldom lost an opportunity, in prose or in poetry, to laud slavery as a God-given institution for the betterment of the negro race. The development of the sectional spirit in the South sowed the seeds of a unity that might have, under different conditions, produced a great literature. Southern talents, however, gravitated toward political controversy, leaving the literary field, in the main, to the less-gifted sentimentalists and moralists.

5. GEOGRAPHICAL DISTRIBUTION OF MAGAZINES

It is interesting to observe the various literary centers of the State in which the most important magazines began. Of the twenty-four discussed in this work, by far the greatest number were established in Middle Georgia. In that section of the State were found the densest population before 1865, the largest number of slaves in proportion to the white population, and the lowest percentage of illiterate whites. And there, too, were found the leading institutions of higher learning: Franklin College (the State university), Emory College, Mercer University, Oglethorpe College, and the Georgia Female College (later Wesleyan College). In at least two cities the presence of a college or university was the dominant influence in these journalistic experiments. Savannah, the largest city until the middle of the nineteenth century, was the home of the first two literary periodicals: the *Georgia Analytical Repository* (1802–03) and the *Ladies' Magazine* (1819). Its position on the Atlantic seaboard gave it a contact with the North that the inland towns could not have until the railroads were built. We know, too, that in 1802 Joseph Dennie's *Port Folio* (Philadelphia) was being widely read there, and that Georgia magazines later had many subscribers in that city. Yet after 1819 not a single literary periodical of importance began publication in Savannah before 1865. The *Friend of the Family*, which appeared there from 1849 to 1851, attracted little attention, and only one writer of any prominence contributed to its pages. William Tappan Thompson, who began publication of the Savannah *Morning News* in 1850, contributed several humorous tales, but no other writer apparently showed any interest in the magazine. Even the transfer of the *Southern Ladies' Book* (1840-42) from Macon to Savannah with the new title of *Magnolia* failed to arouse any enthusiasm, and the periodical was removed to Charleston, where it died. The Georgia city, which grew in population from 5,000 in 1800 to 11,000 in 1840, with its libraries and people of wealth and culture, was probably too near Charleston to be able to establish any literary publications. Yet some of Georgia's leading citizens were living there in *ante-bellum* days. Richard Henry Wilde, author of the famous lyric "My Life Is Like the Summer Rose," as well as of other short poems and translations, was at one time Attorney General of Georgia, and from 1827 to 1835 was a representative in the United States Congress. Robert M. Charlton, contributor to the New York *Knickerbocker* and to numerous Southern periodicals, was, at different times, United States District Attorney, Judge of the Superior Court of Georgia, United States Senator, and Mayor of Savannah. Henry Rootes Jackson, author of *Tallulah, and Other Poems*,[15] and of many poems appearing in Southern magazines, was a lawyer, soldier, diplomat, and editor. William Bacon Stevens, an Episcopal minister, was the State historian and author of a two-volume *History of Georgia*.[16] Besides other Savannah writers of minor importance several men were owners of large libraries: Alexander A. Smets, Israel K. Tefft, and George Wimberley-Jones DeRenne. Yet the city, with all its culture and interest in magazines elsewhere, could not, or at least did not, initiate or inspire the establishment of any important literary periodical before the Civil War.

In the period 1837-46 the leading city in the production of periodical literature was Macon, situated almost in the center of the State. The *Southern Post and Literary Aspirant* (1837-39?) was the first of its three magazines, but the next two were among the best produced in *ante-bellum* Georgia: the *Southern Ladies' Book* (1840-42) and the *Family Companion and Ladies' Mirror* (1841-43). Macon at this time was a small city of about four thousand people, but it was the seat of the Georgia Female College (later Wesleyan College), whose pre-eminence in the education of women was the probable inspiration for the attempts to make the city a literary center. In this same period Augusta, with no college or university, gave the *Mirror* (1838-41) to the State; and Penfield, the village home of Mercer University, with its versatile William C. Richards, established the *Orion* (1842-44). Madison, with its *Southern Miscellany* (1842-46?), produced some good periodical literature during the few months when William Tappan Thompson was editor of the journal. The predominant position of Macon was not due to the labor of any one editor or of any particular writer. The work, however, of Mrs. Sarah Lawrence Griffin, who launched the *Family Companion and Ladies' Mirror*, probably best symbolizes the new interest in education for women.

Between 1848 and 1854 the focus of periodical literature was Athens, a town of two or three thousand people in Middle Georgia about a hundred miles north of Macon. For many years it had been the seat of Franklin College (the State university), and with the coming of William C. Richards to its midst in the late 1840's, it began to show such an interest in the launching of magazines that it produced five of the most important in this period. Richards began his labor with the *Southern Literary Gazette* (1848-49) and then added the *Schoolfellow* for juveniles in 1849. He soon transferred both publications to Charleston, but his journalistic connections with Charles L. Wheler and T. A. Burke almost certainly inspired, respectively, *Wheler's Magazine* (1849-50?) and the *Mistletoe* (1849). In Athens, too, T. A. Burke published his *Horn of Mirth* (1849-50), a humorous monthly which had a subscription list of 1,200 in 1850, according to Census figures. This periodical occasioned much favorable comment in contemporary magazines, but no files of it have been located—not even a single issue. The last work begun in Athens was *Roath's Monthly Magazine* (1853–?), a magazine of a fair degree of excellence. Nothing else of importance occurred in this period except the publication of the *Southern Eclectic* (1853–54) in Augusta, a periodical devoted principally to reprinting material from British magazines.

From 1859 to 1865, experiments in periodical literature were carried on in the towns of Middle Georgia, from Augusta on the east, to Newnan, near the Alabama border. More were conducted, it seems, in Atlanta, the fast-growing railroad center of the State, than anywhere else. With a population of about twelve thousand people at the outbreak of the Civil War, this city, soon to be made the capital of the State, was the center of a commercial activity that may have encouraged the publication of magazines. Its *Medical and Literary Weekly* (1859), *Hygienic and Literary Magazine* (1860), and *Georgia Literary and Temperance Crusader* (1860–?) were all mediocre works, but they were steps in the direction of a wider appreciation of literature. The Augusta *Southern Field and Fireside* (1859–64) was perhaps the best magazine of the period, with its decidedly varied reading matter. The most colorful journalistic figure of these years was the energetic Joseph Addison Turner, who published in 1860 four numbers of Georgia's only quarterly, the *Plantation,* founded mainly to defend slavery against Northern attacks. His next publication was the *Countryman* (1862–66), printed at Turnwold, nine miles from Eatonton, home of the *Plantation*. Turnwold was forty miles northeast of Macon, and it was in Turner's printing office there that Joel Chandler Harris got his first lessons in printing and writing. The *Countryman* was the only periodical published on an *ante-bellum* Southern plantation, and it attracted many subscribers, chiefly because Southerners during the war were cut off from receiving reading matter from the North. In 1863 the *Bugle-Horn of Liberty* appeared for several issues in Griffin, forty miles south of Atlanta. It was a humorous monthly with contributions from Bill Arp (Charles Henry Smith). The years between 1859 and 1865 could scarcely have produced any important literary magazines. After 1861 or 1862 paper and ink were almost impossible to get, and labor was often scarce. And, too, the South was intent on winning the Civil War, and there was little time for literary activity.

6. IMPORTANCE AND INFLUENCE OF GEORGIA MAGAZINES

Georgia *ante-bellum* periodicals are important, first of all, because they furnished a medium wherein authors of the State could get their writings published. Some of these writers were rank amateurs who were trying their wings in literary flight, and who were delighted if only their names appeared in print. Some were amateurs with a touch of genius, who welcomed an opportunity to test their wares in the magazine laboratory. Some writers of talent, such as William Tappan Thompson and Augustus Baldwin Longstreet, found their magazine contributions popular enough to be issued in book form in later months. All in all, these literary periodicals became the repository of some short stories and poems that are not only interesting today, but worth preserving as cameos of literature.

In the next place, from Georgia magazines we learn something about the culture of the State before and during the Civil War—a culture that paralleled that of most other Southern states. Georgians apparently liked the same kind of sentimental, emotion-arousing literature being read all over the country, excluding, of course, only what tended to criticize their cherished institutions. Contents of Georgia periodicals were similar to what was found in the lighter magazines of the North, and the periodicals themselves were seldom stiff and pedantic, usually light and entertaining, yet containing some solid reading matter for the instruction of the reading public.

In comparison with the best periodical literature in other sections, that of Georgia cannot rank high. Northern magazines were concentrated in the large cities of New York, Philadelphia, and Boston, and it is to be expected that some of these cities, with their cultural advantages, resident professional men of letters, and large publishing houses, would surpass in production all that the entire State of Georgia produced with its amateur writers before the war. Philadelphia, between 1833 and 1865, could claim such excellent magazines as *Godey's Lady's Book* (1830–98), *Burton's Gentleman's Magazine* (1837–40), *Graham's Magazine* (1840–58), *Peterson's Ladies' National Magazine* (1842–98), and the *Union Magazine of Literature and Art* (1847–52). Besides these were many others of less importance, as short-lived as most Georgia periodicals. New York and Boston also produced a number of magazines. It must not be forgotten, however, that in the smaller Northern towns, in rural New England, and in the newly-settled West many periodicals were begun that lasted no longer and were of no greater literary importance than those of Georgia, with its small towns and widely-scattered population.

Among the literary periodicals of the immediate South before 1865 the best was doubtless the *Southern Literary Messenger* (Richmond). Several of Charleston's best periodicals were short-lived, but some were above the average and superior to those of Georgia: the *Southern Review* (1828–32), the *Southern Literary Journal* (1835–38), the *Southern Quarterly Review* (1842–57), and *Russell's Magazine* (1857–60). Aside from the above-mentioned periodicals, those of Georgia are not below the general average, but are superior in some instances. Of Georgia periodicals it can at least be said that they exceed in number those established in Charleston. William Stanley Hoole lists eighty-two periodicals published in the latter city between 1732 and 1864.[17] Georgia, between 1802 and 1865, published 134 periodicals of all kinds, fifty-seven of which claimed literary interests.[18] What the story would have been if the State had had one or more great literary centers is problematical. Certainly there was commendable activity for the development of culture in the State; the magazines in Georgia attest this.

The influence of Georgia magazines outside the State was doubtless inconsiderable. Beyond commendatory notices in the periodicals of other states, we find few references to them. Their circulation was confined mainly to Georgia, though there is evidence that Charlestonians and people from Alabama and Mississippi subscribed to some of the better works. Contributions from Northern writers probably indicate a passing interest in what was going on in the South, for the latter section was generally regarded elsewhere as without education and with little culture worthy of the name. Even cultured Charleston looked upon Georgia as a new and crude country and did little to encourage Georgia editors except to contribute to their periodicals or to send a few subscriptions to the magazines.

The main contribution to American literature made by Georgia periodicals consists in its humorous tales, more distinctly Georgian than anything else appearing in print. The list of important humorous writings has been given earlier in the chapter and needs no repetition. In these humorous tales are preserved humorously realistic pictures of pioneer life in the State, with little attempt at artistry, and often with little exaggeration; but no attempt was made to play up the negro, as did Joel Chandler Harris after the war.

7. REASONS FOR THE COMPARATIVE FAILURE OF GEORGIA MAGAZINES

What were the reasons for the comparative failure of Georgia literary periodicals before 1865? The conditions that existed all over the South, a few of which were found in large areas of the North, may be advanced to explain the failure:

Summary and Conclusion 207

1. Lack of large literary centers to foster periodicals, as Boston did the *North American Review,* New York the *Knickerbocker,* and Philadelphia *Godey's Lady's Book.*
2. Almost exclusive Southern interest in political controversy.[19]
3. Policy of sending periodicals to subscribers on credit.
4. Lack of sufficient advertisements in periodicals.
5. Lack of good business management on the part of editors. Most Southern editors were amateurs.
6. Non-support by the people of the South. Southern readers apparently preferred to subscribe to Northern periodicals.
7. Authorship not a profession in the South. Not enough good material could be obtained from Southern writers. Planters and people of leisure would not write.
8. Northern publishers had better facilities for printing, illustrating, distributing, and marketing their periodicals, even in the South.

Little remains to be said concerning the literary periodicals of Georgia. They undoubtedly fostered an interest in literary production that would otherwise have remained latent, for among the many poems and tales appearing in their pages are some of unusual excellence. One thing is certainly true: these *ante-bellum* periodicals sowed the seed that produced much of the literature for which the New South has become famous, especially in the realm of humor and local color. Particular examples of this carry-over from the Old South are Bill Arp (Charles Henry Smith), Richard Malcolm Johnston, and Joel Chandler Harris. Bill Arp's "Letters" continued to multiply after their first appearance in 1861, and were published in the North in 1866 as *Bill Arp, So Called* and in 1873 as *Bill Arp's Peace Papers.* Later publications were *Bill Arp's Scrap Book* (1884) and *Bill Arp: From the Uncivil War to Date* (1903). Bill Arp handled the negro and the Georgia cracker dialects in a trustworthy manner. Dialect was less used in his later writings, but the rustic philosophy was unchanged. Richard Malcolm Johnston, learning after the Civil War the financial value of his stories, embarked upon a career of writing local color tales, his popular *Dukesborough Tales* appearing in 1871. He spent most of his *post-bellum* days in the North and aided in popularizing the humorous local-color story. Joel Chandler Harris, who had learned the printer's trade in the printing office of Turner's *Countryman* during the Civil War, and who had studied the negro on the plantation of Turner, began writing his humorous sketches while working with the Atlanta *Constitution* in the 1870's. Learning that negro characters had a vast appeal, he issued many of his sketches in book form: *Uncle Remus: His Songs and His Sayings* (1880) and *Nights with Uncle Remus* (1883), both of which were popular in the North. Thus humor, mixed with local color, in the hands of Harris ties up very definitely with *ante-bellum* humorous sketches, typically Georgian. Sectionalism had changed to regionalism in literature with Bill Arp, Johnston, and Harris, but the seeds of the Old South had not been planted in vain. Georgia has reaped a substantial harvest from her literary periodicals before the Civil War.

APPENDICES

Appendix A

Georgia Literary Periodicals to 1865 [1]

City	Title	Years	Periodicity	Editors
Athens	*Athenian	1836 (Prospectus)	Monthly	?
	*Georgia Home Gazette	1852?–53?	?	Messrs. Smythe and Whyte
	Georgia University Magazine	1851–?	Monthly	Members of Senior Class
	*Horn of Mirth	1849–50	Monthly	T. A. Burke
	Mistletoe	1849	Monthly	J. W. and T. A. Burke
	Richards' Weekly Gazette (see Athens Southern Literary Gazette)			
	Roath's Monthly Magazine	1853	Monthly	David L. Roath
	Schoolfellow	1849–57?	Monthly	William C. Richards
	Southern Literary Gazette	1848–49	Weekly	William C. Richards and D. H. Jacques
	Wheler's Monthly Magazine	1849–50	Monthly	C. L. Wheler

[1] No files have been located for periodicals marked with asterisk (*).

City	Title	Years	Periodicity	Editors
Atlanta	Georgia Literary and Temperance Crusader	1860–?	Weekly	W. H. Stokes (?) John H. Seals (?) Mrs. Mary E. Bryan Mrs. L. Virginia French
	Hygienic and Literary Magazine	1860	Monthly	Mrs. Dr. Riley (Le Ferve)
	Medical and Literary Weekly	1859	Weekly	Dr. V. H. Taliaferro Dr. A. G. Thomas
	Monthly Miscellany	1849–?	Monthly	Joseph S. Baker
	Scott's Monthly Magazine	1865–69	Monthly	J. J. Toon Rev. W. J. Scott
	Soldiers' Friend	1863–64	Weekly	J. J. Richards
Augusta	Georgia Home Gazette	1851–52	Weekly	Messrs. Smythe and Whyte
	Mirror	1838–41	Semi-Monthly	William Tappan Thompson Augustus Baldwin Longstreet
	Southern Eclectic	1853–54	Monthly	J. H. Fitten James M. Smythe Daniel K. Whitaker
	Southern Field and Fireside	1859–64	Weekly	W. W. Mann, John R. Thompson James Nathan Ells

Appendix A

City	Title	Years	Periodicity	Editors
Augusta				S. A. Atkinson
	*Southern Pioneer	1839 (Prospectus)	Weekly	Charles Wyatt Rice
	*Youth's Friend	1850	Monthly	Miss W. C. Tyson
Buena Vista	*Literary Vade Mecum	1852-53	?	James W. Gaulding (?)
Columbus	*Southern Bee	1839 (Prospectus)	Weekly	William J. Ellis and James H. Ticknor
	*Youth's Companion	1843	Monthly	Rev. Thomas M. Slaughter (?)
Covington	*College Miscellany and Orphan's Advocate	1858-59	Monthly	?
Eatonton	Plantation	1860	Quarterly	Joseph Addison Turner
	Turner's Monthly	1848	Monthly	Joseph Addison Turner
Fayetteville	*Literary Casket	1859-60?	Weekly	?
Greenville (?)	*Georgia Weekly	1860	Weekly	William Henry Peck
Griffin	Bugle-Horn of Liberty	1863	Monthly	Messrs. Hill and Swayze
La Grange	*Rose-Bud	1848?	Monthly	Young ladies
Macon	Army and Navy Herald	1863-65	Weekly	Robert J. Harp
	Children's Guide	1864-?	Monthly	?
	Child's Index	1862-65	Monthly	Samuel Boykin
	Family Companion and Ladies' Mirror	1841-43	Monthly	Mrs. Sarah Lawrence Griffin

Early Georgia Magazines

City	Title	Years	Periodicity	Editors
Macon				William Tappan Thompson
	Southern Ladies' Book (later the Magnolia, Savannah)	1840–42	Monthly	George F. Pierce Philip C. Pendleton William Gilmore Simms
	Southern Post and Literary Aspirant	1837–39	Weekly	Cornelius R. Hanleiter Philip C. Pendleton
	*Tomahawk	1853	Monthly ?	Peter Pickle (Joseph Addison Turner)
	*Youth's Gem and Southern Cadet	1850	Semi-Monthly	J. C. Reagan
Madison	Southern Miscellany	1842–49?	Weekly	Cornelius R. Hanleiter William Tappan Thompson
Marietta	*Kennesaw Gem	1859	Quarterly	Students of Marietta Female College
	Masonic Journal	1849–52	Monthly	?
	Masonic Signet and Journal	1855–60	Monthly	Samuel Lawrence
Milledgeville	*Day Star of Truth	1850	Monthly	Rev. Mr. Reagan
	*Gem	1850	Monthly	J. C. Reagan
Newnan	*Fly Leaf	1854?	Quarterly	Senior Class of College Temple
	Southern Literary Companion	1860–65	Weekly	Miss C. W. Barber

Appendix A 215

City	Title	Years	Periodicity	Editors
Oxford	*Southern Literary Journal	1850	?	Mrs. Rebecca Haynes Riley
Penfield	Orion	1842–44	Monthly	William C. Richards
Savannah	Friend of the Family	1849–51	Weekly	E. J. Purse
	Georgia Analytical Repository	1802–03	Bi-Monthly	Rev. Henry Holcombe
	Ladies' Magazine	1819	Weekly	William C. Barton Richard W. Edes Henry P. Russell
	Magnolia (see Macon Southern Ladies' Book)			
	*Literary Messenger	1842–?	Weekly	H. S. Bell
Turnwold	Countryman	1862–66	Weekly	Joseph Addison Turner
Waynesboro	*Gopher	1860	Semi-Weekly	?
?	Youth's Repertory and Child's Magazine	1831	Monthly	?

Appendix B

Georgia Non-Literary Periodicals to 1865 [1]

City	Title	Years	Classification	Periodicity
Athens	*American Mechanic	1850	Industrial	Weekly
	*Southern Silk Grower and Agricultural Register	1839 (Prospectus)	Agricultural	Monthly
	*Sunday School Advocate	1850	Religious	Weekly ?
Atlanta	*Cherokee Baptist	1860–?	Religious	Weekly
	*Educational Journal and Family Monthly	1857–?	Educational	Monthly ?
	Educational Repository and Family Monthly	1860–61	Educational	Monthly
	Georgia Blister and Critic	1854–55	Medical	Monthly
	*Knight of Jericho	1855–?	Temperance	Weekly
	*Lita National	1860–?	Masonic	?
	*Luminary	1846?–?	Religious	?
	Medical and Surgical Journal	1855–81?	Medical	Monthly
	*Olive Branch	1857	Religious	?
	Southern Dental Examiner	1860–61	Dental	Monthly
Augusta	Baptist Banner	1859–64	Religious	Weekly
	Christian Union	1856–?	Religious	Monthly

[1] No files have been located for periodicals marked with asterisk (*).

Appendix B

City	Title	Years	Classification	Periodicity
Augusta	Gleanings of Husbandry	1840–42?	Agricultural	Monthly
	*Harp	1839 (Prospectus)	Musical	Semi-Monthly
	Herald	1838–?	Business	Monthly
	*Masonic Journal	1842–?	Masonic	Monthly
	*Pacificator	1864–?	Religious	Weekly
	Southern Christian Advocate	1862	Religious	Weekly
	Southern Cultivator	1843–71?	Agricultural	Monthly and Semi-Monthly
	*Southern Farmer's Register	1842 (Prospectus)	Agricultural	Monthly
	Southern Medical and Surgical Journal	1836–69?	Medical	Monthly
	Unitarian Christian	1831	Religious	Quarterly
	Washingtonian, or Total Abstinence Advocate	1842–45?	Temperance	Semi-Monthly
Columbus	Baptist Expositor and South-Western Intelligencer	1842–?	Religious	Monthly
	*Farmer's Register	1840–?	Agricultural	?
	Soil of the South	1851–57	Agricultural	Monthly
	*Southern Silk Journal: and Farmers' Register	1839–?	Agricultural	Monthly
Covington	Southern Baptist Messenger	1851–61?	Religious	Semi-Monthly
	*Southern Family Journal	1850?–?	Religious	Weekly
Forsyth	*Educational Journal	1857–61?	Educational	Weekly
	Evangelical Pulpit	1862–?	Religious	Monthly
	*Gazette	1840–?	Agricultural, etc.	Weekly
	Southern Botanico Journal	1841–42?	Medical	Monthly

Early Georgia Magazines

City	Title	Years	Classification	Periodicity
Forsyth	Southern Botanico-Medical Journal	1842–43?	Medical	Semi-Monthly
	Southern Medical Reformer	1845	Medical	Monthly
	*Georgia Baptist	1854?	Religious	?
?	*Georgia Gazette	1860?	?	?
?	Planters' Weekly	1860–61?	Agricultural	Weekly
Greensboro	*Educational Monthly	1861?–?	Educational	Monthly
Lumpkin	Park's Reform Medical and Family Journal	1853	Medical & Family	?
	*Champion	1860?	?	Bi-Monthly
	*Crusader	1849 (Prospectus)	Religious, etc.	?
Macon	Evangelical Universalist	1838?–40?	Religious	?
	Georgia Botanic Journal and College Sentinel	1847–48	Medical	Monthly
	Georgia Christian Repertory	1831–32	Religious	Weekly
	*Georgia Citizen Advertiser	1860	Political	Monthly
	*People's Reform Medical Journal	1856 (Prospectus)	Medical	Weekly
	*Reformer	1850?	Medical	Monthly
	*Southern Christian Spectator	1834 (Prospectus)	Religious	Weekly
	Southern Medical Reformer and Review	1852–60	Medical	Monthly
	*Southern Planter and Horticultural Lyceum	1834 (Prospectus)	Agricultural	Semi-Monthly
	Southern School Journal	1853–55?	Educational	Monthly

Appendix B

City	Title	Years	Classification	Periodicity
Macon	*Spiritualist	1860?	?	Bi-Monthly
Madison	*Bantling	1842?	?	?
Marietta	South Countryman	1859–?	Agricultural	Monthly
Milledgeville	*Christian Pioneer	1830 (Prospectus)	Religious	Semi-Monthly
	*Presbyterian	1847?–53?	Religious	Weekly
Mount Zion	Missionary Weekly	1819–?	Religious	Weekly
Newnan	*Progressionist	1859–?	?	Monthly
Penfield	Christian Index	1821–current	Religious	Weekly
	*Southern Baptist Review	1847 (Prospectus)	Religious	?
	Temperance Banner	1834–?	Temperance	Semi-Monthly and Weekly
Rome	Arminian Magazine	1848–49	Religious	?
	*Landmark Banner and Cherokee Baptist	1859–61?	Religious	?
Sandersville	Georgia Medical and Surgical Encyclopedia	1860	Medical	?
Savannah	Oglethorpe Medical and Surgical Journal	1858–61	Medical	Bi-Monthly
	Journal of Medicine	1858–66	Medical	Bi-Monthly
Scottsboro	*Georgia Academician and Southern Journal of Education	1834 (Prospectus)	Educational	Semi-Monthly
?	Southern Journal of Education	1833–?	Educational	Monthly

City	Title	Years	Classification	Periodicity
Sparta	Georgia Reporter and Christian Gazette	1826	Religious	Weekly
Trenton	*Methodist	1850–?	Religious	?
?			?	
Waresboro	* ?	1860?	?	Monthly
Washington	Southern Baptist Preacher	1840–41?	Religious	Monthly
Waynesboro	*Sky Rocket	1860	?	Monthly

Appendix C

Contributors to Georgia Literary Periodicals to 1865 [1]

Abbreviations Used

AM: Augusta *Mirror;* BHL: *Bugle-Horn of Liberty* (Griffin); C: *Countryman* (Turnwold); CI: *Child's Index* (Macon); FC: *Family Companion* (Macon); FF: *Friend of the Family* (Savannah); GAR: *Georgia Analytical Repository* (Savannah); GLTC: *Georgia Literary and Temperance Crusader* (Atlanta); HLM: *Hygienic and Literary Magazine* (Atlanta); LM: *Ladies' Magazine* (Savannah); M: *Mistletoe* (Athens); MLW: *Medical and Literary Weekly* (Atlanta); O: *Orion* (Penfield); P: *Plantation* (Eatonton); SE: *Southern Eclectic* (Augusta); SF: *Schoolfellow* (Athens); SFF: *Southern Field and Fireside* (Augusta); SLB: *Southern Ladies' Book* and *Magnolia* (Macon and Savannah); SLC: *Southern Literary Companion* (Newnan); SLG: *Southern Literary Gazette* (Athens); SM: *Southern Miscellany* (Madison); SP: *Southern Post* (Macon); TM: *Turner's Monthly* (Eatonton); WM: *Wheler's Magazine* (Athens).

Abdy, Mrs.—SP, SLB
Ada—SP
*Addisine, Nina—SFF
*Addison (see Joseph Addison Turner)
Adele—SFF
Adolphus—SP
Aglaus (see Henry Timrod)
*Albanio—AM
Alceus—SP
*Aleck—SLG

Alexander, James E.—SLB
*Algeroy—AM
Alguno—SFF
Allan—AM
*Alligator—AM
*Allspice, Josiah—SLG
Alpha—AM, SLG, SE
Alphonso—SLG
Alteram Partem—SE
Alton (see A. L. Taveau)
Amateur, An—SLG

[1] Asterisks indicate Georgia writers. Included among them are those known only through a Georgia address.

American in Paris, An—SFF
*Anders, Hon. G.—SLB
Ann E.—SLG
Annette—SLB
Anthropos—SP
Archaeus—AM
Arena—SFF
Aria—SF
Arion—SLB
Aristeus—SLB
Armstrong, Mrs. M.—GLTC
Arnell, David R.—SLG
Aros—SLB
Arthur, T. S.—FC, WM
Ashman—AM
Ashton, Ellen—SLC
Austin, Mrs. Sarah (A Disappointed Man)—FC

Baber, George—GLTC
Baber, Mrs. M. F.—SLG
Bachelor—SLG
*Baldwin (see Augustus Baldwin Longstreet)
Baldwin, Rev. J. D.—SLG
*Barber, Miss Catherine W.— TM, SLG, SF, M, WM, SLC
Bard of Saratoga—SLG
Barlow, Billy—SP
*Barnard—AM, FC
Barrick, Hon. J. R.—GLTC
Bates, Mary—O, SLG
Bayard (see Benedict Bayard)
Bayard, Benedict—SLG
Belisle, D. W.—SLG
Benjamin, Park—O
Benton, Mrs. E. C.—SFF
Bernardo—SFF
Berry, Mrs. H. L.—SLC
Berryhill, S. Newton—SFF
*Bertha—AM
Bessie B.—HLM, SFF
Beta—O

Bethune, Rev. G. W.—AM
*Bigby, Mrs. Mary C.—SFF
*Billups, Col. Jorn—SLB
Bkocksbank (sic), Miss L. A.—SLC
*Black, Hon. Edward J.—SLB
Blondel—SP
*Blount, Annie R. (Jennie Woodbine)—MLW, HLM, SFF, SLC, GLTC
Boatwright, Dr. J. W.—SLB
Botanist—AM
Bradley, Thomas Bibb—SE
Branch, Mrs. Caroline Hentz —SFF
Brown, Rev. J. Newton—O
Brown, Mrs. Martha W. (Estelle)—GLTC
Bryan, Mrs. Madeline V. (Melodia)—SLB
*Bryan, Mary E.—MLW, SFF, SLC, GLTC
Buena Vista—SFF
*Burke, Thomas A.—M, WM
Butler, Gen. William O.—SLG
*Butt, E. W.—SLB
Butt, Martha Haynes—GLTC
Butterball, Col.—SLB

Calla, A Lady of A——WM
*Cameron, Leila (see Mrs. C. W. DuBose)
Campbell, C. K.—SLB
Campbell, Mrs. M. A.—SLC
Campbell, Major Calder—SLB
Campbell, W. H.—SM
Canedo, Margarita J.—SFF
Carlos—HLM
Carolina—SP
Carolina Contributor, A—O
Carolina Girl, A—SFF
Carolinian, A—AM
Carr, Henry A.—SFF

Appendix C

Carra, Emma (see Mrs. Agnes Jean Stibbes)
Carrie (see Mary Caroline Griswold)
Carter, Mrs. E.—FC
Caruthers, Dr. William A.—SLB, FC, O
Catlin, S. W.—FC
Chapman, Mrs. A. T. D.—SLC
*Chapman, S. T.—SLB
*Chappell, A. H.—SLB
Charles—AM
*Charlton, Robert M.—SP, AM, SLB, FC, O, SLG, WM
Child, L. Maria—SLG
Chilton, Emily C. S.—GLTC
*Chips (see T. Addison Richards)
*Chittenden, D. A.—SLB, FC, O, SM
*Chivers, Thomas Holley—O, SLG
*Church, Alonzo—SLB
*Clara (see Mrs. Clara Cole)
Claude—O
Claudia—SFF
Clements, H. H.—SLG
Cleveland, Henry—SFF
Clifford—SLB
*Clifton—SLB, FC, O
Clifton, Mrs.—SLB
Clinch, Rev. J. H.—SLB, SLG
*Clio (see George F. Pierce)
Clyde, Kitty—MLW
*Cole, Mrs. Clara (Clara)—GLTC, SLB
Cole, F. W.—O
Collins, John D.—WM
*Colquitt, W. T.—SLB
Comus—LM
Conjux—SLG
Cooke, John Esten—SFF
*Cora—AM

*Countryman's Devil (see Joel Chandler Harris)
*Cousin Betsy (see Mrs. Sarah Lawrence Griffin)
*Cousin Leila (see Mrs. C. W. DuBose)
Crean, Mary W.—GLTC
Crossley, M. Louise (Currer Lyle)—SLC
Crowquill, Alfred—SLG
Curry, Rev. Daniel—SLB
*Curtis, Dr. Thomas—FC

*Daisy—SFF
Dallas, Alabama—SFF
Dalton, De Louis—SFF
Dana, Mrs. Mary S. B.—AM, SLB, FC, SLG
Dana, Matilda F.—WM
Dana, Rev. W. C.—O
*Darby, Prof. J.—FC
Davidson, James Wood—SE, SFF
Davis, William E.—SLG
Dawson, Col. A. H. H.—GLTC
Deen, Ethel (see Mrs. Augusta DeMilly)
De'esting—SFF
*Delta—SLB, SLG, WM
DeMilly, Mrs. Augusta (Ethel Deen)—SFF
DeWitt, B. M.—GLTC
Dick, Thomas—SLB
Dickson, Dr. John—SLB
Dillard, A. W.—SFF
Disappointed Man, A (see Mrs. Sarah Austin)
Dod, Charles S., Jr.—SFF
Dogwood—MLW
Doyal, L. T.—SLG
*DuBose, Mrs. C. W. (Leila Cameron; Cousin Leila;

Mrs. Kate A. DuBose)—
SLG, SF, SFF
Dulany, Mrs.—SP
Dwight, Dr.—SLB

Eames, Mrs. E. Jessup—SLG
Edith—SFF
Edwards, J. C.—FC
Edwards, S. B.—AM
Elder, Abraham—SLB
Eliza—SLB
*Eliza N.—SLB
Ellet, Mrs. E. F.—AM, FC, O, SLG, WM
Ellis, John P.—SLG
*Ellison, William B.—SLB, FC
Elton—SFF
Elwin—SLB
Embury, Mrs. Emma C.—FC, TM
Emerald, Emmie—SFF
Enid—SFF
Eola—SFF
Ephemerus—SLB
Epsilon—SLG, SFF
*Eremus—SLG
Erwin—SLG
Estelle (see Mrs. Martha W. Brown)
Eton, Etta—SFF
Etowah Bard—SLB
Eufaula—SFF
Eugine (sic)—FC
Evelyn—SFF

Fabian—SFF
Fairfax, Richard—SLG
*Falstaff, Jonathan (see Joseph Addison Turner)
Ferguson, Jessie—GLTC
*Few, Rev. I. A.—SLB
Fidelis—SFF

*Filicaja—SLB
Fleming, J. H.—M
*Fleming, Robert—SFF
Flit—SLG
Florio—SLG
*Fonerden, Rev. William H.— AM, SLB
Forrest, Florida—SFF
*Forrest, Floy—SFF
*Frank—SP, AM, SFF
*Franklin, Leonidas—SLB
Freeman—SLB
Freeman, Mrs. Ellen B. F.— SLB
French, L. Virginia—SFF, GLTC
Fudge, Tim—SP
Fusbos Secundus—SLB

Gamma of Natchez—SLC
Gaultier, Gertrude—SLG
*Georgia Woman, A—FC
*Georgian—SFF
Geraldine—SLB
Gertrude—SLG
Gifford, Mrs. M. E.—SLB
Gilman, Mrs. Caroline—SLB, SLG
Gilman, S.—SLG
*Giovanni—SLB
Glenmore—WM
*Goosequill, Abraham (see Joseph Addison Turner)
*Gorman, John B., Jr.—SFF
*Gorman, Ossian D.—SFF
Gothamite, A—AM
Gould, Hannah F.—O
Gould, Theodore A.—WM
Grandfather, A—SLB
Grey, Helen—SFF
*Griffin, Mrs. Sarah Lawrence (Cousin Betsy)—FC

Appendix C

Griswold, Mary Caroline (Carrie)—SFF
Griswold, Walter H.—SLG
Gulnare—SFF

Hackleton, Mrs. Minnie W.—GLTC
*Hadermann, C. J.—SLB
Hal—SFF
Hall, Rev. C. H.—SLG
Hall, Katie—SFF
Hall, Mrs. S. C.—SLG
Hallock, Charles—SFF
Hamblin, Louisa Medina—AM
Hamett, Alphonso O.—SFF
Hamilton—FC
Hamilton, Mrs. Leila A.—SFF
Hammond, Gen. James H.—SLB
Hansell, Gen. Andrew J.—O
Hanson, J. W.—SLG
Happy, John—BHL
Harden, John M. B.—SLB
*Harietta—AM
Harmonia—SFF
*Harold—SLB
Harrell, E. M.—SFF
*Harris, Joel Chandler (Countryman's Devil)—CI, C
Hatcher, John E.—GLTC
Hawkins, Mary E.—SFF
Hawkins, Col. William S.—SFF
Hayne, Paul Hamilton (as P. H. H.?)—SLG, SFF
Hazard, W. W.—O
Hedas—SP
Heinfred—SP
*Henri—SLB, SFF
Henry—SP, SFF

Henry, James Edward—SLB, FC
Hentz, Mrs. Caroline Lee—SP, SLB, FC, SLG, SF
Herbert—C
Herbert, Grace—SLC
Heriot, Edwin—SLG, M, WM
Hermit, The—C
Hetty—SLG
Hewitt, J. H.—SFF
Hill, Miss E. H.—GLTC
Hill, Mrs. Martha J.—GLTC
*Hilliard, Henry W.—AM
Hinda—AM
Holcomb—AM
Holcombe, Rev. Henry—GAR
Holmes, George Frederick—FC
Holroyd, C. Vavasour—SLG
*Holt, Harry (see Clara LeClerc)
*Holt, Polly (see Clara LeClerc)
Homer—AM
Homes, Mrs. Mary Sophie Shaw (Millie Mayfield)—GLTC
Hooper, J. J.—WM
Hoplegg, Achilles—SFF
Houser, Rev. William—FC
Howard, Caroline (Mrs. Caroline Gilman Jervey)—SLG, SF
*Howard, Prof. William G.—FC
Howitt, Mary—SLG
Hungerford, James—O
Hunt, Mrs. Sue E.—SFF
Hunter, J. L.—SLB

Imlac—SLB
Ines—SP
Inez—SLB

*Inisfael—SLB
Inkle, Ludwig—SLB
Irene—SLB
Ireneus—SP

*Jackson, Henry Rootes—AM, SLB, FC, O, SM, SLG, WM
*Jacques, D. H. (Jacques Journot)—SLG, SF, WM
James, G. P. R.—SLB
*Jamie—SP, AM
Janett—SLB
Janue—SP
Jennings, Miss V. A.—SLC
Johnson, Finley—MLW, HLM
Johnson, Mrs. Rosa Vertner—GLTC
*Johnston, Richard Malcolm (Philemon Perch)—SFF, GLTC
Jones, Rymmon—HLM
*Journot, Jacques (see D. H. Jacques)
Julien—SE
Juliet—SP
*Juvenis—AM, SLG
Justitia—SFF

*Kaluptonoma—SFF
Katy-Did—SFF
Keem, B. A. (see A. B. Meek)
Kendall, R. C.—SFF
Kendrick, Rev. J. R.—O
*Kennedy, Crammond—SFF
Ketchum, Mrs. Annie C.—GLTC
Keyes, Mrs. Julia L.—SFF, GLTC
Knox, Miss M. J. E.—WM
Kyle, Charles—SLB
*Kyle, Maria Gertrude—SLB, O

*Ladd, Mrs. C.—SP
Lady, A—SLB, SFF
*Lady of Augusta, A—AM
*Lady from Georgia, A—AM
*Lady of Georgia, A—SLG
*Lady of Milledgeville, A—SLB
Lady of South Carolina, A—FC, O, WM
*La Georgienne—O
La Josse—MLW
*Lamar, John B.—FC
*Lamar, Mary—WM
*Lamar, Mirabeau B.—FC
Lane, Thomas W.—SLG
Lanman, Charles—O, SLG
Larry—C
LaTaste, L.—SLG
LaTaste, Victor—SLB
Laurence—SFF
*Law, Judge (William)—SLB
Law, Annie F.—SF
Lawrence, E.—FC
*Lawrie, John Love—SLB, O
Learner, A—SLG
*LeClerc, Clara (Harry Holt, Polly Holt)—SLC, GLTC
Lee, Annie—FF
Lee, Mary E.—SLB, FC, O, SLG
Leelin—SP
*Le Ferve (see Mrs. Dr. Riley)
Legaré, J. M.—SLG, WM
Leila—AM
Leola (see Mrs. Loula Kendall Rogers)
Leole—HLM
Leon—AM
Le Vert, Madame Octavia—GLTC
Lightheart, Lily—SFF
Lilly-Bell—SFF
Lincoln, Laura—SFF

Appendix C

L'Inconnue (see Janie Ollivar and Mrs. L. Virginia French)
Lind, Eva—SFF
Lippard, George—M
*Lochrane, O. A.—SLG, WM
Lois—SFF
Longfellow, Henry W.—WM
*Longstreet, Augustus Baldwin (Baldwin)—AM, SLB, SM, SFF
Lothaire—SLB
Lou Bell—SFF
Lucas, S. D.—SFF
Lufton, Charles—SLG
*Lumpkin, Col. J. L.—SLB
Lyle, Currer (see Mrs. M. Louise Crossley)

Mabel—SFF
McBride, Archd. Arne—SFF
*McCrimmon, Mrs. Mary A.—SFF, SLC, GLTC
Macdonald, Miss H. B.—SLB
Magnolia—SFF
*Manhiem, Louise—SFF
Marah—SFF
Marcus—AM
Marengo—SFF
*Marinda (see Virginia M. O. Minor)
Marion—SFF
Martin, Mrs. Margaret—AM, SLB
Martin, Miss Mary—AM
Mary—SFF
Mattie—SFF
*Maussenet, Adolphus—SLB
May—SFF
May, Minnie—SFF
Mayfield, Millie (see Mrs. Mary Sophie Shaw Homes)

*Means, Alexander—AM, SLB, HLM, SFF
Medicus—SLB
Meek, A. B. (B. A. Keem)—SLB, O, FF, AM
Mellen, Grenville—O
Melodia (see Mrs. Madeline V. Bryan)
Memet—SFF
*Mercer, Rev. Jesse—SLB
Mercer, S. C.—GLTC
Mernet—SFF
Merrill, A. K.—SLB
Merriwether, Mrs. Lide—GLTC
*Mifflin, J. H.—SP, AM, SLB, FC, O
Mignionette—SFF
Mills, Cotton Mather—SLG
Milward, Mrs. Maria G.—FC
*Miner, Mrs. Serena A.—SFF
Minister's Wife, A—SFF
*Minor, Virginia M. O. (Marinda)—MLW
Miot, Emma—SFF
Miriam—HLM
Moragne, Miss M. E.—AM, O
Moreton, Clara—SLG, SF
Moreton, Maud—SFF
*Munroe, N. C.—SLB
Mustapha—SP
Muza—SP
Myrtle, May—SFF

Nadamia—SFF
Neal, John—FC, WM
Neal, Mrs. Joseph C.—SLG, SF
Nettleton, Abiel L.—O
Nichols, Eliza G.—SLG
Nina—SFF
*Nisbet, Eugenius A.—SLB
Noble, Louis L.—O

Nobody, Nettie—SFF
*Nom de Plume—SFF
Novissimus—SFF

Oliver, Dr. Samuel C.—AM, FC
Ollivar, Janie (L'Inconnue)—SFF
O'Neall, Judge John Belton—O
*Orionis (see William C. Richards)
Orne, Mrs. Caroline—FC
Orne, Miss Caroline F.—FC
*Orthopolitan, Olinthus—WM
Oscar—SP
Osgood, Mrs. Frances S.—AM, SLB, FC
Oswald—SFF
Ouvrier—SFF
Overall, John W.—GLTC

*Paedagogus, Ludovic (see Lovick Pierce)
Paine, Miss Phebe—SLB
*Panola—SFF
Pardoe, Miss—AM
Parker—SFF
Patten, Lieut. G. W.—SP, SLB, FC
*Pendleton, E. M.—SP, AM, SLB, SM, SFF
*Pepper, Peter—AM
*Perch, Philemon (see Richard Malcolm Johnston)
Percy, Dr. Eugene—SLG
*Philander—SLB
*Philologus—SP
*Pierce, George F. (Clio)—SP, SLB, FC
*Pierce, Lovick (Ludovic Paedagogus)—SLB
Pires—SFF

*Poke, Sally (see Joseph Addison Turner)
Porter, Hon. Benjamin F.—SLG, WM
Porter, Edward J.—SLG, WM
Postell, D.—SLB
Pradt, Emma F.—SFF
Preacher, The—AM
Prentice, George D.—SLG
Proportion, Polly—LM
Psyche—FC

Queerfish, Tom—LM
Quintard, C. F.—SLG
Quintus—SFF

Rab—SLG
Raiford, Hamilton—AM
Rambler—AM, SFF
Randall, James R.—SFF
Randolph, Jessie—HLM, SFF
Reed, Dr.—SLB
Reedy, Miss Sallie Ada—SLC, GLTC
Requier, A. J.—SFF
Rice, Charles Wyatt—AM
Richards, Mrs. C. H. (same as Mrs. William C. Richards?)—SF
*Richards, T. Addison (Chips)—AM, O, SLG.
*Richards, William C. (Orionis)—AM, SLB, FC, O, SLG
*Richards, Mrs. William C. (C.H.B.R.; Mrs. Manners)—O, SF
Rigel—O
*Riley, Mrs. Dr. (LeFerve)—MLW, HLM
Rinaldo—FC
Ritchie, Anna Cora—SFF
Rockwell, J. O.—M
Rockwell, William S.—FC

Rogers, Laura Bibb—SFF
*Rogers, Mrs. Loula Kendall (Leola)—MLW
Rogers, Mrs. M. Louise—MLW, HLM
*Round, Rev. G. H.—SLB
*Rymmon—HLM

Saffronia—LM
Sallie—SFF
Saluda—SFF
*Samivel—SLG
Sass, George H.—SFF
Saunders, J. Henry Dmochowski—SFF
Saxe, John G.—SLG
Saxon, Parish—SLG
Screven, William E.—SFF
Senex—AM
Seroc—AM
Shiras, Charles P.—WM
Sigma—SFF
Sigourney, Mrs. L. H.—AM, SLB, FC, O, SLG, M
Silver Age—HLM
Simmons, James W.—SLB
Simms, William Gilmore (G. B. Singleton)—SLB, FC, O, SLG, WM, SFF, AM
*Sinclair, Carrie Bell—SFF
Singleton, G. B. (see William Gilmore Simms)
Slaughter, James Summerfield—HLM
Slow, Dean—HLM
*Smith, G. G.—SLB
*Smith, O. L.—FC
Smith, Mrs. Seba—SLB
Smith, Mrs. Susan A.—FC
Smith, W. Wragg—AM, SFF
Snelling, Mrs. Anna L.—O
Snodgrass, Dr. J. Evans—SLB, FC

Snubs, Mark Anthony—SP
Somers—FC
Son, The—SFF
South Carolina—SFF
*Southman, Charles—SLG, M, WM
Spain, H. P.—SFF
*Sparks, W. H.—C
Spofford, H. M.—O
Squier, E. G.—O
*Stafford—SP, SLB
Stanford—SFF
*Starnes, Judge—SFF
Statham, Mrs. C. L.—SFF
Stella—SFF
*Stephens, Alexander H.—SLB
Stevens, Mrs. Ann S.—AM, FC, SLG
*Stevens, William Bacon—SLB, O, SLG
Stewart, J. A.—HLM
Stibbes, Mrs. Agnes Jean (Emma Carra)—SFF
*Stokes, Rev. W. H.—SLB
Stranger, The—SLB
*Strong, Samuel M.—AM, SLB
*Stuart, Susan A.—FF
*Studens—SLB
Student at Law, A—O
Suarez, M. R.—AM
Sylvanus—LM
Symmetry, Benajmin—LM

Tallulah—MLW
Taveau, A. L. (Alton)—SLG
Telescope—SLB
Terence—SFF
Theolian—SFF
*Thomas, Rev. J. R.—SLB
Thompson, Ed. Porter—BHL
*Thompson, James M.—SFF
Thompson, John R.—SFF

*Thompson, William Tappan—AM, FC, SM, FF
Thomson, Charles West—AM
Timrod, Henry (Aglaus)—SLG
Tirtium (sic) Quid—AM
Tomlin, J.—SLB
Toulmin, Camilla—SLG
Trippe, Mrs. Kate—SLC
*Turner, Joseph Addison (Abraham Goosequill; Addison; Jonathan Falstaff; Sally Poke?)—TM, SLG, SFF, P, C
*Turner, William Wilberforce—SFF, P, C

Ursula—SFF

V——, Caroline—SP
*Valeria—SP, AM
Vaughan, Mrs. S. A.—GLTC
*Veazey, L. L.—GLTC
Venator—AM
Vere-Dicus—SLB
Verena—SFF
*Viator—AM, SLB, SFF
Village Bard—SP
Vindex Veritatis—SLB
Viola—SLB, SFF
Virginian, A—SFF
Voigt, L. T.—FF

*Waddel, Prof. James P.—SLB, WM
Wade, J. A.—SLB
Wakelee, Kate C.—SFF
Wallace (see William Wallace Webster)
Walley, Miss Mary E.—FC
Warfield, Mrs. C. A.—GLTC
Washington, Augusta—SFF

Watkins, Gen. James—FC
*Watson, A. R.—SFF
Watts, James R.—C
Waybridge, W.—AM
Webster, William Wallace (Wallace)—O
Welby, Amelia B.—SLB
*Wheler, Charles L.—SLG, SF, M, WM, FF
Whetstone, Tim—SLG
Whitaker, Daniel K.—SE
Whitaker, Mrs. D. K. (same as Mrs. Mary S. Whitaker)—SE, WM
Whitaker, Mrs. Mary S. (see Mrs. D. K. Whitaker)
White, Robert A.—SLG
*White, William N.—SLG, WM
Wildbrier—SFF
*Wilde, Richard Henry—AM, SLB, FC, O
Wilde, William Cumming—SLG, SFF
Wilfred—SLG
Wildwood, Charles—SFF
*Willhelmine—SLG
*Willie, of Camp Bird—SFF
Willison, M. G.—SFF
Wilson—SFF
Wilson, Miss Leonora—O
*Windsor, Robert—SFF
*Wittich, E. L.—AM, SLB
Wood, Mrs. Charlotte M.—FC
*Woodbine, Jennie (see Annie R. Blount)
Woodville—SFF
Woodworth, Samuel—FC
Wooten, H. V.—AM, SLB, FC, O

Xemia—SFF
Xenia—SFF

Appendix C

*Xury—SLG
*Xylon—SLB

Yeames, Eliza—LM
*Yona—O
Youl, Edward—SLG
Young—AM
*Young, Edward—SFF

*Young Lady of Columbus, A
  —SLB
*Young Lady of Hamilton, A—
  SLB

Zena—SFF
Ziola—SFF

BIBLIOGRAPHY

Bibliography

Books and Collected Works

Allibone, S. Austin. *A Critical Dictionary of English Literature and British and American Authors.* Philadelphia: J. B. Lippincott & Company. 1871. 3 vols.
American Newspapers 1821–1936. A Union List of Files Available in the United States and Canada. Edited by Winifred Gregory. New York: The H. W. Wilson Company. 1937.
Andrews, Garnett. *Reminiscences of an Old Georgia Lawyer.* Atlanta: Franklin Steam Printing House. 1870.
Appletons' Cyclopaedia of American Biography. New York: D. Appleton & Company. 1888–89. 6 vols.
Avery, I. W. *History of the State of Georgia from 1850 to 1881.* New York: Brown & Derby, Publishers. 1881.
Barrow, Elfrida DeRenne, and Laura Palmer Bell. *Anchored Yesterdays.* Savannah: Review Publishing Company. 1923.
Baskervill, William Malone. *Southern Writers.* Nashville: Publishing House of the Methodist Episcopal Church, South. 1902. 2 vols.
Battey, George Magruder, Jr. *History of Rome and Floyd County.* Atlanta: Webb & Vary Company. 1922.
Beer, William. *Checklist of American Periodicals, 1741–1800.* Worcester, Mass.: Published by the American Antiquarian Society. 1923.
Beveridge, Albert J. *Abraham Lincoln.* Boston and New York: Houghton Mifflin Company. 1928. 2 vols.
Biographical Souvenir of the States of Georgia and Florida. Chicago: F. A. Battey & Company. 1889.
Blount, Annie R. *Poems.* Augusta: H. D. Norrell. 1860.
Bowden, Haygood S. *Two Hundred Years of Education. Bicentennial 1733–1933. Savannah, Chatham County, Georgia.* Richmond: Press of the Dietz Printing Company. 1932.

Bradshaw, Sidney Ernest. *On Southern Poetry Prior to 1860.* Richmond: B. F. Johnson Pub. Co., 1900.

Brantley, Rabun Lee. *Georgia Journalism of the Civil War Period.* Nashville: George Peabody College for Teachers. 1929.

Bremer, Fredrika. *Homes of the New World; Impressions of America.* New York: Harper & Bros., Publishers. 1854. 2 vols.

Brooks, R. P. *Preliminary Bibliography to Georgia History.* Athens: McGregor. 1910.

Buckingham, J. S. *The Slave States of America.* London. 1842. 2 vols.

Bullock, Henry Morton. *A History of Emory University.* Nashville: Parthenon Press. 1936.

Bureau of the Census. *A Century of Population Growth.* Washington: Government Printing Office. 1909.

Bureau of the Census. *Statistical View of the United States. . . . A Compendium of the 7th Census (1850).* Washington: Government Printing Office. 1854.

Burke, Mrs. Emily P. *Reminiscences of Georgia.* Oberlin, Ohio: James M. Fitch. 1850.

Burke, Thomas A. (ed.). *Polly Peablossom's Wedding; and Other Tales.* Philadelphia: T. B. Peterson & Bros. 1851.

Butler, John C. *Historical Record of Macon and Central Georgia.* Macon: J. W. Burke. 1879.

Cain, Andrew W. *History of Lumpkin County for the First Hundred Years. 1832-1932.* Atlanta: Stein Printing Company. 1932.

Cairns, William B. "Later Magazines." *Cambridge History of American Literature.* III (1921), pp. 299-318.

Cairns, William B. "Magazines, Annuals, and Gift Books, 1783-1850." *Cambridge History of American Literature.* II (1918), pp. 160-175.

Campbell, Jesse H. *Georgia Baptists: Historical and Biographical.* Richmond: H. K. Ellyson. 1847.

Candler, Allen D., and Clement A. Evans (eds.). *Georgia. Comprising Sketches of Counties, Towns, Events, Institutions, and Persons, Arranged in Cyclopedic Form.* Atlanta: State Historical Association. 1906. 3 vols.

Cardozo, J. N. *Reminiscences of Charleston.* Charleston: Joseph Walker. 1866.

Cardwell, Guy Adams, Jr. *Charleston Periodicals, 1795-1860: A Study in Literary Influences, with a Descriptive Check List of Seventy-five Magazines.* Unpublished University of North Carolina dissertation. 1936.

Cassels, Samuel Jones. *Providence and Other Poems.* Macon: Griffin & Purse. 1838.
Cate, Wirt Armistead. *Lucius Q. C. Lamar.* Chapel Hill, N.C. 1935.
Chappell, Absalom H. *Miscellanies of Georgia.* Atlanta: James F. Meegan. 1874.
Charlton, Robert M., and Thomas J. Charlton. *Poems.* Boston: Charles C. Little & James Brown. 1839.
Chew, S. C. *Byron in England.* New York: Scribners. 1924.
Clemens, Samuel Langhorne (Mark Twain). *Life on the Mississippi.* New York and London: Harper & Bros. 1917. (Originally published in 1875.)
Coad, Oral Sumner. *William Dunlap.* New York: The Dunlap Society. 1917.
Cohen, Sidney J. *Three Notable Ante-Bellum Magazines of South Carolina.* New York: Columbia University Press. 1915.
Cook, Mrs. Anna Maria Green. *History of Baldwin County, Georgia.* Anderson, S.C.: Keys-Hearn Printing Company. 1925.
Cook, Elizabeth Christine. *Literary Influences in Colonial Newspapers, 1704–1750.* New York: Columbia University Press. 1912.
Cooper, Walter G. *Official History of Fulton County.* Atlanta: Walter G. Cooper. 1934.
Coulter, E. Merton. *College Life in the Old South.* New York: Macmillan. 1928.
Coulter, E. Merton. *A Short History of Georgia.* Chapel Hill: University of North Carolina Press. 1933.
Cyclopaedia of American Biographies. Edited by John Howard Brown. Boston: The Cyclopaedia Publishing Company. 1897–1903. 7 vols.
Damon, S. Foster. *Thomas Holley Chivers, Friend of Poe.* New York and London: Harper & Bros. 1930.
Davidson, James Wood. *Living Writers of the South.* New York: Carleton, 1869.
Davis, Richard Beale. *Francis Walker Gilmer: Life and Learning in Jefferson's Virginia.* Richmond. 1939.
DeBrahm, John Gerar William. *History of the Province of Georgia.* Wormsloe (Printed at Philadelphia, by C. Sherman). 1849.
Derby, J. C. *Fifty Years among Authors, Books and Publishers.* New York: G. W. Carleton & Company; Publishers, London: S. Low, Son & Company. 1884.
Dictionary of American Biography. New York: Charles Scribner's Sons. 1928–36. 20 vols.

Dictionary of National Biography. London: Macmillan & Company. 1885–1900. 63 vols.

Dodd, William E. *The Cotton Kingdom.* New Haven: Yale University Press. 1921.

Duyckinck, Evert A., and George L. *Cyclopaedia of American Literature.* New York: Charles Scribner. 1856. 2 vols.

Dyer, G. W. *Democracy in the South before the Civil War.* Nashville & Dallas: Publishing House of M. E. Church, South. 1905.

Eaton, Clement. *Freedom of Thought in the Old South.* Durham, N.C.: Duke University Press. 1940.

Elliott, Rt. Rev. Stephen. *A Reply to a Resolution of the Georgia Historical Society, Read before the Society at Its Anniversary Meeting, February 12th, 1860.* Savannah: Purse & Son, Printers. 1866.

Evans, Augusta J. *Beulah.* New York: Carleton. 1868. (Originally published 1859.)

Fitzgerald, Oscar Penn. *Judge Longstreet.* Nashville: Publishing House of the Methodist Episcopal Church, South. 1891.

Flanders, Ralph Betts. *Plantation Slavery in Georgia.* Chapel Hill: University of North Carolina Press. 1933.

Forrest, Mary (Mrs. Julia Deane Freeman). *Women of the South Distinguished in Literature.* New York: Charles B. Richardson. 1866.

French, Mrs. L. Virginia. *Wind-Whispers; a Collection of Poems.* Nashville: Published for the Author. 1856.

Fries, Adelaide L. *The Moravians in Georgia, 1735–40.* Raleigh, N.C.: Edwards & Broughton. 1905.

Gaines, Francis Pendleton. *The Southern Plantation.* New York: Columbia University Press. 1925.

Gamble, Thomas. *Savannah Duels and Duellists 1733–1877.* Savannah: Review Publishing & Printing Company. 1923.

Garwood, Irving. *American Periodicals from 1850 to 1860.* Macomb, Ill.: n.p. 1931.

Gay, Miss M. A. H. *Prose and Poetry.* Nashville: South-Western Publishing House. 1859.

Gay, Miss M. A. H. *The Transplanted. A Story of Dixie before the War.* New York and Washington: Neale Publishing Company. 1907.

Georgia: A Pageant of Years. Edited by Elfrida DeRenne Barrow, et al. Richmond: Garrett & Massie, Inc. 1933.

Gibbs, John Ernest, Jr. *William Gilmore Simms and The Magnolia.* M.A. thesis, Duke University. 1931. Unpublished.

Gilman, Samuel (ed.). *Poetical Remains of the Late Mary Elizabeth Lee.* Charleston: Walker & Richards. 1851.
Gilmer, George R. *Sketches of Some of the First Settlers of Upper Georgia.* New York: D. Appleton & Company. 1855.
Gilmer, Gertrude C. *Checklist of Southern Periodicals to 1861.* Boston: The F. W. Faxon Company. 1934.
Grayson, William John. *The Hireling and the Slave, Chicora, and Other Poems.* Charleston: McCarter & Company. 1856.
Harden, William. *History of Savannah and South Georgia.* Chicago and New York: The Lewis Publishing Company. 1913. 2 vols.
Harris, Joel Chandler. *Georgia.* New York, 1896.
Harris, Joel Chandler. *On the Plantation.* New York: D. Appleton & Company. 1903.
Harris, Julia Collier. *Life and Letters of Joel Chandler Harris.* New York: Houghton Mifflin Company. 1918.
Hart, Albert Bushnell (ed.). *American History Told by Contemporaries.* New York: Macmillan. 1926. Vol. II.
Hart, Albert Bushnell. *Slavery and Abolition.* New York and London: Harper & Bros. 1906.
Hart, Bertha Sheppard (Mrs. Jack Hart). *Introduction to Georgia Writers.* Macon: J. W. Burke Company. 1929.
Hart, John S. (ed.). *Female Prose Writers of America.* Philadelphia: E. H. Butler & Company. 1864.
Hill, Frank Pierce. *American Plays Printed 1714–1830.* Stanford University Press. 1934.
Hillyer, Rev. Shaler Granby. *Reminiscences of Georgia Baptists.* Atlanta: Foote & Davies Company. 1902.
History of Atlanta and Its Pioneers. Atlanta: Byrd Printing Company. 1902.
History of the Baptist Denomination in Georgia. Atlanta: J. P. Harrison & Company. 1881.
Holcombe, Henry. *The First Fruits, in a Series of Letters.* Philadelphia: Printed for the author, by Ann Cochran. 1812.
Holliday, Carl. *A History of Southern Literature.* New York and Washington: The Neale Publishing Company. 1906.
Hoole, William Stanley. *A Check-List and Finding-List of Charleston Periodicals 1732–1864.* Durham, N.C.: Duke University Press. 1936.
Hornaday, John R. *Atlanta Yesterday, Today and Tomorrow.* American Cities Book Company. 1922.
Hornblow, Arthur. *A History of the Theatre in America.* Philadelphia and London: J. B. Lippincott Company. 1919. 2 vols.

Howe, M. A. DeWolfe. *The Atlantic Monthly and Its Makers.* Boston: The Atlantic Monthly Press, Inc. 1919.

Howe, Will D. "Early Humorists." *Cambridge History of American Literature.* II (1918), pp. 148–159.

Howell, Clark. *History of Georgia.* Chicago, Atlanta: The S. J. Clarke Publishing Company. 1926. 4 vols.

Hubbell, Jay B. "Southern Magazines." *Culture in the South,* edited by W. T. Couch. Chapel Hill: University of North Carolina Press. 1934, pp. 159–182.

Hudson, Frederic. *Journalism in the United States from 1690 to 1872.* New York: Harper & Bros., Publishers. 1873.

Hull, Augustus Longstreet. *Annals of Athens, Georgia, 1801–1901.* Athens: Banner Job Office. 1906.

Hull, Augustus Longstreet. *Historical Sketch of the University of Georgia.* Atlanta: Foote & Davies Company. 1894.

Hundley, D. R. *Social Relations in Our Southern States.* New York: Henry B. Price. 1860.

Incidents of a Journey from Abbeville, South Carolina, to Ocala, Florida, By an Observer of Small Things. Edgefield, S.C. Printed at the Advertiser Office. 1852.

Ingle, Edward. *Southern Sidelights, A Picture of Social and Economic Life in the South a Generation before the War.* New York: Thomas Y. Crowell & Company. 1896.

Jackson, David Kelley. *Contributors and Contributions to the Southern Literary Messenger (1834–1864).* Charlottesville, Va.: The Historical Publishing Company, Inc. 1936.

Jackson, Henry Rootes. *Tallulah and Other Poems.* Savannah: John M. Cooper. 1850.

Jacobs, Thornwell (ed.). *Oglethorpe Book of Georgia Verse.* Oglethorpe University Press. 1930.

The Jeffersonian Cyclopedia, ed. by John Foley. New York and London: Funk & Wagnalls Company. 1900.

Jenkins, William Sumner. *Pro-Slavery Thought in the Old South.* Chapel Hill: University of North Carolina Press. 1935.

Johnson, James Gibson. *Southern Fiction Prior to 1860; An Attempt at a First-Hand Bibliography.* Charlottesville, Va.: The Michie Company. 1909.

Johnson, Thomas Cary, Jr. *Scientific Interests in the Old South.* New York and London: D. Appleton-Century Company. 1936.

Johnston, Richard Malcolm. *Autobiography.* Washington: The Neale Company. 1901.

Johnston, Richard Malcolm. "Early Educational Life in Middle

Georgia." *Report of the Commissioner of Education.* Washington: Government Printing Office. 1896.
Jones, Charles Colcock, Jr. *History of Georgia.* Boston: Houghton, Mifflin & Company. 1883. 2 vols.
Jones, Charles Colcock, Jr. *Memorial History of Augusta, Georgia.* Syracuse, N.Y.: D. Mason & Company, Publishers. 1890.
Jones, Charles Edgeworth. *Education in Georgia.* U.S. Bureau of Education Contributions to American Educational History, edited by Herbert B. Adams. No. 5. Washington: Government Printing Office. 1889.
Jones, Mary G., and Lily Reynolds. *Coweta County Chronicles for One Hundred Years.* Atlanta: Stein Printing Company. 1928.
Jones, Stephen (ed.). *Biographia Dramatica.* London: Longman. 1812. 3 vols.
Judge, Jonathan J. (compiler). *Southern Orator.* Macon: Benjamin F. Griffin. Charleston: M'Carter & Allen. 1851.
Kennedy, J. P. *Life of William Wirt.* Philadelphia: Lea & Blanchard. 1850. 2 vols.
Knight, Lucian Lamar. *Georgia and Georgians.* Chicago and New York: Lewis Publishing Company. 1917. 6 vols.
Koch, G. Adolf. *Republican Religion.* New York: Henry Holt. 1933.
Le Conte, Joseph. *Autobiography.* Edited by William Dallam Armes. New York: D. Appleton & Company. 1903.
Lee, F. D., and J. L. Agnew. *Historical Record of Savannah.* Savannah: Estill. 1869.
Lee, James Melvin. *History of American Journalism.* Boston and New York: Houghton Mifflin Company. 1917.
Leonard, William Ellery. *Byron and Byronism in America.* Boston: Columbia University thesis. 1905.
Library of Southern Literature. Edited by E. A. Alderman, Joel Chandler Harris, *et al.* New Orleans, Atlanta, Dallas: The Martin & Hoyt Company. 1907-23. 15 vols.
Link, Samuel Albert. *Pioneers of Southern Literature.* Nashville & Dallas: Publishing House of the Methodist Episcopal Church, South. 1900.
Living Female Writers of the South. Edited by Ida Raymond (pseud. of Mary T. Tardy). Philadelphia: Claxton, Remsen & Haffelfinger. 1872.
Longstreet, Augustus Baldwin. *Georgia Scenes, Characters, Incidents, etc.* Augusta: State Rights' Sentinel Office. 1835.

Longstreet, Augustus Baldwin. *Master William Mitten.* Macon: J. W. Burke. 1889.

Lyell, Sir Charles. *A Second Visit to the United States of North America.* New York: Harper & Bros. 1849. 2 vols.

Mallard, R. Q. *Plantation Life before Emancipation.* Richmond: Whittet & Shepperson. 1892.

Martin, John H. (compiler). *Columbus, Geo., from Its Selection as a Trading Town in 1827, to Its Partial Destruction by Wilson's Raid, in 1865.* Columbus, Ga.: Thomas Gilbert. 1874.

Mayes, Edward. *Lucius Q. C. Lamar.* Nashville: Smith & Lamar. 1896.

McCain, James Ross. *Georgia as a Proprietary Province.* Boston: Richard G. Badger. 1917.

McCall, Hugh. *History of Georgia.* Atlanta: Reprinted by A. B. Caldwell. 1909.

McMurtrie, Douglas Crawford. *History of Printing in the United States.* New York: R. R. Bowker Company. 1936. 2 vols.

Meine, Franklin J. (ed.). *Tall Tales of the Southwest.* New York: A. A. Knopf. 1930.

Memoirs of Georgia. Atlanta: The Southern Historical Association. 1895. 2 vols.

Mercer, Jesse (ed.). *Cluster of Spiritual Songs, Divine Hymns, and Sacred Poems.* Philadelphia: J. J. Woodward. 1835.

Merriam, C. Edward. *A History of American Political Theories.* New York: Macmillan. 1920.

Miller, Stephen Frank. *Bench and Bar of Georgia.* Philadelphia: Lippincott. 1858. 2 vols.

Mims, Edwin. *Sidney Lanier.* Boston and New York: Houghton Mifflin. 1905.

Minor, Benjamin Blake. *The Southern Literary Messenger, 1834–1864.* New York and Washington: Neale Publishing Company. 1905.

Morais, H. M. *Deism in Eighteenth Century America.* New York: Columbia Press. 1934.

Moses, Montrose J. *The Literature of the South.* New York: Crowell. 1910.

Mott, Frank Luther. *American Journalism.* New York: Macmillan. 1941.

Mott, Frank Luther. *A History of American Magazines, 1741–1850.* New York: D. Appleton & Company. 1930.

Mott, Frank Luther. *A History of American Magazines, 1850–1865.* Cambridge, Mass.: Harvard Press. 1938.

Bibliography

National Cyclopaedia of American Biography. New York: James T. White & Company. 1892–1937. 26 vols.

Negro Population. Bureau of the Census. Washington: Government Printing Office. 1918.

Nottingham, Carolyn Walker, and Evelyn Hannah. *History of Upson County, Georgia.* Macon: J. W. Burke Company. 1930.

Odell, George C. D. *Annals of the New York Stage.* New York: Columbia Press. 1927–37. 9 vols.

Olmsted, Frederick Law. *A Journey in the Seaboard Slave States.* New York: Dix & Edwards. 1856.

O'Neall, John Belton. *Biographical Sketches of the Bench and Bar of South Carolina.* Charleston: S. G. Courtenay & Company. 1859. 2 vols.

Parrington, Vernon Louis. *The Romantic Revolution in America, 1800–1860.* New York: Harcourt, Brace & Company. 1927.

Parsons, C. G. *Inside View of Slavery: Or a Tour among the Planters.* Boston: John P. Jewett & Company. 1855.

Pattee, Fred Lewis. *The Feminine Fifties.* New York: D. Appleton-Century Company. 1940.

Phillips, Ulrich B. "The Literary Movement for Secession." *Studies in Southern History and Politics; Inscribed to William Archibald Dunning.* New York: Columbia Press. 1914. pp. 33–60.

Pioneer Citizens' History of Atlanta, 1833–1902. Atlanta: Byrd Printing Company. 1902.

Powell, Nettie. *History of Marion County, Georgia.* Columbus, Georgia. 1931.

Quinn, Arthur Hobson. *A History of the American Drama from the Beginning to the Civil War.* New York and London: Harper & Bros. 1923.

Redding, Mrs. J. H. *Life and Times of Jonathan Bryan, 1708–1788.* Savannah: The Morning News Print. 1901.

(Rembert, W. R.). *Manolia; or, The Vale of Tallulah, by a Georgia Huntsman.* Augusta: McKinne & Hall. 1854.

Rhea, Linda. *Hugh Swinton Legaré.* Chapel Hill: University of North Carolina Press. 1934.

Richardson, Lyon N. *A History of Early American Magazines.* New York: Thomas Nelson & Sons. 1931.

Roath, David L. *Zara: A Romance.* Athens: Christy, Kelsea & Burke. 1851.

(Robinson, Francis James). *Kups of Kauphy.* Athens: Christy & Kelsea. 1853.

Roden, Robert F. *Later American Plays 1831–1900.* New York: The Dunlap Society. 1900.

Rogers, Edward Reinhold. *Four Southern Magazines.* University of Virginia Studies in Southern Literature. 1902.

Roorbach, O. A. *Bibliotheca Americana.* New York: O. A. Roorbach. 1852.
- (a) *Supplement.* Oct., 1852, to May, 1855. New York: O. A. Roorbach, Jr. 1855.
- (b) *Addenda.* May, 1855, to Mar., 1858. New York: Wiley & Halsted. 1858.
- (c) Vol. IV. 1858–61. New York: Orville A. Roorbach. 1861.

Rowe, H. H. (publisher). *History of Athens and Clarke County.* Athens: McGregor Company. 1923.

Rutherford, Mildred Lewis. *The South in History and Literature.* Atlanta: The Franklin-Turner Company. 1907.

Sabin, Joseph, et al. *A Dictionary of Books Relating to America,* New York: Sabin. 1868–1936. 29 vols.

Scott, Frank W. "Newspapers, 1775–1880." *Cambridge History of American Literature.* II (1918), pp. 176–195.

Seilhamer, George O. *History of the American Theater before the Revolution.* Philadelphia: Globe Printing House. 1888–91. 3 vols.

Sherwood, Adiel. *Gazetteer of the State of Georgia.* Charleston: W. Riley. 1827.

Sherwood, Adiel. *Gazetteer of the State of Georgia.* Philadelphia: W. K. Boden. 1829.

Sherwood, Adiel. *Gazetteer of the State of Georgia.* Washington: P. Force. 1837.

Sherwood, Adiel. *Gazetteer of the State of Georgia.* Macon & Atlanta: n.p. 1860.

Shipp, J. E. D. *Giant Days, or The Life and Times of William H. Crawford.* Americus, Ga.: Southern Printers. 1909.

Sholes, Albert E. (compiler). *Directory of the City of Augusta, for 1877.* Augusta: A. E. Sholes. 1877.

Shryock, Richard H. *Georgia and the Union in 1850.* Durham, N.C.: Duke University Press. 1926.

Shryock, Richard H. (ed.). *Letters of Richard D. Arnold, M.D. 1808–1876.* Papers of the Trinity College Historical Society, Double Series XVIII–XIX. Durham, N.C.: The Seeman Press. 1929.

Smith, Charles Alphonso. *Southern Literary Studies.* Chapel Hill: University of North Carolina Press. 1927.

Smith, Charles Henry (Bill Arp). *Bill Arp, So Called. A Side Show of the Southern Side of the War.* New York: Metropolitan Record Office. 1866.

Bibliography

Smith, George Gilman, Jr. *Life and Times of George Foster Pierce*. Sparta, Ga.: Hancock Publishing Company. 1888.
(Smythe, James M.). *Ethel Somers, or The Fate of the Union*. Augusta: H. D. Norrell. 1857.
South in the Building of the Nation, The. Vol. VII, "History of the Literary and Intellectual Life of the Southern States," edited by S. C. Mitchell. Richmond: Southern Historical Publication Society. 1909.
Sparks, Andrew. *A History of the Theatre in Savannah, 1800–1836*. Unpublished University of Georgia M.A. thesis. 1940.
Sparks, W. H. *The Memories of Fifty Years*. Philadelphia: Claxton, Remsen & Haffelfinger. Macon: J. W. Burke & Company. 1870.
Starke, Aubrey Harrison. *Sidney Lanier*. Chapel Hill: University of North Carolina Press. 1933.
Stevens, Rev. William Bacon. *History of Georgia*. New York: D. Appleton & Company. Savannah: William Thorne Williams. 1847. 2 vols.
Stewart, George R. *John Phoenix, Esq., the Veritable Squibob*. New York: Henry Holt. 1937.
Tailfer, Patrick, et al. *A True and Historical Narrative of the Colony of Georgia*. Charles Town, S.C.: P. Timothy. 1741.
Tandy, Jennette. *Crackerbox Philosophers in American Humor*. New York: Columbia University Press. 1925.
Tardy, Mary T. (pseud. "Ida Raymond"). *Southland Writers*. Philadelphia: Claxton, Remsen & Haffelfinger. 1870. 2 vols.
Tassin, Algernon. *The Magazine in America*. New York: Dodd, Mead & Company. 1916.
Temple, Sarah Blackwell Gober. *The First Hundred Years. A Short History of Cobb County, in Georgia*. Atlanta: Walter W. Brown Publishing Company. 1935.
Thomas, Isaiah. *History of Printing in America*. Albany, N.Y.: Joel Munsell, Publisher. 1874. 2 vols.
Thompson, William Tappan. *John's Alive; or, The Bride of a Ghost, and Other Sketches*. Philadelphia: David McKay. 1883.
Thompson, William Tappan. *Major Jones' Courtship*. Philadelphia: T. B. Peterson & Bros. n.d.
Thompson, William Tappan. *Major Jones' Sketches of Travel in His Tour from Georgia to Canada.* Philadelphia. 1849.
Thwing, Charles F. *A History of Higher Education in America*. New York: D. Appleton & Company. 1906.
Trent, William P. *Southern Statesmen of the Old Regime*. New York: Thomas Y. Crowell. 1897.

Trent, William P. *William Gilmore Simms.* Boston and New York: Houghton, Mifflin & Company. 1892.

Turner, Joseph Addison. *The Discovery of Sir John Franklin, and Other Poems.* Mobile and New York: Goetzel & Company. Athens: William N. White. 1858.

(Turner, Joseph Addison). *A Hasty Plate of Soup.* Edited by Peter Pickle. Cassville, Ga.: John W. Burke. 1852.

Turner, William Wilberforce. *Jack Hopeton, or the Adventures of a Georgian.* New York: Derby & Jackson, Publishers. 1860.

Union List of Serials in the United States and Canada. Edited by Winifred Gregory. New York: The H. W. Wilson Company. 1927.
    (a) *First Supplement, 1925–31.* Edited by G. E. Malikoff. New York, 1931.
    (b) *Second Supplement, 1931–32.* Edited by G. E. Malikoff. New York, 1933.

Van Doren, Carl. *The American Novel.* New York: The Macmillan Company. 1921.

Wade, John Donald. *Augustus Baldwin Longstreet.* New York: Macmillan Company. 1924.

Wauchope, George Armstrong. *The Writers of South Carolina.* Columbia, S.C.: The State Company, Publishers. 1910.

Wegelin, Oscar. *Early American Fiction, 1774–1830, etc.* New York: Peter Smith. 1929.

Wegelin, Oscar. *Early American Plays, 1714–1830.* New York: The Literary Collector Press. 1905.

White, George M. *Historical Collections of Georgia.* New York: Pudney & Russell. 1855.

White, George M. *Statistics of the State of Georgia.* Savannah: W. Thorne Williams. 1849.

Wiggins, Robert Lemuel. *Life of Joel Chandler Harris.* Nashville: Publishing House of the Methodist Episcopal Church, South. 1918.

Willis, Eola. *The Charleston Stage in the XVIII Century.* Columbia, S.C.: The State Company. 1924.

Wilson, Adelaide. *Historic and Picturesque Savannah.* Published for the Subscribers by the Boston Photogravure Company. 1889.

Young, Edward. *The Ladye Lillian and Other Poems.* Lexington, Ga.: E. Young. 1859.

Bibliography 247

Articles and Manuscript Material

Blair, Walter. "Burlesques in Nineteenth Century American Humor," *American Literature,* II, 236–247 (1930).

Blair, Walter. "The Popularity of Nineteenth Century American Humorists," *American Literature,* III, 175–194 (1931).

Brantley, Rabun Lee. "History of the Telegraph," Macon *Telegraph* Centennial Edition, 1826–1926, Section A.

Chew, Samuel C. "Byron in America," *American Mercury,* I, 335–344 (1924).

Corry, John P. "Education in Colonial Georgia," *Georgia Historical Quarterly,* XVI, 136–145 (June, 1932).

Coulter, E. Merton. "The Ante-Bellum Academy Movement in Georgia," *Georgia Historical Quarterly,* V, 11–42 (March, 1921).

Coulter, E. Merton. "A Georgia Educational Movement during the Eighteen Hundred Fifties," *Georgia Historical Quarterly,* IX, 1–33 (March, 1925).

Dodd, William E. "The Social Philosophy of the Old South," *The American Journal of Sociology,* XXIII, 735–746 (1918). Later included in the author's *Cotton Kingdom,* New Haven: Yale University Press. 1921.

Eckenrode, Hamilton James. "Sir Walter Scott and the South," *North American Review,* CCVI, 595–603 (1917).

Flanders, Bertram Holland. "An Uncollected Longfellow Translation," *American Literature,* VII, 205–207 (1935).

Flanders, B. H. "Two Forgotten Youthful Works of Joel Chandler Harris," *South Atlantic Quarterly,* XXXVIII, 278–283 (July, 1939).

Gilmer, Gertrude. "A Critique of Certain Georgia Ante Bellum Literary Magazines Arranged Chronologically, and a Checklist," *Georgia Historical Quarterly,* XVIII, 293–334 (Dec., 1934).

Harris, Joel Chandler. Manuscript letter to William Malone Baskervill, dated April 15, 1895. In Duke University Library.

Hoole, William Stanley. "The Gilmans and the *Southern Rose,*" *North Carolina Historical Review,* XI, 116–128 (1934).

Hoole, William Stanley. "William Gilmore Simms's Career as Editor," *Georgia Historical Quarterly,* XIX, 47–54 (1935).

Hubbell, Jay B. "Cavalier and Indentured Servant in Virginia Fiction," *South Atlantic Quarterly,* XXVI, 22–39 (1927).

Hubbell, Jay B. "Two Letters of Uncle Remus," *Southwest Review,* XXIII, 216–223 (1938).

Kennedy, Fronde. "Russell's Magazine," *South Atlantic Quarterly*, XVIII, 125–144 (1919).
Landrum, Grace Warren. "Notes on the Reading of the Old South," *American Literature*, III, 60–71 (1931).
Landrum, Grace Warren. "Sir Walter Scott and His Literary Rivals in the Old South," *American Literature*, II, 256–276 (1930).
McMurtrie, Douglas C. "Pioneer Printing in Georgia," *Georgia Historical Quarterly*, XVI, 77–113 (June, 1932).
Orians, G. Harrison. "The Romance Ferment after *Waverley*," *American Literature*, III, 408–431 (1932).
Orians, G. Harrison. "Walter Scott, Mark Twain, and the Civil War," *South Atlantic Quarterly*, XL, 342–359 (Oct., 1941).
Purvis, J. D. "Georgia Buys Historic Library," Atlanta *Journal*, April 3, 1938, Magazine Section, p. 9.
Smart, George K. "Private Libraries in Colonial Virginia," *American Literature*, X, 24–52 (1938).
Smithsonian Institution. *Appendix to the Report of the Board of Regents*. Washington: Government Printing Office. 1850.
Stearns, Bertha-Monica. "Southern Magazines for Ladies, 1819–1860," *South Atlantic Quarterly*, XXXI, 70–87 (1932).

NOTES

Notes

INTRODUCTION

1 Bureau of the Census, *A Century of Population Growth* (Washington, 1909), p. 11.
2 For sketches and criticism of all periodicals mentioned in this paragraph see Frank Luther Mott, *A History of American Magazines, 1741–1850* (New York, 1930), chs. I–II. A fuller discussion of early magazines is found in Lyon N. Richardson, *A History of Early American Magazines* (New York, 1931).
3 For sketches of these magazines see Mott, *op. cit.*, Part II, with Supplement. For the *North-American Review*, see Frank Luther Mott, *A History of American Magazines, 1850–65* (Cambridge, Mass., 1938), pp. 219–261.
4 U.S. Census. Of this number 2,367 were slaves.
5 Haygood S. Bowden, *Two Hundred Years of Education* (Richmond, 1932), p. 34.
6 *Ibid.*, ch. III.
7 Elfrida DeRenne Barrow and Laura Palmer Bell, *Anchored Yesterdays* (Savannah, 1923), p. 101.
8 Adelaide Wilson, *Historic and Picturesque Savannah* (Boston, 1889), p. 98.
9 Eola Willis, *The Charleston Stage in the XVIII Century* (Columbia, S.C., 1924), pp. 103–104. The popularity of the drama in Savannah may be noted in Andrew Sparks, *A History of the Theatre in Savannah, 1800–1836*, 1940, an unpublished University of Georgia M.A. thesis.
10 Statement of the editor in the *Port Folio*, II, 367 (Nov. 20, 1802). See also II, 383 (Dec. 4, 1802); III, 359 (Nov. 5, 1803); III, 47 (Feb. 5, 1803); III, 167 (May 21, 1803).
11 J. H. Campbell, *Georgia Baptists* (Richmond, 1847), p. 33. See also Henry Holcombe's own *The First Fruits, in a Series of Letters* (Philadelphia, 1812) for an account of his Savannah experiences.
12 *Cyclopaedia of American Biographies*, IV (1901), 109. I have been unable to find anywhere a corroboration of the above claim.
13 *A History of American Magazines, 1741–1850* (New York, 1930), p. 792.
14 Often written "Midway."
15 Jan. & Feb., 1803, p. 238. These lines strongly suggest the influence of the hymns of John and Charles Wesley.
16 Mar. & Apr., 1803, pp. 245–246. Holcombe himself was the author, says *The First Fruits, op. cit.*, p. 51.
17 Sept. & Oct., 1802–Jan. & Feb., 1803.
18 Sept. & Oct., 1802, p. 99.
19 *Ibid.*, p. 100.
20 Nov. & Dec., 1802, pp. 168–174.

[21] Nov. & Dec., 1802, p. 174. The "patronage" probably refers to Thomas Jefferson, then president.
[22] Jan. & Feb., 1803, pp. 221–222.
[23] *Ibid.*, p. 231.
[24] Herbert M. Morais, *Deism in Eighteenth Century America* (New York, 1934), p. 84.
[25] For details see G. Adolf Koch, *Republican Religion* (New York, 1933), p. 281.
[26] Clement Eaton, *Freedom of Thought in the Old South* (Durham, N.C., 1940), pp. 280–281.
[27] Wilson, *op. cit.*, p. 110.
[28] *Ibid.*, p. 111.
[29] *Ibid.*, p. 110.
[30] Elfrida DeRenne Barrow and Laura Palmer Bell, *op. cit.*, p. 115.
[31] Feb. 13, 1819, p. 8.
[32] Frank Luther Mott, *A History of American Magazines, 1741–1850* (New York, 1930), pp. 789–791.
[33] *Ibid.*, p. 792.
[34] *South Atlantic Quarterly*, XXXI, 70 (Jan., 1932).
[35] This letter, together with similar ones appearing in later issues, is in the tradition also of Benjamin Franklin. For the latter's use of this form in his *Pennsylvania Gazette*, see Elizabeth C. Cook, *Literary Influences in Colonial Newspapers, 1704–1750* (New York, 1912), pp. 95–99.
[36] I have been unable to locate the place of publication.
[37] Feb. 27, 1819.
[38] Feb. 20, 1819. Concerning this and the following three "Letters," Miss Gertrude Gilmer, in "A Critique of Certain Georgia Ante Bellum Literary Magazines, etc.," *Georgia Historical Quarterly*, XVIII, 293–334 (Dec., 1934), contends that "The prototype of the matrimonial bureau of today may have been the Ladies' Magazine." Even a casual reading reveals an unmistakable spirit of humorous distortion. There is nothing serious in "Proclamation" or "Letters."
[39] Feb. 27, 1819.
[40] *Ibid.*
[41] Mar. 6, 1819.
[42] Mar. 13, 1819. No title is given.
[43] *Ibid.*
[44] Mar. 20–Apr. 17, 1819.
[45] Apr. 24, 1819.
[46] Apr. 17, 1819.
[47] Apr. 10, 1819.
[48] May 1, 1819.
[49] June 12, 1819.
[50] Aug. 7, 1819. In the magazine the author's name is written "Geoffry Crayton." It is interesting to note the early appearance in Savannah of the first number of the *Sketch Book*, which the author dispatched from England in March, 1819, for New York publication. See Stanley T. Williams, *Life of Washington Irving* (New York, 1935), I, 173.
[51] June 19–26, 1819.
[52] Feb. 20, 1819.
[53] Feb. 27, 1819.
[54] Mar. 6, 1819.
[55] *Ibid.*

Notes 253

[56] Apr. 10, 1819.
[57] Apr. 17, 1819.
[58] May 15, 1819.
[59] July 31, 1819.
[60] June 26, 1819, p. 158.
[61] The U.S. Census of 1820 gives a total population in Savannah of 7,523, of which number 3,075 were slaves.
[62] July 10, 1819.
[63] Aug. 7, 1819.

CHAPTER I

[1] William Sumner Jenkins, *Pro-Slavery Thought in the Old South* (Chapel Hill, N.C., 1935), p. 65. This work contains a full discussion of the Southern arguments for slavery.

[2] The only extant copy, dated July 9, 1823, in the Duke University Library, states that it was published by M. J. Kappel, semi-weekly from November to May, and weekly the rest of the year.

[3] The magazine is referred to in Guy Adams Cardwell, Jr., *Charleston Periodicals, etc.*, Ph.D. thesis, University of North Carolina, 1936, p. 360; and in William Stanley Hoole, *A Check-List and Finding-List of Charleston Periodicals, 1732–1864* (Durham, 1936), p. 33. Cardwell declares it "reasonable to suppose the magazine was printed in Georgia" (*loc. cit.*).

[4] It had no connection with the newspaper of the same name.

[5] See Gertrude Gilmer, *Checklist of Southern Periodicals to 1861* (Boston, 1934).

[6] For a full account see Frank Luther Mott, *History of American Magazines, 1741–1850* (New York, 1930), pp. 544–555.

[7] See Mott, *op. cit.*, p. 547.

[8] Mott, *op. cit.*, p. 549.

[9] *Ibid.*, p. 555.

[10] *Ibid.*, pp. 606–614.

[11] Mott, *op. cit.*, pp. 629–657.

[12] I, 2 (Sept. 9, 1837) is the earliest number extant. Hereinafter I shall give, in referring to Georgia periodicals, both volume number and issue number followed by the date in parentheses, except in case of short-lived magazines, which are usually indicated solely by date of issue. Page numbers are always preceded by *p.* or *pp.* This departure from the usual method of indicating files of periodicals is due to the fact that some libraries record files only by the number of volume and issue; and such a departure facilitates the checking and identification of references in such cases. Needless to say, the usual method is followed with out-of-the-state periodicals.

[13] The subscription price was raised to $3 in 1838.

[14] I, 6.

[15] Augusta *Mirror*, II 4 (June 29, 1839). About one half of each issue was devoted to literature.

[16] The last number located is II, 46 (Oct. 26, 1839), though this issue gives no intimation of an early discontinuance.

[17] His own statement in II, 24 (Apr. 6, 1839).

[18] I, 38 (July 14, 1838).

[19] Most of the biographical details are from the *Cyclopaedia of American*

Biographies, VII (1903), 331, though this source contains some inaccuracies that had to be corrected from miscellaneous other sources.

20 Thompson here means "young men and women," not "children and adolescents."

21 Later installments appeared in I, 10–11 (Sept. 8–22, 1838).

22 May 19, 1838.

23 See Prospectus of the *Southern Bee* in the *Southern* Post, II (July 13, 1839).

24 Augusta *Mirror,* II, 6 (July 27, 1839).

25 *Southern Literary Messenger,* IV, 404 (June, 1838).

26 *Southern Post,* I, 29 (May 12, 1838).

27 Quoted in the Augusta *Mirror,* I, 26 (Apr. 20, 1839). The formats of the two periodicals are similar. Except for the fact that the Augusta journal contains more original matter, its New York contemporary is superior in every respect.

28 Quoted in Augusta *Mirror,* II, 6 (July 27, 1839).

29 Thompson's own statement in *Southern Miscellany,* I, 21 (Aug. 20, 1842).

30 III, 8.

31 III, 9.

32 Augusta *Mirror,* II, 14 (Feb. 8, 1840).

33 May 11, 1839.

34 II, 4 (June 29, 1839).

35 II, 26 (July 25, 1840).

36 I, 5 (June 30, 1838).

37 I, 10 (Sept. 8, 1838).

38 II, 8.

39 II, 9.

40 Statement of his personal physician in Thompson's "Open Letter" in the *Southern Miscellany,* I, 21 (Aug. 20, 1842).

41 III, 8.

42 III, 9.

43 Published, I, 17–20 (Dec. 15, 1838–Jan. 26, 1839).

44 Published, I, 18 (Dec. 29, 1838).

45 See I, 12 (Oct. 6, 1838).

46 I, 1 (May 5, 1838).

47 I, 22 (Feb. 23, 1839). This is the only uncollected tale by Thompson to appear in the *Mirror.*

48 I, 25 (Apr. 6, 1839).

49 II, 5 (July 13, 1839).

50 II, 6 (July 27, 1839).

51 II, 10 (Dec. 14, 1839).

52 Ran serially in III.

53 I, 1 (May 5, 1838).

54 I, 2 (May 19, 1838).

55 I, 6 (July 14, 1838).

56 Sometimes written as "Stephens."

57 I, 5 (June 30, 1838).

58 I, 4–8, 15–16 (June 16–Aug. 11, Nov. 17–Dec. 1, 1838).

59 I, 14, 24 (Nov. 3, 1838; Mar. 23, 1839).

60 II, 8 (Aug. 24, 1839).

61 II, 9–12 (Nov. 30, 1839–Jan. 11, 1840).

62 II, 14–20 (Feb. 8–May 2, 1840).

63 I, 1–2, 4 (May 5–19, June 16, 1838).

[64] I, 11–13 (Sept. 22–Oct. 20, 1838).
[65] II, 11 (Dec. 28, 1839).
[66] II, 25 (July 11, 1840).
[67] II, 7 (Aug. 10, 1839).
[68] II, 2 (May 25, 1839).
[69] II, 6 (July 27, 1839).
[70] I, 25 (Apr. 6, 1839).
[71] II, 5 (July 13, 1839).
[72] II, 15 (Feb. 22, 1840).
[73] Serially in II, ending in No. 11 (Dec. 28, 1839).
[74] III, 1 (Sept. 19, 1840).
[75] Began in III, 16 (July 31, 1841).
[76] II, 3 (June 8, 1839).
[77] II, 4 (June 29, 1839).
[78] II, 7 (Aug. 10, 1839).
[79] II, 24 (June 27, 1840).
[80] II, 9 (Nov. 30, 1839).
[81] George G. Smith, Jr., *Life and Times of George Foster Pierce* (Sparta, Georgia, 1888), p. 100. Pierce (1811–84) was the son of a Methodist preacher, a native of Georgia, and President of Georgia Female College (later Wesleyan College), 1839–42. He was later President of Emory College, 1849–54, and in 1854 was elected bishop of the Methodist Episcopal Church, South.

[82] Jesse Mercer (1769–1841), though born in North Carolina, early came to Georgia as a Baptist preacher, laboring for many years in that state, so much so that Mercer University, the Baptist institution in Georgia, was named in his honor. He also edited what was called *Mercer's Cluster,* a collection of hymns and sacred poems.

[83] Quoted in G. G. Smith, Jr., *op. cit.,* pp. 102–103.

[84] Adiel Sherwood, *Gazetteer of the State of Georgia* (Washington, 1837), p. 189.

[85] U.S. Census.

[86] Sherwood, *op. cit.,* 1837, p. 190.

[87] *Ibid.,* p. 191.

[88] Statement of George F. Pierce in *Southern Ladies' Book,* I, 2 (Feb., 1840), pp. 68–69.

[89] See back cover of I, 1 (January, 1849); also Washington (Georgia) *Independent Press,* Aug. 12, 1840.

[90] *Southern Ladies' Book,* I, 2 (Feb., 1840), pp. 127–128.

[91] *Godey's Lady's Book,* XXI, 192 (Oct., 1840).

[92] *Southern Ladies' Book,* II, 3 (Sept., 1840), p. 190. The apparent discrepancy of replying in Sept., 1840, to an article appearing in Oct., 1840, may be explained by the fact that the *Southern Ladies' Book* was sometimes published months after the date on the cover. In fact, the issues for Nov. and Dec., 1840, were not actually printed until the summer of 1841.

[93] Frank Luther Mott, *History of American Magazines, 1741–1850* (New York, 1930), pp. 699–700.

[94] See editorial comment in *Magnolia,* III, 1 (Jan., 1841).

[95] *Southern Ladies' Book,* II, 6 (Dec., 1840). See "Editor's Table," p. 346.

[96] *Magnolia,* III, 1 (Jan., 1841), p. 48.

[97] P. 43. The U.S. Census for 1840 shows a population of 11,214 in Savannah, against 3,927 in Macon.

[98] III, 1 (Jan., 1841), pp. 42–43.

[99] U.S. Census for 1840 gives Charleston a population of 29,261.
[100] P. 55.
[101] I, 3 (Mar., 1840).
[102] I, 2 (Feb., 1840).
[103] II, 2 (Aug., 1840).
[104] G. G. Smith, Jr., *op. cit.*, p. 104.
[105] I, 6 (June, 1840); II, 2 (Aug., 1840).
[106] I, 3 (Mar., 1840), "The Reaper and the Flowers."
[107] I, 5 (May, 1840), "Abderahman: the Washington of Spain."
[108] I, 2 (Feb., 1840), p. 128. Georgia periodicals contain all too many amateurish works that show "the want of exercise."
[109] III, 1 (Jan., 1841), p. 43.
[110] II, 3 (Sept., 1840).
[111] I, 6 (June, 1840).
[112] II, 3 (Sept., 1840).
[113] I, 1–2 (Jan.–Feb., 1840).
[114] II, 4 (Oct., 1840).
[115] III, 1 (Jan., 1841), p. 42. The tale was later published as *The Knights of the Horse-Shoe*, in Weptumpka (*sic*), Ala., in 1845. In 1841 it was entered at the District Court of Georgia for publication by Philip C. Pendleton, but whether it actually came out in book form then is uncertain. See "An Ancient Record," *Scott's Monthly Magazine*, III, 473 (June, 1867).
[116] III, 11 (Nov., 1841), p. 524.
[117] So far Simms had been editorially connected with four Charleston journals and periodicals: the *Southern Literary Gazette* (1828–29), *The Pleiades and Southern Literary Gazette* (1829, one issue), the *City Gazette and Commercial Advertiser* (1830–32), and the *Cosmopolitan: An Occasional* (1833, two issues). See William Stanley Hoole, "William Gilmore Simms's Career as Editor," *Georgia Historical Quarterly*, XIX, 47–54 (March, 1935).
[118] III, 5–7 (May–July, 1841).
[119] III, 6 (June, 1841), pp. 285–286.
[120] (Boston and New York), pp. 131–132.
[121] *Magnolia*, III, 6 (June, 1841), pp. 286–287.
[122] The "Letter" is found in *ibid.*, III, 8 (Aug., 1841), pp. 376–379.
[123] II, 3, pp. 187–188.
[124] He was probably the "Ludovic Paedagogus," whose name was appended to several articles.
[125] II, 4, p. 256.
[126] Quoted on inside of back cover to II, 5 & 6 (Nov. & Dec., 1840).
[127] Quoted in *Southern Ladies' Book*, II, 6 (Dec., 1840), p. 348. It must be remembered that this number was not issued until the summer of 1841, after the *Magnolia* had already begun in Savannah.
[128] *Ibid.*
[129] XVII, 357 (Apr., 1841).
[130] *Knickerbocker*, XVIII, 461 (Nov., 1841).
[131] IV, 4, p. 249.
[132] II, 3 (Sept., 1840), p. 192.
[133] IV, 3 (Mar., 1842), p. 191.
[134] I, 1–6 (Jan.–June, 1840); II, 6 (Dec., 1840).
[135] I, 3 (Mar., 1840).
[136] I, 6 (June, 1840); II, 1 (July, 1840).
[137] II, 3 (Sept., 1840).

Notes

138 *Ibid.*
139 II, 4 (Oct., 1840).
140 II, 6 (Dec., 1840).
141 III, 1–10 (Jan.–Oct., 1841).
142 III, 3–4 (Mar.–Apr., 1841).
143 III, 5–7 (May–July, 1841).
144 III, 7–9, 11–12 (July–Sept., Nov.–Dec., 1841); IV, 1 (Jan., 1842). No name is attached. For authorship see J. B. O'Neall, *Biographical Sketches, etc.* (Charleston, 1859), II, 525.
145 III, 8–12 (Aug.–Dec., 1841). For authorship see O'Neall, *op. cit.*, p. 524.
146 IV, 1–4, 6 (Jan.–Apr., June, 1842).
147 IV, 3–6 (Mar.–June, 1842).
148 IV, 2–5 (Feb.–May, 1842).
149 I, 1 (Jan., 1840).
150 *Ibid.*
151 *Ibid.*
152 I, 2 (Feb., 1840).
153 I, 3 (Mar., 1840).
154 *Ibid.*
155 *Ibid.*
156 I, 4 (Apr., 1840).
157 I, 5 (May, 1840).
158 I, 6 (June, 1840).
159 *Ibid.*
160 II, 1 (July, 1840).
161 *Ibid.*
162 II, 2 (Aug., 1840).
163 *Ibid.*
164 *Ibid.*
165 III, 1–2 (Jan.–Feb., 1841).
166 III, 7–10 (July–Oct., 1841).
167 III, 10 (Oct., 1841).
168 IV, 1 (Jan., 1842).
169 IV, 4 (Apr., 1842).
170 IV, 5 (May, 1842).
171 IV, 6 (June, 1842).
172 I, 1 (Jan., 1840).
173 I, 3 (Mar., 1840).
174 *Ibid.*
175 I, 5 (May, 1840).
176 *Ibid.*
177 *Ibid.*
178 I, 5–6 (May–June, 1840).
179 II, 1 (July, 1840).
180 II, 3 (Sept., 1840).
181 II, 5 (Nov., 1840).
182 III, 7 (July, 1841).
183 III, 3–9, 11–12 (Mar.–Sept., Nov.–Dec., 1841).
184 III, 11–12 (Nov.–Dec., 1841); IV, 2–5 (Feb.–May, 1842).
185 IV, 6 (June, 1842).
186 III, 12 (Dec., 1841), p. 572.
187 IV, 1 (Jan., 1842), p. 64.

[188] IV, 3 (Mar., 1842), p. 188.
[189] IV, 5 (May, 1842), p. 320.
[190] IV, 4 (Apr., 1842), p. 248.
[191] See Prospectus of *Magnolia* in Griffin *Georgia Jeffersonian and Griffin Gazette,* July 9, 1842, p. 4.
[192] *Ibid.*
[193] For an account of its career in Charleston see Sidney J. Cohen, *Three Notable Ante-Bellum Magazines of South Carolina* (Columbia, 1915); John E. Gibbs, Jr., *William Gilmore Simms and The Magnolia* (M.A. thesis, Duke University, 1931); and Guy Adams Cardwell, Jr., *Charleston Periodicals, etc.* (Ph.D. thesis, University of North Carolina, 1936).
[194] Information from inside front cover of *Family Companion,* II, 3 (June, 1842). Nothing is known about the Griffins except what can be learned from their publications.
[195] Editor's note in the first issue, Oct. 15, 1841.
[196] I, 3 (Dec. 15, 1841).
[197] *Southern Miscellany,* first issue, Apr. 5, 1842.
[198] *Ibid.,* I, 8 (May 21, 1842).
[199] Quoted on inside front cover of *Family Companion* for June, 1842. Even *Godey's Lady's Book* declared that "if the succeeding Numbers resemble the first, it must succeed." XXIII, 237 (Nov., 1841).
[200] They appeared in I, 1–3, 5–6 (Oct. 15–Dec. 15, 1841; Feb. 15–Mar. 15, 1842); III, 1 (Dec., 1842).
[201] I, 6 (Mar. 15, 1842).
[202] *Ibid.* This was before Dickens' *American Notes,* which did not appear till Oct., 1842.
[203] *Southern Miscellany,* I, 21 (Aug. 20, 1842).
[204] *Ibid.,* II, 3 (Apr. 15, 1843).
[205] II, 3.
[206] I, 1 (Oct. 15, 1841).
[207] I, 2–3 (Nov. 15–Dec. 15, 1841).
[208] I, 2–4 (Nov. 15, 1841–Jan. 15, 1842).
[209] I, 2–5 (Nov. 15, 1841—Feb. 15, 1842).
[210] I, 3–4 (Dec. 15, 1841–Jan. 15, 1842).
[211] I, 1–3, 5 (Oct. 15–Dec. 15, 1841; Feb. 15, 1842).
[212] I, 4 (Jan. 15, 1842).
[213] I, 5 (Feb. 15, 1842).
[214] I, 6 (Mar. 15, 1842).
[215] *Ibid.*
[216] *Ibid.*
[217] *Ibid.*
[218] II, 1 (Apr., 1842).
[219] II, 3 (June, 1842).
[220] *Ibid.*
[221] *Ibid.*
[222] II, 5 (Aug., 1842).
[223] III, 1 (Dec., 1842).
[224] *Ibid.*
[225] III, 1–3 (Dec., 1842–Feb., 1843).
[226] I, 1 (Oct. 15, 1841).
[227] *Ibid.*
[228] II, 3 (June, 1842).

229 *Ibid.*
230 III, 1 (Dec., 1842).
231 *Ibid.*
232 I, 1 (Oct. 15, 1841).
233 *Ibid.*
234 I, 3 (Dec. 15, 1841).
235 II, 2 (May, 1842).
236 II, 3 (June, 1842).
237 II, 6 (Sept., 1842).
238 III, 3 (Feb., 1843).
239 Biographical material, in the main, from the *Cyclopaedia of American Biographies*, VI (1903), 467.
240 For biographical sketches of Thomas Addison Richards, Mrs. C. W. DuBose, and Mrs. William C. Richards see, respectively: *National Cyclopaedia of American Biography*, VIII (1898), 425–426; *Appletons' Cyclopaedia of American Biography*, II (1888), 238; Allibone, *Critical Dictionary* (Philadelphia, 1871), II, 1791.
241 I, 6 (Sept., 1842).
242 II, 2 (Dec., 1842).
243 II, 4 (Feb., 1843).
244 II, 5 & 6 (Mar. & Apr., 1843).
245 See his statement in I, 5 (Aug., 1842), p. 323.
246 P. 54.
247 *Ibid.*
248 *Ibid.*
249 Richards does not say that the *Orion* was printed in New York, but William Gilmore Simms states it as a fact in the *Magnolia* (Savannah), IV, 6 (June, 1842), p. 278.
250 *Southern Miscellany*, I, 15 (July 9, 1842).
251 I, 1 (Mar., 1842), p. 63.
252 I, 4 (July, 1842), p. 248.
253 Nov., 1842.
254 I, 6 (Sept., 1842), p. 399.
255 I, 2 (May, 1842), pp. 123–124.
256 *Ibid.*, p. 124.
257 *Magnolia*, III, 11–12 (Nov.–Dec., 1841); IV, 2–5 (Feb.–May, 1842).
258 *Orion*, I, 4 (July, 1842), p. 251. To this criticism Simms never made any reply, so far as can be learned.
259 II, 1 (Nov., 1842), p. 58.
260 I, 4 (July, 1842), p. 241.
261 II, 3 (Jan., 1843), pp. 175–176.
262 II, 5 & 6 (Mar. & Apr., 1843), pp. 370–372.
263 *Magnolia*, IV, 6 (June, 1842), p. 378.
264 I, 1–5 (Mar.–Aug., 1842).
265 I, 1–3 (Mar.–June, 1842).
266 I, 1–2 (Mar.–May, 1842).
267 I, 3–4 (June–July, 1842).
268 I, 5–6 (Aug.–Sept., 1842).
269 II, 1–4 (Nov., 1842–Feb., 1843).
270 II, 4–5 & 6 (Feb.–Mar. & Apr., 1843).
271 III, 1–6 (Sept., 1843–Feb., 1844).
272 IV, 1–2 (Mar.–Apr., 1844).

273 IV, 1–5 (Mar.–July, 1844).
274 IV, 5–6 (July–Aug., 1844).
275 *Ibid.*
276 I, 6 (Sept., 1842).
277 *Ibid.*
278 II, 1 (Nov., 1842).
279 II, 2 (Dec., 1842).
280 *Ibid.*
281 II, 3 (Jan., 1843).
282 II, 4 (Feb., 1843).
283 II, 5 & 6 (Mar. & Apr., 1843).
284 *Ibid.*
285 IV, 3 (May, 1844).
286 IV, 6 (Aug., 1844).
287 I, 2 (May, 1842).
288 I, 1 (Mar., 1842).
289 I, 1 (Mar., 1842).
290 *Ibid.*
291 I, 3 (June, 1842).
292 I, 4 (July, 1842).
293 *Ibid.*
294 I, 5 (Aug., 1842).
295 *Ibid.*
296 I, 6 (Sept., 1842).
297 II, 1 (Nov., 1842).
298 *Ibid.*
299 II, 2 (Dec., 1842).
300 II, 3 (Jan., 1843).
301 II, 4 (Feb., 1843).
302 II, 5 & 6 (Mar. & Apr., 1843).
303 *Ibid.*
304 IV, 5 (July, 1844).
305 IV, 6 (Aug., 1844).
306 I, 2 (May, 1842).
307 *Ibid.* "The Whip-Poor-Will" is reprinted in Henry Rootes Jackson's *Tallulah, and Other Poems* (Savannah, 1850), but "Harold," though doubtless by the same poet, is nowhere attributed to him.
308 I, 4 (July, 1842).
309 I, 3 (June, 1842).
310 I, 1 (Mar., 1842).
311 I, 3 (June, 1842).
312 I, 4 (July, 1842).
313 III, 6 (Feb., 1844).
314 IV, 5 (July, 1844).
315 I, 4 (July, 1842).
316 I, 5 (Aug., 1842).
317 *Ibid.*
318 I, 6 (Sept., 1842).
319 II, 4 (Feb., 1843).
320 II, 5 & 6 (Mar. & Apr., 1843).
321 *Ibid.*
322 IV, 1–4 (Mar.–June, 1844).

323 IV, 5 (July, 1844).

324 I, 1 (Mar., 1842). This is only a book notice, appearing less than a year after the work first appeared (1841). It shows, however, an interest in the poems of the popular Longfellow.

325 I, 1 (Mar., 1842).

326 I, 2 (May, 1842).

327 I, 4 (July, 1842).

328 I, 6 (Sept., 1842). Though only an article praising the *Poems*, this "review" indicates the editor's close contact with literature in England, where he had spent the early years of his life.

329 II, 3 (Jan., 1843).

330 II, 4 (Feb., 1843).

331 II, 5 & 6 (Mar. & Apr., 1843). Robert M. Charlton (1807-54), native of Savannah, was at different times U.S. District Attorney, Superior Court Judge of the Eastern Circuit, U.S. Senator, Member of the State Legislature, and Mayor of Savannah. He was at one time a contributor to the New York *Knickerbocker*. His brother, Dr. T. J. Charlton, contributed several poems to the above-mentioned *Poems*.

332 II, 5 & 6 (Mar. & Apr., 1843).

333 *Ibid.*

334 IV, 2 (Apr., 1844).

335 *Ibid.*

336 IV, 3 (May, 1844).

337 *Ibid.*

338 IV, 6 (Aug., 1844). The author of this collection was Frances Anne Kemble, an English actress, who had married Pierce Butler, a Georgia planter. She was born in 1809 and died in 1893. Her most famous work was the *Journal Residence on a Georgia Plantation* (New York: Harper & Bros., 1857), in which she attacked the institution of slavery.

339 IV, 6 (Aug., 1844).

340 *Ibid.*

341 *Ibid.*

342 *Ibid.*

343 *Southern Miscellany*, I, 10 (June 4, 1842), Editorial Department.

344 I, 30 (Oct. 22, 1842).

345 *Magnolia*, IV, 6 (June, 1842), p. 378.

346 *Southern Literary Messenger*, IX, 639 (Oct., 1843).

347 *Ibid.*, X, 264 (Apr., 1844).

348 *Knickerbocker*, XIX, 496 (May, 1842).

349 *Orion*, II, 5 & 6, (Mar. & Apr., 1843), p. 361.

350 *Ibid.*

351 *Orion*, III, 6 (Feb., 1844). Editorial Department.

352 *Ibid.*, I, 3 (June, 1842), p. 186.

353 *Southern Miscellany*, Aug. 20, 1842.

354 All that is known about Hanleiter is that he was born in Savannah in 1815 and died in Atlanta in 1897.

355 *Family Companion*, II, 3 (June, 1842), p. 188.

356 See Hanleiter's statement in II, 48 (Feb., 16, 1844).

357 They appeared in the following issues: I, 12 (June 18, 1842); I, 23 (Sept. 3, 1842); I, 37 (Dec. 10, 1842); I, 39 (Dec. 24, 1842); I, 41 (Jan. 7, 1843); I, 42 (Jan. 14, 1843); I, 46 (Feb. 11, 1843); II, 11 (June 10, 1843); II, 13 (June 24, 1843); II, 20 (Aug. 12, 1843); II, 22 (Aug. 26, 1843); II, 25

(Sept. 16, 1843); II, 37 (Dec. 8, 1843); II, 39 (Dec. 22, 1843); II, 42 (Jan. 12, 1844); II, 44 (Jan. 26, 1844); II, 46 (Feb. 9, 1844).
  358 I, 13 (June 25, 1842).
  359 I, 25–28 (Sept. 17–Oct. 8, 1842).
  360 I, 33 (Nov. 12, 1842). Uncollected.
  361 I, 38 (Dec. 17, 1842). Uncollected.
  362 II, 32 (Nov. 4, 1843).
  363 I, 25–28 (Sept. 17–Oct. 8, 1842).
  364 Quoted in *Southern Miscellany*, I, 21 (Aug. 20, 1842).
  365 Editor's statement in II, 51 (Mar. 15, 1844).
  366 *Memoirs of Georgia* (Atlanta, 1895), II, 65.

CHAPTER II

1 See Prospectus in *Southern Literary Gazette* (Athens), I, 15 (Aug. 19, 1848), p. 120.

2 See Prospectus for *Wheler's Monthly Journal* in *Southern Literary Gazette*, I, 16 (Aug. 26, 1848), p. 128.

3 See advertisement of William N. White in *Southern Literary Gazette* (Athens), I, 50 (Apr. 28, 1849), p. 402.

4 See *Richards' Weekly Gazette* (Athens), II, 37 (Jan. 26, 1850); also Gertrude Gilmer, *Checklist of Southern Periodicals to 1861* (Boston, 1934), p. 34.

5 Atlanta, in this instance, was probably only a distributing center for the magazine.

6 Referred to in *Georgia University Magazine*, November, 1852. See also John Donald Wade, *Augustus Baldwin Longstreet* (New York, 1924), p. 212.

7 Commended in *Southern Baptist Messenger* (Covington), III, 6 (Mar. 15, 1853), p. 47; and in *Masonic Signet and Journal* (Marietta), N.S. I, 9 (Sept., 1855).

8 See Nettie Powell, *History of Marion County, Georgia* (Columbus, Georgia, 1931), p. 46.

9 R. L. Wiggins, *Life of Joel Chandler Harris* (Nashville, 1918), p. 44.

10 So reviewed in *Southern Banner* (Athens), Oct. 27, 1853.

11 Wiggins, *op. cit.*, p. 44.

12 A full biographical sketch of Turner is given in the discussion of the *Plantation* in ch. III.

13 Biographical details from *Biographical Souvenir of the States of Georgia and Florida* (Chicago, 1889), pp. 799–801.

14 Wiggins, *op. cit.*, p. 44, says that the periodical failed after three months.

15 The editor says that he had agents in fifteen Georgia towns and one Alabama town, and one traveling agent, F. J. Robinson. He lists the following as making payments for the magazine: Edward T. Terrell, Samuel Farrer, Dr. J. Wright, Dr. J. B. Hudson, John R. Hudson, R. A. Flournoy, Jefferson Adams, J. C. Denham, W. C. Davis, J. M. Adams, W. B. Carter, T. F. Cowles, Miss Ann Hudson, B. F. Adams, D. H. Reid, John B. Trippe, Joseph Turner, Miss Louisa Reid, J. A. Bright, Mrs. C. L. Rees, and Lewis Coffer. We judge, then, that the above constituted the subscription list, at least for that month.

16 This title had been used by W. G. Simms for a Charleston periodical, 1828–29.

17 George W. White, *Statistics of the State of Georgia* (Savannah, 1849), p. 76.

18 *Southern Literary Gazette*, I, 7 (June 24, 1848), p. 56.

19 White, *op. cit.*, p. 76.

Notes 263

20 A. L. Hull, *Annals of Athens, Georgia, 1801–1901* (Athens, 1906), p. 113.
21 *Ibid.*, p. 137. J. S. Buckingham, an Englishman who visited Athens in the 1840's, was very much impressed by the town, where the cultural level appeared to him to be high. See his *The Slave States of America* (London, 1842), II, chs. III–VII.
22 Hull, *op. cit.*, p. 149.
23 I, 1 (May 13, 1848), p. 5.
24 Prospectus in *ibid.*, p. 8.
25 *Ibid.*
26 *Ibid.*, p. 5.
27 *Southern Literary Messenger*, XIV, 390–391 (June, 1848).
28 Quoted in *Southern Literary Gazette*, I, 11 (July 22, 1848), p. 86.
29 *Ibid.*
30 *Ibid.*
31 *Ibid.*
32 The two periodicals differ in format. While the *Mirror* often contains music and engravings, the *Gazette* has a greater popular appeal.
33 Quoted in I, 11 (July 22, 1848), p. 87.
34 Quoted in *Richards' Weekly Gazette*, II, 3 (May 19, 1849).
35 Last group quoted in *ibid.*, II, 5 (June 2, 1849).
36 I, 1 (May 13), 2 (May 20), 6 (June 17), 9 (July 8), 32 (Dec. 16), 1848.
37 I, 39–43 (Feb. 10–Mar. 10, 1849).
38 I, 2–3 (May 20–27, 1848).
39 I, 3 (May 27), 5 (June 10), 7 (June 24), 9 (July 8), 12 (July 29), 14 (Aug. 12), 16 (Aug. 26), 1848; 40 (Feb. 17), 41 (Feb. 24), 1849.
40 I, 18 (Sept. 9), 19 (Sept. 16), 21 (Sept. 30), 24 (Oct. 21), 26 (Nov. 4), 29 (Nov. 25), 1848.
41 I, 47–48 (Apr. 7–14, 1849).
42 I, 6 (June 17, 1848.)
43 I, 8 (July 1, 1848).
44 I, 11 (July 22, 1848).
45 I, 15 (Aug. 19, 1848).
46 I, 17 (Sept. 2, 1848).
47 I, 18 (Sept. 9, 1848).
48 I, 44 (Mar. 17, 1849).
49 II, 1–2 (May 5–12, 1849).
50 I, 4 (June 3, 1848).
51 I, 10 (July 15, 1848).
52 I, 4 (June 3, 1848). Previously published in *Orion*, II, 5 & 6 (Mar. & Apr., 1843).
53 I, 17 (Sept. 21, 1848).
54 I, 27 (Nov. 11, 1848).
55 II, 1 (May 5, 1849).
56 II, 6 (June 9, 1849).
57 I, 1 (May 13, 1848).
58 *Ibid.*
59 I, 9 (July 8, 1848).
60 I, 15 (Aug. 19, 1848).
61 I, 16 (Aug. 26, 1848).
62 I, 21 (Sept. 30, 1848).
63 I, 25 (Oct. 28, 1848).
64 I, 27 (Nov. 11, 1848).

65 I, 29 (Nov. 25, 1848).
66 I, 30 (Dec. 2, 1848).
67 I, 31 (Dec. 9, 1848).
68 I, 32 (Dec. 16, 1848).
69 I, 38 (Feb. 3, 1849).
70 I, 41 (Feb. 24, 1849).
71 The tale was later collected in Whitman's *Complete Prose Works* (Philadelphia, 1897).
72 I, 17 (Sept. 2, 1848), p. 135.
73 *Ibid.*
74 I, 9 (July 8, 1848), p. 71.
75 I, 7 (June 24, 1848).
76 I, 10 (July 15, 1848).
77 I, 12 (July 29, 1848).
78 I, 41 (Feb. 24, 1849).
79 I, 6 (June 17, 1848).
80 I, 8 (July 1, 1848).
81 I, 15 (Aug. 19, 1848).
82 I, 16 (Aug. 26, 1848).
83 I, 18 (Sept. 9, 1848).
84 I, 20 (Sept. 23, 1848).
85 I, 21 (Sept. 30, 1848).
86 I, 29 (Nov. 25, 1848).
87 I, 30 (Dec. 2, 1848).
88 I, 37 (Jan. 27, 1849).
89 I, 40 (Feb. 17, 1849).
90 I, 45 (Mar. 24, 1849).
91 I, 47 (Apr. 7, 1849).
92 *Southern Literary Gazette*, I, 50 (Apr. 28, 1849), p. 401.
93 See Prospectus in *ibid.*, p. 402.
94 I, 23, p. 182.
95 According to Lyle H. Wright, *American Fiction, 1774–1850* (San Marino, Calif., 1939), p. 158, the two prize tales were reprinted in Athens, Georgia, by William C. Richards in 1849 in a 38-page book entitled *The Prize Articles Contributed to Richards' Weekly Gazette*. The Huntington Library in California has the only known copy of the latter work. In this work the "New Aria" is attributed to J. M. Legaré.
96 *Southern Literary Gazette*, I, 40 (Feb. 17, 1849), p. 319.
97 Timrod's only contribution to Richards' magazine in Georgia was a poem entitled "Song" ("We walk'd beneath the shadow"), in II, 18 (Sept. 1, 1849). It is rather an amateurish poem, written when the author was about twenty, and apparently uncollected.
98 *Southern Literary Messenger*, XIX, 59–60 (Jan., 1853).
99 See William Stanley Hoole, *A Check-List and Finding-List of Charleston Periodicals 1732–1864* (Durham, N.C., 1936), pp. 55–56.
100 See Prospectus in *Southern Literary Gazette*, I, 26 (Nov. 4, 1848), p. 207.
101 *Ibid.*
102 *Richards' Weekly Gazette*, I, 2 (May 12, 1849), editorial column.
103 Hoole, *op. cit.*, p. 57, states that the last number located is IX (July, 1857), and that the magazine was later merged with *Merry's Museum*.
104 *Richards' Weekly Gazette*, II, 9 (June 30, 1849).
105 *Ibid.*

Notes

106 XLVI, 375 (Apr., 1853).
107 By Mrs. Manners (Mrs. William C. Richards), I, 3 (Mar., 1849).
108 By Mrs. Manners (Mrs. William C. Richards), I, 4 (Apr., 1849).
109 I, 2-3, 9 (Feb.-Mar., Sept., 1849).
110 I, 4-5 (Apr.-May, 1849).
111 I, 6-7 (June-July, 1849).
112 I, 10 (Oct., 1849).
113 I, 11-12 (Nov.-Dec., 1849).
114 *Ibid.*
115 Her maiden name was Cornelia Holroyd Bradley.
116 Charleston, 1852. Biographical material is taken from the *National Cyclopaedia of American Biography*, II (1921), p. 173.
117 U.S. Census.
118 Published in Philadelphia.
119 Jan., 1849.
120 Feb.-Mar., 1849.
121 Feb., 1849.
122 *Ibid.*
123 *Ibid.*
124 Mar., 1849.
125 *Ibid.*
126 Notice of its appearance may be found in the *Southern Literary Gazette* (Athens), I, 22 (Oct. 7, 1848), p. 175.
127 *Southern Literary Gazette*, I, 22 (Oct. 7, 1848), p. 175.
128 Statement of *Wheler's Magazine*, I, 4 (Oct., 1849), p. 95.
129 *Ibid.*, p. 100.
130 *Southern Literary Gazette*, I, 22 (Oct. 7, 1848), p. 175.
131 *Ibid.*, I, 1-12.
132 I, 16.
133 P. 22.
134 II, 1 (Jan., 1850).
135 As we learn from the Table of Contents for Vol. I, appearing in I, 6 (Dec., 1849).
136 I, 2 (Aug., 1849).
137 *Ibid.*
138 *Ibid.*
139 *Ibid.*
140 *Ibid.*
141 I, 3 (Sept., 1849).
142 *Ibid.*
143 *Ibid.*
144 *Ibid.*
145 I, 4 (Oct., 1849).
146 I, 4-5 (Oct.-Nov., 1849).
147 I, 5 (Nov., 1849).
148 I, 6 (Dec., 1849).
149 *Ibid.*
150 II, 1 (Jan., 1850).
151 *Ibid.*
152 *Ibid.*
153 *Ibid.*
154 I, 1 (July, 1849).

155 *Ibid.*
156 I, 2 (Aug., 1849).
157 *Ibid.*
158 I, 3 (Sept., 1849).
159 *Ibid.*
160 I, 4 (Oct., 1849).
161 *Ibid.*
162 *Ibid.*
163 *Ibid.*
164 I, 5 (Nov., 1849).
165 *Ibid.*
166 II, 1 (Jan., 1850).
167 See Bertram Holland Flanders, "An Uncollected Longfellow Translation," *American Literature*, VII, 205–207 (May, 1935).
168 I, 17 (June 28, 1849). Editor's page.
169 II, 7, 23, 27 (June 23, Oct. 5, Nov. 3, 1849).
170 XV, 638 (Sept., 1849).
171 *Wheler's Magazine*, I, 5 (Nov., 1849), p. 99.
172 I, 3.
173 I, 4 (Oct., 1849), p. 98.
174 I, 3 (Sept., 1849), p. 68.
175 I, 6 (Dec., 1849), pp. 133–137.
176 I, 4 (Oct., 1849), p. 97.
177 *Ibid.*
178 U.S. Census.
179 II, 9 (May 4, 1850). Uncollected.
180 II, 10 (May 11, 1850).
181 II, 11 (May 18, 1850).
182 II, 3–7.
183 I, 37.
184 I, 5 (Nov., 1849).
185 The opinion of the *Caddo Gazette* (Shreveport, Louisiana). Quoted in *A Friend of the Family*, I, 20 (July 19, 1849).
186 *Southern Baptist Messenger* (Covington), III, 2 (Jan. 15, 1853), p. 8.
187 Published in Athens.
188 (New York, 1852). Mentioned in Joseph Sabin, *A Dictionary of Books Relating to America* (New York, 1888), XVII, 329. No copy has yet been located.
189 *Southern Baptist Messenger*, III, 2 (Jan. 15, 1853), p. 8.
190 "Editor's Table," p. 42.
191 Pp. 41–42.
192 I, 1 (Jan., 1853), p. 46.
193 *Ibid.*, pp. 13–20.
194 *Ibid.*, pp. 28–31.
195 *Ibid.*, pp. 33–35.
196 I, 2 (Feb., 1853), pp. 57–70.
197 I, 1–2 (Jan.–Feb., 1853), pp. 1–9, 49–60.
198 I, 1 (Jan., 1853), pp. 23–26.
199 I, 2 (Feb., 1853), pp. 72–81. Note that pp. 65–88 are numbered wrongly.
200 I, 1 (Jan., 1853), p. 36.
201 I, 2 (Feb., 1853), p. 71.
202 I, 1 (Jan., 1853), pp. 10–12.

203 I, 2 (Feb., 1853), pp. 61–65.
204 I, 1 (Jan., 1853), p. 22.
205 *Ibid.*, p. 27.
206 *Ibid.*, p. 32.
207 *Ibid.*, p. 21.
208 Roath writes "William Edmondstowne Aytown."
209 I, 1 (Jan., 1853), pp. 43–44.
210 I, 2 (Feb., 1853), pp. 82–86.
211 *Ibid.*, pp. 86–87. "Bon Gualtier" is the pseudonym for two British writers: William Edmondstoune Aytoun and Sir Theodore Martin.
212 I, 1 (Jan., 1853), pp. 46–48.
213 I, 2 (Feb., 1853), p. 82.
214 *Ibid.*
215 Statement on inside of back cover to I, 3 (May, 1853).
216 *Ibid.*
217 Augusta, 1857.
218 Biographical material from *National Cyclopaedia of American Biography*, I (1892), 274.
219 Inside of back cover to I, 3 (May, 1853).
220 *Ibid.*
221 See inside back covers to I, 2, 7, 8 (Apr., Sept., Oct., 1853).
222 N.S. VIII, 15 (July, 1853), p. 277.
223 XIX, 252 (Apr., 1853). The *Living Age* was, of course, a superior magazine. Its weekly issues contained 48 pages each of selected matter.
224 *Southern Eclectic*, II, 10 (Dec., 1853).
225 *Ibid.*, II, 12 (Feb., 1854), p. 480.
226 I, 1 (Mar., 1853).
227 I, 2 (Apr., 1853).
228 *Ibid.*
229 I, 3 (May, 1853).
230 I, 4 (June, 1853).
231 *Ibid.*
232 *Ibid.*
233 I, 5 (July, 1853).
234 *Ibid.*
235 *Ibid.*
236 I, 4, 6 (June, Aug., 1853); II, 7, 9–12 (Sept., Nov., 1853–Feb., 1854); III, 13–15 (Mar.–May, 1854).
237 II, 7–8 (Sept.–Oct., 1853).
238 II, 8 (Oct., 1853).
239 II, 9 (Nov., 1853).
240 II, 7, 9, 11 (Sept., Nov., 1853, Jan., 1854).
241 II, 7, 10–12 (Sept., Dec., 1853–Feb., 1854); III, 13–14, 16 (Mar.–Apr., June, 1854).
242 II, 12 (Feb., 1854).
243 III, 13 (Mar., 1854).
244 II, 7 (Sept., 1853).
245 *Ibid.*
246 II, 8 (Oct., 1853).
247 II, 10 (Dec., 1853).
248 II, 12 (Feb., 1854); III, 16 (June, 1854).

249 III, 14 (Apr., 1854).
250 III, 15 (May, 1854).
251 *Ibid.*

CHAPTER III

1 *Southern Field and Fireside* (Augusta), N.S. I, 8 (Feb. 21, 1863), p. 60. For biographical sketch of Hewitt see *Dictionary of American Biography*, VIII (New York, 1932), 606–607.
2 *Southern Field and Fireside*, N.S. I, 8 (Feb. 21, 1863), p. 60.
3 *Ibid.*, N.S. I, 11 (Mar. 14, 1863), p. 84.
4 See the Atlanta *Daily Intelligencer*, Sept. 13, 1862; June 10, 1863.
5 Probably Matilda Heron's version of Dumas' *Camille*.
6 Macon *Telegraph Centennial Edition, 1826–1926*, Section A, p. 12, col. 8.
7 II, 2 (Feb., 1861), pp. 72–73.
8 *Ibid.*, p. 75.
9 See Fronde Kennedy, "Russell's Magazine," *South Atlantic Quarterly*, XVIII, 125–144 (Apr., 1919). Also F. L. Mott, *A History of American Magazines, 1850–1865* (Cambridge, Mass., 1938), pp. 488–492.
10 William B. Cairns, "Later Magazines," *Cambridge History of American Literature*, III (1921), 302.
11 M. A. DeWolfe Howe, *The Atlantic Monthly and Its Makers* (Boston, 1919).
12 See Cairns, *op. cit.*, pp. 307–310.
13 See Adiel Sherwood, *Gazetteer for 1860* (Macon and Atlanta, 1860).
14 *Ibid.* Also see Gertrude Gilmer, *Checklist of Southern Periodicals to 1861* (Boston, 1934), p. 27.
15 See Sherwood, *Gazetteer for 1860, op. cit.*
16 Walter G. Cooper, *Official History of Fulton County* (Atlanta, 1934), p. 88.
17 I, 1–4 (May 7–28, 1859).
18 I, 2 (May 14, 1859).
19 *Ibid.*, p. 15.
20 I, 4 (May 28, 1859).
21 I, 24, p. 191.
22 Obviously a pseudonym.
23 Entitled "Zella." Published in *Hygienic and Literary Magazine*, I, 1–3 & 4 (Jan.–Mar. & Apr., 1860).
24 Entitled "A Vision of the Millenium." Published in *Hygienic and Literary Magazine*, I, 2 (Feb., 1860).
25 Professor of Anatomy in Atlanta Medical College.
26 Unidentified resident of Atlanta.
27 Atlanta lawyer.
28 I, 25.
29 *Hygienic and Literary Magazine*, I, 1 (Jan., 1860), p. 55.
30 I, 2–4 (May 14–28, 1859).
31 I, 14–17 (Aug. 6–27, 1859).
32 I, 13–14 (July 30–Aug. 6, 1859).
33 I, 17–25 (Aug. 27–Oct. 22, 1859).
34 I, 18–19, 21–22 (Sept. 3–10; Sept. 24–31 [*sic*], 1859).
35 I, 21–24 (Sept. 24–Oct. 15, 1859).
36 I, 24 (Oct. 15, 1859).
37 I, 24–25 (Oct. 15–22, 1859).
38 I, 4 (May 28, 1859).

39 I, 14 (Aug. 6, 1859).
40 *Ibid.*
41 I, 17 (Aug. 27, 1859).
42 I, 19 (Sept. 10, 1859).
43 I, 24 (Oct. 15, 1859).
44 I, 25 (Oct. 22, 1859).
45 Probably an error for "Miranda," the pseudonym of Virginia M. O. Minor.
46 *Southern Field and Fireside,* I, 1 (May 28, 1859), p. 8.
47 (New York, 1856).
48 *Southern Field and Fireside,* I, 1 (May 28, 1859), p. 8.
49 It was printed in book form in Macon in 1864.
50 Reprinted in book form by Derby & Jackson, New York, 1860.
51 June 11, 1859.
52 I, 7.
53 Resigned in 1862 to edit the Atlanta *Banner & Baptist.*
54 I, 12, 14, 16 (Aug. 13, 27, Sept. 10, 1859).
55 I, 8 (July 16, 1859).
56 I, 9 (July 23, 1859).
57 I, 7 (July 9, 1859).
58 I, 9 (July 23, 1859).
59 I, 2 (June 4, 1859), p. 12. This part of the article, entitled "American Literature," states a footnote, was written on Mar. 16, 1856. At that time Turner was editing the Eatonton (Georgia) *Independent Press.*
60 *Ibid.*
61 I, 20.
62 *Ibid.,* p. 156.
63 N.S. I, 20 (May 16, 1863), p. 139.
64 N.S. II, 45 (Nov. 5, 1864), p. 4.
65 *Southern Literary Messenger,* XXVIII, 318–319 (Apr., 1859).
66 *Ibid.,* XXIX, 77–78 (July, 1859).
67 *Russell's Magazine,* II, 96 (Oct., 1859).
68 I, 51 (May 12, 1860), p. 404.
69 Statement of the editor in N.S. II, 12 (Mar. 19, 1864), p. 4.
70 N.S. I, 22.
71 I, 1–26 (May 28–Nov. 19, 1859).
72 I, 1–27 (odd numbers only), 28 (May 28–Nov. 26, Dec. 3, 1859).
73 I, 1–2, 4, 6, 8, 10–11 (May 28–June 4, 18, July 2, 16, 30, Aug. 6, 1859).
74 I, 1–3 (May 28–June 11, 1859).
75 I, 12, 14, 16 (Aug. 13, 27, Sept. 10, 1859).
76 I, 18, 20, 22 (Sept. 24, Oct. 8, 22, 1859).
77 I, 24, 26 (Nov. 5, 19, 1859).
78 II, 1(?), 8, 11–12 (May 19 [?], July 14, Aug. 4, 11, 1860).
79 II, ?, 42, ? (?, Mar. 9, 1861, ?).
80 N.S. I, 1–5 (Jan. 3–31, 1863).
81 N.S. I, 1–4 (Jan. 3–25, 1863).
82 N.S. I, 6–8, ? (Feb. 7–21, ?, 1863).
83 N.S. I, 10(?)–13 (Mar. 7[?]–28, 1863).
84 N.S. II, 1–19 (Jan. 2–May 7, 1864). For authorship see James Wood Davidson, *Living Writers of the South* (New York, 1869), pp. 313–314.
85 N.S. II, 22–26 (May 28–June 25, 1864).
86 N.S. II, 27–42 (July 2–Oct. 15, 1864).
87 I, 1 (May 28, 1859).

88 I, 2 (June 4, 1859).
89 I, 11 (Aug. 6, 1859).
90 I, 15 (Sept. 3, 1859).
91 N.S. I, 6 (Feb. 7, 1863).
92 N.S. I, 14 (Apr. 4, 1863). Previously published in *Hygienic and Literary Magazine* (Atlanta), I, 2 (Feb., 1860).
93 N.S. I, 22 (May 30, 1863).
94 N.S. I, 38 (Sept. 19, 1863).
95 N.S. II, 17 (Apr. 23, 1864).
96 N.S. II, 27 (July 2, 1864).
97 N.S. II, 28 (July 9, 1864).
98 N.S. II, 32 (Aug. 6, 1864).
99 N.S. II, 33 (Aug. 13, 1864).
100 N.S. II, 36 (Sept. 3, 1864).
101 I, 2 (June 4, 1859).
102 I, 5 (June 25, 1859).
103 *Ibid.*
104 I, 10 (July 30, 1859).
105 N.S. I, 4 (Jan. 25, 1863).
106 N.S. I, 7 (Feb. 14, 1863).
107 N.S. II, 9 (Feb. 27, 1864).
108 N.S. II, 39 (Sept. 24, 1864).
109 N.S. II, 42 (Oct. 15, 1864).
110 II, 8 (July 14, 1860).
111 II, 11 (Aug. 4, 1860).
112 *Ibid.*
113 II, 11 (Aug. 4, 1860), p. 84.
114 For a sketch of Thompson's journalistic experiences see *Dictionary of American Biography*, XVIII (New York, 1936), 464.
115 N.S. II, 22 (May 28, 1864), p. 4.
116 Prospectus on outside of back cover to I, 2 (Feb., 1860).
117 I, 1-3 & 4 (Jan.-Mar. & Apr., 1860). Prize awarded by *Medical and Literary Weekly* (Atlanta) in I, 24 (Oct. 15, 1859).
118 I, 1 (Jan., 1860).
119 I, 2 (Feb., 1860).
120 I, 3 & 4 (Mar. & Apr., 1860).
121 *Ibid.*
122 *Ibid.*
123 *Ibid.*
124 I, 1 (Jan., 1860).
125 *Ibid.*
126 I, 2 (Feb., 1860). Prize awarded by *Medical and Literary Weekly* (Atlanta), in I, 24 (Oct. 15, 1859).
127 I, 2 (Feb., 1860).
128 I, 3 & 4 (Mar. & Apr., 1860).
129 No copy has as yet been located.
130 (Mobile and New York, 1858).
131 Most of the biographical material is from the *Biographical Souvenir of the States of Georgia and Florida* (Chicago, 1889), pp. 799-801.
132 *Countryman*, XIX, 2 (Jan. 12, 1864).
133 His father had curiously named him Joseph Addison, and a brother, William Wilberforce.

Notes

134 (New York, 1857).
135 Turner's own words in the preface.
136 *Countryman*, XX, 7 (Feb. 14, 1865), p. 93.
137 Pp. 500–501.
138 XXX, 476 (June, 1860).
139 Quoted in *Plantation*, II, 2 (Dec., 1860). Inside of back cover. Whether this was the opinion of William Cullen Bryant, then editor of the *Post*, is unknown.
140 P. 3.
141 *The Magazine in America* (New York, 1916), p. 155.
142 I, 1 (March, 1860).
143 II, 1 (Sept., 1860).
144 *Ibid.*
145 *Ibid.*
146 II, 2 (Dec., 1860).
147 II, 1 (Sept., 1860).
148 II, 2 (Dec., 1860).
149 Pp. 219–220.
150 See "Editor's Table."
151 P. 665.
152 P. 670. Turner is probably referring to the later "Jack Downing Letters" by Charles A. Davis.
153 P. 682.
154 Miss Gertrude Gilmer, in "A Critique of Certain Ante Bellum Literary Magazines, etc.," *Georgia Historical Quarterly*, XVIII, 333 (Dec., 1934), claims that a copy of the issue for Dec. 18, 1863, is in the possession of the Columbus (Georgia) *Ledger-Enquirer*, but a careful search has failed to locate it, and the editor of the above paper denies that it has ever been in his or the paper's possession. Miss Gilmer, in the same article, is also in error in the date of the issue in possession of the University of Texas, which is June 1, 1864, instead of Jan. 1, 1864, as she states.
155 New York, 1859.
156 Cassville, Georgia, 1857.
157 Biographical material from *Appletons' Cyclopaedia of American Biography*, VI (1889), 147.
158 *Southern Field and Fireside*, N.S. I, 11 (Mar. 21, 1863), p. 88.
159 VI, 15.
160 For authorship see *Living Female Writers of the South* (Philadelphia, 1872), p. 204.
161 VI, 19.
162 See *Living Female Writers, op. cit.*, p. 343.
163 See Augusta *State Rights' Sentinel*, Aug. 11, 1834.
164 U.S. Census.
165 That of July, 1838, in the private possession of Prof. E. Merton Coulter, Athens, Georgia; and that of May 29, 1852, in the Duke University Library. Neither issue is in any sense "literary."
166 See *Living Female Writers, op. cit.*, p. 321.
167 *Ibid.*
168 *Ibid.*
169 Not to be confused with the periodical of the same name published in Macon in 1840, which later became the *Magnolia*.
170 XXVI, N.S. VI, 35.

171 XXVI, N.S. VI, 42.
172 *Living Female Writers, op. cit.,* p. 204.
173 Quoted in XXVI, N.S. VI, 35 (Sept. 12, 1861), p. 3.
174 Author of *Dukesborough Tales,* under pseudonym of "Philemon Perch" (Baltimore, 1871), and other humorous tales later.
175 Quoted in XXVI, N.S. VI, 35 (Sept. 12, 1861), p. 3.
176 *Ibid.*
177 *Ibid.*
178 Statement of Joel Chandler Harris in his *On the Plantation* (New York, 1903), p. 25.
179 Biographical material from Julia Collier Harris, *Life and Letters of Joel Chandler Harris* (New York, 1918), and from R. L. Wiggins, *Life of Joel Chandler Harris* (Nashville, 1918).
180 Statement of Harris in *On the Plantation, op. cit.,* p. 21.
181 I, 10. Johnson did not publish the *Adventurer* but wrote essays for it.
182 II, 1 (June 17, 1862).
183 I, 6 (Apr. 8, 1862).
184 II, 1 (June 17, 1862).
185 I, 3 (Mar. 18, 1862).
186 I, 4 (Mar. 25, 1862).
187 I, 9 (Apr. 29, 1862).
188 *On the Plantation, op. cit.,* p. 22.
189 The experiences of Harris at Turnwold are related in his *On the Plantation,* in which Joe Maxwell is really the author himself.
190 Wiggins, *op. cit.,* p. 49.
191 III, 10 (Dec. 1, 1862).
192 III, 12 (Dec. 15, 1862).
193 V, 2 (Apr. 14, 1863), etc.
194 *Op. cit.,* pp. 155–158.
195 XIX, 24 (June 14, 1864). For a full discussion of this article see B. H. Flanders, "Two Forgotten Youthful Works of Joel Chandler Harris," *South Atlantic Quarterly,* XXXVIII, 278–283 (July, 1939).
196 XX, 4 (Jan. 24, 1865).
197 XXI, 3 (Feb. 13, 1866).
198 III, 8 (Nov. 17, 1862), p. 57.
199 IV, 1 (Dec. 22, 1862), p. 6.
200 XIX, 2 (Jan. 12, 1864).
201 With III, 1 (Sept. 29, 1862).
202 Wiggins, *op. cit.,* p. 26.
203 Quoted in *ibid.,* p. 48. I have been unable to locate this last copy. Members of the Harris family state their ignorance of its whereabouts.
204 III, 1 (Sept. 29, 1862), p. 1. Probably written by Turner himself.
205 IV, 1 (Dec. 22, 1862), p. 6.
206 V, 1 (Apr. 7, 1863), p. 2.
207 Statement of Harris in *On the Plantation, op. cit.,* p. 22.
208 III, 8–10 (Nov. 17–Dec. 1, 1862).
209 III, 6–IV, 2 (Nov. 3, 1862–Jan. 5, 1863).
210 It ran irregularly from XIX, 20 (May 17, 1864) to XX, 14 (Apr. 4, 1865).
211 Beginning in XIX, 4 (Jan. 26, 1864).
212 (Mobile, New York, and Athens, 1858).
213 IV, 3–4 (Jan. 12–19, 1863).

Notes 273

[214] V, 2 (Apr. 14, 1863).
[215] In the issues for Feb., 1866, says Wiggins, *op. cit.*, p. 21, footnote.
[216] IV, 1–9 (Dec. 22, 1862–Feb. 24, 1863).
[217] XX, 2 (Jan. 10, 1865).
[218] Preface to poem in III, 5 (Oct. 27, 1862). There is also a suggestion of Goldsmith's *The Traveller*. Traces of Wordsworth can be detected in the description of the young camp-meeting preacher, suggestive of "The Pastor" in Wordsworth's *Excursion*.
[219] III, 5–12 (Oct. 27–Dec. 15, 1862).
[220] III, 5 (Oct. 27, 1862), p. 37.
[221] III, 9 (Nov. 24, 1862), p. 65. A similar picture of slavery in the Old South, especially as compared to the lot of manual laborers in other parts of the world, is found in a poem of about the same length: "The Hireling and the Slave," by William J. Grayson, of South Carolina. It was published in the collection called *The Hireling and the Slave, Chicora, and Other Poems*, in Charleston in 1856.
[222] III, 9 (Nov. 24, 1862), p. 70.
[223] III, 8 (Nov. 17, 1862), p. 60.
[224] III, 9 (Nov. 24, 1862), p. 65.
[225] *Ibid.*
[226] III, 4–5; IV, 1–2, 6 (Apr.–May, July–Aug., Dec., 1867).
[227] Source not indicated.

CHAPTER IV

[1] From the back cover of the *Messenger* for Dec., 1843.
[2] *Godey's Lady's Book*, XXXVIII, 226 (Mar., 1849).
[3] See cover page of *Whitaker's Magazine* for Sept., 1850.
[4] These figures are compiled from the cover pages of the *Messenger* for 1834–49, the only years in which paid subscription lists were published. I have been aided in this compilation by Miss Mary F. Goodwin, an experienced investigator of Richmond, Virginia.
[5] See cover page of the *Messenger* for Apr., 1842.
[6] Cassville, Ga., 1852.
[7] Athens, 1853. The author has been identified by the late William Kenneth Boyd, of Duke University, as Francis James Robinson, Clerk of the Court, Lexington, Ga.
[8] Published in collected form in Augusta, 1835.
[9] Frank Luther Mott, *A History of American Magazines, 1741–1850* (Cambridge, Mass.: Harvard University Press, 1938), p. 424.
[10] Fred Lewis Pattee, in *The Feminine Fifties* (New York, 1940), describes, in detail, this period in American fiction.
[11] J. S. Buckingham, *The Slave States of America* (London, 1842), II, 80–81.
[12] See Appendix C for a list of contributors, with Georgians marked with an asterisk (*).
[13] First printed in 1859.
[14] Ch. XXIII.
[15] Savannah, 1850.
[16] I (New York and Savannah, 1847); II (Philadelphia, 1859).
[17] *A Check-List and Finding-List of Charleston Periodicals, 1732–1864* (Durham, N.C., 1936).

18 See Appendices A and B.
19 William Gilmore Simms claimed that "No *purely* agricultural people, any where, has ever produced a national literature . . . ; though they have produced great orators, politicians, warriors, and even philosophers." See his "Literary Prospects of the South," *Russell's Magazine*, III, 194 (June, 1858).

General Index

(Italicized figures following a Georgia magazine refer to the historical and critical sketch of the magazine.)

Abdy, Mrs., 29, 46, 54, 57
Abolitionism, 23, 77, 94, 153, 155, 181, 194, 195, 199-200
Ada, 29
Addisine, Nina, 146
Addison (*see* Turner, Joseph Addison)
Addison, Joseph, influence of, in Georgia magazines, 151, 155, 166, 172-173, 183, 188, 192
Adele, 146
Adolphus, 29
Advertising in Georgia magazines, 19, 20, 28, 33, 53, 89, 90, 95, 98, 103, 116-117, 134, 137, 148, 149, 154-155, 158, 185, 188-189, 207
Aglaus (*see* Timrod, Henry)
Albanio, 36
Alceus, 29
Aleck, 104, 114
Alexander, James E., 55, 57
Algeroy, 36
Alguno, 146
Allan, 31, 36
Alligator, 36
Allspice, Josiah, 105
Alpha, 36, 104, 128
Alphonso, 104
Alteram Partem, 128
Alton (*see* Taveau, A. L.)
Amateur, An, 105
American Anti-Slavery Society, founding of, 23
American in Paris, An, 146
American Magazine, 1787-88 (New York), 4
American Magazine and Historical Chronicle, 1743-46 (Boston), 4

American Magazine and Monthly Chronicle, 1757-58 (Philadelphia), 4
American Magazine, or A Monthly View of the Political state of the British Colonies, 1741 (Philadelphia), 4
American Museum (Philadelphia), 5
American Review and Literary Journal (New York), 5
Americus (Ga.), 147, 198
Anders, Hon. G., 57
Ann E., 105
Annette, 56
Anon, 146
Anthropos, 29
Archaeus, 36
Arena, 146
Aria, 107
Arion, 56
Aristeus, 56
Armstrong, Mrs. M., 163
Army and Navy Herald (Macon, Ga.), *132*
Army, magazines for the, 132
Arnell, David R., 104
Arnold, Rev. William, 176
Aros, 56
Arp, Bill (Charles Henry Smith), 177, 193, 194, 204, 207, 208
Arthur, T. S., 67, 115, 116, 196, 197
Arts, Fine, interest in the, 18, 37, 54, 55, 71, 73, 103, 110, 191, 198
Ashman, 36
Ashmore, T. P., 93
Ashton, Ellen, 158, 160
Athenian (Athens, Ga.), 25
Athens (Ga.), 4, 25, 27, 36, 38, 57, 69, 89, 91, 92, 93, 95, 96, 99, 100, 104,

Athens (Ga.), *Continued*
105, 106, 108, 109, 110, 111, 112, 116, 118, 119, 120, 123, 138, 142, 150, 173, 180, 183, 187, 202, 203, 263 n
Atkinson, S. A., 137, 139
Atlanta (Ga.), 90, 92, 130, 132, 133, 134, 135, 136, 142, 146, 147, 148, 149, 160, 161, 162, 177, 183, 185, 186, 198, 203, 204, 208
Atlanta Medical College (Atlanta, Ga.), 163
Atlantic Monthly (Boston), 132, 153, 186
Augusta (Ga.), 3, 9, 16, 25, 29, 30, 31, 32, 33, 34, 35, 36, 37, 38, 40, 56, 60, 67, 70, 71, 87, 92, 93, 104, 105, 120, 123, 124, 129, 133, 136, 137, 138, 140, 142, 145, 146, 147, 158, 181, 183, 184, 187, 188, 189, 190, 191, 192, 198, 202, 203
Augusta Mirror (Augusta, Ga.), 28, 29, *30-38*, 40, 52, 70, 71, 72, 181, 187, 188, 191, 192, 202
Austin, Mrs. Sarah (A Disappointed Man), 66, 67

Baber, Dr. A., 41
Baber, George, 163
Baber, Mrs. M. F., 104
Bachelor, 104
Baker, Joseph S., 92
Baldwin (*see* Longstreet, Augustus Baldwin)
Baldwin, Rev. J. D., 104
Barber, Miss Catherine W., 94, 100, 104, 108, 109, 110, 115, 116, 157, 158, 159, 160, 185, 198, 199
Bard of Saratoga, 104
Barlow, Billy, 29, 192
Barnard, 36, 67
Barrick, Hon. J. R., 163
Barton, William C., 13, 14, 18
Bates, Mary, 87, 104
Bayard (*see* Bayard, Benedict)
Bayard, Benedict, 104, 105
Belisle, D. W., 101, 104
Bell, H. S., 26, 38
Benjamin, Park, 87, 182, 197
Benton, Mrs. E. C., 147
Bernardo, 146
Berry, Mrs. H. L., 160
Berryhill, S. Newton, 147

Bertha, 36, 37
Bessie B., 146, 149
Beta, 86
Bethesda College (Savannah, Ga.), 5, 14
Bethune, Rev. G. W., 35
Bigby, J. S., 157
Bigby, Mrs. Mary C., 140, 147, 198
Billups, Col. Jorn, 57
Bi-monthlies in Georgia, 6, 187
Bkocksbank (*sic*), Miss L. A., 159, 160
Black, Hon. Edward J., 57
Blondel, 29
Blount, Annie R. (Jennie Woodbine), 136, 139, 140, 143, 144, 146, 147, 149, 160, 163, 198
Blue Ink, use of, in Georgia magazines, 120, 122
Boatwright, Dr. J. W., 57
Book Reviews in Georgia magazines, 37, 63, 66, 67, 70, 71, 75-76, 84-85, 98, 101, 121-122, 139, 144-145, 149, 150, 156, 167, 169, 189, 192
Boston Magazine, 4
Botanist, 36
Bowen, T. P., 5
Boykin, Samuel, 133
Bradford, Andrew, editor, 4
Bradley, Thomas Bibb, 128
Branch, Mrs. Caroline Hentz, 147
Brontë, Charlotte, criticism of, 158-159
Brooksville (Ga.), 36
Brother Jonathan (New York), 27-28, 63
Brown, Charles Brockden, editor, 5
Brown, Gov. Joseph E., 167, 173, 174, 183, 194
Brown, Rev. J. Newton, 87
Brown, Mrs. Martha W. (Estelle), 164
Bryan, Mrs. Madeline V. (Melodia), 56, 146
Bryan, Mary E., 136, 143, 147, 159, 160, 161, 162, 163, 185, 198, 199
Buena Vista (contributor), 146
Buena Vista (Ga.), 93
Bugle-Horn of Liberty (Griffin, Ga.), *177-178*, 187, 193, 204
Burke, John W., 108-110, 111, 132, 179
Burke, Thomas A., 91, 92, 108-110, 111, 115, 116, 180, 202
Burns, A. D., 136
Burton's Gentleman's Magazine (Philadelphia), 26, 36, 191, 205

General Index

Butler, Frances Anne (see Kemble, Frances Anne)
Butler, Gen. William O., 104
Butt, E. W., 57
Butt, Martha Haynes, 163
Butterball, Col., 54, 56

Calhoun (Ga.), 147
Calla, A Lady of A—, 115, 116
Cameron, Leila (see DuBose, Mrs. C. W.)
Campbell, C. K., 57
Campbell, Mrs. M. A., 160
Campbell, Major Calder, 57
Campbell, W. H., 90
Campbell, W. T. C., 135, 136
Canedo, Margarita J., 147
Capers, Bishop William, 176
Carlisle, W. B., 131
Carlos, 149
Carolina, 29
Carolina Contributor, 86
Carolina Girl, A, 146
Caroline V—, 29
Carolinian, 36
Carr, Henry A., 147
Carra, Emma (see Stibbes, Mrs. Agnes Jean)
Carrie (see Griswold, Mary Caroline)
Carter, Mrs. E., 67
Caruthers, Dr. William A., 46, 50, 52, 54, 57, 67, 84, 87, 256 n
Casket (Philadelphia), 26, 27
Cassville (Ga.), 108, 109, 110, 111
Catlin, S. W., 67
Catoosa Springs (Ga.), 178
Chapman, Mrs. A. T. D., 160
Chapman, S. T., 57
Chappell, A. H., 57
Charles, 36
Charleston (S.C.), 18, 27, 44, 59, 60, 61, 69, 70, 73, 74, 76, 85, 87, 95, 104, 105, 106, 108, 110, 115, 124, 125, 131, 142, 146, 147, 152, 172, 180, 184, 186, 187, 188, 189, 190, 201, 202, 205, 206, 256 n
Charlton, Robert M., 29, 35, 44, 45, 57, 67, 70, 81, 84, 87, 100, 104, 115, 116, 191, 196, 201, 261 n
Charlton, Thomas J., 84, 261 n
Child, L. Maria, 104

Children, magazines for (see Juvenile Magazines)
Children's Guide (Macon, Ga.), *133*, 187
Child's Index (Macon, Ga.), *133*, 187
Chilton, Emily C. S., 163-164
Chips (see Richards, T. Addison)
Chittenden, D. A., 57, 67, 80, 87, 90
Chivers, Thomas Holley, 77-80, 87, 100, 101, 104, 191
Christian Review (Boston), 70
Church, Alonzo, 57
Circulation of Georgia magazines, 9, 19-20, 31-32, 33, 51, 53, 58, 59-60, 65, 74, 90, 92, 93, 95, 97, 103, 106, 109, 118, 120, 126, 130, 133, 135, 143, 157, 160, 161, 171, 172, 183, 185, 187, 189, 199, 202-204, 206, 207
Clara (see Cole, Mrs. Clara)
Clarke, John G., 93
Clarksville (sic) (Ga.), 86
Classics, Ancient, interest in the, 37, 55, 66
Claude, 86
Claudia, 146
Clements, H. H., 104
Cleveland, Henry, 140, 147
Clifford, 44, 56
Clifton, 54, 56, 66, 67, 86
Clifton, Mrs., 57
Clinch, Rev. J. H., 57, 104
Clio (see Pierce, George F.)
Clyde, Kitty, 135, 136
Coelebs, 18
Cole, Mrs. Clara (Clara), 56, 162, 164
Cole, F. W., 87
Colleges in Georgia, 4, 5, 14, 25, 39, 41, 44, 45, 51, 54, 61, 63, 68, 91, 93, 96, 105, 114, 115, 133, 138, 150, 160, 163, 182, 187, 200, 202
College Magazines in Georgia, 25, 92, 93, 133, 160, 187
College Miscellany and Orphan's Advocate (Covington, Ga.), *133*, 187
College Temple (Newnan, Ga.), 91, 93, 160, 187
Collins, John D., 116
Colquitt, W. T., 57
Columbian Magazine (Philadelphia), 5
Columbus (Ga.), 26, 36, 57, 86, 104, 157, 187, 190
Comer, 146

Comus, 18
Conjux, 104
Contributions to Georgia magazines, payment for, 35, 51, 113, 118, 141-142, 161, 199
Contributors to Georgia magazines, lists of, 29, 35-36, 56-58, 67-68, 86-87, 90, 93, 94, 95, 100, 104-105, 108, 110, 116, 128, 136, 146, 147, 149, 160, 163-164, 172, 177-178, 190-191, 196-198
Cooke, John Esten, 143, 147
Cora, 36
Countryman (Turnwold, Ga.), 130, 151, *164-177*, 182, 183, 184, 187, 188, 192, 193, 194, 195, 203, 208
Countryman's Devil (*see* Harris, Joel Chandler)
Cousin Betsy (*see* Griffin, Mrs. Sarah Lawrence)
Cousin Dick, 146
Cousin Jessie, 146
Cousin Leila (*see* DuBose, Mrs. C. W.)
Covington (Ga.), 57, 58, 87, 133, 140, 147, 187
Covington Female College (*see* Masonic Female College, Covington, Ga.)
Crawfordville (Ga.), 32, 36
Crean, Mary W., 164
Criticism (*see* Literary Criticism)
Crossley, M. Louise (Currer Lyle), 160, 198
Crowquill, Alfred, 105
Curry, Rev. Daniel, 57
Curtis, Dr. Thomas, 63, 67
Cygriet, 146

Dahlonega (Ga.), 36
Daisy, 146
Dallas, Alabama, 146
Dalton, De Louis, 147
Dana, Mrs. Mary S. B., 35, 38, 57, 67, 71, 104
Dana, Matilda F., 116
Dana, Rev. W. C., 84, 87
Darby, Prof. J., 63, 66, 67
Dargan, Clara V., 140
Davidson, James Wood, 128, 133, 147
Davis, Jefferson, 167, 173, 174, 183, 194
Davis, William E., 104
Dawson, Col. A. H. H., 164

Day Star of Truth (Milledgeville, Ga.), 92
DeBow, J. B. D., 27
DeBow's Review (New Orleans), 150, 182
Deen, Ethel (*see* DeMilly, Mrs. Augusta)
De'esting, 146
Deism, 12-13
Delinquent Subscribers, 20, 33, 40, 51, 111
Delta, 56, 105, 116
DeMilly, Mrs. Augusta (Ethel Deen), 146
Democratic Review (New York), 102
Dennie, Joseph, editor, 5, 6, 200
DeRenne, George Wimberley-Jones, 201
DeWitt, B. M., 164
Dick, Thomas, 57
Dickens, Charles, visit to the U. S., 53-54, 64, 76-77
Dickson, Dr. John, 57
Dillard, A. W., 144, 147
Disappointed Man, A (*see* Austin, Mrs. Sarah)
Dod, Charles S., Jr., 147
Dogwood, 136
Doyal, L. T., 104
Drama in Georgia, 5-6, 14, 129, 130, 251 n
Dramatic Criticism, 85, 98
DuBose, Mrs. C. W. (Leila Cameron; Cousin Leila; Mrs. Kate A. DuBose), 69, 98, 101, 104, 107, 144, 147, 198
Duelling in Georgia, 18
Dulany, Mrs., 29
Dwight, Dr., 55, 57

Eames, Mrs. E. Jessup, 104, 197
Eatonton (Ga.), 93, 95, 150, 151, 152, 165, 166, 173, 174, 182, 183, 203
Ebenezer (Ga.), 3
Eclecticism in Georgia magazines, 16, 17, 18, 19, 29, 36-37, 45, 98, 101, 102, 108, 110, 123-128, 134-135, 155, 158, 178, 191
Edes, Richard W., 13, 14
Edith, 146
Editors, problems of, 8, 18-20, 32, 33, 34, 40, 43, 48, 50-51, 53, 58-59, 64, 65,

General Index

71, 72, 73, 74-75, 89, 102, 110, 111, 112, 113, 121, 128, 130, 135, 143, 145-146, 149, 151, 152, 158, 160, 170, 171, 172, 185, 186, 189, 204, 205, 207
Editors, women (see Women Editors in Georgia)
Education, journals of, 4-5, 25, 93, 132-133, 148
Education of Women (see Women, education of)
Educational Institutions (see Colleges in Georgia)
Educational Journal (Forsyth, Ga.), *133*
Educational Monthly (Lumpkin, Ga.), *133*, 185
Educational Repository and Family Monthly (Atlanta, Ga.), 130-131, *133*
Edwards, J. C., 67
Edwards, S. B., 35
Elder, Abraham, 57
Eliza, 56
Eliza N., 56
Ellet, Mrs. E. F., 35, 66, 67, 87, 104, 115, 116, 197
Ellis, John P., 104
Ellis, William J., 26
Ellison, William B., 57, 67
Ells, James Nathan, 137, 139
E. Louise W., 146
Elton, 146
Elwin, 56
Embury, Mrs. Emma C., 67, 94, 197
Emerald, Emmie, 146
Emory College (Oxford, Ga.), 4, 44, 45, 54, 57, 91, 150, 163, 182, 200
English Magazines, influence of, 5, 29, 36, 123, 187, 203
Engravings (see Illustrations)
Enid, 146
Eola, 146
Ephemerus, 56
Epsilon, 105, 146
Eremus, 105
Erwin, 105
Estelle (see Brown, Mrs. Martha W.)
Etchings (see Illustrations)
Eton, Etta, 146
Etowah Bard, 56
Eufaula, 146
Eugine (sic), 67
Evans, Augusta J. (Augusta Evans Wilson), 145, 149, 156, 169, 190, 196, 199
Evelyn, 146

Fabian, 146
Failure of Georgia magazines, reasons for, 13, 18-20, 90, 111, 112, 113, 118, 130, 135, 148, 149, 150, 152, 156, 158, 160, 184, 185, 201, 204, 206-207
Fairfax, Richard, 104
Falstaff, Jonathan (see Turner, Joseph Addison)
Family Companion (see *Family Companion and Ladies' Mirror*, Macon, Ga.)
Family Companion and Ladies' Mirror (Macon, Ga.), 30, 32, 52, 60, 61-68, 70, 72, 89, 181, 187, 188, 191, 192, 202
Family Visitor (Madison, Ga.), 111, 185
Fayetteville (Ga.), 133
Ferguson, Jessie, 164
Few, Rev. I. A., 57
Fidelis, 146
Files of Georgia magazines, location of, 6, 13, 25, 26, 28, 30, 39, 61, 68, 88, 92, 93, 95, 106, 108, 110, 118, 119, 123, 132, 133, 134, 137, 148, 150, 157, 160, 164, 177
Filicaja, 56
Fitten, J. H., 123, 124, 125, 126
Flash, Henry Linden, criticism of, 168, 169
Fleming, J. H., 110
Fleming, Robert, 147
Flit, 98, 105
Florence (Ga.), 29
Florio, 100, 104
Fly Leaf (Newnan, Ga.), 93, 160, 187
Fonerden, Rev. William H., 35, 57
Format of Georgia magazines, 6, 15, 25, 26, 28, 30, 44, 46, 60, 62, 70, 88-89, 92, 94, 97, 106, 109, 110, 112, 118, 120, 123, 125, 133, 134, 137, 140, 148, 154, 157-158, 165, 170, 177
Forrest, Florida, 146
Forrest, Floy, 146
Forsyth (Ga.), 56, 57, 133
Frank, 29, 36, 146
Franklin, Benjamin, editor, 4
Franklin, Leonidas, 57

Franklin College (University of Georgia), (Athens, Ga.), 4, 25, 57, 58, 91, 93, 96, 105, 114, 116, 138, 163, 187, 200, 202
Franklin Printing House (Atlanta, Ga.), 186
Freeman, 56
Freeman, Mrs. Ellen B. F., 57
French, Mrs. L. Virginia (L'Inconnue), 144, 147, 160, 162, 163, 164, 185
French Literature, translations from, 37, 67, 70, 81, 84, 100, 191
Friend of the Family, A (Savannah, Ga.), 92, 111, 116, *118-119*, 188, 193, 200-201
Fryer's Pond (Ga.), 36
Fudge, Tim, 29
Furman, Rev. Richard, 140, 144
Fusbos Secundus, 56

Gamma of Natchez, 158, 160
Garrison, William Lloyd, editor, 23
Gaulding, James W., 93
Gaultier, Gertrude, 104
Gem (Milledgeville, Ga.), 92
General Magazine and Historical Chronicle, for all the British Plantations in America (Philadelphia), 4
Gentlemen and Lady's Town and Country Magazine (Boston), 4
Georgia, population 1790-1830, 21
Georgia Academician and Southern Journal of Education (Scottsboro, Ga.), *25*
Georgia Analytical Repository (Savannah, Ga.), *6-13*, 186, 200
Georgia Female College (Wesleyan College), (Macon, Ga.), 4, 39, 41, 45, 50, 51, 57, 61, 63, 91, 200, 202
Georgia Home Gazette (Athens, Ga.), 92-93, 124, 184
Georgia Illustrated (collection of engravings), 63, 86
Georgia Literary and Temperance Crusader (Atlanta, Ga.), *160-164*, 185, 203
Georgia Woman, A, 67
Georgia University Magazine (Athens, Ga.), *93*, 187
Georgia Weekly (Greenville, Ga.), *133*
Georgian, 146
Geraldine, 56

German Literature, translations from, 66, 100, 124, 191, 195
Gertrude, 105
Gifford, Mrs. M. E., 57
Gilman, Mrs. Caroline, 57, 60, 74, 104, 108, 197
Gilman, S., 104
Giovanni, 56
Glenmore, 116
Godey's Lady's Book (Philadelphia), 15, 26, 27, 42, 56, 62, 63, 107, 113, 132, 148, 150, 182, 188, 190, 191, 205, 207
Goosequill, Abraham (*see* Turner, Joseph Addison)
Gopher (Waynesboro, Ga.), *133*, 187
Gorman, John B., Jr., 147
Gorman, Ossian D., 147
Gothamite, 36
Gould, Hannah F., 87, 197
Gould, Theodore A., 116
Goulding, Rev. F. R., 191
Graham's Magazine (Philadelphia), 26, 60, 112, 113, 132, 187, 188, 205
Grandfather, A, 56
Greensboro (Ga.), 68
Greenville (Ga.), 56, 133
Grey, Helen, 147
Griffin (Ga.), 146, 177, 187, 204
Griffin, Benjamin F., 38, 61-68, 93
Griffin, Mrs. Sarah Lawrence (Cousin Betsy), 33, 61-65, 67, 68, 202
Griswold, Mary Caroline (Carrie), 144, 146
Griswold, Rufus W., 75, 76, 84, 114, 169
Griswold, Walter H., 104
Gulnare, 146

Hackleton, Mrs. Minnie W., 164
Hadermann, C. J., 55, 57
Hal, 146
Hall, Rev. C. H., 104
Hall, Katie, 147
Hall, Mrs. S. C., 104
Hallock, Charles, 147
Hamblin, Louise Medina, 35
Hamett, Alphonso O., 147
Hamilton, 67
Hamilton (Ga.), 57
Hamilton, Mrs. Leila A., 147
Hammond, Gen. James H., 57

General Index

Hanleiter, Cornelius R., 28, 29, 38, 65, 88, 89, 90, 167, 186, 261 n
Hansell, Gen. Andrew J., 87
Hanson, J. W., 104
Happy, John, 178
Harden, John M. B., 57
Harietta, 36
Harmonia, 146
Harold, 56
Harp, Robert J., 132
Harper's Monthly Magazine (New York), 132, 186
Harrell, E. M., 147
Harris, Joel Chandler (Countryman's Devil), 165, 166, 167, 168, 169, 171, 172, 182, 203, 206, 207, 208, 272 n
Hatcher, John E., 164
Hawkins, Mary E., 147
Hawkins, Col. William S., 147
Haygood, Atticus G., 130-131, 133
Haygood, Greene B., 133
Hayne, Paul Hamilton, 104, 105, 131, 147
Hazard, W. W., 87
Hedas, 29
Heinfred, 29
Henri, 56, 146
Henry, 29, 146
Henry, James Edward, 54, 57, 67
Hentz, Mrs. Caroline Lee, 29, 46, 54, 57, 67, 100, 104, 108, 140, 143, 195
Herbert, 144, 146, 172
Herbert, Grace, 159, 160
Heriot, Edwin, 104, 110, 115, 116, 197
Hermit, The, 172
Hetty, 105
Hewitt, J. H., 129, 147
Hill, Miss E. H., 164
Hill, Mrs. Martha J., 164
Hilliard, Henry W., 35
Hinda, 36
Historical Tales in Georgia magazines, 35, 38, 54, 80, 81, 84, 90, 107, 110, 121, 143, 149, 190, 195
Holcomb, 36
Holcombe, Rev. Henry, 6, 7, 8, 9, 10, 11, 12, 13, 179, 251 n
Holden's Magazine (New York), 112
Holmes, George Frederick, 67
Holroyd, C. Vavasour, 98, 104
Holt, Harry (*see* LeClerc, Clara)
Holt, Polly (*see* LeClerc, Clara)

Homer, 36
Homes, Mrs. Mary Sophie Shaw (Milly Mayfield), 163, 164
Hooper, Johnson J., 109, 115, 116, 193, 194
Hoplegg, Achilles, 146
Horn of Mirth (Athens, Ga.), 91, *92*, 109, 187, 202
Houser, Rev. William, 67
Howard, Caroline (Mrs. Caroline Gilman Jervey), 100, 104, 107, 108, 197
Howard, Prof. William G., 67
Howitt, Mary, 104, 108
Humor, magazines of, in Georgia, 91, 92, 109, 133, 177, 187, 202-203, 204
Humor in Georgia magazines, 15, 17, 18, 19, 31, 35, 37, 54, 64, 66, 69, 70-71, 74, 80, 81, 88, 90, 91, 92, 98, 100, 109, 114, 115, 119, 121, 123, 138, 141, 143, 144, 154, 155, 165, 172, 173-174, 177, 178, 181, 182, 191, 192-194, 201, 204, 206, 207, 208, 252 n
Hungerford, James, 80, 81, 87
Hunt, Mrs. Sue E., 143, 147
Hunter, J. L., 57
Hunter, Theodore, 136
Hygienic and Literary Magazine (Atlanta, Ga.), 135, *148-150*, 185, 203

Illustrations in Georgia magazines, 26, 62, 63, 71, 73, 85, 86, 106, 111, 112, 114, 143, 177, 189, 191
Imlac, 56
Indamird, 146
Ines, 29
Inez, 56
Inisfael, 56
Inkle, Ludwig, 57
Irene, 56
Ireneus, 29
Irish Protestant Settlers in Georgia, 3
Irving, Washington; early appearance of *Sketch Book* in Georgia, 18, 252 n

Jackson, Henry Rootes, 35, 37, 38, 45, 55, 57, 67, 70, 76, 81, 84, 87, 90, 99, 100, 101, 104, 115, 116, 191, 196-197, 201, 260 n
Jacksonboro (Ga.), 57
Jacques, D. H. (Jacques Journot), 95-105, 108, 113, 114, 115, 116, 117

James, G. P. R., 44, 46, 57, 76, 196, 197
Jamie, 29, 36
Janett, 56
Janue, 29
Jefferson, Thomas, and Deism, 12
Jennings, Miss V. A., 160
Jervey, Mrs. Caroline Gilman (see Howard, Caroline)
John Donkey (New York), 98
Johnson, Finley, 136, 149
Johnson, Mrs. Rosa Vertner, 164
Johnston, Richard Malcolm (Philemon Perch), 144, 147, 163, 164, 193, 194, 207, 208
Jones, Prof. B. L., 136
Jones, Nette, 136
Jones, Rymmon, 149
Journot, Jacques (see Jacques, D. H.)
Judges in prize contests, 35, 104, 135, 140
Julien, 128
Juliet, 29
Juvenile Magazines in Georgia, 26, 69, 92, 106, 133, 187, 202
Juvenis, 36, 38, 105
Justitia, 146

Kaluptonoma, 146
Katy-Did, 143, 146
Keem, B. A. (see Meek, A. B.)
Kemble, Frances Anne (Frances Anne Butler), 85, 261 n
Kemble, Frank (see Turner, Joseph Addison)
Kendall, R. C., 147
Kendrick, Prof. A. C., 87
Kendrick, Rev. J. R., 84, 87
Kennedy, Crammond, 147
Kennesaw Gem (Marietta, Ga.), *133*, 187
Ketchum, Mrs. Annie C., 164
Keyes, Mrs. Julia L., 140, 147, 164
King, Mrs. Sue Pettigru, 144
Knickerbocker (New York), 26, 29, 36, 52, 60, 70, 85, 99, 132, 180, 187, 188, 191, 201, 207
Knowles, Rev. J., 133
Knox, Miss M. J. E., 115, 116
Kyle, Charles, 54, 57
Kyle, Maria Gertrude, 57, 80, 81, 87, 198

Ladd, Mrs. C., 29
Ladies' Companion (New York), 27, 36, 60, 191
Ladies' Garland (Philadelphia), 27
Ladies' Literary Cabinet (New York), 18, 19
Ladies' Magazine (Boston), 27
Ladies' Magazine (Savannah, Ga.), *13*-*20*, 25, 187, 192, 200, 252 n
Ladies' Magazine and Musical Repository (Philadelphia), 15
Ladies' Museum (Philadelphia), 15
Ladies' Pearl (Lowell, Mass.), 28, 61, 74
Ladies' Repository (Cincinnati), 28, 52, 60
Ladies' Wreath (New York), 28
Lady, A, 50, 144, 146
Lady of Augusta, A, 31, 36, 37
Lady from Georgia, A, 36, 37
Lady of Georgia, A, 104
Lady of Milledgeville, A, 56
Lady of South Carolina, A, 66, 67, 86, 115, 116
Lady's Magazine (Philadelphia), 15
Lady's Weekly Miscellany (New York), 15, 19
La Georgienne, 86
LaGrange (Ga.), 91, 92
LaGrange Female College (LaGrange, Ga.), 91, 92
La Josse, 136
Lamar, John B., 66, 67, 192
Lamar, Mary, 113, 116
Lamar, Mirabeau B., 67
Lane, Thomas W., 104
Lanman, Charles, 70, 87, 104-105
Larry, 172
LaTaste, L., 105
LaTaste, Victor, 54, 57
Laurence, 146
Law, Annie F., 108
Law, Judge (William), 57
Lawrence, E., 67
Lawrie, John Love, 55, 57, 81, 82, 87
Learner, A, 105
LeClerc, Clara (Harry Holt, Polly Holt), 159, 160, 163, 164, 198, 271 n
Lee, Annie, 118
Lee, Dr. Daniel, 138
Lee, Mary E., 56, 57, 63, 66, 67, 73, 80, 81, 87, 98, 100, 101, 105, 197

General Index 283

Leelin, 29
Le Ferve *(see* Riley, Mrs. Dr.)
Legare, J. M., 99, 100, 101, 104, 105, 115, 116, 197
Leila, 36
Leola *(see* Rogers, Mrs. Loula Kendall)
Leole, 149
Leon, 36
Leslie, Charles Robert, criticism of *Autobiographical Recollections*, 145, 155
Le Vert, Madame Octavia, 164
Lexington (Ga.), 57
Liberator (Boston), 23
Libraries in Georgia, 5, 41, 55, 96, 165, 168, 201
Lightheart, Lily, 146
Lilly-Bell, 146
Lincoln, Laura, 147
L'Inconnue *(see* French, Mrs. L. Virginia; and Ollivar, Mrs. Janie)
Lind, Eva, 147
Lippard, George, 110
Literary Casket (Fayetteville, Ga.), *133*
Literary Criticism in Georgia magazines, 37, 48-49, 55, 56, 63, 64, 66-67, 70, 71, 74, 75, 76, 77-80, 84-85, 98, 102, 103, 117-118, 121-122, 123, 139, 141, 144, 145, 155-156, 158-159, 161-162, 167, 168, 169, 173
Literary Magazine and American Register (Philadelphia), 5
Literary Vade Mecum (Buena Vista, Ga.), *93*
Local Color in Georgia magazines, 29, 119, 181, 193-194, 207, 208
Lochrane, O. A., 105, 114, 115, 116
Lois, 146
Longfellow, Henry W.: contributor to *Wheler's Magazine* (Athens, Ga.), 115-116, 197, 266 *n;* criticism of, 115, 117
Longstreet, Augustus Baldwin (Baldwin), 27, 30, 31, 34, 35, 36, 39-40, 45, 54, 57, 90, 138, 141, 143, 147, 181, 191, 192, 193, 194, 204
Lothaire, 56
Lou Bell, 146
Lucas, S. D., 147
Lufton, Charles, 105
Lumpkin (Ga.), 133, 185, 198
Lumpkin, Col. J. L., 57

Lyceum in Georgia, 41
Lyle, Currer *(see* Crossley, Mrs. M. Louise)

Mabel, 146
Macaulay's *History of England*, sale in Athens, Ga., 92
McBride, Archd. Arne, 147
McCrimmon, Mrs. Mary A., 133, 147, 160, 164, 185, 198
Macdonald, Miss H. B., 57
McIntosh, Maria J., 191, 198
Macon (Ga.), 4, 22, 28, 29, 30, 32, 33, 36, 38, 39, 40, 41, 42, 44, 46, 52, 54, 56, 57, 58, 60, 61, 63, 64, 67, 68, 70, 88, 91, 92, 93, 109, 114, 116, 130, 132, 133, 146, 147, 160, 169, 171, 181, 187, 190, 201, 202, 203, 255 *n*
Madison (Ga.), 4, 26, 29, 30, 36, 58, 65, 71, 85, 88, 89, 90, 93, 94, 95, 111, 157, 181, 182, 185, 202
Magnolia (contributor), 146
Magnolia (see Southern Ladies' Book, Macon, Ga.)
Malsby, M. A., 148
Manhiem, Louise, 147
Mann, W. W., 136, 138
Manners, Mrs. *(see* Richards, Mrs. William C.)
Marah, 146
Marcus, 36
Marengo, 146
Marietta (Ga.), 105, 128, 133, 187
Marietta Female College (Marietta, Ga.), 133, 187
Marinda *(see* Minor, Virginia M. O.)
Marion, 146
Martin, Mrs. Margaret, 35, 57
Martin, Miss Mary, 35
Mary, 146
Masonic Female College (Covington, Ga.), 133, 187
Massachusetts Magazine (Boston), 5
Mattie, 146
Maussenet, Adolphus, 57
May, 146
May, Minnie, 146
Mayfield, Milly *(see* Homes, Mrs. Mary Sophie Shaw)
Means, Alexander, 35, 44, 54, 57, 135, 140, 144, 147, 149, 191

Medical and Literary Weekly (Atlanta, Ga.), *134-136*, 148, 185, 203
Medicus, 56
Medway (near Savannah, Ga.), 9, 251 n
Meek, A. B. (B. A. Keem), 35, 38, 55, 56, 57, 87, 118
Mellen, Grenville, 87, 197
Melodia (see Bryan, Mrs. Madeline V.)
Memet, 146
Mercer, Rev. Jesse, 40, 57, 255 n
Mercer, S. C., 164
Mercer University (Penfield, Ga.), 4, 56, 68, 91, 163, 200, 202
Merle, Cyrille, 146
Mernet, 146
Merrill, A. K., 57
Merriwether, Mrs. Lide, 164
Microcosm (Athens, Ga.), *91*, 262 n
Middle Georgia, 3, 4, 22, 88, 91, 150, 181, 193, 200, 202, 203
Midway (near Milledgeville, Ga.), 4, 105
Mifflin, J. H., 29, 35, 57, 67, 70, 81, 87
Mignionette, 146
Milledgeville (Ga.), 4, 36, 56, 92, 172, 173, 190, 191, 192
Mills, Cotton Mather, 105
Milward, Mrs. Maria G., 67
Miner, Mrs. Serena A., 140, 144, 147
Minister's Wife, A, 146
Minor, Virginia M. O. (Marinda), 136
Miot, Emma, 140, 147
Miriam, 149
Miss Barber's Weekly (Newnan, Ga.), 157, 185
Mistletoe (Athens, Ga.), *108-110*, 111, 202
Mobile Literary Gazette (Mobile), 36
Monroe (Ga.), (see Munroe, Ga.)
Monthlies in Georgia, 25, 26, 38, 61, 68, 92, 93, 106, 108, 110, 119, 123, 133, 148, 177, 187, 188, 202, 204
Monthly Magazine and American Review (New York), 5
Monthly Miscellany (Atlanta, Ga.), 92
Moragne, Miss M. E., 34, 35, 70, 87
Moravian Settlers in Georgia, 3
Moreton, Clara, 105, 108
Moreton, Maud, 139, 140, 143, 147
Mount Zion (Ga.), 29, 56
Munroe (sic), (Ga.), 116
Munroe, N.C. (contributor), 57

Music in Georgia magazines, 26, 30, 37, 189, 191
Mustapha, 29
Muza, 29
Myers, Rev. E. H., 93
Myrtle, May, 146

Nadamia, 146
Navy, magazines for the, 132
Neal, John, 66, 67, 115, 116, 197
Neal, Mrs. Joseph C., 98, 105, 107, 108, 197
Neal's Saturday Gazette (Philadelphia), 98, 99
Nettleton, Abiel L., 87
Newnan (Ga.), 91, 93, 144, 146, 157, 158, 160, 185, 187, 198, 203
Newton (Ga.), 36
New York Magazine, 5
New York Mirror, 27, 29, 32, 36, 37, 99, 191, 263 n
Nichols, Eliza G., 100, 105
Nina, 146
Nisbet, Eugenius A., 55, 57
Noble, Louis L., 81, 87
Nobody, Nettie, 146
Nom de Plume, 146
North American Review (Boston), 5, 27, 132, 152, 207
Northern Magazines, influence of, 26, 27, 29, 36, 37, 62, 70, 71, 99, 187-188, 254 n
Novel-reading, editorials on, 76, 122
Novissimus, 146

Oak Grove (Ga.), 136
Observer, An, 18
Oglethorpe College (Midway, near Milledgeville, Ga.), 4, 91, 200
Oliver, Dr. Samuel C., 35, 38, 67
Oliver, Thaddeus, 93
Ollivar, Janie (L'Inconnue), 146
O'Neall, Judge John Belton, 84, 87
Orion (Penfield, Ga.), 27, 60, *68-88*, 96, 108, 180, 181, 186, 188, 191, 193, 202, 259 n
Orionis (see Richards, William C.)
Orne, Mrs. Caroline, 67
Orne, Miss Caroline F., 67
Orthopolitan, Olinthus, 114, 115, 116
Oscar, 29

General Index

Osgood, Mrs. Frances S., 35, 55, 57, 67, 197
Oswald, 146
Ouvrier, 146
Overall, John W., 164
Oxford (Ga.), 4, 44, 56, 67, 92, 150, 182, 185

Paedagogus, Ludovic (see Pierce, Lovick)
Paine, Miss Phebe, 57
Paine, Thomas, 4, 11, 12
Panola, 147
Pardoe, Miss, 31, 35
Parker, 147
Patten, Lieut. G. W., 29, 52, 57, 67
Peck, William Henry, 133
Pendleton, E. M., 29, 35, 55, 57, 90, 146, 191
Pendleton, Philip C., 29, 38, 39, 41, 42, 43, 45-54, 58-61, 62, 74, 151, 167, 256 n
Penfield (Ga.), 4, 27, 36, 60, 68, 69, 71, 160, 161, 180, 202
Pennsylvania Magazine (Philadelphia), 4
Pepper, Peter, 36
Perch, Philemon (see Johnston, Richard Malcolm)
Percy, Dr. Eugene, 105
Peterson's Ladies' National Magazine (Philadelphia), 28, 150, 182, 205
Philander, 56
Philologus, 29
Pickle, Peter (see Turner, Joseph Addison)
Pierce, George F. (Clio), 29, 39-42, 44-46, 50, 51, 54, 57, 61, 67, 179, 255 n
Pierce, Lovick (Ludovic Paedagogus), 45, 51, 54, 55, 57, 256 n
Pires, 147
Plantation (Eatonton, Ga.), 72, *150-157*, 165, 167, 173, 182, 183, 186, 187, 188, 193, 194, 195, 203
Poe, Edgar Allan, editor, 26, 27, 56, 77, 117
Poke, Sally (see Turner, Joseph Addison)
Porter, Hon. Benjamin F., 105, 115, 116
Porter, Edward J., 105, 116

Port Folio (Philadelphia), 5, 6 (circulation in Georgia), 200
Portico (Baltimore), 5
Postell, D., 58
Pradt, Emma F., 147
Preacher, The, 36
Prentice, George D., 105
Price, Prof. W. H. C., 133
Printers in Georgia (see Publishers and Printers in Georgia)
Prize Contests (see Prizes for Contributions)
Prizes for Contributions, 34-35, 38, 66, 101, 103-104, 109, 135, 139, 140, 144, 149, 199, 270 n
Proportion, Polly, 17, 192
Pseudonyms, lists of, in Georgia magazines, 17-18, 29, 36, 56-57, 67, 86, 94-95, 104, 105, 116, 128, 136, 140, 146-147, 149, 160, 164, 188, 198-199
Psyche, 66, 67
Publishers and Printers in Georgia, 6, 13, 18-19, 25, 26, 28, 30, 38, 40, 61, 68, 88, 92, 93, 94, 95, 106, 108, 109, 110, 111, 118, 119, 123, 132, 133, 134, 136, 137, 138, 139, 148, 150, 152, 157, 160, 161, 164, 177, 183, 186, 203, 207, 208
Puritan, A, 48
Purse, E. J., 118
Putnam's Magazine (New York), 186

Quarterlies in Georgia, 72, 93, 133, 150, 152, 165, 167, 183, 187, 188, 195, 203
Queerfish, Tom, 15, 192
Quintard, C. F., 105
Quintus, 147

Rab, 105
Raiford, Hamilton, 35
Rambler, 36, 37, 147
Randall, James R., 147
Randolph, Jessie, 135, 136, 147, 149
Reagan, J. C., 92
Reed, Dr., 58
Reedy, Miss Sallie Ada, 160, 164
Repository and Weekly Register (Philadelphia), 15
Requier, A. J., 147
Rice, Charles Wyatt, 25, 35
Richards, Mrs. C. H. (see Richards, Mrs. William C.)
Richards, J. J., 132

Richards, T. Addison (Chips), 35-36, 37, 63, 69, 70, 71, 73, 80, 81, 86, 87, 96, 98, 100, 105, 193
Richards, William C. (Orionis), 24, 27, 36, 38, 55, 58, 63, 67, 68-81, 84-88, 89, 95-105, 106-108, 111, 167, 173, 179, 180, 181, 182, 185, 186, 188, 189, 191, 192, 193, 194, 203
Richards, Mrs. William C. (C. H. B. R.; Mrs. C. H. Richards; Mrs. Manners), 69, 70, 80, 81, 84, 86, 96, 98, 108, 198
Richards' Weekly Gazette (see *Southern Literary Gazette*, Athens, Ga.)
Richmond (Va.), 27, 39, 60, 85, 92, 116, 125, 131, 139, 142, 150, 187, 188, 190, 191, 205
Rigel, 86
Riley, Mrs. Dr. (Le Ferve), 136, 148, 149, 160, 198
Riley, Mrs. Rebecca Haynes, 92, 185
Rinaldo, 67
Ritchie, Anna Cora, 147
Roath, David L., 108, 119-122, 140, 193
Roath's Monthly Magazine (Athens, Ga.), 93, *119-123*, 180, 193, 203
Rockwell, J. O., 110
Rockwell, William S., 67
Rogers, Laura Bibb, 147
Rogers, Mrs. Loula Kendall (Leola), 136
Rogers, Mrs. M. Louise, 135, 136, 149
Rome (Ga.), 177
Rose-Bud (LaGrange, Ga.), *92*
Roswell (Ga.), 104
Round, Rev. G. H., 58
Royal American Magazine (Boston), 4
Russell, Henry P., 18, 19
Russell's Magazine (Charleston), 131, 142, 188, 205
Rymmon, 149

Saffronia, 17
Salaries of Georgia editors, 64, 89
Sallie, 147
Saluda, 147
Salzburger Settlers in Georgia, 3
Samivel, 105
Sandersville (Ga.), 36, 151
Sass, George H., 147
Satire, magazines of, in Georgia, 91, 93

Satire in Georgia magazines, 81, 121, 123, 155, 165, 173-174, 177, 178, 194, 195
Saunders, J. Henry Dmochowski, 147
Savannah (Ga.), 3, 5, 6, 7, 9, 13, 14, 15, 16, 17, 19, 20, 22, 26, 30, 32, 35, 36, 42, 43, 44, 45, 49, 50, 51, 52, 54, 56, 57, 58, 59, 60, 61, 68, 74, 82, 87, 92, 100, 105, 116, 118, 130, 136, 146, 147, 182, 187, 190, 197, 198, 200, 201, 251 n, 252 n, 253 n, 255 n
Savannah *Literary Messenger* (Savannah, Ga.), 26
Savannah *Times* (Savannah, Ga.), 25, 253 n
Saxe, John G., 105
Saxon, Parish, 105
Schoolfellow (Athens, Ga.), 69, 105, *106-108*, 111, 180, 187, 202, 264 n
Science in Georgia magazines, 44, 54, 55, 102, 110, 114, 191, 195
Scotch Highlander Settlers in Georgia, 3
Scott's Monthly Magazine (Atlanta, Ga.), *133-134*, 150, 177, 183
Scottsboro (Ga.), 25
Screven, George P., 136
Screven, William E., 147
Seals, John H., 160, 161, 162
Sears, Robert, 86
Sears' New Monthly Family Magazine (New York), 86
Semi-monthlies in Georgia, 25, 30, 92, 187, 188
Semi-weeklies in Georgia, 133
Senex, 36
Seroc, 36
Seward, William H., 175-176
Shiras, Charles P., 116
Sigma, 147
Sigourney, Mrs. L. H., 36, 45, 58, 67, 87, 105, 109, 110, 197
Silver Age, 149
Simms, William Gilmore (G. B. Singleton), 27, 35, 36, 39, 44, 45, 47-49, 52, 54-56, 58-60, 66, 67, 73, 75, 80, 84, 85, 87, 98, 100, 101, 105, 112, 113, 115, 116, 144, 147, 188, 196, 197, 256 n, 259 n, 274 n
Sinclair, Carrie Bell, 144, 147, 191, 198
Singleton, G. B. (see Simms, William Gilmore)

General Index 287

Slaughter, James Summerfield, 135, 136, 149
Slaughter, Mrs. T. I., 136
Slaughter, Rev. Thomas M., 26
Slavery, 23, 24, 84, 126, 128, 152-153, 154, 155, 169-170, 175, 180, 183, 194-195, 196, 197, 199-200, 203, 273 n
Sledge, James A., 91
Slow, Dean, 149
Smets, Alexander A., 55, 201
Smillie, James, engraver, 71
Smith, Charles Henry (*see* Arp, Bill)
Smith, George G., Jr., 58
Smith, M. A., 93
Smith, O. L., 67
Smith, Mrs. Seba, 58, 197
Smith, Mrs. Susan A., 67
Smith, W. Wragg, 36, 144, 147
Smythe, James M., 92, 93, 123, 124, 125
Snelling, Mrs. Anna L., 73, 80, 81, 87, 197
Snodgrass, Dr. J. Evans, 55, 58, 68
Snubs, Mark Anthony, 29
Social Criticism in Georgia magazines, 7-8, 10-12, 17, 18, 67, 76, 102-103, 107, 115, 181, 185, 194
Soldiers' Friend (Atlanta, Ga.), *132*
Somers, 67
Son, The, 147
South Carolina (contributor), 147
South Carolina Weekly Museum (Charleston), 5
Southern Bee (Columbus, Ga.), 26
Southern Eclectic (Augusta, Ga.), 93, *123-128*, 184, 188, 191, 203
Southern Field and Fireside (Augusta, Ga.), 130, 133, *136-148*, 150, 158, 161, 183, 185, 189, 193, 199, 203
Southern Ladies' Book (*Magnolia*), (Macon and Savannah, Ga.), 28, 29, *38-61*, 62, 68, 70, 72, 74, 75, 80, 85, 187, 188, 201, 202, 258 n
Southern Ladies' Book (New Orleans), 162, 271 n
Southern Ladies' Companion (Nashville), 92
Southen Literary Companion (Newnan, Ga.), *157-160*, 185, 271 n
Southern Literary Gazette (*Richards' Weekly Gazette*), (Athens, Ga.), 27, 69, 89, 92, *95-105*, 106, 107, 108, 111, 114, 116, 118, 150, 172-173, 180, 181, 183, 188, 191, 192, 193, 202, 263 n
Southern Literary Journal (Charleston), 124, 184, 188, 205
Southern Literary Journal (Oxford, Ga.), *92*, 185
Southern Literary Messenger (Richmond), 27, 29, 32, 36, 39, 52, 56, 60, 63, 85, 95, 98, 116, 125, 131, 139, 142, 150, 152, 155, 156, 182, 187, 188, 190, 191, 205, 273 n
Southern Literature, pleas for, 24, 31, 33, 37, 39, 41, 45, 47, 48, 53, 55, 60, 62, 72-73, 94, 97, 103, 113, 116, 120-121, 123, 125-126, 130-131, 137-138, 151, 170
Southern Magazines, influence of, 27, 29, 36, 53, 60, 187-188
Southern Miscellany (Madison and Atlanta, Ga.), 26, 29, 30, 63, 65, 71, 85, *88-90*, 181, 182, 188, 193, 202
Southern Pioneer (Augusta, Ga.), 25
Southern Post and Literary Aspirant (Macon, Ga.), 25, 26, *28-29*, 32, 88, 188, 192, 202
Southern Quarterly Review (New Orleans and Charleston), 27, 53, 70, 124, 125, 152, 180, 184, 188, 205
Southern Review (Charleston), 205
Southern Rose (Charleston), 60, 74, 189
Southern School Journal (Macon, Ga.), *93*
Southman, Charles, 105, 110, 114, 116
Southron (?), 36
Southwest Georgia, 22
Spain, H. P., 147
Sparks, W. H., 172
Sparta (Ga.), 29, 36, 57, 69, 104, 198
Spofford, H. M., 84, 87
Squier, E. G., 87, 197
Stafford, 29, 56
Stanford, 147
Starnes, Judge, 147
State Rights' Sentinel (Augusta, Ga.), 25, 30, 39-40, 181, 191, 192
Statham, Mrs. C. L., 147
Stella, 147
Stephenia, 100
Stephens, Alexander H., 32, 58, 163
Stephens, J. V. D., 157
Stevens, Mrs. Ann S., 36, 38, 68, 105, 197

Stevens, William Bacon, 55, 58, 84, 87, 105, 201
Stewart, J. A., 149
Stibbes, Mrs. Agnes Jean (Emma Carra), 146
Stokes, Rev. W. H., 58, 160, 161
Story, W. W., 115, 146
Stowe, Harriet Beecher, criticism of *Uncle Tom's Cabin*, 156, 196
Stranger, The, 57
Strong, Samuel M., 36, 45, 55, 58
Stuart, Susan A., 118, 198
Studens, 56
Student at Law, 86
Suarez, M. R., 36
Subscription Prices for Georgia magazines, 9, 15, 28, 42, 62, 89, 94, 97, 106, 109, 111, 112, 118, 120, 132, 137, 143, 152, 158, 171, 188, 253 n
Summerfield, James, 135
Symmetry, Benjamin, 17, 18, 192

Taboos for contributors to Georgia magazines, 195
Talbotton (Ga.), 58, 147
Taliaferro, Dr. V. H., 134, 135, 148
Tallulah, 135, 136
Taveau, A. L. (Alton), 104, 105
Tefft, Israel K., 201
Telescope, 56
Temperance Movement in Georgia, interest in, 50, 102, 108, 109, 111, 117, 118, 160, 161, 162, 194
Terence, 147
Theaters in Georgia, 6
Theolian, 147
Thomas, Dr. A. G., 134, 135
Thomas, Rev. J. R., 58, 163
Thomas, Miss O. L., 136
Thompson, Ed Porter, 178
Thompson, James M., 147
Thompson, John R., 98, 99, 137, 139, 145, 147
Thompson, William Tappan, 24, 28, 29, 30-35, 37, 38, 40, 64-66, 68, 71, 89-90, 108, 119, 167, 179, 180, 181, 182, 186, 191, 192, 193, 194, 201, 202, 204, 254 n, 262 n
Thomson, Charles West, 36
Ticknor, James H., 26
Timrod, Henry (Aglaus), 104, 197, 264 n

Tirtium (*sic*) Quid, 36
Tomahawk (Macon, Ga.), 91, *93*
Tomlin, J., 58
Toon, J. J., 133
Toulmin, Camilla, 105
Travel Articles and letters in Georgia magazines, 55, 67, 71, 84, 98, 100, 101, 139, 163, 191
Trippe, Mrs. Kate, 160
Turner, Joseph Addison (Frank Kemble; Abraham Goosequill; Addison; Jonathan Falstaff; Peter Pickle; Sally Poke), 38, 72, 93-95, 100, 104, 105, 139, 140, 144, 147, 150, 151, 152, 153, 155, 156, 164, 165, 166, 167, 168, 169, 170, 171, 172, 173, 174, 175, 177, 179, 182, 183, 184, 186, 188, 190-191, 192, 193, 194, 195, 197, 200, 203, 208
Turner, Nat, insurrection of, 23
Turner, William Wilberforce, 139, 143, 147, 155, 165, 172, 190
Turner's Monthly (Eatonton, Ga.), *93-95*, 151, 182, 183, 188, 262 n
Turnwold (Ga.), 141, 151, 164, 165, 166, 168, 177, 182, 183, 203
Tyson, Miss W. C., 92

Union Magazine of Literature and Art (New York), 205
University of Georgia (*see* Franklin College, Athens, Ga.)
Ursula, 147

Valeria, 29, 36
Vaughan, Mrs. S. A., 164
Veazey, L. L., 164
Venator, 36
Vere-Dicus, 56
Verena, 147
Viator, 36, 56, 147
Village Bard, 29
Vindex Veritatis, 55, 56
Vineville (Ga.), 29
Viola, 56, 147
Virginian, A, 147
Voigt, L. T., 118

Waddel, Prof. James P., 58, 114, 116
Wade, J. A., 58
Wakelee, Kate C., 140, 144, 146, 147
Walker, Joseph, 105, 106
Wallace (*see* Webster, William Wallace)

General Index

Walley, Miss Mary E., 66, 67, 68
Walnut Grove (Ga.), 144, 146
Warfield, Mrs. C. A., 164
Warrenton (Ga.), 29, 34, 36
Washington (Ga.), 36, 57, 58, 87, 160, 161
Washington, Augusta, 147
Watkins, Gen. James, 68
Watson, A. R., 144, 147
Watts, James R., 172
Waybridge, W., 36, 37
Waynesboro (Ga.), 133, 187
Webster, Noah, editor, 4
Webster, William Wallace (Wallace), 86
Weeklies in Georgia, 13, 25, 26, 28, 88, 95, 118, 132, 133, 134, 136, 138, 157, 160, 161, 164, 170, 187, 188
Welby, Amelia B., 55, 58
Wesley, Charles, 251 n
Wesley, John, 12, 251 n
Wesleyan College (see Georgia Female College, Macon, Ga.)
Western Continent (Baltimore), 182
Western Literary Messenger (Buffalo), 99
Westmoreland, Mrs. W. F., 136
Wheler, Charles L., 38, 93, 95, 105, 107, 108, 109, 110-112, 113, 114, 115, 116, 117, 118, 180, 202
Wheler's Magazine (Athens, Ga.), *110-118*, 119, 142, 188, 193, 197, 199, 202
Wheler's Monthly Journal (Athens, Ga.), 91, 110, 111
Whetstone, Tim, 104
Whitaker, Daniel K., 27, 114, 123, 124, 125, 126, 128, 179, 180, 184
Whitaker, Mrs. D. K. (Mrs. Mary S. Whitaker), 114, 115, 116, 124, 128, 184, 197
Whitaker, Mrs. Mary S. (see Whitaker, Mrs. D. K.)
Whitaker's Magazine (Columbia), 124, 184, 190
White, Robert A., 105
White, Thomas W., 27, 32
White, William N., 98, 105, 116, 138
Whitefield, Rev. George, 5, 14
Whitehead, J. P. C., 136
Whitman, Walt, reference to "Death in a School-Room," 101-102
Wildbrier, 147
Wilde, Richard Henry, 35, 36, 52, 58,
67, 68, 70, 81, 84, 87, 190, 191, 197, 201
Wilde, William Cumming, 105, 147
Wildwood, Charlie, 147
Wilfred, 105
Willhelmine, 105
Willie, of Camp Bird, 147
Willison, M. G., 147
Wilson, 147
Wilson, Augusta Evans (see Evans, Augusta J.)
Wilson, Miss Leonora, 87
Windsor, Robert, 147
Wise, Daniel, editor, 61, 74
Wittich, E. L., 36, 38, 46, 54, 58
Women Editors in Georgia, 61, 92, 93, 133, 157, 160, 161, 162, 185, 187
Women, education of, 14, 39, 41, 44, 45, 54, 55, 133, 195, 202
Women, magazines for, 4, 13, 14, 15, 19, 28, 38, 61, 92, 93, 133, 187
Wood, Mrs. Charlotte M., 66, 68
Woodbine, Jennie (see Blount, Annie R.)
Woodcuts (see Illustrations)
Woodville, 147
Woodworth, Samuel, 66, 68, 197
Wooten, H. V., 36, 58, 67, 68, 86
Worrell, A. S., 132

Xemia, 147
Xenia, 147
Xury, 105
Xylon, 57

Yeames, Eliza, 18
Yellow Fever in Augusta, 34
Yona, 86
Youl, Edward, 105, 146
Young, 36
Young, Edward, 147
Young Lady of Columbus, A, 56-57
Young Lady of Hamilton, A, 57
Youth's Companion (Columbus, Ga.), 26, 187
Youth's Friend (Augusta, Ga.), 92, 187
Youth's Gem and Southern Cadet (Macon, Ga.), 92, 187
Youth's Repertory and Child's Magazine (?), 25, 187, 253 n

Zena, 147
Ziola, 147

www.ingramcontent.com/pod-product-compliance
Lightning Source LLC
Chambersburg PA
CBHW021214240426
43672CB00026B/83